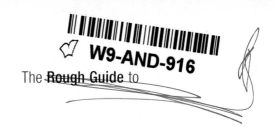

W9-AND-916

The Rough Guide to

First-Time Europe

written and researched by

Doug Lansky

with additional contributions by

Henrik Harr

ROUGH GUIDES

www.roughguides.com

Contents

Colour section   1

Introduction 6
Reasons to go 12

The big adventure   17

1. Planning your big trip 19
2. Getting there and around 38
3. Travelling alone or
   with others 65
4. Costs and savings 71
5. Working, volunteering and
   studying 88
6. Documents and
   insurance 109
7. Before you leave home 119
8. Packing 123
9. Carrying valuables 139
10. Guidebooks and
    other reading.................... 146
11. When you arrive 150
12. Culture shock.................... 164
13. Staying in touch 169
14. Security............................. 178
15. Health 187
16. Travellers with special
    considerations 200
17. Documenting your trip 208
18. Returning home 215

Where to go   219

Austria 221
The Baltic States.................... 225
Belgium and Luxembourg...... 230
Britain 235

Bulgaria 241
Croatia................................... 245
The Czech and
   Slovak republics 249
Denmark 254
Finland................................... 258
France.................................... 262
Germany 267
Greece 272
Hungary 276
Ireland.................................... 280
Italy 285
Montenegro 290
Morocco 292
The Netherlands 293
Norway 298
Poland 303
Portugal 307
Romania 311
Russia.................................... 315
Slovenia................................. 320
Spain 324
Sweden.................................. 329
Switzerland 333
Turkey 337

Directory   341

Transport 343
Accommodation...................... 346
Red tape 346
Money.................................... 347
Travel tools 348
Health and safety................... 348
Working abroad 349

Small print & Index   351

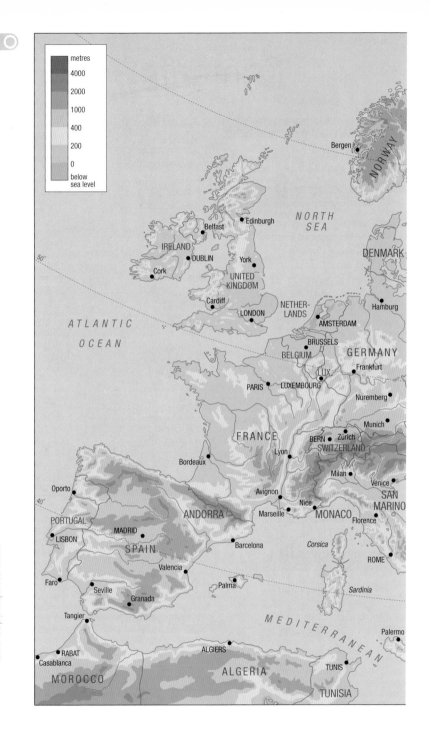

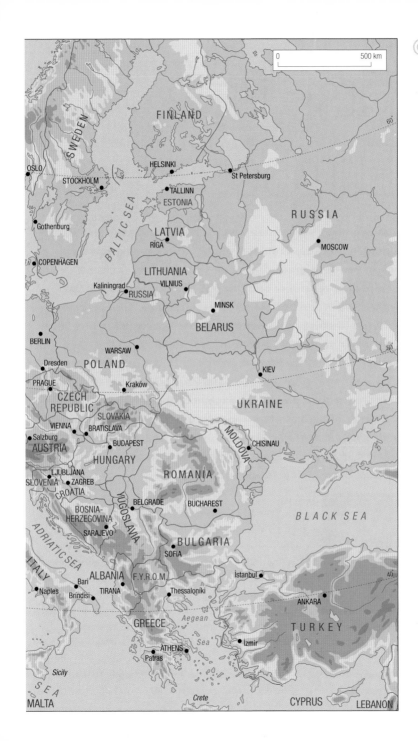

0   500 km

FINLAND

SWEDEN

OSLO
STOCKHOLM

HELSINKI

St Petersburg

BALTIC SEA

TALLINN
ESTONIA

RUSSIA

Gothenburg

LATVIA
RĪGA

MOSCOW

COPENHAGEN

LITHUANIA
VILNIUS

Kaliningrad
RUSSIA

MINSK

BELARUS

BERLIN

WARSAW

Dresden

POLAND

KIEV

PRAGUE

Kraków

CZECH
REPUBLIC

UKRAINE

SLOVAKIA

VIENNA   BRATISLAVA

MOLDOVA

Salzburg

BUDAPEST

CHISINAU

AUSTRIA

HUNGARY

LJUBLJANA

ROMANIA

SLOVENIA   ZAGREB

CROATIA

BELGRADE

BUCHAREST

BLACK SEA

BOSNIA-
HERZEGOVINA

YUGOSLAVIA

SARAJEVO

BULGARIA

ADRIATIC SEA

SOFIA

ITALY

ALBANIA   F.Y.R.O.M.

İstanbul

Bari

Naples   Brindisi

TIRANA

Thessaloniki

ANKARA

GREECE   Aegean

TURKEY

Sicily

Sea

İzmir

ATHENS

Patras

SEA

Crete

MALTA

CYPRUS   LEBANON

60

60

40

First-Time Europe

Italians don't serve "deep pan" pizza. Swedes aren't all blondes. And the French probably won't French-kiss you when you first greet. But none of these little cultural realities is reason enough to put off your trip to Europe – the "Old World" offers more architecture, wine, music, fashion, theatre and gastronomy per square kilometre than any other continent. Which means heading off the main routes will still land you waist-deep in cultural treasures. The continent (including Russia) boasts over seven hundred million people, in excess of three hundred World Heritage Sites and more renowned paintings than you can point your camera at. And it's usually just a matter of a short bus or train ride to get from one place to the next – though even a bicycle will often suffice.

Europe stretches 3900km from the Greek island of Crete to Hammerfest, on the northeastern coast of Norway, and just as far from Lisbon to Moscow. But with the reunification of East and West at the end of the 1980s leading to widespread improvements in roads and rail, Europe became more accessible than ever. The introduction of the euro has made spending easier and means you're no longer giving away fistfuls of commission to the moneychangers every time you cross a border. What you put this saving towards is quite limitless: climbing a Swiss Alp, tasting wine at a French chateau, renting a surfboard in Portugal, having tea and scones in England, chilling out in Sweden's *Ice Hotel* or sipping a local Karlovacko beer while soaking your toes in the Adriatic off the Croatian coast. For more clever budgeting tricks and strategies to help cut costs along the way, see p.72.

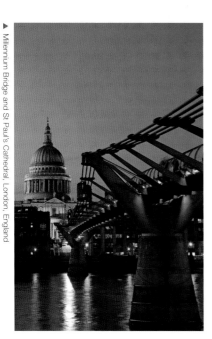

Europe's riches are waiting; the decision to find them is yours. In other words, this book is not going to try to persuade you to travel, nor try to convince you that stomping around with a backpack will fulfil whatever may be missing from your life. Travel is an urge best cultivated from within. In fact, one of the biggest favours you can do for yourself is to travel when you want to, not when someone else thinks you should. The more eager you are to open yourself up to life on the road, the more willing you'll be to shrug off the prepacked experience and reap real rewards.

Of course, that first trip overseas can be intimidating, and few people ever feel completely ready. You'll invariably make some mistakes along the way – we all have – but with this book you'll be able to sidestep the major pitfalls.

Fact file

- **Biggest countries**: France (547,030 sq km), Spain (504,782 sq km), Sweden (449,964 sq km), Russia (17,075,200 sq km; over two thirds of which lie in Asia) and Ukraine (603,700 sq km)

- **Smallest countries**: Vatican (0.44 sq km), Monaco (1.95 sq km), San Marino (61.2 sq km)

- **Highest point**: Mt Elbrus, Russia (5642m)

- **Lowest point**: Lemmefjord, Denmark and Prins Alexander Polder, the Netherlands (both 7m below sea level)

- **Highest temperature**: Seville, Spain (50°C)

- **Lowest temperature**: Ust'Shchugor, Russia (-55°C)

- **Most sunshine**: Rhodes, Greece (3480hr per year)

- **Most rainfall**: Crkvica, Bosnia-Herzegovina (4650mm per year)

- **Biggest economy**: Germany (€2.69 trillion)

- **Highest per capita GDP**: Luxembourg (€79,578)

- **Highest life expectancy**: Andorra (82.67 years)

- **Biggest beer consumers**: Czech Republic (160 litres per man, woman and child a year – half a litre daily)

- **Biggest coffee consumers**: Finland (more than four cups per day)

- **Most paid vacation time**: Sweden (33 days a year)

- **Most "connected" internet users**: Sweden (76.9%)

The **Big Adventure** section will walk you through some of the more baffling bits of the planning process that tend to trip up many travellers, show you how to enrich parts of your travels that commonly get glossed over, and help to make sure you have your gear and documents in order before leaving, as well as to bring the entire overseas experience together well within your budget. You might start by opening the map on pp.4–5 and letting your eyes wander over the possibilities. Then flip to Chapter 1 and learn how to start customizing your journey.

The country profiles in the **Where to Go** section provide a glimpse into each country to assist with your preparation, highlighting landmarks and festivals, providing more detailed weather info and letting you know if there are any bus or train passes you should consider buying before your arrival. Of course, you'll want more specific information eventually, either from websites or publications listed in the **Directory** section at the end of the book or from your guidebook once you arrive, but at this point such facts and figures would bog down the planning process rather than help it along, and you'd barely be able to lift this book. Besides, there is such a thing as too much planning. One of the greatest thrills of travel is making your trip up as you go.

▼ Spanish Steps, Rome, Italy

What's the European Union?

It's not a federal government, like the United States. Nor a continent. They like to call it "a family of democratic European countries, committed to working together for peace and prosperity". It started with a proposal by French foreign minister Robert Schuman in 1950 and originally consisted of six countries: Belgium, Germany, France, Italy, Luxembourg, and the Netherlands. There are now 27 **EU member states**; Switzerland, Iceland, and Norway are the most notable countries that opted not to join (but they, along with Liechtenstein, are members of the European Free Trade Area, which keeps them from economic seclusion). Not all EU members decided to adopt the **euro** – Sweden, Denmark and Great Britain, for example, still use their own currencies, while unofficial state members like Andorra, Monaco, San Marino and the Vatican have taken on the euro. All in all, 22 states and territories use the euro. The European Parliament, with 788 members, works from Brussels, Belgium and Strasbourg, France. The Central Bank is run out of Frankfurt, Germany. And the Court of Justice is based in Luxembourg.

Little-known fact: even though Denmark is part of the EU, the Danish island of Greenland isn't. It became a reluctant member when Denmark joined in 1973, but left in 1985 after gaining home rule in 1979. It is the only region to ever leave the European Union without leaving its mother state.

FAQ

Will I manage travelling around Europe only speaking English?

English and, when necessary, a few hand gestures will get you by just fine in most situations. Remember to keep your speech slow and basic, skip the slang, and don't take a puzzled look as a sign to speak louder. That said, if you make the effort to pick up a language, you'll enrich your experience tenfold. At the very least, take twenty minutes to learn "please", "thank you", "excuse me", "where?", "toilet" and "how much?" in the local languages. For more info on language schools, see p.105.

I've got US$4500 saved up. Will that be enough?

No problem. The question is: for what kind of trip and for how long? To figure out a daily budget that fits your comfort level and to discover which countries offer the best value, turn to the "Costs and savings" chapter (see p.71). You'll pick up savings tips there as well.

How do I figure out where to sleep each night and what to see during the day?

Easy. Carry a guidebook (or a smartphone and download the guides – or try the old-fashioned way still popular with guidebook writers: asking other travellers). There are extensive lists of places to stay at various price ranges in each city, with short descriptions to help you narrow down your selection. In peak periods such as summer, you may want to find an internet café and book a few days or weeks in advance for central hostels in popular cities. At most tourist offices (often conveniently located at the train station), they'll call around and find an available room for you once you've arrived. Of course, you can always just show up at the front door with your pack. For more on accommodation, see p.155.

I'm thinking of going with my best friend. Is that a good idea?
Possibly not. Travelling with a partner or two should be a carefully weighed decision. Turn to p.65 to make sure you know what you're getting into and how to minimize the potential pitfalls.

There's just two weeks left before my trip and I haven't done a thing. I don't even have a passport. Am I too late?
Nope, but you've got your work cut out. Step 1: sort out your passport. You'll need expedited service (see pp.110–111). Step 2: get some credit cards. You'll probably want two. Or at least one credit card and one cash card – both with pin numbers to access cash machines. Step 3: get hold of a budget card like ISIC or another you qualify for. Step 4: buy your plane ticket. Step 5: organize rail and bus passes. There are a few other things you'll need, and you can find all that on p.123.

▼ Reichstag, Berlin, Germany

What if everything gets stolen, even my passport?

Go to the local police and report it. Have them call your nearest embassy. Call your parents collect and get some funds wired. There are a few other important things to do (see p.182), but the message is this: you'll be OK. To prevent it from happening in the first place, check out the "Carrying valuables" chapter (see p.139).

Is there anything I should leave at home?

Yep, many things. Starting with your "going out" shoes. If you find you need a pair of dress shoes for a night or two, you can pick up a pair for €5 at a secondhand store. Textbooks are a popular pack-along with well-intentioned students, but these cumbersome tomes rarely get opened. For more items better left behind, see p.135.

Do I really need travel insurance?

Only if you get injured. Or very sick. Or sued for some driving accident. If this happens and you don't have insurance, you're screwed. Well, not just you. Possibly your parents and employer as well, depending on how shrewd and aggressive their lawyers are and how much you owe. The real question is which insurance to get. Turn to p.114 to find out what to look for and why you shouldn't just buy the one your travel agent tries to sell you on the spot. For European citizens, if you've got a European Health Insurance Card (EHIC), which has replaced the E111 and E128 forms, you've got your medical expenses covered, at least for emergency services.

18

reasons to go

Adventure and cultural insights can be found almost anywhere. How you decide to travel and what you decide to do is far more important than where you decide to go and what you intend to see. Thinking in terms of "doing" rather than "seeing" will enhance that most vital and often elusive dimension to your travels: depth.

01 Participate in a festival La Tomatina, Spain.

02 **Travel by ferry** Leaving Korčula, Croatia.

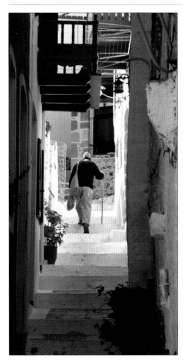

03 **Wander the backstreets** Nisyros, Dodecanese Islands, Greece.

04 **Check out a sporting event** Wimbledon Tennis Championships, England.

05 **Learn a foreign language** Spanish class in Salamanca, Spain.

06 View attractions early, before the crowds

arrive St Mark's Square, Venice, Italy.

08 Learn how to make a local dish
Making pizza in Rome.

07 Try the local firewater
Polish vodka.

09 Climb a mountain
Durmitor National Park, Montenegro.

10 Take a painting course
Painting in the garden of Matisse's villa, France.

11 **Visit a European traveller you met along the way and let them show you their home town** Catania, Sicily.

12 **Hunt for bargains at the local market** Rialto Market, Venice, Italy.

13 **Taste some wine at a chateau** Kuehn winery, Alsace, France.

14 **Try a family stay** Provence, France.

15 **Discover a place that's not in the guidebook** Lac Combal, Val Veny, Italy.

16 **Try the street food wherever you go** Sweet seller, İstanbul, Turkey.

17 **Volunteer to do something you're passionate about** Cleaning a ruin in Greece.

18 **Rent a bike and explore** Amsterdam, the Netherlands.

First-Time Europe

The big adventure

1	Planning your big trip	19
2	Getting there and around	38
3	Travelling alone or with others	65
4	Costs and savings	71
5	Working, volunteering and studying	88
6	Documents and insurance	109
7	Before you leave home	119
8	Packing	123
9	Carrying valuables	139
10	Guidebooks and other reading	146
11	When you arrive	150
12	Culture shock	164
13	Staying in touch	169
14	Security	178
15	Health	187
16	Travellers with special considerations	200
17	Documenting your trip	208
18	Returning home	215

Planning your big trip

D
eciding where to go, how to get there, what to do and how long to stay is a lot easier than it sounds. In this chapter, the planning process is chopped into smaller, easier-to-chew pieces that will get you under way, from figuring out what activities are available in each place to avoiding troublesome weather and catching the festivals you don't want to miss. Because prices change from year to year, sometimes from peak season to low season, and exchange rates fluctuate on a daily basis, many guides are reluctant to list specific prices. That's an easy way out, but doesn't make it easy to calculate your budget or get a sense of prices as you read. In this guide, you'll find prices listed in euros (€) in nearly all cases. At the time of research, the rates were approximately €1: $1.34 and £0.89 ($1: €0.75; £1: €1.12).

How much time do you need?

Here's a better question: how much time can you spare? You could easily spend a lifetime hopping around Europe and not experience all it has to offer. So, carve out whatever time you can and worry later about what you'll do with it. Besides, it's easier to come home early than try to push back deadlines once you're on the move.

The truth is, you won't know how long you'll want to go for until you get out there. You might meet someone who will invite you along on a camping trip, or you may stumble across a great course that lasts two months, or suddenly have a burning desire to sketch Italy's most famous frescoes. The trick at this point is to structure

I don't have much money – should I travel cheap or wait until I've got the funds to do it in style?

Independent budget travel in Europe isn't for everyone. Especially if you're not thrilled about eating most of your meals picnic-style on park benches or in youth hostel kitchens, or spending the night in a place that considers the urine stain on the mattress all the decoration the room needs. If this doesn't seem like it would faze you, you're in luck; the cultural and social payoff of budget travel is enormous, the experience invaluable. As nice as it may sound to travel in comfort, a thick wallet has a tendency to **insulate** you from the very culture you're trying to experience. That is, you don't want the only locals you meet to be the ones checking you into the hotel and serving you drinks. A tight budget will encourage you to seek out places you perhaps would normally overlook.

If you're not ready to travel on the cheap, you'll still find plenty of essential information and itinerary ideas from the ensuing pages, but you may have to limit your time on the road, or knock off a bank. Three months of air-conditioned tours, meals served on real tablecloths, and comfortable hotel rooms could set you back €24,500, whereas it can be done for €5000 or even less with a few tips from the "Costs and savings" chapter (see p.71).

your trip so that those unforeseen experiences can happen. So, how do you do this?

If you already know how long you've got, you should be thinking about the pace of your trip. How many countries, cities and activities should you try to tackle in that amount of time? A good guideline is this: don't plan more than four multi-day activities per month in advance. (Sorry, visiting Spain doesn't count as a single activity; but things like a two-day cooking class, a short stay with a relative, a few days exploring a major city or a hiking trip do.) Less than four is even better. If you plan to see, say, Paris and Rome in June, that doesn't necessarily mean you're only going to see these two cities. It means you get to make up the rest of your plans on the move as you travel between the two. This approach allows for ample **flexibility**, plus any transport delays you may encounter (when it comes to transportation strikes, the French and Italians are in a league of their own).

If the length of your trip is largely dictated by budget, check out the "Costs and savings" chapter (see p.71) to help calculate your time on the road and maximize the funds you have. However, you don't need to let your initial funds shorten your trip. "Working, volunteering and studying" (see p.88) covers jobs and volunteer projects, so you can leave home with minimal money or stretch your trip for years.

Any amount of time is better than none, but less than a month doesn't give you much of a chance to get into the rhythm of travel. You may get accused by "hardcore" travellers of not getting a real taste of the road on a short trip, but don't be put off by their comments; if you concentrate your trip in one area and take a course in something or stay with locals,

you'll get a more culturally enriching experience than those with a year
of travel grime under their belts who merely look the part.

A year off has a nice ring to it, but that's not a realistic time frame
for those with jobs to return to or student loans that need paying off.
Two to six months is a reasonable target. It will give you a chance to
do some exploring and even allow you to dig a little deeper with one
or more cultures. The best option is to have a flexible ticket so you can
return when you're ready.

How much time do you need in each place?

Two days. That is, two days longer than you think. Maybe even two weeks.
The faster you go and the more ground you cover, tempting though it
may be, the less you'll see. According to the author Wendell Berry, "Our
senses . . . were developed to function at foot speeds." The same way that
slowing down improves your peripheral vision when driving, **reducing
your speed** enables you to take more in while you travel. Or take the
advice of travel author Peter Moore: "If you're having a good time – stay.
If you've met someone you fancy and who fancies you – stay. If you're
too buggered to move – stay. If the police are closing in on you – go."
If you're not pressed to press on, you might forge a friendship with the
traveller you met over breakfast or find out that your favourite musician
is giving a concert in an ancient amphitheatre nearby, or that the local
cultural centre is offering free palm-tree-climbing lessons. With enough
time and curiosity, something interesting is bound to happen.

Why you need a pit stop and when you should take it

Travel can be romantic and adventurous, but finding your way around a city,
coordinating train schedules, locating a place to stay, taking the stairs up every tall
structure for a scenic overview, using perplexing toilets, sampling palate-numbing foods
and testing each country's unique beers – the things that give independent travel its bite
– combine to form an exhausting experience. Give yourself a chance to relax.

To some extent, **taking a break** is going to happen on its own. You might stumble
upon a place you can't resist, get stuck waiting for a ferry that's not running due to
inclement weather, find a fun person or group of travellers to hang out with or just hit
the sensory-overload wall.

The last one will occur if the first four don't. This exhaustion – think of it as cultural
burnout – typically occurs after two to four months of continuous, fairly fast-paced
travel. There's one main symptom: you spend increasingly more time in cafés and
hostel lounges and less time out exploring towns and museums. There's also one
simple remedy for recharging your wanderlust: stay put. Give yourself a chance to
absorb and process what you've seen. Write some long letters. Get to know a few
locals. Volunteer. Earn some money. Fall in love. Whatever.

Give yourself the flexibility to stop when you need it, or plan ahead so you end up at
your dream hangout, or take an interesting course. A decent formula is two weeks of
"down time" for every three months on the road.

www.roughguides.com

Where to go

Here's the good news: you can't miss. That is, there's **no wrong place to go**. It's what you decide to do there that makes the real difference. Want to spend two weeks in France? Two weeks at a farmstay learning French, two weeks visiting the tourist attractions in Paris, and two weeks at an intensive cooking school are so different they can hardly be summed up as "spending a fortnight in France". Even on that same farm, at those same attractions and at that same cooking school, you'd have a hard time replicating the experience of someone else who did those things. There are simply too many variables. Forget about trying to find the "Top 10" this and the "best-of" that – you *can* find a magical experience, but if you don't push yourself off the tourist trail and do something that moves you, there will be very little "top" or "best" or "magical" of anything, unless you count "best staged photo in front of famous sculpture". And remember: what may seem awful at the time might, in retrospect, prove to be the most life-changing event of your journey.

To find the best places, the only person to consult is yourself. Grab a pencil, take a look at the five points below, and start jotting down places, sights and activities that sound appealing. You can figure out how to connect them later.

Go where you speak the language

No, not English. A **second language** (although an English-speaking country is a fine place to begin your travels). Even if you can just read a menu and a few street signs, you're off to a good start. Europe is a great place for the lingual novice; you can almost always find an English speaker when you need one. However, tapping into these ubiquitous translators should be your safety net, not your crutch. The idea is that

---

What is adventure travel?

These days, with 70-year-olds waiting for hip replacements signing up for "adventure tours", it's hard to know exactly what the term means. An adventure used to involve exploring uncharted waters and lands with hidden dangers.

"**Adventure travel**" is typically applied to white-water rafting, bungy jumping, trekking and getting spun about in jet boats, especially when these activities take place in foreign countries – that is, foreign from our own. The fact remains that they're completely packaged activities with a predictable outcome, rendering them closer to a fairground ride than what any explorer would dub an adventure. Does that mean you should avoid them? No. A little adrenaline is healthy and good fun. Does that mean there are no "real" adventures left? No. Just make sure you understand which kind you're signing up for. Come to think of it, if you need to sign up for an adventure, that's a pretty good indication of what kind it is.

once you start using a language, once you start looking around and trying to decipher the words or communicate where you need to go, the learning curve becomes nearly vertical and you're taking a big step into the culture you've come to experience.

Go where you have family or friends

Don't be afraid to look up that childhood pen pal in Estonia or your third cousin once removed in Portugal. To cover your bets, bring along some kind of document or a snapshot to help bridge any gaps. Despite any present-day politics, you'll find Europeans have a special place in their hearts for relatives and old friends who have been separated by oceans for years. With a little luck, you'll find you've got yourself a cultural guide. You'll almost certainly get a free place to stay and, if nothing else, an inside look at the way they live, from food and interior decor to bowling or strip clubs – whatever, in fact, your relatives happen to do for fun.

If you're still at university, take the opportunity to get involved with **international groups**. Students visiting your university from other countries for a year (or several years) are typically members of an international club, and tend to want to make friends with locals. Hanging out with club members is a nice way to start travelling while still at home and, better yet, you'll have some new friends to visit (and maybe free places to stay) during your trip.

Go somewhere you've longed to see

A little **wanderlust** goes a long way. If there's some place you've read about, heard people talk about for ages, or had some sort of childhood fascination with, then that's not a bad reason to go – at the very worst, it's a decent starting point. Let James Joyce's *Ulysses* be your tour guide through Dublin, or jumpstart your wandering in Salzburg with the sites from *The Sound of Music*. If it seems too trivial, keep in mind that many of the travellers who end up in Transylvania are there just because they like the sound of it.

www.roughguides.com

23

Are you a tourist or a traveller?

Why on earth should you go out of your way to try some sport or activity you've never heard of and will probably never do again? Why bother with any slower, less comfortable mode of transport? Why go anywhere near a squat toilet or, for that matter, a Parisian roundabout in a rented car? Because, if you're not **doing something new**, you're doing something you've done before. If you're not using the local language (or hand gestures and phrase books), you're often speaking with professional guides and concierges. If you're not eating local food, you're probably eating food you know from home. The creature comforts of Europe are likely to be similar to the ones where you come from, but finding the differences and trying them is up to you. If you don't, you'll be getting a Disneyfied view of the place you're trying to see. It's often the "strange" food and more uncomfortable elements that give travel its extra dimension, and separate the Eiffel Tower in Paris from the one at the Epcot Centre, the gondola ride in Venice from the one in Las Vegas – and the tourists from the travellers.

Attractions of the world

When you start travelling, you hear a lot about "attractions" and "must-sees" and "wonders". Is it tourist-bureau hype or is there something to it? In reality, it's a bit of both. When the hype is old enough, it seems to become legend, or even fact. The classic is the "**Wonders of the World**". For the record, Europe had two of the original Seven Wonders of the Ancient World: the Statue of Zeus in Olympia and the Colossus of Rhodes, both in Greece. Unfortunately, they've both been destroyed.

None of the twelve Natural Wonders is located in Europe, only five of the nineteen so-called "Forgotten" Wonders and just three "Modern" Wonders (see below). What's left? Plenty – Europe has 401 of UNESCO's 878 **World Heritage Sites**, more than any other two continents combined. These are the world's architectural and archeo-logical treasures, as defined by this special United Nations body. There's a wide range of sites. Many, like the Cathedral of Notre-Dame in Paris or the archeological areas of Pompeii, you're familiar with. Others, like France's fortified city of Carcassonne or Italy's Botanical Garden in Padua, you may have never heard of. Are they less impressive than the more famous sights? Perhaps, but there are almost certainly fewer crowds. To find out where they are and their historical significance, visit ⓦ whc.unesco.org.

"Forgotten" Wonders

The Colosseum, Rome, Italy
The Leaning Tower of Pisa, Italy
Mont-Saint-Michel, Normandy, France
The Parthenon, Athens, Greece
Stonehenge, Wiltshire, England

"Modern" Wonders

The Eiffel Tower, Paris, France
The Channel Tunnel, under the English Channel
Big Ben, London, England

Follow your interests

This is perhaps the best tool to use to start picking your destinations. The concept is simple enough: instead of thinking about what you'd like to see, think about **what you'd like to do**. Approach the trip as a chance to collect unique experiences, not passport stamps, postcards and snapshots in front of famous monuments. If you're a golfer, you might pursue the sport to its roots with a round at the Old Course in St Andrews in Scotland. Or try a twist, and stop for a game of ice golf in Finland, where you can play with a bright-orange ball, tee up on an ice cube, hack out of the fairway and putt on icy "whites". If you like to cook, you might take a crepe-making course in Brittany or try a day of pasta preparation at a villa in Tuscany. The more original your approach, the more unique your experience is likely to be.

Go somewhere you know nothing about

Consider Croatia. Maybe Lativa? How about Slovenia? Head off the beaten path and chances are that's where you'll find the highlights of your journey.

When to go

On a long trip, you can't be everywhere at just the ideal time. Don't knock yourself out trying. Usually, if it's too hot inland, you can head for the coast. And if it's too hot on the coast you can move to higher elevations, where temperatures are milder. Sweating it out in

---

Want to try something new?

Can't think of something active to do while travelling? Here are a few ideas. To find out where, simply enter the activity and the place you're heading into your favourite search engine.

Alpine skiing • Beer tasting • Bike touring • Birdwatching • Bungy jumping • Canal barging • Canoeing • Canyoning • Caving • Cross-country skiing • Deep-sea fishing • Fly-fishing • Golfing • Horseback riding • Ice diving • In-line skating • Kayaking • Kiteboarding • Learning meditation • Long-distance ice-skating • Mountaineering • Off-road driving • Painting • Paragliding • Rock climbing • Roller-coaster riding • Sampling haute cuisine • Scotch tasting • Scuba diving • Snowboarding • Studying martial arts • Studying photography • Surfing • Trekking • Visiting castles/palaces • White-water rafting • Windsurfing • Wine tasting • Yachting

---

Rome? It's only 25km from the beaches of Fregene and Ostia in the coastal town of Fiumicino. Or take an overnight train into the Alps and hike around Lugano. It's pretty impossible to avoid a day or two of rain, but finding good weather typically requires just two things: keeping your eye on the **weather reports**, and a **flexible schedule**. What you need to investigate, therefore, is not the ideal time to be in each location, but if there are any dates you should absolutely avoid (see p.28).

Much of this depends on **what you plan to do**. Southern Italy in January may be chilly but it's fine for city exploring, especially if you plan to be inside museums and churches, whereas the weather in Chamonix in January may render mountain biking impossible. If you

Museum heavyweights

British Museum
Where: London, England
What: artefacts, architecture and other items uprooted (read: looted) by the British Empire.
Most famous pieces: its mummy collection and the Rosetta Stone
Cost: free, donation requested
ⓦ www.thebritishmuseum.ac.uk

Deutsches Museum
Where: Munich, Germany
What: natural sciences, technology and industry
Most famous piece: its aeroplane collection
Cost: €8.50
ⓦ www.deutsches-museum.de

Hermitage Museum
Where: St Petersburg, Russia
What: classics, sculptures and artefacts
Most famous piece: possibly Cézanne's *Girl at the Piano*
Cost: €8
ⓦ www.hermitagemuseum.org

Kremlin and Armoury
Where: Moscow, Russia
What: royal carriages, guns and tsars' clothing
Most famous pieces: Fabergé eggs, Orlov Diamond and Tsar cannon and bell
Cost: €8 (Kremlin) €16 (Armoury)

Kunsthistorisches Museum
Where: Vienna, Austria
What: classics
Most famous pieces: its Goya, Titian and Giorgiones collections
Cost: €10
ⓦ www.khm.at

plan to hitch sections of your journey on boats, make sure you check out the seasonal schedule. Similarly, you'll want to know if there are any dates not to miss. If you're applying for a seasonal job, there's usually a tight window. And it's a pity unwittingly to arrive in Venice a day after Carnevale has ended; you're stuck with the crowds but have missed the event. See the individual country profiles for more specific information on local weather and events.

Travel seasons

Travelling in the **peak season** is climatically favourable, but the advantages of touring Europe out of season are numerous: low-cost (sometimes over fifty percent less) and less crowded flights, better

Louvre
Where: Paris, France
What: classics, sculptures and artefacts
Most famous pieces: *Mona Lisa*, *Winged Victory* and *Venus de Milo*
Cost: €9, €6 after 6pm
Ⓦ www.louvre.fr

Prado
Where: Madrid, Spain
What: classics
Most famous piece: *Las Meninas* by Velázquez (Picasso's *Guernica* is in Museo Reina Sofia)
Cost: €6 (free 6–8pm)
Ⓦ www.museoprado.es

Tate Modern
Where: London, England
What: modern art
Most famous piece: whatever's in the Turbine Hall (exhibitions every six months)
Cost: free, donations encouraged
Ⓦ www.tate.org.uk

Uffizi
Where: Florence, Italy
What: frescoes and sculptures
Most famous piece: any number of masterpieces, from Botticelli's *Birth of Venus* to Da Vinci's *Adoration of the Magi*
Cost: €6.50
Ⓦ www.uffizi.firenze.it

Vatican Museums
Where: Rome, Italy
What: maps, frescoes and classics
Most famous piece: The Sistine Chapel
Cost €14
Ⓦ www.vatican.va/phome_en.htm

www.roughguides.com

Off-season travel

It's not all gravy during the off-season. Some places just never quieten down. I was in Florence, Italy, one November and it felt as if I had taken a bus to Chicago, but for the old buildings and marble statues of pantless men. English, not Italian, was by far the dominant language on the streets, and the people walking around without a camera were in the minority. Florence (and Venice) aside, I found off-season travel to be hugely rewarding. I got into sites faster, my pictures weren't spoiled by people resting their behemoth bums on the 2000-year-old ruins and, above all, a surprising amount of local flavour surfaced, even in places like Paris.

Leif Pettersen

chances of finding a room at the cheapest hostels, shorter queues at museums, less need for reservations and – best of all – fewer visitors to distract you from the culture you came to observe. However, you may be looking at a few hidden expenses. Some of the cheapest hotels shut down in the **off-season**, so you may be forced into more expensive digs. If it's cold enough to rattle your teeth loose at night, expect to pay extra for a room with heat. If you've arrived in the hot and sweaty season, be prepared to pay more for air conditioning. Sure, you can combat these with a good sleeping bag or a cold, wet sarong wrap, but you might not always be in the mood. As a general rule, the best times to visit are at the beginning and end of the tourist cycles, the so-called **shoulder seasons** (March 1–June 1 and Sept 1–Nov 1 for southern Europe; April 15–June 1 and Sept 1–Oct 1 for northern Europe), when you get the good weather without the crowds. For skiers, the season slows down for a few weeks just after the Christmas/New Year rush and again at the end of March when the spring skiers head back to work. If there's any decent snow left on the slopes in April, it can be a great time to surf the slush.

When not to go

Rather than aiming for the perfect time to go, focus on **avoiding the wrong time**, bearing in mind that there are degrees of right and wrong to consider as well. For example, you might want to steer clear of Rome in August – all the Italians have left on vacation and the country is invaded by scores of tourists and sweltering temperatures. It's not a great time to be there, but it's hardly a catastrophe. However, if you plan on cycling across Scandinavia, you absolutely don't want to be doing it between November and March.

In general, winter (Nov–Feb) in northern Europe is cold and rainy, and snowstorms are common. Southern Europe can get chilly, but is typically quite mild. Summer (June–Aug) is pleasant in northern Europe (though the occasional rainy days can be difficult to avoid) and very hot in southern Europe.

▲ Acqua Alta floods, St Mark's Square, Venice

Planning around local holidays and events

Your overnight train pulls into the station, you stagger over to the tourist information bureau and say you're looking for some budget accommodation for a night or two, and the person behind the counter is nodding their head like a paint shaker before you even finish your sentence. There's a Rotary Club convention and a national youth volleyball competition in town and they've taken up all the rooms. The best the tourist office can do is a double room at the *Ritz* for €285. Or you can stay an hour out of town at a little hostel situated next to a minimum-security psychiatric ward.

Occasionally, **scheduling conflicts** occur. A rock concert, business convention or sporting event unexpectedly disrupts your travel plans. So what do you do? First, try to avoid the situation by keeping an eye on your guidebook for national holidays or other events that might cause a hotel-booking frenzy (such as the festivals on pp.30–31). Then, if you expect the city's accommodation to fill up, email ahead for a reservation, or try booking rooms in advance via a site like Ⓦwww.hostelworld.com or www.hotels.com, or delay your arrival until a more auspicious day. If you're already there, the easiest thing to do is to simply move on to the next town. For this, the tourist office can be quite helpful. It's the perfect time to head somewhere

European festivals and events

Cities and towns come alive during **festivals**. The locals are more upbeat and the experience is often more interactive. But if you miss a festival by a day or two, you'll arrive just in time to watch the streets get cleaned while you pay for the still-inflated hotel prices. Festival planning usually takes some advance legwork. Last-minute accommodation, if indeed there is any, gets snatched up several days before the event, but the extra effort it takes to attend a festival is almost always worthwhile. There are hundreds to choose from around Europe. In some you can participate, in others the spectators become part of the spectacle, but the exuberance is nearly always palpable.

Here are a few of the major events around the continent. To find some of the lesser-known festivals, turn to the country profiles at the back of the book and see ⓦwww .festivals.com and ⓦwww.whatsonwhen.com.

Carnevale, Venice, Italy. A decadent renaissance festival, pyjama party and three-day rager played out against the backdrop of the world's most picturesque sinking city. The costumes are as elaborate as they are expensive. And guess what? They're for sale. Feb–March (the week prior to Ash Wednesday); ⓦwww.carnevale.venezia.it

St Patrick's Day, Dublin, Ireland. If you're not in green, you'd better have a good excuse. There's everything from Skyfest, an enormous fireworks display, to a treasure hunt that has families scurrying around the city. The full week of "craic" culminates with over 500,000 people lining the streets for Ireland's biggest parade. March 12–17; ⓦwww.stpatricksday.ie

Las Fallas, Valencia, Spain. Two million people unite in Valencia to honour St Joseph by building six-metre-high papier-mâché effigies of local or national celebrities, parading them through town, then stuffing them with fireworks and explosives and setting them ablaze. Sound like fun? Grab some earplugs and join the riot. March 15–19; ⓦwww .fallas.com

Cooper's Hill Cheese Roll, Brockworth, England. Maybe the local hospital was running low on patients but, for whatever reason, people have been chasing a cheese down a sixty-degree slope here for over 200 years. Most tumble in a blur of legs, hands and dislocated shoulders all the way to the bottom, where there are plenty of ambulances standing by. Last Mon in May; ⓦwww.cheese-rolling.co.uk

Notting Hill Carnival, London. Europe's largest street fest is getting bigger every year. Each summer, west London overflows with costumed dancers, tripped-out floats and half a million spectators as the spleen-shaking sound systems fill the air. Last weekend in Aug; ⓦwww.thenottinghillcarnival.com

Roskilde Festival, Denmark. The biggest, baddest jam-fest in Scandinavia, probably all of Europe (provided England's Glastonbury isn't underway at the end of June). Expect to stand tattoo-to-tattoo with 100,000 or so concert-goers while you share the

not mentioned in a guidebook, but before you do, ask for a list of accommodation the tourist office represents and a phone book. Cross-check their list with the one in the *Yellow Pages*. Often, there are several hotels, especially the cheaper digs, not on the list. Give those places a call first; they're the most likely to have a room. Or look for less conventional places to stay, such as university dormitories or campgrounds that rent tents. Don't forget to ask about rooftop sleeping at hostels if the weather is favourable.

same beer-soaked camping ground. Recent performers include Nine Inch Nails, Kanye West and Coldplay. First week of July; @www.roskildefestival.dk

Montreux Jazz Festival, Geneva, Switzerland. Expanding from its jazz roots, this world-famous music event now bursts with blues, rock and pop acts as well. Each summer around 200,000 people congregate on the eastern shore of Lake Geneva to watch some of the best musicians on the planet jam in the Alps. The festival has its own currency, so be sure to exchange your euros for "Jazz" when entering. First two weeks of July; @www.montreuxjazz.com

Il Palio, Siena, Italy. Combining bribes, religion and dirty tricks, this horse race is straight out of the Middle Ages. To be precise, 1147. Riders representing Siena's different neighbourhoods battle and race around the town square for three laps. The party starts for days before each of the two big races. Early July & mid-Aug; @www .ilpaliodisiena.com

Edinburgh Fringe Festival, Scotland. It's the largest arts festival on the planet (it breaks the attendance record each year), with a dizzying display of thousands of performances in nearly 300 venues around the Scottish capital. It started in 1947, and the quality of the drama, comedy, and everything else in between only seems to get better. Three weeks in August; @www.edfringe.com

Running of the Bulls, Pamplona, Spain. People have been testing out their insurance polices at this event for years. Eight days of drinking, revelling in the streets and, oh yes, attempting to avoid stampeding bulls on a narrow, winding, cobblestoned street armed with nothing more than a pair of running shoes, a rolled-up newspaper and a hangover. Second week of July; @www.sanfermin.com

Love Parade, the Ruhr, Germany. At the world's largest rave, you'll see mosaic tattoos, blinding hair colours, and more body piercings than you can shake a . . . well, you'd better think twice before you shake anything at them. Millions of technophiles dance nonstop as they squirm through the über-fest, exchanging sweat, drugs and exotic diseases. July; @www.loveparade.de

La Tomatina, Buñol, Spain. Take one small cement-producing town, one plaza, 30,000 mostly drunk lunatics and 40,000kg of tomatoes. Mix aggressively for one hour or until town is sufficiently red, then rinse at a local watering hole. Last Wed in Aug; @www.latomatina.org

Oktoberfest, Munich, Germany. Just grab a seat and a frothy *mas* and start slidin' back the brew. The atmosphere in the fourteen tents with a combined capacity for almost 100,000 happy drinkers makes the beer taste even better. But don't let the name fool you; most of the event takes place in September. Sept–Oct; @www .oktoberfest.de

Researching special activities

The internet works a treat for **trip planning**. Let's say you speak Spanish and you like scuba diving: start at your favourite web search engine, type in "scuba" and "Spanish" and see what pops up, then narrow the search with words like "shark" or "tapas" or whatever diving aspects you deem essential. You can often find reviews and references online as well just by adding the words "reviews" or "references" to the search.

For specific **activities**, look in specialized magazines and newsletters. For a cooking course or fine dining, for example, you might look in *Gourmet Magazine*; for photography trips, *Outdoor Photographer*. If you're looking for general ideas, major-city newspaper travel sections are invaluable. A similar assortment, often with more edgy writing, can be found in adventure magazines, with some of the best ideas located among the tour advertisements listed in the back. That doesn't necessarily mean you ought to sign up for their tours – many of those things you can do on your own for a fraction of the price.

For information directly from other travellers, try forums such as ⓦwww .virtualtourist.com and ⓦwww.lonelyplanet.com's Thorn Tree, where you can post and read messages on thousands of specific travel topics.

Preparing your parents and employers

Not everyone may be as excited about your big trip as you are. Some parents might need a bit of convincing on the merits of such an endeavour, especially if you're making a large request for funding. Some employers will wonder what they'll gain by keeping your position available. So here's a little ammunition to help fight your corner.

Pre-talk

Start by softening them up with some early **hints**. Weeks, months or years before you reveal your plans, try to let it slip during conversation that you've always wanted to travel to Europe, see a bit of the world. Or, if you have specific interests like learning a language or taking a cooking course, drop that in as well. Keep it casual and speculative. You don't want a conversation about it at this point; you just want to plant a few seeds.

Passion

Let your enthusiasm shine through. Few people like to get in the way of someone pursuing their dreams. Often, it's infectious, and you'll find parents and employers wishing they could take a journey of their own.

Educational value

Travelling through Europe will help instil many of the essentials you just don't get at university: self-reliance, confidence in navigating through new surroundings, a chance to experience paintings and architecture and develop new language skills.

Use role models

The strongest examples you can find may be friends of your parents who have taken such trips, and still went on to successful careers. Do some research into some of your parents' favourite authors, cooks and TV personalities. Chances are more than one of them has taken such a

Dear Mom and Dad,

I know you want what's best for me. I know you want me to be safe. And I know you want me to earn a living/attend university/stop moonlighting as an erotic dancer. We both want those things. But as I see it, life isn't about racing to the finish line. I'll get a job/degree eventually, but I want to appreciate life first. Just now, I have a few things I need to work out, and there's no better place to get a taste of life's options than the world's biggest classroom. This is the perfect time in my life for free-spirited travel. I don't have kids. This may be the one chance in my life to do it on my own terms. And Europe is one of the world's safest destinations. Besides, plan B is to move back in with you.

trip in their youth and has probably brought it up during an interview you'll be able to find archived on the internet.

Tie it to a university program

If you can find a study-abroad program that enables you to transfer credit, you may find you have a better argument for staying in Europe over the summer after the program ends or going a few months before it begins. For many parents, the university connection cements the educational value of the entire experience overseas.

Know what you're talking about

Read through this book and you'll have all the background info you'll need to answer your parents' questions about how you're going to get around, what you're going to do and how you can make it the safest possible experience. If you can demonstrate that you've done your homework, then they'll be able to see this is something you've put time and thought into, not just your heart.

Talking money

If asking parents for money, borrow a tactic from the politicians. First sell the concept, then worry about the funding. If they ask what it will cost, tell them you're not sure, still looking into it, but that you'll take all steps to keep it as cheap as possible. Even with generous parents, as a show of good faith, you may offer to put your own money into it to the extent that you can.

Prepare for your return

Some parents may worry that you won't come back for years. Or will become some sort of vagabond, drifting back overseas and never taking what they might consider a "real job" (for my parents, this turned out to be a legitimate concern). Put them at ease by talking about what you'll do when you return. Explain that the trip will help focus your plans for the future. Of course, this will require the daunting task of coming up with some plans. Remember: nothing is set in stone, so if there are

①

> ### Dear boss,
>
> I value my job and hope I'll be working here for years to come. But just now, I can feel I need an educational break. Some companies send employees to business school or to various workshops and courses. I'd like the education that comes from travel – an edification investment I plan to pay for myself on an upcoming extended trip to Europe. I will make sure all pressing projects are completed before departing and help train any transition personnel you'd care to bring in. However, if you would take me back upon my return, I believe the company will benefit from my experience. I know I can bring new value to the job: an international perspective, a familiarity with meeting people, more confidence and street smarts. And, with a long-time dream fulfilled, I think you'll find I'll have more focus and renewed energy for the tasks. On paper, it may not look as tidy as sending me to business school, but in real terms it will be more practical. And it will come at just a fraction of the cost with far less time away from the company.

some career buzz words you know they like to hear (such as "medical school"), this would be the time to toss them around. Point out that a gap in your CV (résumé) will not hurt. Employees often find journeys like these fascinating, especially if your passion for travel shines through.

Your itinerary

OK, you've got a few places in mind, some weather you want to miss and a few dates you want to hit for festivals or seasonal activities. Before you start stringing it together, there are a few more things to consider.

If it's your first big trip, **start out gently**. If you're going to Turkey, Germany and England, for example, Turkey is the most challenging of the three and won't make the best starting point. Besides, after Turkey, Germany and England won't seem nearly as exciting. If you start in England, it'll still be exhilarating, but much easier. Once you get a feel of getting around on your own, move on to a more challenging country like Germany, where there's a solid infrastructure, but (perhaps) a language barrier. After that, navigating the bus stations and markets of Turkey will be significantly easier to handle.

Take a moment and consider the **balance of your trip**. You want a good mix of attractions, adventure, a course or two, a little wandering, a break, maybe a ferry or canal passage, a measure of hiking, and possibly even a dose of meditation. Chances are your trip may be thin in a few of these areas. Look back at the activity list on p.25 for some ideas on how you might round out your experiences. Just remember to space them out. You don't want to feel like you're trapped in an adventure race, trying to tick a slew of attractions off your list before jumping on your flight back home.

A word of warning, it's not in your best interest to "do" Paris in two days, then "do" Rome in two days, then "do" Prague, and so on. The most you'll be "doing" with such an itinerary is getting a blurry view out of the train window and less cultural depth than can be found on a postcard.

To find out how to connect the dots with the best-suited transportation, see the "Getting there and around" chapter on p.38.

Checking political stability

Europe is extremely stable, but there's no shortage of strikes and – depending on how you feel about watching protesters put cobblestones through a *McDonald's* window – you might not want to be in a city during a G8 meeting or World Bank gathering. Try to get into the habit of picking up an international newspaper and scanning the headlines. America's State Department tends to play up the dangers, which may help prevent lawsuits but can also scare people away from a reasonably safe destination. Instead, or at least as a comparison, try the UK's foreign office (Ⓦwww.fco.gov.uk), Australia's advisories (Ⓦwww.dfat.gov.au) or Canada's department of foreign affairs (Ⓦvoyage.dfait-maeci.gc.ca), for a more sensible assessment.

Activity booking

Just because you find the ideal **activity**, that doesn't mean you have to book it there and then. In fact, you can often save more than fifty percent of the cost by foregoing the middlemen and making arrangements once you arrive. However, there are some courses and tours that fill up well in advance. You can't always tell which these are, but it's possible to make a decent guess. You could reason, for example, that there's a steady stream of overnight hiking trips heading out in the Alps so, if you're not too particular about which peak, you'll find a tour that fits your level, even last-minute. If you're after something a bit more celebrated, and something specific, such as a short pastry course at Le Cordon Bleu cooking school (Ⓦwww.lcbparis.com), it's worth booking ahead. You can always call or email, say you're not sure about your arrival dates just yet and ask if they anticipate a problem booking a week or two ahead of time.

Ease of travel

Easy (strong traveller infrastructure, many locals speak English):
Denmark, England, Finland, the Netherlands, Northern Ireland, Norway, Republic of Ireland, Scotland, Sweden, Switzerland, Wales

Moderate (fair to good traveller infrastructure, some language barriers):
Austria, France, Germany, Italy, Portugal, Spain

Tougher (mixed traveller infrastructure, considerable language barrier):
Albania, Bulgaria, Hungary, Romania, Russia, Turkey

Sample itineraries

1. One month

Start in Dublin; bus to Limerick; bus to Doolin, ferry to Aran Islands; ferry to Galway, horseback riding tour; bus to Belfast; bus to Dublin.

2. One month

Start in Zürich; train to Interlaken, adventure activities; train to Montreux for the Jazz Festival; train to Zermatt, climbing course and hiking; back to Zürich.

3. Two months

Start in London; fly to Barcelona; train to Marseille; train to Florence, take cooking course; train to Venice; train to Italian Alps, mountain-biking tour; train to Vienna, visit relative; fly back to London.

Lessons learned

This entire book is filled with lessons learned, but here are seven most noticeable things that have changed in the way I travel.

- I am no longer that interested in travelling someplace simply to see something, so going to a new city just to have a look around now holds much less appeal. These days, my motivation for travel is what I'm going to do when I get there: hike a specific trail, volunteer with an interesting project, try my hand at some new thing, or get to do one of my favourite things (such as kitesurfing) in a new spot.

- I'm more comfortable with a small pack. For some reason I thought I needed more stuff – you know – just in case. The more you travel, the more you realize you can find virtually anything you need on the road.

- I don't need to conquer as much territory. I used to think, for example, that a month in New Zealand was loads of time, and I'd start trying to figure out how much ground I could cover in that time. Now I'm happy (and realize I get more out of it) if I visit fewer places, stay longer in each one and try more of the local things in each spot.

- I plan longer pit stops, even look forward to them. If I travel quickly for a bit, I know I'll get sensory overload and appreciate the travel less. I count on this now and make some interesting plans to stay put a while.

- I take more pictures of the details along the way (road signs, toilets, meals, doorways) and fewer postcards and posed shots.

- I always find out the approximate price for any taxi ride, then make sure I'm getting in the right type of taxi and that we've agreed on the price (or meter) before getting in. Even in the most developed nations (like Sweden), getting in the wrong taxi will cost you dearly.

- I'm less worried about the micro savings. I realized I don't sit around after a trip and think, oh, I should have walked an extra 3km for that slightly cheaper bakery that day I was hanging out in Rome. It's good to be frugal, but I'm better at not letting the tiny expenditures dictate my entire trip.

4. Two months

Start in Amsterdam; train to Bruges; train to Paris, pantomime lessons; train to Bordeaux, wine tasting; train to Pamplona, Running of the Bulls; train to Barcelona; ferry to Ibiza, club hopping; fly to London; hitchhike to Edinburgh, single-malt Scotch tour; ferry to Amsterdam.

5. Four months

Start in Berlin; train and ferry to Copenhagen, rent bicycle and ride and take trains to Frederikshavn; ferry to Oslo; train to fjords, hiking and white-water rafting; train to Stockholm, kayak in archipelago; ferry to Helsinki, train to St Petersburg; train to Vilnius; train to Kraków, visit Auschwitz; train to Prague, beer tasting; train to Berlin.

6. Four months

Start in Rome, study Italian; train to Brindisi, Greek island-hopping around the Aegean Sea; ferry to Athens, cooking class; train to Belgrade; train to Budapest; train to Vienna, take photography course; train to Salzburg, *Sound of Music* tour; train to Munich, Oktoberfest; train to Venice; train to Rome.

Not planning at all

Here's another way to go about it: get a passport, rustle up some cash and hop on the next plane to Europe and head in whichever direction cries out. If you need a visa to get into the next country, no worries; just pick somewhere else. Or fill out a visa application, find a cheap hotel and wait for the visa to be processed. While you're waiting, you might study the language and meet a few locals. Or don't. Go with the wind and your whims.

The drawback to planning your trip, free spirits claim, is that, to a large extent, you decide in advance what you're looking for. So, while you'll probably find "it", you'll likely miss many of the unpredictable things that are subtly trying to find you. The drawback to NOT planning is that you may miss things you would have liked to see because you were simply unaware of them, or because courses, volunteer projects or hotel rooms during festivals were already booked up.

Getting there and around

You can get a consolidated flight to Europe, buy a motorcycle in London, ride around Britain, sell it, take a ferry to Ireland and then buy a horse. Ride down the coast, sell it, take a ferry over to the European continent, zip along the Mediterranean with a one-month rail pass, then hitchhike to Paris and catch the Eurostar under the Channel to London for your return flight. The price, length of journey, reliability of arrival and comfort vary enormously with each. This chapter will help you compare the most popular choices so you can find the one that best fits your budget and itinerary (or lack thereof).

Getting to Europe

There's some truth to the famed airline axiom that savings come with restrictions, discomfort and stopovers. But only some truth. You can get **reduced prices** on tickets on major airlines with direct flights as well.

If you're not tied to one particular destination, you should check prices on flights to the cheapest gateways in Europe. Start with London, Amsterdam and Paris, then try Rome, Milan, Madrid and Frankfurt. Trying to begin your journey with a flight into, say, the Swiss Alps, isn't going to do much more than make your travel agent light up with dollar signs.

If prices are relatively equal, book with a well-informed travel agent and get their email address and phone number. They can point out things you never thought of and provide access to consolidator fares. Besides, it's nice to have someone to contact in case you're in a jam.

But before you call an agent, do a little online checking on your own so you'll know a good price when you see one. Start looking on the major online booking engines (see p.343) and check out the lowest published fares for a particular flight. Here are a few tips that will help keep down the costs:

Using one-way tickets

If I'm flying into Europe with a one-way ticket, I always get a flight to Amsterdam. You may want to buy a train, bus or plane ticket out of the country in advance, just in case the immigration officials ask. Don't fly into the UK (especially Heathrow or Gatwick airports) without a return ticket. If you are going to be working or studying in Europe (and therefore spending a year or longer) you'll probably want to get a one-way ticket and then take advantage of the cheap tickets out of London to come home.

Tim Uden,
Editor, Ⓦ www.bugeurope.com

- Take a couple of hours researching combinations of dates into different major cities (Amsterdam, London, Madrid, Paris, Frankfurt and Milan are good hubs) at one or more of the online booking engines. Sometimes, just leaving a day later or flying into a different city can make a difference of €125. In this sense, a little flexibility can translate into substantial savings.
- Often, the cheapest tickets are sold far in advance. Call a trusted travel agent and ask him/her to book the cheapest fully refundable ticket available. Then keep looking. If you find something cheaper, simply cancel the first ticket.
- For internet bookings, consider purchasing the ticket on a Wednesday (when airlines offer special promotions), not on a weekend (when the prices shoot back up).
- Once you find a good deal, go directly to that airline's site to see if they're offering any other special promotions to places nearby that are even cheaper, or any frequent-flier bonuses. Strange as it may seem, flights and prices can differ between the airlines' sites and the site where you originally spotted the flight. You might, for example, find a great fare on a Virgin Atlantic Airways flight through Expedia that Virgin doesn't offer on its own site. Air India also offers cheap deals, and Iceland Air has been offering cheap fares to Europe for backpackers since the 1960s.
- Keep in mind the cheapest fares are often less direct, less conveniently scheduled and may involve an airline you've never even heard of. If you have more time than money, this is a fine way to grab a deal.

- Don't let your frequent-flier plan get in the way of finding the best ticket. First, look for the best deal, then if two or three offer similar fares pick the one that fits with your mileage plan.
- If you don't live in a hub city (such as Los Angeles, New York, Toronto, Sydney), look for ads in the mainstream press of the nearest one to you (*New York Times*, *San Francisco Chronicle Travel*, *LA Times*, *Washington Post*, *Toronto Star*, *Melbourne Age*, *Sydney Morning Herald*), plus any student newspapers or the free and alternative newspapers such as *Village Voice*, *Montreal Mirror* and *San Francisco Bay Guardian*. If you find a great price, but you've never heard of the company, buy with a credit card so you can stop payment if need be.
- Consider an open-jaw ticket (see box opposite). If you know your itinerary, you may be able to save by not backtracking.

Travel agents

Don't assume, just because you're speaking with a "discounter" or "consolidator" (including those listed below), that you're getting the best deal. And don't assume all will spend a lot of time with your questions – many deal in bulk and are looking for a quick booking. Do a good deal of searching before you speak with an agent so you can ask better questions and act quickly (if there are limited seats left). Don't pay with cash or deal with a company that doesn't take credit cards.

- **Adventure World** Based in Sydney, Australia (☎02 8913 0755), with offices in Perth (☎08 9226 4524) and Auckland, New Zealand (☎09 524 5118); ⓦwww.adventureworld.com.au.
- **Air Brokers** International consolidator; ⓦwww.airbrokers.com.
- **AirTreks** Multi-stop international low-price ticket seller based in the US (☎1 877 247 8735); ⓦwww.airtreks.com.
- **Flight Centre** Discount flight specialist with offices in Australia (☎133 133), Canada (☎1 888 967 5302), New Zealand (☎0800 243 544), South Africa (☎0860 400 727), the UK (☎0870 499 0040) and the US (☎1 866 967 5351); ⓦwww.flightcentre.com.
- **Moment's Notice** Discount travel club based in the US (☎1 888 241 3366); ⓦwww.moments-notice.com.
- **STA Travel** UK-based agent with hundreds of offices in the US (☎1 800 781 4040) and coverage in all English- and German-speaking markets as well as Scandinavia, Switzerland, Thailand, Singapore, China and Japan. Specializes in student and independent travel. Also sells ID cards, insurance and rail passes; ⓦwww.sta.com.

What's what

APEX: Advance Purchase Excursion Fare. This standard budget ticket usually needs to be purchased 7–21 days before departure and you stay between 7 and 90 days at your destination before returning. Changes come with penalty fees.

Bucket shops: these travel agencies are unbonded (ie uninsured) discount ticket sellers that operate mainly in large gateway cities like Singapore, Bangkok, San Francisco, New York and London. Many bucket shops are small-time operators that may go out of business overnight or try to pull a fast one. Insist on a receipt that lists complete restrictions and refunds and – just in case – purchase by credit card so you can stop payment if the ticket never materializes. How do you find them? Try the newspaper travel sections of the major cities mentioned above. Just look for the smallest ads with the lowest prices. The insured version is called a "consolidator" (see below).

Charter flights: some agents can make arrangements on charter flights at incredible savings. However, changing plans can mean high penalties.

Consolidator: these travel agents buy blocks of tickets from the airlines at a reduced rate (on certain popular flights), and pass on that saving to you.

Discount clubs: a fee-based membership service that offers discounts in the range of twenty to sixty percent. Just check to make sure they offer discounts on the types of services you are likely to use. For example, great deals on four-star hotel suites may not be for you.

Discounter: they work with special student and youth fares and often deal in consolidated tickets as well. Many offer related services like rail passes and ID cards. STA Travel and Travel Cuts are typical examples.

Open-jaw ticket: these are two one-way flights sold for half their round-trip value, with an overland connection in between that you provide. For example, if you fly into London and then travel around southern Europe by train, instead of using two travel days to zip back to London to catch your flight home you can buy an open-jaw ticket and fly back from, say, Rome.

Super APEX: not an action figure with unlimited powers. Like APEX but a bit cheaper and limits the stay to 7–21 days at your destination. Sometimes also called "Eurosaver".

- **Student Universe** US-based (☎1 800 272 9676). Also sells insurance and rail passes; ⓦwww.studentuniverse.com.
- **Trailfinders** UK-based all-round travel agent (☎0845 050 5945) with offices in Australia (☎1300 780 212); ⓦwww.trailfinders .co.uk.
- **Travel Cuts** Canada-based (☎866 246 9762) with offices in the US (☎1 800 592 2887). Specializes in student and independent travel. Also sells ID cards, insurance and rail passes; ⓦwww .travelcuts.com.
- **YHA Travel** The same people that sell YHA membership cards also book budget travel. Offices around Australia; ⓦwww .yha.com.au.

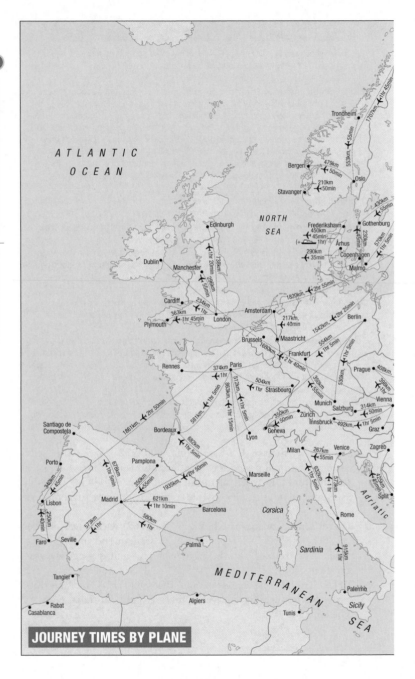

JOURNEY TIMES BY PLANE

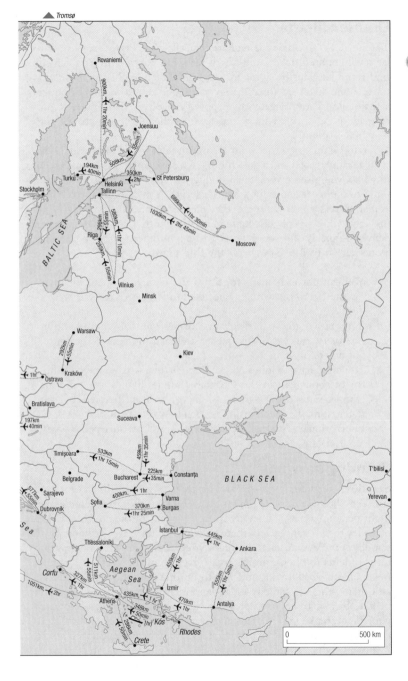

▲ Tromsø

Rovaniemi
900km
1hr 20min
Joensuu
508km, 55min
Turku 194km 40min
Stockholm
Helsinki 350km 2hr St Petersburg
Tallinn
698km 1hr 30min
BALTIC SEA
1030km 2hr 45min
Moscow
590km 1hr 10min
295km 55min
Riga
Vilnius
Minsk
Warsaw
292km 55min
Kraków
Kiev
1hr
Ostrava
Bratislava
197km 40min
Suceava
459km 1hr 35min
Timişoara 533km 1hr 15min
225km 35min
Belgrade Bucharest Constanţa
BLACK SEA
T'bilisi
400km 1hr
Sofia Varna
Sarajevo 577km 55min
Dubrovnik 370km 1hr 25min Burgas
Yerevan
İstanbul 445km 1hr
Sea
Thessaloniki Ankara
459km 1hr
Aegean Sea
Corfu 511km 55min
327km 1hr
İzmir
558km 1hr 5min
1051km, 2hr
Athens 435km 1hr
470km 1hr Antalya
348km 50min
Kos
1hr
50min
Crete Rhodes

0   500 km

Courier flights

The heydays of **courier travel** are basically over. Prices are now similar to discounted tickets, only with far more restrictions. You can still find some bargains by flying as a courier, but it applies to those who travel alone, live near (or can very easily get to at a moment's notice) a major international gateway airport (Vancouver, San Francisco, Los Angeles, New York, Sydney) and have a schedule looser than a yoga master on Valium.

Serving as an air courier – for a company, not for an independent guy with a leather jacket and a gold tooth – is a completely legal arrangement in which you give up your check-in luggage space (leaving you carry-on only) to transport goods for a courier service. You carry an invoice (plus as many layers as you can wear), they handle all the actual carrying – and they give you a heavily discounted ticket in return. They get their freight delivered quickly and you get a good deal. In other words, you become a one-person FedEx. Now, here's the **fine print**:

- You can put in requests for times and destinations, but for most discounted tickets you may be asked to leave on a day's or week's notice.
- You get a round-trip ticket that brings you back home within one or two weeks – this can be stretched up to several months, but don't count on it.
- You often have to join a courier service (that is, pay a membership fee of about €40 in the US, for example) before you can start getting transport assignments. If you're not deterred by the restrictions, the membership fee can be well worth it.
- International Association of Air Travel Couriers; ⓦwww.courier.org.

Standby services

Standby services – such as Airhitch (ⓦwww.airhitch.org) and AirTech (ⓦwww.airtech.com) – are a bit like the arrangement that flight personnel have. (They fly for ten percent of the cost of a ticket, but they're on standby.) If there's no room, they aren't flying. With standby services, you pick the flight you want (there are one-way and return flights to choose from), pay a fraction of the price of a regular ticket (about €200 for a round-trip to Europe from the US or Canada), and then either go standby or get an email 24 hours in advance. You need to be able to get to a departure city in a particular region to catch your flight, or be very patient and wait for a flight from your city to come up. And they may not take you exactly where you want to go. So, if you're very flexible, it's great. If you're trying to plan a trip in advance

GETTING THERE AND AROUND | Getting to Europe

www.roughguides.com

44

FIRST-TIME EUROPE

and need dates to correspond with certain planned events, it's less than ideal. They regularly fly to Europe from New York, Los Angeles, Boston and Washington, DC. There are some flights from Minneapolis, Orlando and other cities in the US, but not many.

Air travel within Europe

The "Costs and savings" chapter (see p.71) explains why augmenting your rail or bus pass with a **cheap flight** within Europe can be a great idea. This section will tell you how to get that cheap air flight. Zipping around on flights, no matter how cheap, is probably not the best way to see Europe (it's hard to make cultural inroads and experience the country at 30,000 feet), but it offers a great chance to connect two or three spots that might otherwise be out of range. For example, you might want to spend the bulk of your trip travelling in Spain and Portugal, but you can hop on a plane in Barcelona and get to Rome or Dublin for a long weekend without breaking your budget.

With cut-throat **budget airlines** battling it out in the skies, your biggest cost for a flight within Europe is likely to be getting yourself out to the airport. Really. It's not uncommon to find flights for €10–30, except for certain routes at certain times of the year, when demand is particularly high, though taxes can add around €25 on top of these prices. Many of these start-up "no-frills" carriers use minor airports located a little further from the city centre, but if you've got more time than money, no worries. However, most of the airports are served by regular transport so getting to and from them is rarely complicated. When they say "no frills", they generally aren't kidding, but since the flights are almost never more than three hours, it doesn't matter that it feels more like a bus. Pack a meal and something to drink and you'll be fine. You might even bring some cheap earphones so you don't have to buy the feeble ones they try to flog you on the plane. No need to worry about safety. Whatever corners they need to cut to streamline their company, there's no getting around the strict EU regulations that govern the flight industry.

Ryanair is the biggest player and London's Stansted Airport the budget epicentre. But if you're in Stockholm, Copenhagen, Birmingham, Venice, Rome, Milan, Stuttgart, Leeds, Cologne, Bonn, Bratislava, Vienna, Budapest, Dublin, Amsterdam, Rotterdam, Glasgow, Brussels, Barcelona, Frankfurt and more … you've got yourself a hub and a range of cheap destinations to choose from.

These new budget start-ups haven't been a big hit with travel agents, though. Many agents won't have anything to do with them (there's no

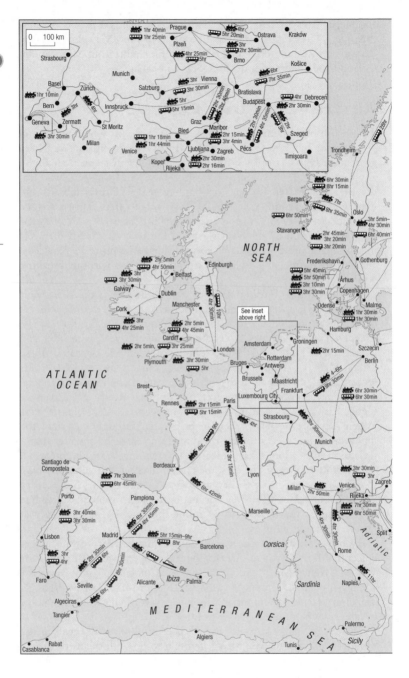

JOURNEY TIMES BY TRAIN & BUS
HIGH-SPEED TRAIN TIMES
Rome–Naples 1hr 30min
Paris–Brest 2hr 15min
Paris–London 2hr 35min
London–Brussels 1hr 25min
Paris–Bordeaux 3hr
Paris–Brussels 1hr 25min
Brussels–Amsterdam 2hr 40min
Amsterdam–Frankfurt 3hr 45 min
Copenhagen–Stockholm 5hr
Barcelona–Alicante 4hr 40min
Berlin–Hamburg 1hr 30min
Geneva–Zürich 2hr 43min
Milan–Zürich 3hr 40min
Madrid–Barcelona 2hr 38min
Madrid–Seville 2hr 30min
0 100 km
Groningen
1hr
2–3hr
Amsterdam
Rotterdam
2hr 35min
2hr 20min
4hr 12min
45min
Antwerp
Bruges
1hr
Brussels
Maastricht
3hr
Luxembourg City
Tromsø
Rovaniemi
12hr
13hr 25min
Joensuu
5hr 30min
7hr 10min
1hr 55min
2hr 30min
Turku
7hr
9hr
Helsinki
St Petersburg
Stockholm
Tallinn
4hr 35min–8hr 50min
4hr 30min–8hr 30min
8hr
5hr 30min
15hr
10hr
15hr 30min
10hr 30min
17hr
19hr
Riga
Moscow
BALTIC SEA
5hr 30min
5hr
Vilnius
Minsk
Gdańsk
5hr
4hr
6hr
Warsaw
2hr 30min
7hr 30min
Kiev
Kraków
See inset above left
Suceava
6hr 30min
6hr 30min
Timişoara
6hr 30min
7hr 30min
3hr
2hr 50min
Belgrade
Bucharest
Constanţa
BLACK SEA
T'bilisi
11hr
Sarajevo
8hr
7hr 30min
Varna
Sofia
7hr 30min
Burgas
Yerevan
Dubrovnik
2hr 30min
5hr 30min
2hr
Plovdiv
Sea
İstanbul
5hr–9hr
5hr 30min
Ankara
Thessaloníki
6hr 30min
(+ 2hr)
5hr
7hr 40min
6hr
0 500 km
Corfu
Aegean Sea
7hr
10hr
İzmir
Athens
7hr
Antalya

commission). And some of the carriers have bypassed agents altogether to save money through more direct sales. Perforce, there's not one agent or website with access to all the discounted fares offered (at least not at the moment), so to check rates you need to surf the internet. For a list of airlines and search engines see "Directory", p.343.

Charter seats

Many Europeans take a holiday with the kids and fly **charter**. Which means you can catch a charter flight from any major city to the major resort destinations (the ones with overcrowded beaches and ski slopes). There are too many to list, though popular destinations include the Canary Islands, Ibiza, Majorca, Cyprus, Greece and Egypt. Simply check the travel section of the local newspaper. You can find great deals on last-minute flights (you don't have to buy the entire hotel package – many offer leftover seats on the plane).

Flight passes

- **Star Alliance Europe Airpass** (Ⓦwww.staralliance.com). Choose among 45 countries with this air pass of three to ten

Sitting on a train

It's not quite as straightforward as it sounds. On most **regular trains**, you can just hop on board with your rail pass, grab a second-class seat (the train cars are marked as such on the outside, and the conductors are typically guarding the first-class entrances) and relax. But like a subway ticket, individual train tickets and rail passes don't guarantee a seat, just passage on the train. On some particularly popular journeys you may end up hopping from one free seat to the next at every stop, or get stuck standing in the aisles or in the noisy passageway between train carriages when the seats completely fill up. You can avoid that by paying to **reserve a seat** (about €9) or getting to the station early (or the day before) and asking at the ticket window how crowded the train will be.

All **high-speed trains** – crowded or not – require a seat reservation, which is going to cost €10–15 per ride, even if you have a rail pass. You also have to pay extra for a sleeper car or couchette on overnight journeys. The **sleeper** is luxury train travel – at least, some of it is. It covers the range from a semi-soft bunk bed in a shared room to a real bed with a washstand and fresh sheets and towels. Prices for one night range from about €40 to €125, depending on the comfort level. The **couchette** is like a small cabin where the seats fold flat and you can sleep side by side with a few fellow passengers. Some turn into double-decker bunk beds with the sort of padding normally found in dental waiting-room furniture. A couchette costs about €30 a night. Some trains also have special reclining seats ("sleeperettes" or, more specifically, "lackofsleeperettes") like you might find in business class on a plane, which can also be reserved. You can find a place to sleep without a reservation, and many do, but you're taking your chances spending a night in an upright seat or getting bumped from your recliner in the middle of the night by someone who boards with a reservation. It could make the difference between a full day of sightseeing and spending your day passed out on a park bench for a four-hour nap.

distance-priced coupons (€65 and up per flight). To qualify, your travels to and from Europe have to be on a Star Alliance carrier. You can change your reservation at any time so long as the routing isn't changed, but you can't visit the same place twice.

- **europebyair** (Ⓦwww.europebyair.com). Travellers heading to Europe can fly on 20-plus different airlines to more than 500 cities within Europe and beyond at the flat rate of €71 per flight plus airport taxes. Each €71 coupon is valid for 120 days on nonstop flights between any two cities within the system. You can buy as few as one, and there are no blackout dates. But – here's the catch – you have to buy the tickets before you enter Europe, and you don't get refunds for the ones you don't use. Reservations (and reservation changes) can be made at any time.

Travelling by train within Europe

If you don't set foot on a **train** at least once while you're in Europe, you're missing out on something. Besides the overpriced stale food they like to serve onboard, Europe is train country. How else would you describe a rail network totalling 240,000km? (By comparison, there's 45,000km of rail in the US and Canada, an area more than twice as big.) It's not necessarily the cheapest way to get around; it's simply the preferred way. And not because the rail routes are often more scenic: the

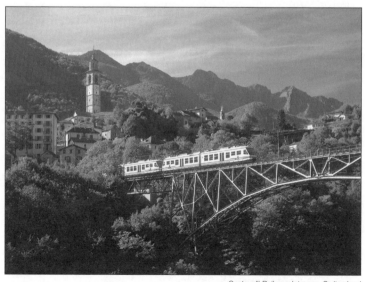
▲ Centovalli Railway, Intragna, Switzerland

facing seats provide an opportunity to meet locals or chat with friends, the aisles allow you to stretch your legs, some carriages allow full reclining at night and the train's chug-chug adds an authentic travel beat to any conversation. Plus, ethically, it beats flying.

Buying a train ticket is as simple as walking up to the ticket window, saying the name of the town you want to go to and handing over a credit card or cash. The biggest problem is that, in most European countries, this is a painfully expensive way to get around.

Europe rail and bus passes

Rail passes

Eurail Global Pass Adult		Global Pass Youth	
15 days	$699	15 days	$445
21 days	$909	21 days	$589
1 month	$1125	1 month	$735
2 months	$1589	2 months	$1035
3 months	$1959	3 months	$1279
Any 10 days within 2 months $825		Any 10 days within 2 months $539	
Any 15 days within 2 months $1085		Any 15 days within 2 months $705	

Eurail Select Pass		Eurail Select Pass Youth	
3 bordering countries within 2 months		3 bordering countries within 2 months	
5 days	$445	5 days	$289
6 days	$489	6 days	$319
8 days	$579	8 days	$379
10 days	$675	10 days	$435
4 bordering countries within 2 months		4 bordering countries within 2 months	
5 days	$495	5 days	$319
6 days	$545	6 days	$349
8 days	$635	8 days	$409
10 days	$725	10 days	$469
5 bordering countries within 2 months		5 bordering countries within 2 months	
5 days	$549	5 days	$355
6 days	$595	6 days	$385
8 days	$685	8 days	$445
10 days	$775	10 days	$499
15 days	$979	15 days	$639

Eurail countries:
Austria, Belgium, Bulgaria, Croatia, the Czech Republic, Denmark, Finland, France, Germany, Greece, Hungary, Ireland, Italy, Luxembourg, Montenegro, Netherlands, Norway, Poland, Portugal, Romania, Serbia, Slovenia, Spain, Sweden, Switzerland.

InterRail Global Pass (second class)
Any five days in ten days €271
Any ten days in 22 days €391
Twenty-two consecutive days €510
One month €652

InterRail Youth Pass (under-26, second class)
Any five days in ten days €174
Any ten days in 22 days €261
Twenty-two consecutive days €337
One month €435

Enter the **rail pass** (Eurail for North Americans and those Down Under; InterRail for Europeans: throughout this book, we've included prices for Eurail in US dollars, and InterRail in euros). There are scores of options. You can buy a pass that allows either unlimited travel during a set period or a fixed number of days during a set period. Some allow travel in multiple countries, some limit travel to just one country.

Prices change, but the box below should give you a good idea. There are several more passes available online at ⓦwww.raileurope.com and

InterRail countries:

Austria, Belgium, Bosnia-Herzegovina, Britain, Bulgaria, Croatia, the Czech Republic, Denmark, Finland, France, Germany, Greece, Hungary, Ireland, Italy, Luxembourg, Macedonia, Montenegro, the Netherlands, Norway, Poland, Portugal, Romania, Serbia, Slovakia, Slovenia, Spain, Switzerland, Sweden, Turkey.

Bus passes

Busabout

The Loops Pass

Northern Loop: Paris–Amsterdam–Berlin–Prague–Vienna–Munich–Paris

Southern Loop: Munich–Venice–Rome–Siena–Florence–Pisa–Nice–Lucerne–Munich

Western Loop: Paris–Alps–Nice–Avignon–Barcelona–Valencia–Madrid–San Sebastian–Bordeaux–Tours–Paris

1 Loop €419 (students €399), 2 Loops €719 (students €689), 3 Loops €879 (students €849)

Flexitrip Pass

Start and finish anywhere on the above Loops routes and stay as long as you want. Additional Flexistops can be bought on board (valid May–Oct). Six Flexistops €369 (students €349), additional Flexistop €39

Busabout countries:

Austria, Belgium, Czech Republic, France, Germany, Italy, the Netherlands, Spain, Switzerland.

Eurolines Adult

15 days: low season €205, mid season €240, high season €345

30 days: low season €310, mid season €330, high season €455

Eurolines Youth

15 days low season €175, mid season €205, high season €290

30 days low season €240, mid season €270, high season €375

Eurolines serves major cities in:

Albania, Austria, Belgium, Bosnia-Herzegovina, Britain, Bulgaria, Croatia, the Czech Republic, Denmark, Estonia, France, Germany, Greece, Hungary, Ireland, Italy, Latvia, Lithuania, Macedonia, Morocco, the Netherlands, Poland, Portugal, Romania, Serbia, Slovakia, Slovenia, Spain, Sweden, Switzerland, Turkey.

@www.interrail.com; see pp.50–51 to compare prices and p.75 to best take advantage of your pass. (Note that InterRail tickets are not valid in your European country of residence.) In general, a flexipass-type ticket will better serve most travellers as you don't want to be taking long train journeys every day (and short journeys will likely be cheaper to buy individually).

Travelling by bus within Europe

There are two **bus passes** worth looking into, and they both undercut the train fares: Eurolines (@www.eurolines.com) and Busabout (@www .busabout.com) – see box on pp.50–51 for a price guide. **Eurolines** is cheaper and functions as Europe's standard long-distance bus line, connecting 500 destinations across Europe, while **Busabout** is aimed specifically at budget travellers – taking you not just around Europe but right to a hostel (one they hope you'll stay at) – and provides onboard movies and a guide. That gives you less reason to look out of the window and less opportunity to meet locals, but it will save you the hassle of finding a hostel and will put you in touch with more travellers. For those just travelling in the UK, there's also Megabus (@www .megabus.co.uk), which is like a discount Eurolines.

Travelling by car within Europe

Driving offers the chance to take control of your itinerary, get to places you can't easily reach (or reach at all) with public transport and (with enough people) even save money. Whether you decide to buy or rent a car (both covered in this section), there are some basic tips that will make the experience more enjoyable:

- **Drive defensively** In Paris, Greece, Italy and several other countries it may seem like most drivers are making up new traffic laws as they go. Stay cool and follow the law, even if those around you aren't.
- **Know how to drive a stick-shift car** Automatics often cost more to rent.

> ## Border crossings
>
> There are **border crossings** in Europe, but chances are you won't notice them on a train or bus. Perhaps you'll spot names on road signs, or the train conductor may start speaking a different language. There won't be any sort of announcement or blinking lights. Few, if anyone, will actually ask to see your passport. And, unless you ask nicely, they won't put a stamp in it.

- **Learn the metric system** FYI it's about four litres of gasoline to a gallon – yes, it is about as expensive as twelve-year-old Scotch. If you're in Germany, Italy or France and near the Austria or Luxembourg border, cross over to fill up and save up to €5 per gallon. Eastern Europe and especially Russia and Ukraine are even cheaper.
- **Don't use the car for city sightseeing** It's usually a lot cheaper and easier to find free parking well outside of the city, and use public transport to get into town. It's quicker, better and greener to get out and wander cities on foot, especially since most European cities have more curves than a bag of pretzels and half of them are one-way streets. There's a simple formula: tiny medieval roads plus stress equals scratches and extra rental fees.
- **Know where you're heading** You'll rarely see north, south, east and west signs to point you in the right direction; just directions to specific towns. Before you tuck the map away, take a good look at the next town's name and the next big city's name.
- **Stick to the back roads** Highways are fast but boring. Take advantage of your mobility and go places rail and bus travellers can't. Most back roads are in excellent shape and offer much more interesting food, and far more scenery (though they're not as well lit for night driving). Many of the major roads come with extra tolls and often they run parallel with the old road they replaced.
- **Be aware of hidden expenses** Super-freeways in France and Italy have tolls (about €5 per hour), and you may be spending up to €20 a day for parking in major cities. Since 2003, you have to pay a "congestion charge" to drive in central London (£8/€12 a day; ⓦwww.cclondon.com). Oslo also has one, as do Stockholm, Milan, Riga, Valletta (Malta) and Durham, England. And driving in Norway and Sweden in winter without proper winter tyres is fineable. Two countries require drivers to get a sticker to use their national motorways (sold at border crossings): €30 for the Swiss highway permit, €11 a week for Austria's. And tax on your rental is typically 18–25 percent (zero in Switzerland, but its rates are higher).
- **Know the signs** Thanks to EU regulations, road signs have been standardized. There are only a few you really need to know, so take five minutes to learn them. To get to the centre of town, you can typically find signs pointing you to *Centre-ville*, *Zentrum* or *Stadtmitte*, while the tourist office is designated by "i", "VVV" or *turismo*. The signs can be found online at ⓦwww.ideamerge.com /motoeuropa/roadsigns.
- **Don't speed** Many European countries take speeding seriously: Germany, because you can go as fast as you like, and other

www.roughguides.com

countries, because they seem to be financing their government with the fines. An €85 ticket is not uncommon. Some places have speed cameras mounted on the side of the road. If one flashes when you go by, just smile. You'll pay the fine later when the rental company tacks it on to your credit card account.

● **Prepare for emergencies** European law now dictates that you must carry the following items in your car: first-aid kit, reflective jacket for each person in the car, hazard triangle, fire extinguisher, spare bulb for every exterior light. Also, UK drivers need to adjust UK cars' headlamps with beam adjusters.

Renting a car

This is probably the most hassle-free way to drive. But then, you're paying for that convenience. If you can put together a group of travellers, however, you may not be paying so much. It depends on how much you drive. With two people in a **rented compact car** with unlimited kilometres driving five hours every other day, a month is going to cost about €850 per person. Driving five hours every fourth day will set you back about €550 each, or roughly the same as a rail pass. With four people driving a slightly larger car five hours every third day, this will bring the costs down to just under €425 per person.

Weekly rentals with unlimited kilometres are the most economical short-term solutions and can be booked over the web, via a travel agent or directly with the company. It's usually cheaper to book from home. Having said that, it's worth taking a look at the pricing of some **rental consolidators** (ⓦwww.autoeurope.com and ⓦwww.kemwel .com). As with flights, these agents buy in bulk and pass on the savings. If you're travelling for more than three weeks, a lease (sometimes called a "buy-back") is going to be the best option. You get a new car and unlimited kilometres, plus breakdown cover and zero-deductible (zero excess) insurance for a great rate. In addition to the sites above, try ⓦwww.europebycar.com and ⓦwww.renaultusa.com.

An **RV** (**Recreational Vehicle**) is another option, especially for families, as it makes the more affordable campsites accessible – some are little cities unto themselves with large swimming pools and waterslides. However, the petrol-guzzling motors make it less than ideal for covering long distances. Figure about €100 per day for rental, not including petrol or campsites.

What you'll need

Remember, when you rent a car, you're liable for the whole shebang. There's a **Collision Damage Waiver** (CDW) supplement, which covers the car (usually with a deductible fee of a few hundred dollars – roof, tyres and windshield aren't usually covered) and costs €11–20

Driving in Italy

"OK," Renato explained, as I adjusted the rear-view mirror of my red Ford Fiesta, "driving in Napoli is like a video game. You just have to relax, stop thinking, and feel it in your stomach."

I fastened my seat belt.

"What are you doing?!" he reprimanded. "No one in Napoli wears seat belts. You want to look like a tourist?"

I unbuckled. Renato told me that about a decade ago when the mandatory seat-belt law was passed and briefly enforced, people started wearing T-shirts with a black stripe painted across the chest.

We came to the first traffic light, but cars were only stopping if there was faster traffic coming from the other direction. It seems red, yellow and green lights are, in the eyes of Napolitano drivers, just colours, and should be obeyed no more than Christmas decorations. I asked Renato why the drivers ignored them. "If they followed rules," he explained, "they'd be stuck in traffic for hours."

"But they are stuck in traffic for hours," I pointed out.

"Well, yes," he admitted, "that's true."

My lesson also had an acoustic component. In Napoli, the horn is not just a warning device, but a musical instrument, and Renato played it beautifully. When we passed a voluptuous woman walking on the sidewalk, he reached over and hit the side of the horn, delivering three short, cute squeaks. No one looked over at us except the woman he was honking at, as if everyone knew only she was the object of the honk. Later, five machine-gun-style honks got the attention of his friend on the other side of the street. One quick blast warned a driver not to cut us off. When we were in a crowd of people, Renato reached over and honked with a short double-tap to the centre of the horn, and people moved. A few were slow to get out of our way, and a two-second blast was required. This longer honk was quite effective, but protocol dictated that they shoot us a nasty look as they stepped aside.

Watching some Napolitano drivers squeeze past me on the right, drive up on the curb, and triple-park, I wondered aloud how they ever passed their driver's tests. "They probably didn't," Renato answered. "Up until a few years ago, anyone could buy a black market license for around €500."

Now that I was getting the hang of it, it was time for a little sightseeing. Renato gave me the three-second tour: "University there, church there, blond there!" (honk).

Doug Lansky

a day, depending on the country, the car and the rental company. There are two ways to do it cheaper. The first is to call your credit-card company and ask if they offer coverage for free with your card if you use it to pay for the rental. Some do, some don't, but always ask them to spell out exactly what happens in case of an accident. Plan B is to buy the CDW elsewhere: Travel Guard (Ⓦ www.travelguard.com), for example, sells it for €7 a day, though check validity for Italy and Ireland, as they may not allow it.

Most rental companies won't hand over the keys if you're under 21 or don't have a credit card. Many want you to be 25, or will stick you with under-age insurance fees. If you're considered too young, leasing may be a better option, as the leasing companies are more relaxed with age limitations. STA Travel (®www.statravel.com) may also be able to help with rentals for the under-25 set.

A valid **driver's licence** is all you need in most European countries to rent a car. In Austria, Bosnia, Bulgaria, the Czech Republic, Greece, Hungary, Italy, Poland, Portugal, Romania, Russia, Spain and Ukraine, you'll need an international driving permit (IDP), which is simply a translation of your licence. It feels better to hand to a police officer if you get pulled over, but it just makes it easier for him to write out the ticket. It's simple enough to get (€10–15 plus one or two passport-size photos) from your national auto association; see p.344 for a list of these.

Airport or town

The surest way of saving money with your rental car is to make sure you don't pick it up at the airport when you land, if you plan to start your trip by exploring a city for a few days. Paying €30–50 a day for the car plus another €17 to park it safely is a quick way to flush around €250 down the drain. Instead, pick up your car after your initial city sightseeing and plan to return it before sightseeing at the end of the trip. And if you're not picking up the car at the airport when you arrive, don't bother to go back there to get it. Pick it up in town (away from the train station, as well), and you may skip an ugly tax (possibly as much as seventeen percent) on the total rental fee.

If you can get a good deal, try renting a car with a built-in GPS system. These are incredible inventions and may never serve you better than they can in Europe. The digital map shows exactly where to go and can even give voice prompts like "Take the second left one hundred metres ahead." Miss a turn and it will recalibrate your route. It can even tap into the public traffic system and automatically replan your route to avoid traffic jams. But it's not as much fun as looking at a map.

Buying a secondhand car

The UK seems like a good place to **buy a used car** because there's a great market for vehicles aimed at travellers; everything is in English, so contracts aren't so intimidating; it's a common point of entry; and if you're going to buy a car, doing it at the beginning of your trip makes the most sense. The problem is European driving can be tricky enough without having to worry about being on the left-hand side of the road. Taking the vehicle over to the Continent (and back if you plan to sell it) gets expensive as well; and you don't really want a right-hand drive there where they drive on the right. Naturally, if you plan to do your driving exclusively in the UK, buy your car there. If not, you might consider picking it up on the Continent. If you have a friend or relative who is willing to help you register the vehicle, let them help. Frankfurt, Amsterdam and Paris are particularly good car-buying cities for travellers. Look on the web (the Netherlands Ⓦwww.zoekertjes.net; France Ⓦwww.jannonce.com; Germany Ⓦwww.zweitehand.de), in classified papers and on notice boards at hostels. You should be able to find a car for under €850 that will get you around. Even if you sell it for €425 after two months, it'll still be cheaper than a rental.

But if you buy a car you need to insure it. And this is the tricky bit. Talk to the sellers and see what they did and if they'll help you sort through the paperwork and provide any tips. Otherwise, consider buying the car in a place where you have friends or relatives who can help with translation and bypassing complex bureaucracy.

How to hitch safely and quickly

In many countries around Europe, **hitchhiking** is an accepted way of getting around and drivers are sympathetic to your roadside plight (as many have done some hitching themselves). In others, such as parts of Scandinavia, you're something of a pariah, although it's still eminently possible to thumb your way around. Bear in mind, though, that there are dangers inherent to hitchhiking beyond the normal traffic risks. The driver who seemed nice enough to stop for you may not in fact be very nice at all. And, once you're in the car with such a person, you're at a serious disadvantage. Female travellers in particular are at a higher risk; it's advisable for women never to hitch alone. Rough Guides doesn't recommend hitching as a safe means of getting around, but if you do choose to hitch, be aware of the risks and check out the "Security" section on p.58 for tips on making hitchhiking as safe as possible.

Presentation

- Start by dressing well. You've only got a few seconds to make an impression. This is the time (in case it's been a while) to wash your clothes and tuck in your shirt. A jacket and tie is out of place – you should look like a budget traveller; just a clean and trustworthy one. Leave the black and camo colours in your pack.
- Remove the hat and sunglasses. They need to be able to see your face clearly, see that you're not hiding anything.
- Don't smoke while waiting for a ride.
- Minimize the luggage. The four-piece custom luggage set with a windsurfer isn't going to get you far. One bag – a midsize backpack – is ideal.
- If you're standing on the side of the road, place your pack neatly in front of you to show that you're a backpacker travelling their country on a budget. Some (not Americans, typically) like to put a flag patch of their home country on their pack to highlight the foreign-traveller angle.

www.roughguides.com

- Hold up a sign. Not a necessity, but it can help. Carry a permanent marker and then just look for an old pizza box or chunk of cardboard. Try to pick a place that's not more than two hours away so you've got an excuse to get out if nine hours with this driver seems intolerable. Similarly, they may be intimidated about spending a full day giving you a ride. If it goes well, you can explain that you're actually going a bit further. Some people use a sign with a giant smile on it. Or "Student traveller". Or "I don't smell funny". If you're standing at or near a stoplight, you might try something humorous on the back, so you can flip it over if you've got someone's eye for a few seconds.

- Hitching is easiest for people travelling on their own, a couple or two women. Three of anybody is too many – it's hard to find anyone with enough room – and intimidating. Two guys can be intimidating to many drivers as well. Although not advisable, if you do decide to hitch as a single woman, see the security section below.

- The typical age range is 18–30. If you're over 30 and look young, you can pull it off, but drivers tend to shy away from people who aren't in this group.

Location

- Usually the best place to hitch is at a petrol station near the motorway. This means getting directions from the tourist office or a website (@www.autostopguide.com and @www.digihitch.com have all the best places in Europe to hitch) and taking a bus or subway there. Simply ask people who are at the pump (ah, a captive audience). Say you're a student trying to see their country cheaply and you'd appreciate a ride. Offer to chip in for some petrol as well. Or buy a coffee/Coke for the journey. With this method, it should take five to thirty minutes to get a ride. Besides, you have plenty to eat and someplace to stay warm/cool while you hitch.

- If you need to stand on the side of the road, make sure there's plenty of room for the driver to stop; that they're going slowly and don't need to concentrate on merging or accelerating; and that you can be seen from a distance.

Security

- Safety starts with your appearance. You're going to likely get safer rides if you look the part. Kind drivers (and owners of nice cars) are far less likely to pick up travellers who look like street urchins or seem even remotely like they might be a threat to their safety.

- If you're hitching on the side of the road and a car pulls over, don't just run after it and jump in. Take a moment to go to the passenger side window (open the door if the driver doesn't put down the electric window) and ask where he/she is going.

Use those precious few seconds to see if the driver looks dangerous in any way; if there are other potentially dangerous people in the car; or if there's any smell of alcohol or open bottles.

- Women are not advised to hitch alone. If you do choose to do it, you should only consider hitching at petrol stations. If anyone looks mildly suspicious, don't even ask them for a ride. In fact, try to restrict your hitching requests to families with young kids and single women drivers who look presentable. Also, non-hitch hitching can be an option (see below).

(see below)

Strategy

- If you're going further down the highway and the driver needs to let you off, ask him to stop at a well-positioned petrol station before the city he's heading to. If he takes you into the city, you can't hitch there, so you'll need to take a bus back out to a petrol station on the other side of town.
- If there's a chance it might rain, buy a cheap umbrella. No one wants a soaking-wet person in the car.
- Bring enough food and drink to last you for several hours.
- As a rule of thumb, give a place two hours before you give up. You'll normally find a ride well before that.
- Learn the local protocol. It's not always a question of putting your thumb out. That's just the standard. In Latvia, you use an open hand instead; in parts of Eastern Europe you flap your arm like a bird with a dislocated wing.

Be a good hitcher

- You represent the hitchhiking community when you accept a ride. If the driver has a good experience, they may stop for more hitchers later so be a good ambassador.
- Don't smoke unless you get permission first.
- If they picked you up because they wanted some company on a long ride and feel like talking, talk back. If you must sit silently and don't feel like making conversation, come up with a good excuse or stop hitching.
- If you arrive at a spot where there are already one or more hitchers, the etiquette is that you head down traffic (the direction cars are headed) and stay 20–100m away. Sometimes drivers zip past the first person, then get a bad conscience and see you and stop (or slow down for the first person but don't like the look of him), so it's not the worst place to be.

Non-hitch hitching

- Put up a notice in your hostel saying that you're looking for a ride and you don't mind sharing petrol expenses. Put up notices in other hostels as well. Often groups of travellers will have rented or bought a car and are looking for some help with the costs.

● Contact a rideshare or lift centre. Some organizations are paid a small fee both for membership and per kilometre driven while others request a donation. In Switzerland, for example, many cities offer a ride service called Mitfahrzentrale. See ⓦwww .hitchhikers.org for more info.

Travelling by ferry around Europe

Obviously, you can't realistically travel the whole of Europe by **ferry**, but the services on offer do provide interesting alternatives and handy little short cuts here and there. For a list of ferry operators see "Directory", p.346. A few routes, including their journey times, are:

Brindisi, Italy–Kefalonia, Greece (12hr)
Copenhagen, Denmark–Oslo, Norway (16hr)
Gdansk, Poland–Nynäshamn, Sweden (18hr)
Harwich, England–Esberg, Denmark (16hr)
Helsingør, Denmark–Helsingborg, Sweden (20min)
Helsinki, Finland–Stockholm, Sweden (15hr)
Helsinki, Finland–Tallinn, Estonia (3hr 30min)
Newcastle, England–Gothenburg, Sweden (25hr)
Newhaven, England–Dieppe, France (1hr 15min)

Travelling by bicycle within Europe

This is a continent that deserves to be seen from a **bike**. The hamlets that tour buses and cars roll past regularly are some of the greatest treasures. With the great road races (Giro d'Italia, Vuelta de Espana, the Tour de France) ripping by at one point or another, you find a great respect for cyclists (though not always much actual room on the road). In fact, taking a bike around Norway or Sweden and camping for free among the fjords or on the coast is quite possibly the single cheapest way to see Europe. You just pay for your plane ticket (plus some of Norway's and Sweden's overpriced food), and out on the back roads expensive restaurants aren't even an option. Denmark offers some of the best biking, with 10,000km of bike trails packed into a country that's not more than 300km wide and 500km long. The Netherlands also has excellent flat bike trails.

Europe's larger cities all have daily and weekly **rentals**. Or you can buy a local bike when you arrive. They have everything from €40 rusty

▲ Cycling in Amsterdam

wrecks that work to the very same top-of-the-line Treks, Cannondales, Giants, Bianchis and the like you can find at home.

And just because your bike holds four **saddlebags**, that doesn't mean you should bring all four. You'll probably need them all if you're camping. But if you're planning to stay at hostels or pensions (and there are plenty along the way to keep you from camping if you'd rather have a comfortable bed after a long ride), two saddlebags should be sufficient. The reduced weight is a godsend going up hills. But, more importantly, it makes security less of an issue. If you want to head into a market or restaurant, or up a flight of stairs to check the availability of a hostel (something you'll be doing daily), it's easy to lock up the bike and carry your two bags along. With four bags (or five, including a front bag), that's not much of an option, so someone will get stuck guarding the gear – or you'll need one impressive security system.

Bringing your **bike on a plane** can be an issue. That is, a cost issue. Some carriers will provide you with a bike box, some won't. You'll need to find out in advance. The easiest thing to do is to get a bike box for free at your local cycle shop and then buy a pedal wrench to remove the pedals yourself (even if they do it for you, you'll still need the wrench to put the pedals back on when you arrive). Take off the handlebars and tape them to the frame of the bike, lower or move the seat as well. And don't forget to let some air out of the tyres. Then make sure the whole thing is well padded. Another option, if it's OK with your airline, is to simply put it on board without a box. Just leave it as is, with a huge "Fragile" note on it. Chances are, handlers will be gentler with it if they can see what it is.

61

Why travel by bike?

Modern transportation, especially in Europe, is reliable. That's the problem. It's so easy, and rather tempting, to book your way as you go. Biking doesn't quite let you get away with that. Bad weather, fatigue and punctures force flexibility into your trip and make you stop where you never thought you would. OK, you look a bit silly interacting with the locals while wearing black spandex shorts with a built-in sweaty maxi-pad. But if you take that next step and shave your legs, it somehow looks more natural. Some countries, like France, have great respect for this type of travel. There's a historical precedent for it – the concept was sold to them long ago as the horse that needs no hay. Trucks make room for you on narrow roads, and the locals cheer you along. Even if, like me, you don't feel that sporty when you start, you'll be in incredible condition by the time it's over. And at the end of a 100-mile day, when you pull into a pub or café and see the people who've just been sitting around, there's a tremendous feeling of accomplishment, and a touch of arrogance. You almost want to sit down next to someone and ask, "So, what did you do today?"

Tim Moore
Author, *French Revolutions: Cycling the Tour de France* and *Travels with My Donkey: One Man and His Ass on the Pilgrimage Way to Santiago*

When biking around Europe, you can put up a tent in a campground or free field (if legal) more easily than if travelling by train or bus, since you'll be passing through the rural areas anyway. You can also easily make hotel reservations by carrying a mobile phone and a guidebook; just call ahead to a hostel or B&B once you get a sense of how far you'll get that day. A phone is also particularly handy to have along in case of any falls in fairly remote areas.

Travelling with a tour

If you'd rather follow a leader than a map, guidebook or your nose, then taking a **tour** will certainly provide some peace of mind and remove any worry of planning. Or maybe you think you'd like to go it alone but want a bit of handholding to start out your trip and boost your confidence. Tours are also a good idea if you want to visit a few places you otherwise couldn't. There are plenty of operators happy to take your money. The tough part is just deciding which tour you want to do.

Regional tours

These include everything from four-star luxury tours to local packages that can be arranged in almost any midsize city. There are thousands of **tour companies** to choose from at any number of levels, and it certainly helps to get a personal recommendation or find some favourable reviews before you sign up to one. In many areas, hostels team up with local tour operators (or allow them to leave posters around, for which the hostel may get a commission); the operators typically offer off-road budget trips to scenic spots in the area that are hard to access by local transport. Often, these tours are good fun, but try to get a sense of what the guide is like beforehand and trust your instincts.

Bicycle tours

A support vehicle and leader provide a good deal of assistance on a long bike trip. However, this turns one of the cheapest ways of seeing Europe into a rather expensive one.

- **BackRoads** Classic upscale tours; about €2500 for one week; ⓦ www.backroads.com.
- **Bicycle Beano Tours** Vegetarian bike tours in Wales; about €620 for one week; ⓦ www.bicycle-beano.co.uk.
- **Bike Rider Tours** Upscale tours; €2000–2500 for one week; ⓦ www.bikeriderstours.com.
- **Butterfield and Robinson** Luxury tours; €3900–6450 for one week; ⓦ www.butterfield.com.
- **Euro-Bike Tours** Mid-range tour company with over thirty years of experience; €1790–2360 for one week; ⓦ www.eurobike.com.
- **Pack and Pedal Europe** Among the cheaper tours; €645–1520 for one week; ⓦ www.tripsite.com.

Guided excursions

Despite the general reluctance of independent travellers to sign up for just about anything, for small portions of a longer trip jumping on a **tour** can be an excellent way to get some professional supervision for something you haven't done before. There are glacier treks in the Alps, kayak trips in Norway's fjords – the list goes on. Some of these activities are difficult to arrange on your own and they can, oddly, be cheaper if done with a tour. You can usually get good, impartial information from your guidebook and from other travellers while you're in the region. A few questions to ask when enquiring about an activity are:

- How easy is it to book on the spot, without a reservation?
- Are there any possible (likely) weather-related conflicts with the intended activities? If so, are there any discounts (if they're not available when you arrive)?
- Does the price include taxes and tips? If not, what's the total cost?
- What are the living conditions like? Private room? Private bathroom? Washing facilities?
- What meals are included?
- For walking and cycling tours, are baggage transfers or porters included?
- What's the cancellation policy, and what kind of insurance is included?

Europe-wide tours

You can get everything from fourteen cities in six days on a bus ("on your right, the blur of lights out of the window is Paris") to a speciality tour that visits the best restaurants in one tiny region for over a week. For speciality travel, take a look at "Planning your big trip" (p.19).

The three main **bus tour companies** shuttling travellers (often at breakneck speed) around Europe are Contiki (ⓦwww.contiki.com), Trafalgar (ⓦwww.trafalgar.com) and Cosmos (ⓦwww.cosmos.com). All three typically start and end in London. One of the main differences is the age of passengers (Trafalgar's and Cosmos's are older). However, Trafalgar has a special "break-away" tour aimed at 21- to 38-year-olds. Contiki caters to 18- to 35-year-olds, and has a slightly more party atmosphere. All companies run more than a dozen tours within Europe, but here's a snapshot of the routes they can provide, and the cost:

- **Sample Contiki tour**: Madrid–Zaragoza–Barcelona–Avignon–Aix-en-Provence–French Riviera–Cinque Terre–Pisa–Florence–San Gimignano–Rome–Vatican City; 13 days; US$1640/€1175.

- **Sample Trafalgar tour**: London–Dover–Paris–Savigny-Les-Beaune–Lucerne–Venice–Rome; 8 days; US$1900/€1340.

- **Sample Cosmos tour**: London–Amsterdam–Rhineland–Lake Lucerne–Paris–London; 11 days; US$1600/€1130.

Travelling alone or with others

For many, this is one of the most difficult decisions of the trip. And understandably so. There are several factors to consider before making this choice, with sizeable pros and cons for each. All things being equal, you'll probably want to travel solo, at least for some portion of your trip. Even if all things aren't equal and there's someone you'd really like to travel with, read through this chapter so you know the risks you'll be taking and how to minimize them. Getting around requires a bit of thinking, but not all that much. Europe has an ingrained culture of travel. They're used to foreigners wandering around, and nearly all Europeans have done it themselves to some degree. Everything is set up to make travel easy.

Travelling alone

Obviously, this is the more intimidating path. It's also the most potentially rewarding. And it's not nearly as frightening as it may sound. First, **travelling alone** does not mean you'll be travelling alone for the bulk of your trip. Quite the opposite, in fact. Most solo travellers just end up travelling with different people for different legs of their journey. Surprising fact for the shy: something about solo travel seems to bring out the outgoing nature in everyone and makes meeting others inevitable. Everywhere you go, from museums to hostels to cafés, you'll run into other solo travellers who'll be delighted to travel with someone and, because there are often significant price breaks on rooms for pairs and in dormitories, there's a good chance you'll be sharing accommodation. Even shy travellers find the dialogue easy to start; you already

Tourists v locals

I first went to Europe just after I graduated from college. I bought a Volkswagen right from the factory in Germany and drove around the continent – drank wine in Pamplona during San Fermin and downed beers in Munich's Hofbrau Haus. But the stronger memories are meeting up with friends from college and doing things I could have done at home. I wasn't in a tour group, but might as well have been.

I learned that you learn far more during your travels if you go alone. Or as a couple. Or with children. When I travel with a film crew, for example, there are typically two campfires: one with me and the film crew and one with the locals. When you're alone, there's just one campfire. You sit with the locals and find out what's important to them. It's moments like that that provide the reason for travel.

Tim Cahill,
Author of *Lost in My Own Backyard*, *Hold the Enlightenment* and *Jaguars Ripped My Flesh*

have your travel destination and independent spirit in common, not to mention doubtless shared frustrating experiences. At times, it can almost be more difficult to find periods to be on your own. For those who are still uncertain about their ability to meet travel partners on the trail, you can, virtually everywhere, sign up for a group tour along the way and surround yourself with an entire platoon of companions.

The benefits of travelling solo

You learn about yourself. You'll find out what your likes and dislikes are. And you'll be able to act on them. Often travellers spur each other on to check off a "to-do" list. With no one looking, maybe you'll give that famous museum a miss and rent a bike and head for the countryside instead. You'll be less distracted and more likely to notice the small things happening around you. With more time to reflect, you'll write better in your journal, take more thoughtfully composed photos, have additional reading time and greater insights from studying the culture – in short, you'll absorb more of the country you're travelling in. Your hair, skin colour, clothes and height may make you stand out to varying degrees depending on the location, but as a single traveller it's easier to blend in. Plus, you're less likely to be attracting attention by speaking English with your partner. Instead, you'll be approached by more locals and other travellers eager to make conversation. They're often anxious to meet foreigners but can be intimidated by couples, not wanting to interrupt your conversation or intrude.

Solo travel

One of my favourite tricks is carrying my small daypack on my front in crowded areas. At least that protects my front from the anonymous hands searching for a quick feel. I'm also no longer afraid to lash out when I do get grabbed – and a little yelling helps get it out of my system.

Beth Wooldridge,
Author of the *Rough Guide to India*

This means solo travellers are much more likely to return home with an address book filled with great contacts from all over Europe and from travellers from around the world. In many ways, travel is about learning what is possible and that's a personal realization. After all, it's your trip. Why compromise?

Women travelling alone

Women can and do **travel solo** throughout Europe. Some countries, such as Norway, Sweden, Denmark, Finland and the Netherlands, make this quite easy and provide a better starting point. In southern Europe, you'll rarely feel threatened (for safety tips, see p.183), but you may be perceived as something of an oddity, so expect numerous enquiries. It's helpful to have a story for the men (you're meeting up with your husband in the next town, for example), but many questions will come from women, which is a great conversation starter and can often offer interesting insights.

The possibility of rape and robbery should be taken seriously, but can be minimized (see p.179). Most likely, the **harassment** you get will be a mild irritant: an admirer on a long train ride who thinks he can charm you with a six-hour story, or a whistle on the street. But it can be more offensive as well: an anonymous hand brushing your breasts or bum in a crowded market. The trick is being able to distinguish between a tactless man and a dangerous one. Always trust your instinct. If any man makes you feel at risk, simply move to a train compartment where there are safer-looking people (preferably women or other travellers), head to a more crowded street, pop into a busy store or stop a police officer.

If you're heading overland into a country or region that you're a little unsure of, you can almost always find a trustworthy **travel companion** to accompany you for at least a few days, if not longer, provided you're going in the same direction. It may take a day or three to find the right person, but in places where the hassle factor is high, such as crossing into Morocco or heading to Turkey, a male companion can make things much easier (especially if you tell people you're married).

Safety lesson

Even if travelling on a tight budget, I keep enough money in my wallet for a cab fare. In Amsterdam, leaving a bar by cab was the fastest way for me to escape a drunken pub-crawler who was trying to get me to give him a Red Light show.

Also, carry a small travel headlamp. I laughed when a friend gave me one as a parting gift, but used it on many nights walking back alone from train stations in Belgium. The extra light helped me feel a little safer, lessened tripping over broken sidewalks, and never left me fumbling with a key in a door.

Jen Leo,
Travel anthology editor,
Sand in My Bra Ⓦ www.writtenroad.com

www.roughguides.com

Travelling with others

Travelling with a companion isn't all bad. In fact, there are some nice **benefits**: minimized culture shock, medical security (they can help get you to a doctor if you get sick or carry you back to the hostel after you've passed out in a bar), money saved when staying in double rooms and taking taxis. For many, though, a travel partner's most important role is offering moral support for the never-ending onslaught of new situations to face. And helping to avoid the fairly frequent party-of-one meals or having your ear bent by some garrulous locals.

The risks of bringing a friend

Just because you're the best of friends, there's no guarantee you'll **travel well together**. Twenty-four hours a day of support and sharing for weeks or months on end can put a serious strain on even the best of friendships. In fact, you're putting that friendship at risk. Having to make constant decisions – often with little sleep, a hangover, or a faulty air-conditioning system on a long train ride – can test the tightest bonds. And here's something else to keep in mind: if you think it would be nice to stumble upon some romance on the road, you'd better pray you meet twins going in the same direction, because your friend isn't going to want to hang around while you fall in love.

Snowballing into large groups

When I arrived at the train station in Madrid, I sat down at a bench beside two Australians. We started talking and decided we'd buy some beer while we waited for our train to Lisbon. One of the Aussies did the buying, so we still had plenty left over when we got on the train and were joined in the couchette by a Dutch couple and two Danish women. The night train turned into something of a night party and by the time our train pulled into Lisbon there was some sort of unwritten rule that we weren't going to split up.

First, we waited for the Aussies to find a bank machine, then the Dutch wanted to buy some stamps and send off a few postcards, while one of the Danes went in search of water. We waited. The Danes had already picked out a hotel they liked from the guidebook, but no one else thought it sounded that appealing, especially since it was on the other side of town and getting there would be a minor logistical hassle, short of chartering our own bus. So, we kept walking and making suggestions and the only ones we could agree on didn't have room for all seven of us. Meanwhile, it felt like I was part of some kind of tourist platoon walking down the street in V-formation with large backpacks. We'd been in Lisbon for well over two hours and at this rate it didn't seem like we'd ever be able to shed our packs, much less find a place to stay without renting an entire floor at the *Hilton*. I half-heartedly suggested we abandon the group lodging idea, find our own hostels and meet up for drinks later. The quick consensus had us all in rooms within twenty minutes.

Doug Lansky

Maintaining your travel relationship

If you do decide to go with another person, there are a few things you can do to increase the chance that you'll still be friends at the end of the journey. For starters, give yourselves the option of **separating** for a while. You may want to plan ahead for it ("After the Running of the Bulls, we'll head our own way, then meet up in Barcelona"). Even just a morning or afternoon apart every few days can be enough breathing room to sustain a travel relationship. Or you could build some regular solo time into the trip, perhaps a week or two apart every other month: sign up for different courses or adventure activities in the same region or tackle a city separately. Pick a meeting time and figure out a few ways to get in touch in case one person can't make it, such as email or by leaving a note at a certain hostel.

What to look for in a travel partner

First, you want someone with the **same budget**. If you don't see eye to eye (or wallet to wallet), it's going to be a straining trip. If one person is going down the comfort route while the other is on a tight budget, you won't be staying at the same places, eating at the same restaurants or doing as many activities together. Or, more likely, you will, but neither of you will be having a good time doing it. The one on a tight budget will feel like a Scrooge, always getting their budget pushed too far, having to eat plain rice at a nice restaurant or sit outside while the other goes to a string of expensive museums. The one on the bigger budget will be roughing it more than they'd like, yet feel they're shamelessly indulging in front of their companion the entire time.

If your budgets are in alignment, then check if your **itineraries** are. Talk about what you hope to do during a typical day. Will you get up early and aggressively pound the pavement of a city, or sleep until noon, then linger in a café and read a book? Will you be pursuing cultural activities or beaches? Are you keeping things flexible or planning all the details? These are not the sorts of things you want to discover after you've started travelling.

Finding a travel partner

Many people find the prospect of travelling alone so daunting they try to line up an unknown travel partner before leaving. (Many parents insist that their kids travel with a partner for the perceived added security.) They place personal ads in travel magazines, newspapers and on websites. These correspondence-arranged partnerships may work out, but all too often they don't: heading out on the road together is

www.roughguides.com

like getting married after one blind date. There's no need to do this, especially without taking at least one short local trip together first. You'll meet so many travellers during your travels, it's much more natural and sensible to make friends first, travel for a while without commitment and only continue together as long as it's working out.

Travelling with a crowd

With more than two people, you're going to find yourself taking votes, which is a fine way to run a democracy but a maddening way to set an itinerary. Whether you leave with a group or simply snowball into an international party on the move, beware: you're going to be about as subtle as a Hare Krishna tambourine parade dancing through a public library. Another potential problem is getting anything done. It's nice to find a social set of people. But instead of corralling yourself into a tour group, a better idea is to pick a bar or restaurant in the next town and say you'll meet them there at a certain time. Then everyone can break up and go their own way.

Travelling on a long organized tour

This locks you in with a group for the duration of the tour, for good and bad. Such trips tend to bring out the best in some people and worst in others. Lifelong friendships are common, but so too are group conflicts, and you won't likely see much about the latter in the brochure. So make sure you ask about free time away from the group then take advantage of it when you get the chance. You might actually want to make substantial independent time part of your criteria when selecting a tour.

Costs and savings

ow much does it **cost** to travel around Europe? Seems like a reasonable question, but it's a bit like asking how much a car costs. It depends very much on the type of car. Or in this case, the type of trip. A personalized, independent journey doesn't come with a standard price tag, so you're going to have to make some fundamental calculations based on your level of travel comfort, the activities you want to do, where you want to go and the length of your trip – and this chapter will show you how.

Without narrowing down these factors, you'll have a hard time getting within €2000 of an accurate figure on a three-month-long trip. Why? Take a typical European budget of €50 per day, plus €700 for a plane ticket (if you're flying from the US or Canada in the summer), €915 for a three-month youth Eurail ticket, €250 for insurance and €400-worth of gear, and you get a total of around €6765. If you stop and work at, say,

Starting costs

Backpack: €100–200 (or borrow one)
Travel gear, toiletries, medical kit (depending on what you have already): €100–350
Passport: €55–115 (depending on where you live)
Insurance: €50–300 (based on a three-month trip)
Discount card: €18
Vaccinations: Not required, though you'll probably want protection from Hepatitis A if heading to less developed areas like rural parts of Turkey or Eastern Europe
Two-month Youth Flexi Pass with fifteen days of travel: €530
Return plane ticket to Europe: €400–1100
Approximate total: €1400–2700

THE BIG ADVENTURE

an ecological farm for two weeks, you're down to €5920, plus whatever you manage to earn. If you stay with relatives/pen pals for a week and spend a week in a cheap hangout collecting your thoughts (and a tan), you're down to €5520. If you confine your travels exclusively to cheaper countries and use other budgeting tricks to bring your daily rate down by €10, and you use a two-month Flexi Rail pass coupled with additional local transport that you pay for along the way, that will cut your costs down to €4520. Conversely, if you decide to have two nice meals a week, stay in two decent hotels a week and take two courses during your trip, you might be looking at a daily budget of €100, which would bump that original trip plan from €6765 to nearly €10,000.

Daily costs on the road

Even with a rail or bus pass, it's possible to spend anywhere between €2500 and €25,000 on a three-month trip. It all depends on how you want to live while you're there. So, you can either make do with what you have or gather more funds before you depart. See the box on pp.76–77 for help calculating your **daily budget**.

How do you travel cheaper?

Without a number of **budget tricks**, you may end up travelling on a high-end budget while only getting mid-range value. The key to saving money on the road is not to concentrate exclusively on the big expenditures, but to find small savings along every step of the way. Beyond picking countries where your funds will last longer (for example, most of the countries without the euro), savvy saving is about using a combination of tricks and making a deliberate lifestyle adjustment that rations out the creature comforts, or drops them altogether. People love to spend countless hours surfing the web and calling around to find the cheapest ticket to Europe. Of course, you don't want to end up paying more than the guy sitting next to you on the plane, but don't knock yourself out in a massive effort that will not likely save you more than €50–200. Why? That's not where the real savings are found. With some self-discipline and a few budget tips, you can reduce your daily budget by as much as €30. Over a three-month-long trip, that's a saving of €2700. Even on a one-month trip, that's €900 you can leave in the bank.

Discount cards

There's no magic wand to wave and guarantee savings everywhere you go, but for €11–18 the widely accepted **International Student Identity Card** (ISIC) comes close (@www.isic.org). There are also

Top ten things you can do to save money

1. Couchsurf: use this network of people willing to let you stay for free each night (see p.79).
2. Spend more time in countries/cities where your money will last you longer. It's cheaper in rural Portugal than central Paris.
3. Eat in. Dine on supermarket food and cook in hostels or with the people you couchsurf with.
4. Work along the way. Take small jobs to earn a bit of cash as you go.
5. Hitchhike. Rough Guides can't officially endorse hitching, but there are safe and quick ways to do it.
6. Fly into hub cities rather than smaller places at the start and end of your trip. For example, think Rome, not Florence; London, not Edinburgh.
7. Surf the web on the cheap. Try libraries instead of internet cafés.
8. Limit your mobile phone charges by using voice mail, text messages and free (or cheap) internet calling services like skype.
9. Use discount cards. Some, like the International Student ID card, can earn back the investment in a few days if you remember to ask for the discounts.
10. Minimize cash withdrawals. Those ATM fees add up, so figure out what you think you'll need before you tap a nice round number.

youth cards (for under-26s) and teacher cards issued by the same organization that offer similar discounts. They provide significant deals for museums, local transport passes, plane tickets and more. You may very well make up the €11–18 on the flight over. The trick is remembering to ask for the discount. It won't help you much in restaurants, but nearly anywhere a ticket is required be sure to ask. Also, use it as a backup ID card you can leave behind when renting bikes and so on.

Another popular card is the **Hostelling International Card** (€21; Ⓦwww.hihostels.com; see p.157 to find out if you like the sound of hostelling). If you want to get this card, you'll need to do so in your home country before leaving. With it, you get discounts on about 2000 affiliated hostels around Europe, plus reductions on transport, including discount car rental, bus and train travel. The card will pay for itself within four nights. The downside is that you can get many of the same transport discounts with an ISIC or youth card, and these official hostels don't pack the party atmosphere of the private hostels and are often not centrally located. But if you're hoping to get some peaceful sleep, it can be ideal.

Once on the road, you may find you're staying at a number of VIP-affiliated private hostels (there are about five hundred in Europe, mostly concentrated in Scandinavia and Ireland). If so, you might as well pick up a VIP Backpackers membership card (€25; Ⓦwww .vipbackpackers.com) and start getting roughly five percent discounts per night – that is, if you think you'll use it more than forty nights, which is what it takes to earn back the card's value.

Where you can stretch your money

The five most expensive (overall) countries

1. Norway 2. Switzerland 3. Finland 4. Sweden 5. France

The five cheapest (overall) countries

1. Romania 2. Bulgaria 3. Poland 4. Turkey 5. Slovakia

Typical cheapest hostel dorm room bed costs per country (average city and rural prices – a city hostel will be €2–5 more)

Most expensive:		Mid-range:		Budget:	
Switzerland	€23	Britain	€19	Estonia	€13
Norway	€23	Spain	€17	Czech Republic	€12
Finland	€22	Austria	€16	Hungary	€12
France	€22	Germany	€15	Latvia	€12
Sweden	€22	Ireland	€15	Turkey	€11
Russia	€21	Slovenia	€15	Slovakia	€10
Denmark	€20	Belgium and		Bulgaria	€9
Greece	€20	Luxembourg	€15	Poland	€9
Italy	€20			Romania	€9
The Netherlands	€20				

Consumables index – cost of living in Europe

(100 = euro zone average)

Most expensive:		Mid-range:		Budget:	
Iceland	153	Austria	105	Hungary	62
Norway	146	The Netherlands	105	Slovakia	59
Denmark	143	Germany	102	Latvia	61
Switzerland	130	Spain	92	Czech Republic	58
Ireland	126	Cyprus	90	Poland	58
Luxembourg	124	Greece	89	Lithuania	55
Sweden	123	Portugal	84	Romania	55
Finland	122	Slovenia	77	Montenegro	50
Britain	112	Malta	69	Serbia	49
France	109	Croatia	66	Bosnia and	
				Herzegovina	47
Belgium	108	Estonia	66	Albania	43
Italy	106	Turkey	64	Bulgaria	41

A few things to consider: Sweden and Norway have free camping rights. France and Italy have more museums you're likely to pay for (at around €7 each). And, in the summer, you'll likely be buying more drinks and ice cream in southern Europe's sweltering heat. Just as you might even be more likely to splash out for an air-conditioned room. Also, in the Scandinavian countries, alcohol is very expensive (helping push up the consumables index) so if you don't drink, or don't drink much, they're more affordable. Since there's not a huge difference in the range of the cheapest supermarket food, these things just mentioned can make a significant difference.

Flights

The "Getting there and around" chapter (see p.38) has more details on how to get the cheapest **flight**, but a good basic guideline to follow before booking any flights is to do a little checking on your own so you'll know a good price when you see one. Start looking around on the web (online search engines are detailed on p.343), and check out the lowest published fares for a particular flight. Then, all things being relatively equal, book with a well-informed travel agent and get their email address and phone number. The advantages of using an experienced travel agent are twofold: they are aware of the finer points that most travellers overlook, such as ease of airport connections, and they are able to access considerably cheaper fares.

Rail passes

Most Europe **rail passes** can only be purchased in your home country, but with the internet this isn't such a problem. If you're already in Europe, or on your way there, you can order a pass online (check out ⓦwww.raileurope.com and ⓦwww.interrail.com), have it sent to your parents or friends and then get them to forward it to you. The more difficult task is selecting the right one. You can't bargain your way to a cheaper rail pass, but there are several ways to get more for your money:

- If you plan to stay in one spot for a while, try to time it at the beginning or end of your journey so your active pass isn't sitting idle more than it need be.
- Consider a Flexi Pass (certain number of travel days allowed within a fixed time period) instead of an unlimited travel pass. You don't want to spend every day on the train anyway.
- Supplement a Flexi Pass with cheap, shorter trips. If you calculate the per-day value of a Flexi Pass, it's €35–40. If you're travelling, say, the 97km from Florence to Siena in Italy, a second-class ticket costs €13. Typically, if the journey is less than an hour and you're not on a high-speed train, it's going to be cheaper to buy a ticket at the window and save travel days on your pass.
- Check for weekend deals before using your Flexi Pass. In Germany, for example, you can land bargains with Deutsche Bahn's €37 "Happy Weekend" ticket.
- Don't be afraid to use flights just because you have a rail ticket. You need to balance this, of course, with your environmental philosophy. But you'd spend a few days of your trip on the train (and use up a few days of your rail pass, plus some not-so-ecological packaged food and drinks) to get, for example, from

www.roughguides.com

London to Portugal or Greece. With cut-throat budget airlines practically giving tickets away, chances are you can find a one-way flight for less than €85, possibly even less than €25. That will save you time and roughly €70-worth of travel on your flexi rail pass; not needing to pay overnight and reserved-seating supplements will push the total saving to over €110.

● As a rule of thumb, the less flexible the rail pass, the cheaper it is. In other words, if you know more or less where you plan to go (and you don't feel obligated to hit every single region or country), you can get a much better deal. However, sometimes it's not much of a bargain. For example, a youth traveller can get ten travel days in two months in five adjoining countries

Calculating your daily budget

Select your level of comfort from the list below, then figure out how many weeks or months you plan to travel and which countries you plan to spend the most time in, then add up the costs. For example, using the information below, if you plan to spend one month in Norway on a low-end budget (€1200), one month in Spain on a medium budget (€1600) and one month in Romania on an upper budget (€2000), it will tally up to a total of €4800.

Wherever you go, your daily budget will reduce significantly if you couchsurf consistently.

Low-end budget

Accommodation: sleeping in hostel dormitory rooms, sharing rooms in the very cheapest hotels (no matter how bad the guidebook description), camping or renting a tent at campgrounds, sleeping on trains and buses.

Transport: your rail or bus pass can be supplemented with some hitchhiking or very short local bus rides, plus a flight or two under €25.

Food: eating cheap food purchased at supermarkets, and the lowest-priced side dishes at budget restaurants or at street stalls.

Lifestyle: no clubbing and nothing more than the occasional beer. Limited museum visits and no leisurely drinks at nice cafés. Consequently more time could be spent at journal writing, sketching and digital photography.

Low-end budget expenses:
Expensive country: daily €40; monthly €1200
Mid-range country: daily €35; monthly €1050
Cheap country: daily €25; monthly €775

Middle budget

Accommodation: cheapest digs, occasionally sharing a two-person room and sleeping on a train or bus without reserved bed.

Transport: bus or rail pass can be supplemented by occasional hitching, but more often side-trips just under one hour by train or bus, plus one or two flights under €50.

Food: eating cheap food purchased at supermarkets and at budget restaurants.

Lifestyle: a few coffees a week at nice cafés. Museums are not limited but adventure activities are. The occasional night on the town, but not more than one reasonably priced drink per day.

for €365 with the Select Pass. To access all seventeen countries with the same number of travel days, it's just €393. Thirty euros seems like good value for the extra flexibility. If you're on a shorter trip or know you're not going to visit more than three adjoining countries, the €318 Three-Country Pass offers a more significant saving.

- If you only want to travel in one country and can't decide which, know that some single-country passes cost more than others. In Portugal or Greece, you get three travel days within one month for €128 (first class); Hungary, ten days within one month for €105 (first class); and Sweden or Norway, three days within one month for €192 (second class).

Middle budget expenses:
Expensive country: daily €70; monthly €2100
Mid-range country: daily €55; monthly €1650
Cheap country: daily €45; monthly €1350

Upper budget

Accommodation: occasional splurge on decent budget hotel; otherwise, private rooms in hostels.

Transport: rail or bus pass can be supplemented by a few additional days of travel. Train beds on overnight journeys.

Food: one decent restaurant meal per day.

Lifestyle: unlimited coffee, liberal drinking, two nights out per week and several adventure activities during the trip.

Upper budget expenses:
Expensive country: daily €105; monthly €3150
Mid-range country: daily €90; monthly €2700
Cheap country: daily €70; monthly €2100

High-end budget

Accommodation: quaint hotels and B&Bs.

Transport: comfortable sleepers on night trains; high-speed trains with mandatory reservation supplements; some taxis in cities; plane travel for short trips to other parts of Europe.

Food: eating out two meals a day at moderately priced restaurants; inexpensive wine with dinner and occasional beer or wine with lunch.

Lifestyle: concerts and clubbing three nights a week, accompanied by moderate drinking; almost daily stops in cafés for coffee and snacks; no limit on museums and occasional adventure activities.

High-end budget expenses:
Expensive country: daily €210; monthly €6300
Mid-range country: daily €180; monthly €5400
Cheap country: daily €130; monthly €3900

Buses

Buses are going to be cheaper than trains almost every time. In England (home of Europe's most expensive trains), they'll be roughly one third of the cost. So, it's a good way to save some money. However, you can't get up and stretch your legs the same way. And, if you're using Busabout, you won't be rubbing elbows with the locals. If you're looking for travel or party partners, however, that can be a good thing. For bus passes, follow the same basic strategy listed on p.75.

Accommodation – the biggest potential savings

Europe is equipped with some of the world's best hotels, and you could blow a month's budget (and then some) on a single night in any one of them. (One Swiss hotel has a suite that goes for over €20,500.)

Your guidebook will steer you to the type of place you're after, but at this planning stage one of the best things you can do to save money on the road is prepare yourself for sleeping in **no-star accommodation**. (If you're travelling for over two months, accommodation will be your single largest expense, thus the first place to look for savings.) That means sleeping in dorm rooms when available, trying to share a room with another traveller if there are doubles with low rates, and not letting yourself be put off by places described in your guidebook as basic, or even grungy. If you're armed with earplugs and a good sleep-sheet, you'll be fine. Or opt for **couchsurfing** (see opposite). Other money-saving ideas for bottom-end digs are:

- Stay in small towns and rural areas – hostels and pensions in large cities pay the most rent, and pass the cost on to travellers.
- Make a point of getting addresses of travellers you meet, then stay with them if you're heading to their home town or city. Try to give a few days' or weeks' notice with an email. Taking a digital camera is good in this respect – it's nice to attach a photo of you together when you request a place to stay. They might have offered their address to dozens of travellers or had a bit too much to drink and have trouble remembering your name when you make contact.
- Cram the rooms full. Go for a quad and find three other travellers to take up the extra beds so you all get a better deal than sleeping in a single or double room.
- Head to campgrounds just out of town and rent their walk-in tents (with real beds).

Free accommodation

In 2001, a 24-year-old Dutch traveller named Ramon Stoppelenburg hitchhiked his way around the world for two years "without any money" by setting up a website called ⓦwww.letmestayforaday.com, through which he found sponsors and took up the 3577 invitations to stay which came in from 77 countries. Seems like a cool idea? Well, these days, it's available for everyone. You may have heard of it; it's called **couchsurfing**, and as well as being a great way to meet locals, it's probably the single most effective thing you can do to save money during your trip.

After all the bogus offers from Nigerian billionaires and Viagra pill salesmen, you'll be happy to know that couchsurfing is proof positive you can get something for nothing on the internet. Visit ⓦwww.couchsurfing.com and you'll find a network of people willing to host travellers for free, and a network of travellers happy to get a free place to crash – it's a 2.0 spin on the concept that Servas (ⓦwww.servas.org) has been conducting for years (though they charge a $30 membership/host list fee and have a face-to-face interview system for qualification). The couchsurfing.com version has proven overwhelmingly popular with younger travellers, and now has over a million members around the world. It works like this: you register your "couch" (or guest room, or your parent's guest room) for free and agree to let travellers stay for free when it's convenient for you; in return, you get access to everyone else's sofas or guest rooms. You're not required to allow anyone stay when you get a request – you can say you're away or the couch is occupied. You can also view the profile of anyone who requests a stay online – people get recommended both as hosts and guests – and see if they seem like the sort of guest you'd like to invite into your home. The site accepts donations, and will use your donation (combined with verification of your mailing address) to give you another level of security recommendation.

It takes a bit of advance planning and a good deal of internet time to make arrangements, but the advantages of couchsurfing are enormous. Travellers on a budget can save $20/£12 to $100/£61 (whatever you normally spend) a day on hotel expenses, which adds up quickly to several thousand on an extended trip. In fact, there's virtually nothing you can do that will save you more money, and into the bargain you'll meet locals, get a look into their home and often try home-made cuisine. (It's even safe for female travellers going it alone, but you should be more picky about your hosts, or take a friend with you the first time for a little extra security.) For hosts, it's a great way of travelling without leaving home.

If you don't mind staying in one place a bit longer, you might consider a **house-sit** via ⓦwww.caretaker.org. For an annual membership of $30 you get access to a list of homeowners looking for someone to water their plants, turn the lights on and off, feed the family pet or help keep an eye on grandma. Some will even pay you for your house-sitting skills.

- Check out housing at universities over the summer. Empty dorm rooms are often rented out at cut-rate prices.
- Hang out around the students' union and look for a friendly group. Introduce yourself and ask if you can crash on someone's floor or sofa in exchange for a beer or two, plus free accommodation at your parents' home if they ever get there. Women can do this safely as well (and will likely have an easier time of it) by approaching a group of women.

www.roughguides.com

Budgetitis syndrome

When you first start travelling, spending comes naturally. Almost too naturally. A beer here, a T-shirt there, a few museum passes, a nice meal. Maybe you're too caught up in the excitement of arriving or spending to cushion your landing into a new culture. Whatever the case, after a few days or weeks, many realize they're over budget and begin to feel the stress of a money belt getting thinner. The natural response to this relentless stream of expenditure is an attempt to stem the outflow. And when travellers meet and compare notes, boasting rights go to the one surviving on the lowest funds. When it gets competitive, that's when **budgetitis** really sets in. Symptoms include: walking an extra twenty minutes to find a bread shop whose loaves are three cents cheaper; full-blown arguments with taxi drivers over the equivalent of 25 cents; and skipping a meal because the local supermarket prices seem a little high. In extreme cases, travellers might party all night (without drinking . . . well, not much), then sleep in a park during the day. They'll only travel by hitchhiking and show up at soup kitchens for food, paying with the minimum donation. This is one of the most common budget travel afflictions (followed closely by exaggerated storytelling), and at some point during a long trip you'll likely suffer from it yourself.

When you sit back and think about your trip in a year or two, you won't be rejoicing over the extra three euros you have in your pocket: with budgetitis, many rationalize spending hundreds to get there, plus lodging and food, then not coughing up the last few euros for the thing they had come to see.

If you can sense this happening, you have to take a step back and remember why you're travelling. It's fine to save money while you're on the road, but you need to balance this with the fact that you're not travelling in order to save money. Better to come home a week or two early and suffer a little less.

- A few places may offer sleeping on the roof for half the price if you have a mat and sleeping bag. It doesn't hurt to ask.
- If staying in private rooms, accepting one without a private WC and shower can save you €17–34 per night.
- Stay with relatives (no matter how distant) and friends of friends.

Museums

With the abundance of world-class **museums** Europe has to offer, chances are you're going to be visiting several. Look into multi-museum passes if you know you'll be visiting a few in the same town. The Paris Museum pass (€32 for 2 days), for example, pays for itself in just a few visits and lets you stroll by the snaking queues. Even a single pass to the Louvre is worth picking up in advance, if only to avoid the long queues during peak season. Tickets are a few euros cheaper when purchased from local vendors, such as a Fnac store (Ⓦwww.fnac.com) in Paris.

Food

Cosy **restaurants** and old-world cafés are tempting places to relax, socialize with other travellers and people-watch. They're also nice places to run down your budget: those double café lattes add up in a hurry.

And fleeing to *McDonald's* isn't always going to help. Switzerland has, on average, the world's most expensive *McDonald's* – over €4 for a Big Mac. Minimizing these little luxuries is going to be the first unpleasant step. Here are a few others:

- Stick to restaurants that don't take credit cards or have English menus. Places smart enough to do this are usually savvy enough to jack up their prices as well. Another approach is to choose places where you don't see other foreigners.
- Look for restaurants near universities. Students worldwide have little money for eating, and there's almost always a cottage industry set up to serve them.
- Sample the street food, find a few favourites, and make meals out of them. Two full days of street- or vendor-bought meals costs the equivalent of one decent restaurant meal.
- Cook in hostels. Check your guidebook for hostels with kitchen access. It's always cheaper to cook as a group, so don't be afraid to stick your head into the lounge and ask if anyone wants to pitch in and make a communal dinner.
- Supermarket-dining works. You'll soon learn how to survive on fruit, yoghurt, sandwiches and crisps.
- Try the samples. During weekends and busy shopping times in large supermarkets in developed countries, you can often find a tremendous range of free samples available. With a little luck, you can get an entire meal, as long as you don't mind getting it in fifteen small servings.
- Walk for ten minutes away from major tourist areas and watch the prices drop by the block.
- To increase your options in markets, keep a kit of salt, pepper, olive oil, knife and spoon in a small container, and use it to prepare salads and the like.
- Think pizza. In Italy and elsewhere, pizzas come in just one size, which more than covers a typical plate. These single servings provide some of the best deals in Europe and can typically be had for €4–6. If you've got a small appetite, they're enough for two.
- If you want a recommendation, ask a construction worker. They're often on a limited budget and know where to find a filling meal nearby.
- Bring food onto trains. Trains throughout the world are united by one common theme: bad food at ridiculous prices. Bring more than you think you'll need, plus water.
- Hit the buffets and salad bars: look for a cheap salad bar or buffet and then stack your plate about 1m high. This may require some advanced engineering skills.

www.roughguides.com

- Pizza gathering – not officially recommended, but it works. Travellers have been known to hang out in franchise pizza joints, order a small salad, then grab the untouched slices from other tables when groups get up to leave.

- Order economically. A restaurant is a great place to rest your feet and socialize, but to keep the bill down consider ordering one appetizer and complementing it with a few filling side dishes instead of a main meal.

- Eat seasonal. Fruits and veggies getting shipped in out of season aren't as fresh, taste worse and cost more.

- Gallery openings typically serve free wine and hors d'oeuvres, but you'll need to make yourself presentable enough to enter.

The price of savings

I was in Crete in a picturesque little fishing port. I had my watch-every-penny mindset going, so when a festive outdoor taverna wanted to charge me $2 for a cold beer, I passed on the apparent rip-off and bought a warm one at a liquor store for 70 cents and sat on the curb and drank it – a savvy budget victory. Now, thirteen years later, I've got an extra $1.30 in my bank account...and my memories from that evening are immeasurably poorer.

John Flinn,
Travel editor, *San Francisco Chronicle*

Saving on restrooms

There are savings to be had here, and not just from trying to hold on to it. It's not often you'll encounter a squatter, or hole in the floor where the **toilet** is supposed to be, but you'll run into restroom attendants everywhere who'll charge for use of their facilities, or automatic WCs that require coin activation.

At some point you'll need to use one, so carry change. Tipping the attendant is often optional, but if you can splash a few small coins in the cup it at least sounds generous. Some have specific fees for things like toilet paper or hand towels and some have outrageous admission rates, as much as €1, no matter what you plan to do.

It's best to find **free toilets**, though they're not always easy to come by. *McDonald's*, traditionally one of the most popular free bathroom options, have more recently set up security measures – typically, keypad locks with codes only available to paying customers. If you're reasonably presentable and not toting a large backpack that denotes you as a budget traveller, you might be able to pop into a nice hotel. If questioned by the doorman, you can say that you're scouting the place for your parents or checking out the restaurant's menu as a possible dining option that evening. One of the best options, especially while waiting in train stations where you almost always have to pay for toilet services, is to spot a train that isn't due to depart for a while, then hop aboard, use the restroom and hop back off.

What's the deal with tipping?

If you can figure out a formula that works for **tipping** across Europe, you should probably be working at NASA or cracking codes for MI6. Tipping in Europe is a confusing affair. In some upscale environments, you might be giving a waiter ten to fifteen percent, while in that same country it would be perfectly fine to leave nothing at a lower-end café.

To generalize, tipping in Europe at the lower levels of service is more about rounding up and token tips than straight percentages. For instance, if your lunch tab comes to €5.60, you might leave an even €6. With a tab of €9.80, round up to €10 for service you could have just as easily done without. In some places, it's just as appropriate to leave a fifty cent or €1 coin, even if that works out to be a two percent tip. The same basic concept applies for taxi rides. If the ride comes to exactly €5, you're fine without a tip (unless carrying bags or other service was provided). If it's €5.70, you should probably just pay €6 and tell the driver to keep the change. In a crunch, you can always ask a fellow diner (especially if you're treating yourself to a meal in a swanky restaurant, where the tip will more likely be ten to twelve percent) or your hotel concierge for some guidance. But the final decision is up to you. Give what you feel is appropriate and leave the restaurant or cab with confidence.

Changing money

Changing money isn't as straightforward as money changers would like you to believe. In fact, in many cases it's a mathematical mind-twister and, like in Vegas, the house has you by the short and curlies. There are a few tips that will help keep more money in your pocket after the transaction is over:

Watch for cons and extra fees

At restaurants, waiters may play more tricks than just serving warm soft drinks and seeming to squeeze in a round of golf before getting the food to your table. They may also incorrectly add up the bill, conveniently in their favour. Always double-check it.

One popular gambit in tourist areas is to place a bread roll on your table right when you sit down, then charge a whopping fee for it if you so much as breathe on it. If you're not interested, have them take it away. It may be as tasty as a stone, but it's difficult to stare at when hungry. Same goes for a plate of rice, which may also be extra.

If you're trying to have an inexpensive meal, make sure you don't pick a place with a cover charge – a fee for just sitting down at the table. Feel free to ask if there is such a fee (sometimes called a "service fee"). If there isn't, make sure it doesn't magically appear on the bill.

If the menu says that tax is included in the prices, they shouldn't be adding the tax fee on top of the total price.

www.roughguides.com

● Avoid changing money at hotels, hostels and bureaux de change.
   They're well situated, have great opening hours and charge you a
   fortune for all that convenience.
● Always compare before changing money. The rates can differ
   even on the same street. Check banks or the post office.
● When you shop around, don't be fooled by nice rates. Money
   changers specialize in fee juggling. They use a few mechanisms
   to make sure they get your money. They either use a flat fee (as a
   minimum) or a percentage of the total amount changed. Which
   one you use often depends on the amount you're changing.
   Typically, if you're exchanging a lot of money (say €500), the
   minimum fee will be irrelevant so you should look at rates and
   commissions. If it's a small amount, you'll want to pay closer
   attention to the minimum fee and rate.
● Look for the buy rate and sell rate. The difference (exchanger's
   profit) is probably around five percent. If it's more or they don't
   show it, something may be fishy.
● Minimize transactions. Take a moment to calculate what you'll
   need, because every time you change cash, traveller's cheques or
   withdraw money from a bank machine, you're probably paying
   for the transaction (see opposite to help calculate the hidden
   exchange fees).

How to bargain like a pro

You can't walk into a European shopping centre and start **bargaining**
for food. But there are a number of excellent handicraft and knick-
knack markets across the continent where you can barter, and these
offer some of the best shopping you'll find. You can also negotiate your
hostel/hotel room rate down during off-season and negotiate book
swaps – the basic bargaining concept is the same for all of these.

The golden rule of bargaining is to keep a **smile** on your face. It's
OK to be firm with your offer, even walk away at an impasse, but if you
think of it as a game and keep the atmosphere light and friendly, it's hard
to go wrong. The other rule is not to start bargaining unless you're truly
interested – it's not fair to waste the seller's time.

Getting an excellent price on an item, however, is another story.
The sellers are the experts, but you hold the cash, so you're in control.
The first thing to do is find out from a local or fellow traveller who's
familiar with the market what the **real going rate** is. In Europe, there
typically isn't a special price for locals, so you have one less barrier
to hurdle. Now you've got a goal. More importantly, this little bit of
research will help you recognize any serious price gouging. That is,

Basic exchange maths you need to learn

Let's say you want to change $100 to euros. Bank #1 is offering €0.70 to the dollar with a two percent commission and a €1 minimum fee. Bank #2 is offering €0.74 to the dollar with a 1.5 percent commission and a €3 minimum fee. And bank #3 is offering €0.76 to the dollar with a six percent commission and no minimum fee. At bank #1, you'll get €68. At bank #2, you'll get €71. And at bank #3 (the one with the misleading best exchange rate) you'll get €70. Earning €3 for a minute of elementary-level maths may sound OK on paper, but it seems like cruel and unusual punishment when you're there. Of course, you can bypass all of this with a cash machine.

sometimes vendors, just for sport, like to see how much they can get for an item and may throw out a completely outlandish price and see if you'll take the bait.

The next step is to take a look at **what you're wearing**. It's hard to haggle a price down with a ring on every other finger or a watch on your wrist that will tell you the time 300m under water. Leave the expensive camera, jewellery and the €200 Gore-Tex jacket in the hotel room (or in your daypack) if you know you're heading to a market to do some bargaining. Then **go early**. Many vendors share the belief that a sale early in the day will bring them good fortune, so they may be more likely to lower their prices than they would otherwise. This also increases your chances that you'll be alone with the vendor, which works to your advantage. With other potential customers browsing within earshot, the vendor may feel pressure to keep prices high.

The next step may be the most difficult: hide the true extent of your **interest**. That is, you don't want to hold something up to show your travel partner and say: "Look at this. It's perfect!" The vendors may not be fluent in English, but this exchange won't escape them. You might start out by lifting the item you're interested in for a moment and casually asking how much it costs. They'll either respond with an inflated price, a decent price or this question: "How much will you give me for it?" If you've done your research, you're in good shape for any of these. If you get an inflated price, make an offer that's equally below your target price. The vendor will immediately dismiss it as unfair, and you – here's where that smile really comes in handy – can say: "Maybe we could start the bargaining over again, but this time at a more realistic level." Your next offer should be 5–10 percent under your target price. On the other hand, if the vendor starts the bargaining at a very reasonable level, don't expect it to go down much. Pick a price just under your target and be prepared to come up in price fairly quickly. Finally, if you're asked to start the bidding, you might say: "Actually, I spoke to a few people who bought these as gifts, and they

www.roughguides.com

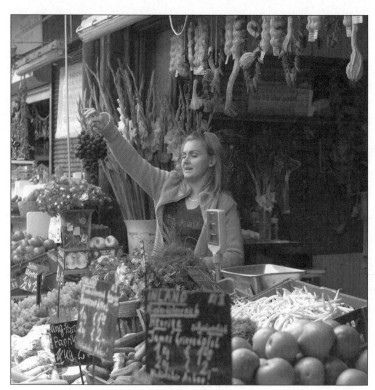

▲ Market, Vienna

told me I shouldn't pay more than €X". The vendor will immediately know that you've been doing your homework, but may not be ready to give it up to you at that price. If that's the sense you get, you can say: "Perhaps that's the local price I heard about. As a visitor to your country, I'd be willing to give you a little more." Then offer a price that's one or two percent higher.

Other bargaining tools

Another trick is to point out the small, obvious **flaws** in the item – cracked glazing, discolouring, etc. This can quickly put vendors on the defensive, so a more clever way to introduce it is (assuming there are several identical items) simply to pick up another one you'd be happy with that has essentially the same minor flaws and say, "how about if I take this one instead, which has some cracks. Surely it's worth less than the other one?" Few vendors will take up the argument that the first one you had was just as flawed. But if they do, you've got a small advantage. "Since you yourself agree that this product is flawed, perhaps you'd be willing to part with it at a fairer rate?"

A more businesslike approach is to introduce yourself to the vendor and tell them that you're considering doing all of your shopping in their boutique and try to get a **bulk discount**. After some small talk, the vendor will probably let you steer the conversation to prices. If you're still not close by the second round, let them know that you're sorry it doesn't sound like it's working out and thank them for their time. They've already put some time into the deal and won't want to lose a fairly substantial customer, so chances are they probably won't let you go that easily.

In the end, it should be a win–win experience. And if you keep the negotiation friendly, keep your cool and only buy at a price you feel good about, it will be. Despite any dramatic claims of losing money, a vendor will never sell you merchandise at a loss, so you shouldn't leave feeling guilty that you obtained an unjustly low price.

5

Working, volunteering and studying

I f you're European, your passport is a ticket to landing jobs around the continent. If you don't have an EU passport, you might find yourself in this typical scenario: you've finished a semester of studies in Europe, you've got two months to bounce around before you need to return home, and you've got some kind of rail or bus pass burning a hole in your pocket with sixteen major cities, twelve beaches and fourteen museums on your wish list. Here are two reasonable questions to ask: is there really time to find a job, volunteer or pick up a new skill? And why should I bother?

You should at least consider making the time. Especially if you want a truly unique, enriching travel experience. Because, no matter how many museums and handicraft markets you hit, no matter how many kilometres you log on buses, trains and ferries, no matter how little you pay for your night's accommodation, you're not likely to get under the skin of a place until you stop and engage yourself. Whether you're **working**, **volunteering** or **studying**, all it takes is some ongoing interaction with locals to develop a connection and make some friends. If you've studied, consider the relationship you've had with your closer classmates compared to the one you've had with people you've shared a bus ride with. It's a different level entirely. Some jobs, volunteer projects and courses immerse you in the culture more than others, and it's not always easy to tell in advance which

www.roughguides.com

▲ Grape picking, Burgundy, France

will and which won't, but at least you'll still be earning money, helping others or learning a skill – not a bad way to pass your time in Europe.

Note to EU passport holders: you may wish to skip ahead to the section on choosing and finding a job.

Working

For years travellers have been running out of money before they've exhausted their wanderlust. Every day, people hit the road with just a few months' or weeks' worth of cash in their pockets. Depending on your age, nationality and professional skills, there are countless options available to keep yourself financially afloat.

Bad news first: the European Union doesn't really want non-EU passport holders to waltz over and land a job. Especially Americans. For New Zealanders, Canadians and Aussies, there are special visas called "**working holiday visas**" that make things quite convenient (see p.91 for a list of "working holiday" countries). Without such agreements, even a very short-term job can come with Himalayan hurdles. Now the good news: you can still get a job almost anywhere.

For a **legal job**, the most important thing to remember is that you need to enter the European country you'll be working in with the proper stamps and papers to be eligible for work. If you don't, and find a job after arriving, you'll still have to return home, fix the paperwork, and then re-enter the country with all your documents in order. Some organizations can help you with the application forms, especially if you're a student or recent graduate.

Work placements for students and recent grads

Several **agencies** have popped up to help students and recent graduates (those who received a degree within the last four months) get special visas. These agencies apply mostly to Americans, but they can help just about anyone if the country you want to work in doesn't have some sort of holiday work-visa arrangement with your country. In which case, they provide the easiest way of taking care of the paperwork. You still have to pound the pavement and find your own job (one where the employer doesn't mind taking you on for just a few months), but at least you can show you've got a work permit. The drawback is that this handy red-tape-cutting service doesn't come free. In fact, it may run you about a month's wages: €450. Typically, the short-term jobs you'll be able to find aren't going to come with meaty pay cheques or bonuses. And you've still got to pay for accommodation and food. In other words, you'll be paying to wait tables full-time in Paris for two months, even if you speak fluent French. Other common jobs include au pair work and teaching English. If the pay cheque isn't as important, some of these organizations offer help arranging interesting internships. You should probably think twice about handing over funds for this. You can call up the companies directly, say you're a student and that you want to work for free to get some first-hand experience, and no paperwork should be necessary.

- **American Scandinavian Foundation** Ⓦwww.amscan.org. Does exchange programs for Americans in research, study or practical training, as well as fellowships and cultural programs.
- **Bunac Working Adventures Worldwide** Ⓦwww.bunac.org. Exactly what the name says. European programs are only offered in Britain, Ireland and France.
- **CDS International** Ⓦwww.cdsintl.org. Programmes in Germany, Switzerland and Spain aimed at young professionals seeking international experience.
- **Council Exchanges** Ⓦwww.ciee.org. Offers teach-abroad programs in Spain.
- **International Cooperative Education Programe** Ⓦwww .icemenlo.com. Eight- to twelve-week paid internships in Belgium, England, Germany and Switzerland, for those with foreign language skills.

- **InterExchange Work Abroad Programs** Ⓦwww
.interexchange.org. Programs for Americans and Canadians 18
and older in France, Germany, the Netherlands and Spain.

The "working holiday"

If you're between 18 and 30 years old and not American, you are eligible to seek employment while "on holiday" in the UK and several other countries. In the UK, the Youth Mobility Visa (£99) allows visitors from Australia, New Zealand, Canada or Japan to work for two years. You will have to prove that you have £1600 to qualify for the so-called "**Tier 5 Visa**", and you have to apply for it before you get to the UK. You also have to leave immediately when your two years is up (and the clock starts ticking the moment your visa is issued); and you can't have dependent children under the age of 18). You can always go back home and apply for a Tier 1 Visa (for highly skilled workers) or Tier 2 (for sponsored skilled workers), but these are much more expensive (£750 for Tier 1) and involve more paperwork and waiting time.

"Working holidays" for Australians

For a UK visa, contact the UK embassy in Australia (Ⓦukinaustralia.fco
.gov.uk). Cost: AUS$484 for a twelve-month visa, or AUS$282 for a Tier 5 Visa. In the rest of the EU, you have "working holiday" arrangements with: Belgium, Cyprus, Denmark, Estonia, Finland, France, Germany, Ireland, Italy, Malta, the Netherlands, Norway, Sweden and the United Kingdom. Surf their embassy websites in your country for application information.

"Working holidays" for New Zealanders

For a UK visa, contact the UK embassy in New Zealand (Ⓦwww
.ukinnewzealand.fco.gov.uk). Cost: A Tier 5 Youth Mobility Visa is NZ$338/€150. A six-month work permit is NZ$581. It takes 5–15 days to process, but there are no guarantees. In the rest of the EU, you have "working holiday" arrangements with: Belgium, Czech Republic, Denmark, Finland, France, Germany, Ireland, Italy, Malta, the Netherlands, Norway and Sweden. Check out their embassy websites in your country for application info.

"Working holidays" for Canadians

For a UK visa, contact the UK embassy in Canada (Ⓦukincanada
.fco.gov.uk). Cost: CAN$387 for a 24-month visa or work permit, or CAN$225 for a Tier 5 Youth Mobility Visa (if you're 18–30). It takes about two to three months to process. In the EU, you have working holiday arrangements with: Austria, Belgium, Czech Republic,

www.roughguides.com

Denmark, France, Germany, Ireland, Italy, Latvia, the Netherlands, Norway, Sweden and Switzerland. Go to their embassy websites in your country for application info.

Britain's ancestry clause

In you're a Commonwealth citizen and you want to work in Britain and have a grandparent who was born in Britain or Northern Ireland (and you can prove it), you can apply for a special UK **Ancestry visa** that enables you to live and work in Britain for an initial period of four years. Visit the website of your nearest British embassy for details.

Starting your job search online

It's not just au pair gigs and private English lessons. You can find IT jobs, translation positions, adventure-guiding jobs, fruit-picking work, wine jobs (grape picking and hauling grapes), ski resort posts and more. Your best starting points on the **web** are probably ⓦwww.jobs-in-europe .com and ⓦwww.workanywhere.com. Even though landing most holiday jobs involves pavement-pounding upon arrival, the web can still be of some help. Once you learn the basics below, you'll be able to fine-tune your web searching. For tips on landing work, see p.100.

Direct employment

The hardest jobs to get are the ones that you set up on your own by **applying directly** to European companies before you leave. To get a job offer without an interview takes some serious legwork, luck or great connections – typically, all three, plus a low-budget miracle. That may mean starting with a bulk mailing of your CV (résumé) and cover letter followed by hours of overseas follow-up calls. Let's say you get a job offer. In order for the company to arrange a work visa for you, they need to be able to show the government that someone from their country or elsewhere in the EU couldn't do the job. Once you understand this position, you can better focus your job search to fit your unique skills. Say, for example, you've got web-programmer skills and have been doing campus promotions at your university. You'd have a good shot landing a job with a European company trying to target English-speaking university-age customers with a new website. And they'd have a good chance of getting you a work visa. Some creative thinking is in order to figure out what marketable skills (in addition to your English speaking and writing) will make you an appealing candidate and also make you an easy sell to the immigration bureau. At any rate, all such permissions must be arranged long before your arrival, so this is one of the first things you'll want to do when planning your trip.

Illegal work

If you do **illegal work**, you could very well – depending on the laws of that country, which are certainly worth looking into – find yourself slapped with a fine, thrown out of the country (guess who gets to pay for the ticket home?) or landed behind bars (picking up free language lessons from your cellmates!). With that little disclaimer out of the way, there are scores of employers who don't mind hiring unregistered foreign help and, from experience, know that the authorities will turn a blind eye. In fact, you may go to great lengths to secure a work permit only to be paid under the table. They often just like knowing you have a permit in case the police show up requesting documents.

Seasonal work

One of your best chances of turning up and landing a decent-paying job with no previous skills (or a work permit) is going to be taking advantage of the **seasonal openings**. It's largely a matter of being in the right place at the right time, and if you know what you're looking for it's easy to coordinate.

Ski jobs

Working in the Alps or Pyrenees can be a fantastic experience, especially if you find a job that allows you to put your **skis** on regularly. Unfortunately, those aren't as common as you'd think. For a job, either apply in writing for work with a tour company in your country six to eight months in advance or arrive at your desired resort around mid-November and start walking the streets (the ski season runs from the beginning of December to May in most places, depending on snowfall for that year). Be especially careful about hiring yourself out as a freelance ski instructor – most resorts keep a keen eye out for unofficial lessons on the slopes and prosecute. Possible jobs include: ski tuning, rental-shop fittings, ski guiding, lift operator, bartender, dishwasher, table waiter, restaurant cook, chalet cook/housekeeping, childcare, singer/guitar player at bars, reception staff, maintenance staff, sales clerk, supply driver, bouncer and DJ. Countries with ski resorts include: Andorra, Austria, Bulgaria, France, Germany, Italy, Norway, Scotland, Slovakia, Slovenia, Spain, Sweden and Switzerland. If you want to find out a bit more on the web first, try ⓦ www.skiconnection.co.uk, ⓦ www.natives.co.uk or ⓦ www.skistaff.co.uk; or look up the resort you want to go to and send out your CV to shops around town. The largest ski resorts include:

- Chamonix Ⓦwww.chamonix.net
- Les Trois Vallées (Courchevel, Meribel, Val Thorens, all interconnected) Ⓦwww.les3vallees.com
- Val d'Isere Ⓦwww.valdisere.com

For other ski areas, try Ⓦwww.resortsonline.com.

Summer-resort work

For **summer resorts**, you may want to turn up two months before the season begins (March–May) to beat the rush for jobs, then go travelling regionally and return when the job starts. On the hotel/bar/restaurant side, women tend to have an easier time finding work. Common jobs include: camp counsellor for kids, bartender, waiter, hotel receptionist, hotel housekeeper, cook, baker, sales clerk, supply driver, singer/guitar player at bars, DJ, rental-shop clerk, cleaner, bouncer, guide, sports instructor, lifeguard, scuba instructor and campground maintainer.

Harvest-season work

If you can eat it, you can probably find work picking it if you turn up at the right place in the right season – from strawberries to dates to apples. Most **harvesting jobs** are in the autumn (fall), but they can be found all summer long. The best place for pre-trip research is the internet: try Ⓦwww.pickingjobs.com. Pay is often based on the amount you pick, and it may take a few days to get up to speed. No one is going to remind you when to drink water or that you should protect yourself from the sun, so take care of that yourself. Bring a good hat, sun cream, and drink throughout the day. And remember to ask for adequate protection when pesticides and other noxious chemicals are sprayed.

Manual labour

Construction jobs tend to be underpaid and overworked. There's often a spot or two in cities where labourers show up each morning and get selected by employers. If no such place exists, or the competition is too fierce, look for large construction sites and ask for work directly from the foreman. There's also plenty of factory work; the nastier tasks usually come with a higher wage. If they don't, don't do them. Possible jobs include: house renovation, road building, landscaping, shrimp peeling and fish packing.

Working independently

Money-making opportunities for the **creative entrepreneur** are almost endless. You could discreetly sell cool drinks on a hot beach or cheap umbrellas on a busy street when it rains. And if you have a trade that allows you to work independently, even better. But unless you have a work permit, do find out about the penalties, assess the risk and keep a low profile. If you're looking for a street to perform on, think about good acoustics, an original act and a place where the police are kind (northern Europe tends to be popular in this regard). Often, small towns, with many pedestrian streets and few buskers (street performers), bring good fortune. Also, keep an eye out for festivals, which attract crowds with ample pocket change and time to stick around until the end of your act, when the hat gets passed. A clever performance with showmanship and a dose of humour will out-earn a talented musician nine out of ten days. Other possible jobs include: masseur/masseuse, private cook, private music instructor, street juggler, house cleaner, window washer, gardener, language tutor, jewellery street-seller, T-shirt designer and peddler, and promotional pamphlet distributor (to other travellers for local bars/hostels).

Teaching English

If English is your mother tongue, you have a university degree of some kind, can dress smartly and carry yourself with confidence, you have a decent shot at landing a job without a TEFL or similar certificate. You can certainly hire yourself out as a private tutor. But there's a lot more to **teaching a language** than just being able to speak it, and any amount of instruction will be helpful. The problem is, the **instruction** isn't that cheap (€1050–1950) or quick (roughly 100hr of coursework), and not all programs are created equal. In Europe, the British-based CELTA (Certificate in English Language Teaching to Adults) is probably the most recognized brand of TEFL/TESOL certificates, and you can take them just about anywhere. (Quick decoder: TEFL is "Teaching English as a Foreign Language" and TESOL is "Teaching English for Speakers of Other Languages" – basically the same thing.) If you decide you want to go after a TEFL certificate, you have a few options:

- **Get it near where you live** – search ⓦwww.cambridge-efl.org for the closest location.
- **Get a certificate online** – a bit shady and probably not as useful in terms of practice and feedback.
- **Take a CELTA or other reliable course in the city or country you want to work in** – you can find out the reputable courses by asking local employers or checking out a TEFL forum like the one at Dave's ESL Café ⓦwww.eslcafe.com, a good source for general job searching and classroom teaching tips and lessons. This is probably the best option because it means spending more time in the country, and the local language schools have the

best job-placement connections. In addition to CELTA, Trinity College London programs (ⓦwww.windsorschools.co.uk) are also well known.

- **Go where it's a bit cheaper to get a TEFL degree** – in places such as Thailand or Egypt, you may get accommodation thrown in for that €1050–1950. (If you're paying €20 a night for six weeks in Europe, that's €840. And you can probably buy a return ticket from London to Bangkok for less than that. Try ⓦwww.teflinternational.com.)

In Europe, most of the jobs these days can be found in Eastern and Central Europe, where the TEFL isn't quite as critical. If you do have a TEFL certificate, though, you'll probably land a better job or beat unqualified competition, and find it easier in the classroom than if you were winging it. Is it worth the money and time to make that "livable wage"? That's your call. But you probably needn't bother with the €290 weekend **introductory course**; those who require a real certificate won't be impressed. Most of the best jobs require a six- to twelve-month contract to prevent you from skipping out and leaving their students with verbs unconjugated and participles dangling.

Teaching diving

Europe may not be anyone's top pick for an exciting dive, but Europeans still want to get certified, and often before they go on holiday. With a **Divemaster certification** (ⓦwww.padi.com), you may be able to find some work, especially in large cities, provided you speak the language. Unlike resorts, schools prefer people for longer stretches, so that may make things a bit more challenging on a traveller's schedule. Greece, Cyprus, Croatia, Malta and the Canary Islands offer the best diving. Go to ⓦwww.scubayellowpages.com for a list of diving companies around Europe. In terms of landing a job, most certified instructors have success making personal contact with dive shops and get paid under the table for their work. Or they return later, once the proper work visa has been processed back home. You might try applying directly to some of the larger, more professional resorts (those destinations with multiple dive shops on the above website, for example).

Telecommute

Depending on the nature of your job, you may be able to reduce your workload to part time and get the work done while you're on the road. Skills like translating, accounting and copy editing don't necessarily require a fixed address. Pack along a **laptop** if need be or just hit the ubiquitous internet cafés and back up your data on a USB jumpdrive.

Journalism and photography

Travel writing and travel **photography** are very competitive fields, and in both cases your chances of supplementing your income or supporting yourself while travelling will be greatly enhanced with well-honed skills from a course or formal education, but no matter how much natural ability or number of course certificates you may have, selling your material without an established track record is extremely tough.

That means, if you're serious about writing or camera-clicking your way around Europe, you'll want to give yourself a head start by making inroads in the industry: get some articles or photos published (no matter what the subject), build a relationship with editors and start putting your portfolio together.

Once you have a solid **client list** of people willing to buy your prose or pictures, you can actually make money during your travels. Unfortunately, it can take months or, more likely, years to develop such contacts. The other, and far more popular, approach is to document your trip and try to sell it upon your return. This can certainly bring in some money, but you're not likely to get it until long after you return. Cold-calling an editor just before you leave and asking if you can, despite your complete lack of experience, report your way around Europe, is a textbook example of how not to go about it.

Otherwise, you might apply to work directly with the large **wire services** (such as Associated Press or Reuters) or, if you plan to stay put for a while, try small English-speaking **newspapers** overseas (Ⓦwww .world-newspapers.com/europe.html).

Multinational jobs

If you happen to live near the headquarters of an international company, surf their website and find out where their **overseas offices** are located and what they do. If you've got some language skills or other marketable training that may interest them, try to arrange for an interview. If you don't live near the headquarters, that doesn't mean you need to give up just yet. Not all require you to interview at their central command centre.

Wine jobs

There's everything from tasting to sales to grape picking to estate management to biology work. Try Ⓦwww.agriseek.com and Ⓦwww.winecountry jobs.com. Or go to Ⓦwww.wineweb.com/mapeuro.html and get the contact info for European wineries and contact them directly yourself.

www.roughguides.com

IT jobs

There are hundreds of **IT recruitment firms** in just about every European country. If you want to go down that route, you might do an internet search with the name of the country you want to work in plus "IT jobs" or "IT recruitment" or "computer jobs". Otherwise, take a look at ⓦwww.dice.com, ⓦwww.cvointernational.com (for placements in Eastern Europe) and ⓦwww.eurosearch.net.

Au pair jobs

Assisting with children can, depending on the family, be a good arrangement. Live-in **au pairs** typically earn less in Europe than in the US, but rates are often adjusted if you have a college degree, childcare education, special language skills and great letters of recommendation. And, of course, if you work more hours or care for more children (for more than three children, wages should go up roughly ten percent for each child). Wages may also be slightly higher in major cities, where there's more competition. The workload varies from one family to the next, but for €70 a week you might expect about five hours of work per day for five days, with two or three babysitting evenings – more for live-out au pairs. Keep in mind that by staying with the family you'll be saving €5000–15,000 in annual accommodation costs. Typically, you get your own room, about €300 a month, and perhaps use of a car and a chance to accompany the family on vacations. So much depends on the family, so ask lots of questions before taking the job. Start your research with these websites:

- ⓦwww.aupair-agency.com
- ⓦwww.greataupair.com
- ⓦwww.aupair.com
- ⓦwww.aupair-world.net

Government and NGO jobs

Landing work for a **government** isn't as intimidating as it might sound. In fact, governments may even offer more opportunities for people to start their careers overseas than any company, and you don't necessarily have to carry a gun, classified microfilm or a pen that doubles as a rocket launcher to get your pay cheque. The US government alone has 50,000 employees working overseas. Non-Governmental Organizations (**NGO**s) are typically major charities, environmental groups or human rights organizations, and they need willing overseas workers – some are volunteers, but most offer paid positions. For a solid listing of NGOs, check out NGO Watch, at ⓦwww.ngowatch.org.

Can you spot a bad travel job?

So many travellers who head abroad end up in the **worst travel jobs**. The reason isn't so surprising. They can't tell a great travel job from a lemon. A great job, they think, is any one they can get. So, they take the first one that comes along without ever checking if it fits with the travel experience they're after.

Let's take a typical job search. Say you want to work in a ski resort. You go to the French Alps, search frantically for a job and land one washing dishes, realizing you were lucky to get anything with your dodgy language skills. You're thrilled to have work, but the minimum wage doesn't get you very far in a pricey resort. After working eight-hour days six days a week (fairly standard), you notice you've only put your skis on a few times and, as the lone washer, you've been kept too busy to meet anyone at the restaurant. Eventually, you'll wonder what the point is. It took me about three weeks.

The fact is, very few jobs in ski resorts pay well (considering the high cost of living) and many don't allow you much time to ski. Savvy ski bums now prefer to work overtime at a better-paying job elsewhere, then head to a ski resort, find some cheap accommodation and ski their asses off for a month.

Contrast this with picking grapes in France. Even if you can't arrange to get paid, you can probably get your room and board covered. Let's say you work a week at a small chateau, meet loads of people, drink as much wine as your liver will permit and leave with a memorable experience that didn't bankrupt you.

Still not sure what a bad job is? If you can't answer "yes" to at least one of the following questions, you'd do well to look for a different job. Factoring in living costs, does the job bring in enough money to cover future travel? Does it make for an interesting experience or provide you with a valued skill? Is it a relatively easy workload and/or does it offer a lenient schedule that allows you to partake in local activities you enjoy?

Australian government jobs

- Australian Public Service Gazette Ⓦ www.apsjobs.gov.au

Canadian government jobs

- Canadian International Development Agency Ⓦ w3.acdi -cida.gc.ca
- Department of Foreign Affairs and International Trade Ⓦ www.international.gc.ca

New Zealand government jobs

- New Zealand's International Aid and Development Agency Ⓦ www.nzaid.govt.nz
- Overseas diplomatic posts Ⓦ www.mfat.govt.nz/about-the -ministry/working-for-us/index.php

UK government jobs

- Department for International Development Ⓦ www.dfid.gov.uk
- Foreign and Commonwealth Office Ⓦ www.fco.gov.uk

US government jobs

- Central Intelligence Agency ⓦwww.cia.gov
- Department of State ⓦwww.state.gov
- Peace Corp ⓦwww.peacecorps.gov
- US Agency for International Development ⓦwww.usaid.gov
- International Information Programs ⓦwww.state.gov/r/iip

United Nations Development Program

- Eight to ten weeks of on-the-job training for enrolled graduate students fluent in two of the United Nations' official languages (see ⓦwww.undp.org).

United Nations Junior Professional programs

- Junior professional posts are given for short assignments. UNICEF has one (requires master's degree, age 32 years or under and fluent French), as do UNESCO and UNDP. See ⓦwww.un.org/esa /socdev/unyin/jobs for more information.

Landing a job while in the country

OK, let's say you've splashed out for a work permit organized by a student work-permit agency (or taken advantage of a "working holiday" visa – see p.91), you still have to **find a job** ... yourself.

Wake up early, check the classified ads in the paper, check notice boards, put up your own messages, dress smartly, don't wear sunglasses, take off the hat, lose the body piercings, cover any tattoos that may frighten small children, dye your hair back to a colour that could at least pass for real hair, leave your shorts in the hostel as well as the loose-fitting jeans that expose your designer underwear, double-check your letters for typos and return calls promptly (easier with a local SIM card for your mobile phone or a local Skype Call-In number see p.171). In short, don't give them a reason to dismiss you.

No potential employer wants to read over a sampling of your term papers. Let's face it, you probably don't want to look at them again, either. Nor are they going to read through a stack of recommendation letters. What you should bring is some **appropriate clothing**, or enough money to pick some up when you arrive. If you think a suit is appropriate for the job, you may wish to cart one along. A current **CV** (résumé) will come in handy. As will a few official copies of your diploma.

If you are rejected, take it with a smile, thank them for their consideration and always take the opportunity to ask them where you might find work. If you've made a good impression, most people won't mind providing a few leads. Furthermore, don't cross off a potential employer just because they said no a few days or a week earlier. Things change.

One of their employees may quit or get sacked. Or perhaps someone they were expecting never showed up. They might even realize that they needed more help than they thought. And as long as your approach is polite, your perseverance will be respected.

If you're going after a more corporate-type job, the best thing you can do once you've arrived is arrange for an **interview**. Buy yourself a phone card or a local SIM card for your phone and start making calls. If you know you really want to work in a certain field, try to arrange a quick meeting even if you've heard they don't have any openings. You might start by saying something like "I expected there weren't any openings at the moment, but as part of my foreign study experience I need to at least do a short interview to get an insider perspective. If you could spare, say, ten minutes in the next day or three I'd be grateful." Or figure out your own way in. Then, when you get the meeting, ask a few questions, see if a free **internship** might be possible. Before you accept an offer for free work, though, say you just need to explore a few other leads. If you like the place, at least you'll have a fall-back opportunity. Or ask if this person knows anyone else in the industry worth contacting. Who knows: if you make a good impression, you might at least get a good referral.

If you're going after a restaurant/bar/resort job, just show up and ask for the manager or owner. They'll want to take a look at you, check that your brain can handle the tasks required and test out your language skills.

If nothing comes along, you'll need some imagination. And funds – a good month's worth or longer if you're prepared to accept a position that doesn't pay. See p.94 for entrepreneurial jobs.

For more info on landing a job, try one or more of the following books or websites:

- *International Jobs* by Erich Kocher
- *International Jobs Directory: 1001 Employers and Great Tips for Success!* by Drs Ron & Caryl Krannich
- *International Job Finder: Where the Jobs Are Worldwide* by Daniel Lauber
- *Live and Work Abroad: A Guide for Modern Nomads* by Huw Francis, Michelyne Callan
- *Work Abroad: The Complete Guide to Finding a Job Overseas* by Clayton A. Hubbs
- *Work Your Way Around the World* by Susan Griffith

- ⓦ www.jobmonkey.com
- ⓦ www.monster.com
- ⓦ www.transitionsabroad.com

www.roughguides.com

You got the job

Once you get a job offer you plan to accept, ask for a few days to fix housing arrangements. Look into family stays, university-room rentals, and enquire at various hostels to see if they'll offer you a long-term deal.

If you work abroad and declare your earnings there, knowing that the amount is too small to be **taxed** in that country, bear in mind that you might be taxed for the amount in your home country, depending upon reciprocal agreements and any other income sources.

Volunteering

It may not seem like Europe needs saving. There's certainly not the level of poverty and disease you'd find in Africa, or other developing countries, but there are people, parks and political groups in need of help and absolutely no shortage of organizations that would like you to come and **volunteer** for them.

Donating your time can be a tremendously fulfilling experience, but picking a good program is not as straightforward as you'd imagine. If you don't select carefully, your time contributed may feel like time wasted. Or it may be fulfilling for you, but little benefit – if any – to the community. The fact is that some organizations' definitions of efficiency and utility will differ substantially from your own, or the flashy review quotes dotted about their website.

And many of the volunteer ventures are almost identical to English-teaching and labour-intensive work projects that you could be getting paid for. You might be moving boxes, doing dishes or shovelling cow dung, which is fine, provided you know what you're getting into. So, before you sign up, make sure you get an exact description of what you'll be doing and what they expect you to accomplish during your visit. You'll want some local orientation before you're dropped off at your project and a reliable local contact for emergency support, supplies and advice. You can ask for these things because you're not just going to be working there for free; you're almost certainly helping **finance** it. And perhaps the most surprising thing about volunteering is that it isn't as cheap as it sounds.

Volunteer projects

Projects change all the time, but here are a few ideas:

Build a school or clinic • help staff an "eco-house" • renovate hiking paths in parks and nature reserves • track animals • assist at a camp for children with learning disabilities • develop ecotourism • promote health-care • work with a women's cooperative • practise sustainable agriculture • teach English • join an archeological dig • help renovate a castle or monastery • develop a small business enterprise or support human rights efforts.

First, there's the air fare or rail/bus transport. Then you often need to pay a fee that covers your lodging, food, insurance and the entire screening and orientation process. It's not uncommon to be shelling out more than €350 a month. As a guideline, the more exotic the project (such as studying dolphins in Europe's aquariums), the more you pay to assist.

Most projects have specific dates for training and transporting new volunteers. Plus, the organizations prefer to screen applicants, so showing up to lend a hand, though well intentioned, can actually backfire. Your best bet is to make arrangements long before you leave. If you're already on the road, your time will be well spent making contact at a nearby internet café. With a more web-advanced organization, you may be able to take care of all the details before you arrive.

Rewards of volunteering

- Feel that you're helping to leave the world in a better condition than when you arrived.
- Live and work in a community where it's easy to make friends.
- Learn customs and language skills.
- Get to know volunteers from around the world.
- Get hands-on practical experience.
- Put your professional skills to use to make a tangible difference in people's lives.

Types of volunteer projects

Some organizations want strong backs, others strong minds. All want good attitudes and your financial support. As you begin your search, you'll find some of the projects are seasonal, some go year-round and some are unique ones that pop up when a university professor has received a major research grant. If possible, try to take advantage of the time of year you'll be volunteering (ie you don't want to be volunteering indoors in Portugal in springtime when the weather is great). If you know where you want to be and what you want to do, try typing some keywords into your favourite search engine. Start with the location, then the type of work, plus "volunteer", "help" or "assist". Meanwhile, here are a few volunteer sites to get you started:

- **Idealist** ⓦ www.idealist.org
- **Taking It Global** ⓦ www.takingitglobal.org
- **Volunteer Abroad** ⓦ www.volunteerabroad.com
- **Volunteer International** ⓦ www.volunteerinternational.org
- **Archelon** (the Sea Turtle Protection Society of Greece) ⓦ www .archelon.gr
- **WWF** ⓦ www.panda.org/how_you_can_help/volunteer

Learning new skills

If you don't have time to work or get involved with a volunteer project during your trip, it's always possible to find time for a course; some take just half a day. **Taking a course** is one of the most enriching things you can do on your trip: it's a chance to learn a new skill that will remain with you long after you've returned home. Education aside, many offer a nice break from the travel scene and provide a chance for you to meet up with some locals or other foreigners with similar interests.

Many courses can be arranged at the last minute, but most often the better programs require some advance booking. Look into this well before you arrive; in some cases, well before you arrange any flights. Unless you're absolutely sure about the soundness of a course, don't pay the entire fee in advance. And pay with a credit card to help protect yourself. The courses listed below are by no means a definitive list; they are meant to provide a sample of some of the activities out there, and are only intended as a starting point.

Learning to cook

Want a great souvenir? Learn how to make one amazing local dish. You'll be impressing friends and family with it for ages, provided you don't keep serving it to the same people. France, Italy and Spain are the most popular destinations for the gastronomically inclined, but **cooking schools** can be found almost anywhere. If you find you're really enjoying a local cuisine, talk to the local tourist office about courses available. Most last from a half-day to a month, with widely varying prices. As well as the listings below, try Ⓦcookforfun.shawguides.com or *The Guide to Cooking Schools* by Dorlene Kaplan.

- **APICIUS Cooking School** Florence, Italy Ⓦwww.apicius.it. Taught in Italian (recipes can be translated, individual courses can be held in English). One-day wine class (in group) €45; three-hour private cooking course €265; one-week summer workshops start at €790.
- **Ballymaloe Cooking School** Cork, Ireland Ⓦwww.cookingisfun.ie. Full-day course in the art of spit-roasting or cooking warm winter stews is €245.
- **Glorious Greek Kitchen** Athens, Greece Ⓦwww.dianekochilas.com. Indoor/outdoor kitchen and class size can vary from five to forty. The price of €1850 for a week includes lodging and meals. One-day culinary walking tours with lunch are available for under €100.

- **Le Cordon Bleu French Cooking** Paris, France Ⓦwww .cordonbleu.com. The Grande Dame of cooking schools. You can take a single-day introductory course for €160–175 on nearly any subject, or a four-day elective course for €920. Also available is a one-month intensive certificate-level course for €7990.

Learning a language

Learning a language isn't as difficult as you might think, even if you've taken a language in school for years, hated it, learned next to nothing and vowed you'd never bother with it again – as I did.

Taking that step back towards language learning can be a humbling experience. And if you get a headache for the first couple of weeks, it just means your brain is working overtime – a sign that you'll have things figured out soon.

One thing you can say about **intensive language schools** is that they work. The combination of small groups or even one-on-one tutoring plus a family stay, or simply living in the country, is a sort of magic formula, and you walk away with a better grasp of the language than you might get in years of regular schooling – and often without the brain-crushing boredom you associate with learning the past imperfect subjunctive gerund form of exceptions to masculine nouns. Again, that doesn't mean it's easy and that you'll be able to down beers at the local pub while you suck up linguistic nuances (unless you count pronouncing the beverages correctly). That bit comes later, after you've picked up the basics.

"Hello", "please" and "thank you" won't take more than five minutes to learn, no matter what the language. If you want to move beyond a few words, a regular language course is a great way to start your travels in a new country. Aside from tools that will help you unlock the cultural codes of the country, you'll meet more locals, be able to get assistance when needed, keep your grey matter active and make your travels far more meaningful. You'll need at least three weeks to make real progress, no matter how intensive the course is. Two months should provide good conversational skills, depending on your study habits.

Many of the better-known language courses take place in towns packed with English-speaking students – great for your social life, but lousy for language discipline. It's better (and cheaper) to select a smaller or less popular town where you'll get an experience far more intensive than the more expensive "intensive" courses offered in major language-learning centres.

If you're set on a specific course, you may need to sign up in advance. Otherwise, you can walk in off the street and usually start the same day. And, naturally, you can find inexpensive private tutors to teach you in nearly any city. Put up a notice near a university and you'll have a few offers within hours.

www.roughguides.com

Credit crisis

OK, you've found the perfect foreign language school and plan to study for about three weeks, all the while enjoying horseback riding and beach parties with your new-found classroom friends. For North Americans, the only thing stopping you now is transferring the classes so your university knows it's actually an educational experience and not just a pseudo-academic vacation.

Attaining credit for studying in a language school takes persistence, though. Make the effort to find the school that's right for you with professional courses and a certified staff, referrals and contacts – basically, anyone that can sell the point that this language school is not one big fiesta, and that you learn more words than just "guacamole" and "cerveza".

These programs can have significant value, even if you don't get academic credit for them. Consider the economics: the average US student spends an average of two years studying another language at university. At the University of California, for example, it takes three consecutive courses for two years to fulfil this requirement. These classes are an hour a day, four days a week. Two years of this instruction will cost over $3000 in the public system (well over $6000 at a private college), and often students (like myself) still feel unskilled in the language. Look at it that way and the intensive programs start to look like a bargain. You can actually become proficient in the language and the average cost for two months (about 120hr) of classroom instruction, room, board and travel excursions runs to about $1500. After one of these intensive courses, it's not unusual for students to test out of language requirements with less time, less money and more fun.

Eric Tiettmeyer,
ⓦ www.studenttraveler.com

Studying photography

Even if you're just taking a pocket camera, learning how to compose your photographs is going to get you a lot further than expensive film and an overpriced lens. You may not learn anything more valuable than the tips on p.210, but you'll need to practise them and develop an eye for what works and what doesn't. That means taking oodles of photos, developing them immediately and having them critiqued. You can find community photography workshops for less than €100, but the upper-end instruction doesn't come cheap. It does, however, often include a trip to Europe, which may be how you'd like to begin your journey, getting comfortable with a group before venturing out on your own.

- **Close Up Expeditions** ⓦ www.cuephoto.com. Workshops in over forty countries concentrating on nature, landscape and traditional cultures; 5–17 days, $250–350/£151–212 per day.
- **National Geographic Expeditions Photo Journey to Provence** ⓦ www.nationalgeographicexpeditions.com/triptypes /photography. Several prominent National Geographic photographers and photo editors come along to hand-deliver personal tips and tricks to budding photographers. Prices for

a week start at US$3985, plus US$700 for a private room (not including flights).

- **Ralph Paonessa Photo Workshops** ⓦwww.rpphoto.com. Specializing in birds, nature, landscapes and travel, these 5- to 15-day programs cost $2000–5995/£1210–3630 with lodging, some meals, and ground transport.
- **Jim Cline Photography** ⓦwww.jimcline.com. Small group (7–10 people) trips mainly to Latin America, India and Southeast Asia. Sometimes in combination with workshops, sometimes with informal tutoring on location. Length: 2–14 days; cost: $240–300/£145–182 per day.

Wilderness survival and alpine courses

You hardly need one of these to get by in Europe, but you never know when **survival skills** will suddenly come in handy. Most survival schools are run by – here's a real shocker – Americans, but many of the programs take place outside the US (and you might feel more confident by taking a course before you leave). Some, such as NOLS and Outward Bound, place more emphasis on the group experience, while others are more technically oriented. If you already speak French, German or Italian, you might feel comfortable jumping right into a European course in the Alps. Make sure you ask plenty of questions (see p.63) before making your decision.

- **NOLS** ⓦwww.nols.edu. US organizer branching out with a sea kayaking and backpacking course in northern Norway at €5700 for thirty days. One-month or two-week courses in the US are $900–2000 per week. Transferable educational credit is possible with some universities.
- **Outward Bound** ⓦwww.outwardbound.org. Roughly €750 per week, with courses of one to eleven weeks. Focuses on wilderness training and team building.
- **Objective Team** ⓦwww.objectiveteam.com. Put your parents at ease by starting your trip with a one-day travel-security course (they specialize not just in backpackers, but corporate training for hostile environments) in London. €175.
- **Adventure Lifesigns** ⓦwww.lifesignsgroup.co.uk. British expedition training, remote medical training and independent travellers' courses that range from 1–2 days from around €120 per day, plus a one-day travel safety seminar for €70.

Before leaving home:

- **Boulder Outdoor Survival School (BOSS)** ⓦwww.totalclimbing.com. Avalanche courses and backcountry skiing safety in the Rocky Mountains. Plenty of one-day courses. From about US$170 per day.

www.roughguides.com

- **LTR (Learn To Return) Training Systems, Inc**. ⓦwww .survivaltraining.com. Alaska-based emergency survival training in arctic, mountain and sea environments, as well as for natural disasters, industrial accidents and terrorist attacks. Over 25 specialized courses that range from 2 to 70 hours. Prices from US$400 for 3 days.
- **Karamat Wilderness Ways** ⓦwww.karamat.com. Canadian wilderness survival specializing in the northern boreal forests. Two-week courses with summer or winter theme. Prices from US$660 per week.
- **Aboriginal Living Skills School** ⓦwww.alssadventures.com. Living off the land in Arizona. Learn desert survival, winter camping and primitive camp-craft skills with one-day to week-long courses. Prices from US$1330 per week.

If you're more interested in staying alive in the mountains and ticking off summits in the process, check out the list of **international mountaineering courses** at ⓦdmoz.org/Recreation/Climbing /Guides_and_Schools, or the two listed below:

- **Bob Culp Climbing School** ⓦwww.bobculp.com. Rock- and ice-climbing trips in Chamonix and the Italian Dolomites; five days or more at €200 per day per person (air fare not included).
- **Swiss Association of Mountaineering Schools** ⓦwww .bergsportschulen.ch. Select schools by speciality (ice-climbing, high-altitude skiing, etc) or region, and the links will put you in touch with professional Swiss guides.

Meditation

If the fast pace of life on the road starts taking its toll on your nerves, the regular pub visits aren't helping and your Valium prescription has run out, consider taking a **personal time-out**. That might mean a couple of yoga classes or a week in silent seclusion. Getting back in touch with your mind and body, however you decide to go about it, can be an invigorating pit stop – just what you need to continue on your physical and inner journey. Many courses are offered in English and the ones that aren't are easy enough to follow by looking at the instructor's movements. Just keep an eye out for local yoga, qi gong and meditation centres as you go. Here are a few links to a variety of yoga schools in Europe to get you started:

- **Ashtanga** ⓦwww.ashtanga.com/html/Europe.html
- **Blue Mountain Center Meditation Centres** (UK and the Netherlands) ⓦwww.easwaran.org
- **Iyengar** ⓦwww.iyengar-yoga.com/Yoga_Centers/Europe
- **Shambhala** ⓦshambhala.org/centers
- **Sivananda** ⓦwww.sivananda.org

6

Documents and insurance

etting your **documents** in order for a big trip to Europe isn't nearly as much of a hassle as it sounds – just a case of sorting out your passport, any necessary visas and some travel insurance. Hardly any European countries require visas (or they make it easy for you to pick them up upon arrival). But take a look on p.112 to see which apply to your nationality and then be sure to check out the box on pp.120–121 for the all-important departure countdown.

Passports

A **passport** is a document issued by your country of citizenship that establishes your identity and enables you to exit and re-enter your country of citizenship. That is to say, without a passport you're looking at a short trip. Probably to the airport and back. See the box on pp.110–111 for how you get one.

Two or more passports

The important thing for dual or triple passport holders is that you **pick one passport** to use during your trip – the one that grants you the most visa-free access or work privileges – and only use the other for emergencies (leave the third one at home with your document copies so it can be mailed to you if a crisis should arise). It may be tempting to swap when you can save a little money on a visa, but if you get questioned by a customs official you need to be able to demonstrate a clear travel history. Any gaps will raise suspicions. To keep the customs

www.roughguides.com

109

process at borders moving smoothly, don't bring up your multiple citizenship unless asked.

Visas

Visas are essentially stamps (but sometimes stickers or entire documents) inserted into your passport by immigration officials or embassies or consulates acting on their behalf, and grant you permission to enter their country for a specified period of time. There are other conditions that can be included as well – such as the right to work, the right to re-enter the country multiple times and the right to extend your visa – which may require special approval. Much of this depends on which passport you hold. Each country has its own set of agreements with other countries, with fees yo-yoing (with diplomacy) in the region of €10–45.

Getting a passport

Australia

Regular service 32-page passport Aus$208, 64-page passport Aus$312; ten working days; can be done online or at a post office, but you must be interviewed.

Expedited Additional fee of Aus$78 to process in two working days (case-by-case basis ☎131 232).

Photo info There are various guidelines and restrictions on Australian passport photos. See ⓦwww.passports.gov.au for details.

Valid For ten years.

Canada

Regular service 24-page passport Can$87, 48-page passport Can$92; 27 days by mail (not including mailing time), ten days in person; no renewal available, new passport must be purchased; photocopies of identity documents (e.g. driver's licence) must be signed by a guarantor.

Expedited Express: two to nine days for an additional fee of Can$30. Urgent: same day or next day (only available on case-by-case emergency basis) for an additional fee of Can$70. Personal pick-up: 10 days; Can$10.

Photo info There are various guidelines and restrictions on Canadian passport photos. See ⓦwww.ppt.gc.ca for details.

Valid For five years.

New Zealand

Regular service Ten working days, NZ$150.

Expedited Three working days, NZ$300. Call-out service, when urgent delivery falls out of working hours, is NZ$650; ☎0800 225 050.

Photo info There are various guidelines and restrictions on New Zealand passport photos. See ⓦwww.passports.govt.nz for details.

Valid For five years.

In Europe, they're not an issue for most passport holders, and once you're on the continent you'll rarely have to show your passport when crossing borders.

Many countries don't require any visas for some passport holders, or simply hand them out at the airport or border crossing for free or a small fee (Turkey's is €10–45, for example). Otherwise, they can take anywhere between a day and a few weeks to process, but they can usually be taken care of within a few days if you opt to pay an additional fee to expedite the application.

Austria, Belgium, Denmark, Finland, France, Germany, Greece, Iceland, Italy, Luxembourg, the Netherlands, Norway, Portugal, Spain and Sweden have joint visas that allow you to spend three months in total in the entire group of countries, known as the **Schengen Area**. The ten new members of the European Union (Cyprus, Czech Republic, Estonia, Hungary, Latvia, Lithuania, Malta, Poland, Slovakia and Slovenia) are also members of the Schengen Area in terms of

UK

Regular service Three-week service at post offices and select travel agents, £72 (48-page passport £85), about two weeks if applying at certain post office branches and Worldchoice travel agents.

Expedited One-week service at passport offices £91 and £97–105 (not possible with first-time passports). Same-day premium service (£123; only when renewing a 48-page "jumbo" passport) is technically not available for standard passports, but you can try calling ☎0870 521 0410 if you think your situation merits special consideration.

Photo info There are various guidelines and restrictions on British passport photos. See ⓦ www.ips.gov.uk for details.

Valid For ten years.

US

Regular service All first-timers must apply in person. Four to six weeks $100; $75 for renewal.

Expedited Two to three weeks expedited processing can be requested, and will add an additional $60 plus overnight shipping both ways. Or make an appointment to visit one of the 15 regional passport agencies (if near you) for US$160. At ⓦ www .americanpassport.com and similar sites, same-business-day service US$159.

Photo info There are various guidelines and restrictions on US passport photos. See ⓦ http://state.gov/travel for details.

Valid For ten years.

visas. As of December 2008, even famously non-aligned Switzerland is a full Schengen member. The UK and Ireland are not.

Americans, Canadians, New Zealanders and UK citizens do not need a visa to enter Europe for less than ninety days. There are, however, a few exceptions, noted below.

● **Americans** require visas for Russia (get in advance) and Turkey (can be obtained at any point of entry).

The notorious thirty-day Russian tourist visa

Russian tourist visas are valid for a period of 14 to 30 days, and obtaining one entails suspending all notions of rational thought. This is the old-school method of tourism – make visitors jump through daunting hoops of red tape.

You need a **passport** that's valid for six months. Easy. A photo or two. Easy. A podtverzdeniye (standard tourist invitation) from an authorized hosting Russian travel agency, registered with the Russian Ministry of Foreign Affairs (MID RF). Huh?! A tour voucher or its copy, attested by said authorized Russian travel agency. Yuck. And a cover letter from your travel agency at home containing dates and points of arrival and departure to and from Russia; means of transport; itinerary in Russia; the name of the hosting Russian agency and its reference number. Double yuck. Plus, the visas aren't cheap: €85 for a basic one that's ready in six business days and good for single entry, quickly escalating to €290 for a double-entry visa processed the same day. Has the Mafia got into the visa office?

What the tourist bureau wants is for you to book everything in advance – preferably an expensive tour. The traditional way around this is to get an **invitation** from a hotel or hostel (who can offer invitations for any length of time, provided you spend one night with them) – typically, a youth hostel in St Petersburg (Ⓦ www.ryh.ru). When contacting any hotel or agency in Russia regarding visas, ask about their recent experience with the particular consulate to which you intend to apply. Also – watch out for this – when contacting the consulates, some like to charge you €8 to reply with information by fax or email. For additional general info on obtaining a Russian visa, see Ⓦ www .russianvisa.org, Ⓦ www.waytorussia.net or Ⓦ www.expresstorussia.com.

Americans
Russian consulates require a two-page application. You should, in theory, contact the consulate nearest you, but they all have their own quirky ways (prices range from US$25–75) and the word on the web is to try to avoid the one in Washington, DC. Most prefer the consulate in San Francisco:
New York: Ⓦ www.ruscon.org
San Francisco: Ⓦ www.consulrussia.org
Seattle: Ⓦ www.netconsul.org
Costs range from US$100 for a single-entry visa that takes six or more working days to process, to US$450 for the same-day processing of a multiple-entry visa.

Australians
You need to apply at the consulate assigned to the state where you live. The basic fee is Aus$85 and takes twelve working days. A single-entry visa issued the same day costs Aus$400 (Aus$485 for double-entry). But, as they like to say on their website (Ⓦ www.sydneyrussianconsulate.com/visa.html), "processing times, requirements and fees are subject to change without notice".

- **Canadians** require visas for Russia (in advance) and Turkey (at any point of entry).
- **New Zealanders** require visas for Romania (at any point of entry), Russia (in advance) and Turkey (at any point of entry).
- **UK citizens** require visas for Russia (in advance) and Turkey (at any point of entry).

Canadians

You can apply at consulates in Ottawa, Toronto and Montreal, though you might consider sending your application to the San Francisco consulate. Contact the Canadian consulate first at ⓦ www.rusembcanada.mid.ru. Costs range from Can$75 for a single-entry visa that takes fourteen days to process to Can$300 for the same-day processing. Toronto does not issue double- or multiple-entry visas:

Toronto: ⓦ www.toronto.mid.ru
Montreal: ⓦ www.montreal.mid.ru
Ottawa: ⓔ ruscon@rogers.com

British citizens

As of June 2006, all visa application forms need to be filled in online and then printed out. Once you've done this, you can show up at the consulate in London in person, but get there very early if you want to avoid the queues. If there are already about twenty people waiting, you may not get processed before closing (if you wait around long enough, you'll probably get approached by people offering visa services for £30, who'll queue up for you). Better yet, mail it in and wait three weeks. Or go to the consulate in Edinburgh. But don't mail your application there without contacting them first (visa@edconsul.co.uk). Costs range from £30 for a single-entry visa that takes eight or more working days to process to £150 for the same-day processing of a multiple-entry visa:

London: ⓦ www.rusemblon.org

New Zealanders

The Russian Embassy in Wellington processes visas in ten working days for NZ$60, same day for NZ$150. See ⓦ www.rus.co.nz for more information.

South Africans

You need to have medical insurance for the entire visa period, plus a copy of a return air ticket. Applications need to be handed in at least three days before the trip. Standard processing time is ten days and costs R280. Urgent three-day handling raises the fee to R455, and same-day treatment will relieve you of R595. Cash only. See ⓦ www.russianembassy.org.za (the website ⓦ http://pretoria.rusembassy.org is not the official government site).

Pretoria: ⓔ rco@pixie.co.za
Cape Town: ⓔ rusco@icon.co.za

The Finnish option

St Petersburg is just a four-and-a-half-hour train ride from Helsinki. Pick up a Russian visa in town when you book a short, on-the-spot tour (try Finnsov Travel at ⓦ www.finnsov.fi). Pay the typically outrageous application fees and away you go.

If you plan to stay **more than ninety days** in any one country, check the website of its embassy in your country (🌐 www.embassyworld.com lists all embassies). New Zealanders, for example, have a special deal: the right to spend three months separately (not just three months in total) in each of the following countries: Austria, Belgium, Denmark, Finland, France, Germany, Greece, Iceland, Italy, Luxembourg, the Netherlands, Norway, Portugal, Spain, Sweden and Switzerland.

Getting visas at home

If you're planning to work legally in a country, apply for that visa first, since it must be arranged from your home country. (For more details on working abroad, see p.88.) Also, if you're planning to stay more than three months, you'll need a visa before you arrive. For instance, Australians heading to France must pay Aus$170 for a visa allowing them a stay of more than three months without a work permit. Getting such a visa is a two-month minimum wait, and also requires a certificate of Police Record, proof of medical coverage while in France, proof that you can support yourself financially, and a signed declaration that you will not take up employment during your stay.

Entry for students on study programs

If you're arriving in Europe to study for a semester or more, you should have all your **study abroad documentation** (eg an official paper stating where and when you'll be studying and living) with you to present to the customs officer. Your study abroad program will tell you if you require a special visa and how to obtain it if you do, but it will be your responsibility to make sure it's processed and ready in time.

Insurance

Here's the most important thing you need to know about **travel insurance** for an extended trip: get some. To find out why, what makes a good policy and what it costs, read on.

Other considerations

Be aware of local **holidays**, as visa-issuing offices at home are likely to be closed on these days.

Don't list your **occupation** if it may give them reason to be suspicious, such as journalist or security analyst. Be vague: writer, editor or data processor gives them less reason to question you.

▲ Waiting out delays, Heathrow Airport

Why get insurance?

Just as experienced drivers still need to get car insurance, experienced travellers know that travel insurance is a **necessity**. All it takes is one mishap – a drowsy bus driver, a patch of sand when you try to brake your rented scooter, a knee twist during a mountain hike – and your family might be stuck selling their home to cover your rescue by helicopter, air-ambulance ride home, surgery, plus ongoing treatment (which may not be covered by your home insurance policy). Any of these things could happen to you in your own country, but at home you're probably covered. Overseas, where your coverage is unlikely to apply, this could easily top €100,000, not including any long-term medical expenses. A comprehensive health-insurance plan may cover some of your medical expenses, even those incurred overseas, but it's unlikely to pick up some of the major rescue and repatriation costs. Even among countries that have **reciprocal health agreements** (such as those with European passports travelling within the EU, who need to carry a EHIC card; which replaced the E111 form in 2006), you will not be fully covered, and certainly not for repatriation.

If, at the last moment before your trip, you get terribly sick, called up for jury duty, robbed or whatever, you don't want to get stuck with **cancellation fees** on top of it. A good policy will cover this, but for this service to kick in you need to get insurance about the time you buy your ticket (not the day you get called up for jury

www.roughguides.com

duty). Also, if your trip is disrupted for an emergency, your insurance company should assist with arrangements to continue your trip once you're ready.

No one plans on legally defending themselves while abroad. But if it happens, it's unlikely to be cheap. Say you hit a local cyclist while driving a rented car on a difficult-to-navigate road. Or scuff the entire length of a new Mercedes with the rusty pedal of your rented bicycle. Travel insurance is about the only way to prepare for such an unfortunate event.

Finding an insurance policy

First, you need to find out what you're insured for already so you can pick out a policy that covers the gaps. Without this knowledge, you'll likely be wasting your money on double coverage. Unfortunately, this means sifting through the fine print. You might start with your **home-owner's insurance policy** to see if it covers lost luggage (even your parents' policy, if their home is still your official residence, may have you covered).

Second, check to see what kind of travel insurance your **credit card company** offers, and whether it is solely for tickets or goods purchased using the card. Some credit cards offer flight insurance in the event of a plane crash or other transportation accidents. Then take a look at your **medical policy**. Will it cover you for illnesses or accidents incurred overseas? If so, photocopy the list of activities it will cover you for (or ask your insurer to send you the list). Finally, check out your life insurance policy. Will it still pay out if you die bungy jumping in France or mountain climbing in Switzerland?

For lost luggage, it's worth noting that airlines will reimburse international travellers for up to 1000 SDR (Special Drawing Rights), which equals about €1100 per passenger, but the process is time-consuming and potentially exasperating.

In terms of dedicated travel insurance, not all policies are created equal. The best don't tend to be cheap, but that doesn't mean the most expensive policies are the best. One sign of a good insurer is a featured list of what they will and won't cover – most prefer to bury this information, knowing you'd rather hack off your arm with an old butter knife than dig through the **fine print** of their policy. Especially since it can be rather gruesome at times – with payouts listed for things like dismemberment or loss of an eye. But it's important to know exactly what you're getting.

No two lists of **activities** seem to be the same. Some policies will require a supplement for an activity that other policies include in the most basic package. And some won't cover you if you get hurt or

Insurance for Europe

The prices below are for a basic **insurance policy** (using Rough Guide's insurance and another provider's calculator) for a trip around Europe without the adventure surplus. Prices vary greatly depending on benefits and who's doing the insuring, so don't take these prices as given – check around.

For Australians (bought in Australia)
Aus$167 for a one-month trip
Aus$259 for a two-month trip
Aus$284 for a three-month trip

For Canadians (bought in Canada)
Can$134 for a one-month trip
Can$213 for a two-month trip
Can$235 for a three-month trip

For New Zealanders (bought in New Zealand)
NZ$167 for a one-month trip
NZ$259 for a two-month trip
NZ$284 for a three-month trip

For Brits (bought in the UK)
£69 for a one-month trip
£118 for a two-month trip
£131 for a three-month trip

For Americans (bought in the US)
US$97 for a one-month trip
US$157 for a two-month trip
US$173 for a three-month trip

More expensive policies will normally cover some of the more "risky" activities or pay out larger amounts.

injured in countries that appear on your foreign office's travel-warning list. Some give you extra money if you're taken hostage on a plane and some won't cough up a cent. Some provide excellent **emergency assistance**, but little **medical coverage**. And many pad their list of benefits with things like "money transfer referrals" and "embassy referrals" – which is nothing more than a referral that you could find in half the time with a search on the internet, or in this book.

It's best to scan through a few brochures or websites and **compare** (start with Ⓦ www.insuremytrip.com or www.worldtravelcenter.com). If you're checking the web, be aware that some policies only apply to certain nationalities. STA Travel's insurance, for example, has a nice package for UK citizens, but its policies for Americans and Australians are rather feeble and more expensive by comparison. Find out who the underwriter of the insurance is (it's almost never the travel agency issuing it), and try to contact that company direct to see if they're offering a deal. Again, check what you're covered for already.

Many policies provide **24-hour emergency assistance** – a collect-call phone number you can ring from anywhere and get access to an English-speaking operator, who will keep you on the line while you sort out your troubles. With standard, inexpensive travel gear, you needn't bother with protection against **theft** unless it's either already included in the policy you want or you're carrying something expensive (a swanky

www.roughguides.com

117

camera, watch, etc). But such items may be covered in your homeowner's insurance. Besides, in the event of a theft, replacing your backpack, some clothes, toiletries and a pair of sandals with items available locally is going to be quite cheap and a lot less hassle than trying to get reimbursed for every little well-worn item. (If you do have theft insurance, take a photo of all your gear, save the receipts and store them in a safe place at home.) Find out if your insurance provider will pay your expenses directly or reimburse you. In either case (but especially the latter), ask for and hang on to receipts for everything.

Another common insurance perk is **cancellation** and **trip interruption coverage**. However, when they say that you have coverage for this, it doesn't mean you get your money back if you suddenly decide not to go. Such expenses are only covered if the reason for cancelling or interrupting your trip is stated in your insurance policy. Typically, it applies if you or your travel partner gets sick or injured, or if there's a death in your immediate family. There are other reasons as well, but you need to read the fine print to discover what they are.

In addition to the comparison sites above, other providers worth investigating are: Rough Guides travel insurance (see below), Ⓦwww.sosinternational.com, Ⓦwww.travelguard.com and Ⓦwww.worldnomads.com.

Insurance for specific activities

It's hard to anticipate what opportunities may come your way while you're travelling. Even timid travellers work up considerable nerve to try new things after a few months on the road. Remember to check the fine print for the **activities** you hope to do, but also try to give yourself as much leeway as possible, in terms of your policy, to try new things. In fact, a quick way to find the relevant section of your policy is to scan through the fine print until you see a list of activities grouped together. There's a good chance you'll have to call and enquire about some specific activities they've left out.

Before you leave home

A ssuming you can't squeeze everything into your backpack, you'll need a place to store the possessions you don't take with you to Europe; preferably, somewhere they'll remain until you return. Keeping your plants green and pets alive is another trick. This chapter will help with the arrangements you'll need to make before you can head out. (To get your finances squared away for the big trip, see p.71.)

Renting out your property

The two best ways to go are renting to a trusted friend, who can take care of things for you while you're away and handle any problems that may arise; or to a corporate company, which will probably be willing to pay more, and provide a guarantee of payments and the safekeeping of your property (of course, not everyone has an apartment that would appeal to an executive).

To avoid the hassles of dealing with tenants, you may wish to work out an arrangement with an estate agent or property manager, who will not only lease your place, but also collect the rent and handle any problems that may arise. This service isn't cheap, but if you're less worried about turning a profit than having to deal with day-to-day problems, this could be the way to go.

Otherwise, you can take out an ad. Ask around before ringing a local newspaper. Often there are much cheaper alternative publications that attract a much better targeted group.

If you do rent your flat to previously unknown tenants, it's worth taking the following precautions:

- While you are with your tenants, take a digital camcorder and walk around the property, taping everything with running commentary. ("There's a little hole in the wall I made while practising my approach shot with an 8-iron. There are eight wineglasses in the cupboard.") This will help protect them against minor damage you may forget about during your trip, and keep you protected against anything new that appears. Plus, it's a nice reminder that you've got the evidence and they should

Departure countdown

You could theoretically get everything together in less than a week. You might pick up an ulcer in the process, but you could do it. You'd also pay more and miss out on valuable pre-trip research. Better to start two to four months in advance.

Miscellaneous

- Suspend your gym membership.
- See if your phone and internet provider will allow you to suspend or cancel your service without penalty.
- Leave a key with a trusted friend.

Three to four months before departure

- Get a passport (see pp.110–111). If you have a passport, make sure it has several blank pages left.
- Figure out what sort of jobs, volunteer programs or courses you'd like to do (see p.88). Gather applications and apply to those that require advance submissions.
- Consider your budget (see p.71). If you don't have the funds for the trip you want, perhaps you should think about picking up some extra work before you leave.
- Start surfing the web for plane tickets (see p.38 & p.343).
- Start looking around for the right insurance policy (see p.114). If you're going to try to reach Europe by yacht or cargo ship, check ideal times and places to start your trip (see p.28).

Two to three months before departure

- If you're flying, book a plane ticket and try to get insurance at the same time to cover you in the event of cancellation.
- Start thinking about the things you'd like to do and see.
- Arrange visas (see p.110) for any extended stays due to work, volunteering or study, plus the first country of entry (if necessary) and any countries with complex visa requirements.
- Make arrangements for your room or flat rental (see p.119).

One to two months before departure

- Get a medical and dental checkup if you haven't had one for a while.

be on good behaviour. If you're going with an estate agent, you may wish to do this before you leave anyway, so you can prove any damage upon returning.

- Agree on anything that requires maintenance, such as plant-watering or garden care.
- Show the tenants that things are in working order (refrigerator, washing machine and so on), and make sure as many of these points as possible are listed in the contract.
- Remove and store personal treasures and anything that would cause the slightest emotional stir were it to break or grow legs and walk off.

- Get credit cards and bank cards (see p.140), and meet with your banker to set up your finances so they can be handled while you're away, either with help from your parents or via internet banking. Try to set up a line of credit.
- Get any discount cards (ISIC, teacher card, youth card, HI card) you need (see p.72).

Two to four weeks before departure

- Buy your travel gear. If you're bringing or sending ahead new hiking boots, start breaking them in (see p.123).
- Arrange for a communication card or kit (see p.174) if you plan to use one, and a mobile phone, if you plan to take one (see p.171).
- If you need to get more rugged glasses, order additional contact lenses or determine your prescription, visit an optician.

One to two weeks before departure

- Leave parents or friends an envelope with photocopies of your documents (credit cards, passport, etc) that can be sent to you in case of an emergency. Take a photo of your travel gear to leave behind.
- Take care of any veterinary needs your pet may have before dropping it off with the pet-sitter.
- Arrange for your mail to be forwarded/held if your parents or roommate aren't willing to handle it.
- Check the CDC website (🌐www.cdc.org) for any medical outbreaks you should be aware of.
- Check the websites of one or two state departments for updated security issues.

Two to three days before departure

- Pack.
- Test your pack (see p.126).
- Reconfirm flight.

Day of departure

- Run over checklist one last time.

● Have some family member or friend keep an eye on the tenants and deal with any emergency situations that may arise. And let your tenants know that someone will be watching them.

● For minor issues, let them know you should be emailed. Bring the number and email address of a trusted electrician and plumber with you, so you can take care of things that pop up with minimal effort.

● Arrange for your mail to be held for you by the post office or forwarded to parents or friends, who can sort out the junk and send on what you need at your next port of call.

Leaving an empty flat

If you're leaving your flat empty, unplug appliances, cancel your newspaper subscription, cancel the cable TV, have your phone turned off, clean out the fridge and make sure someone is coming by every so often to check on the property. If you do leave your phone on, change the message on your answering machine, but keep your whereabouts discreet for security purposes. "Hi, I'm in Europe for the rest of the month. Leave a message and I'll return your call when I get back in August" is only advised for those who want to test the limits of their homeowners' insurance.

Plants

Don't just hand over your plants to a friend, unless you happen to know their horticultural survival record. It's more important to pick someone who's good with plants than pick a good friend. Just about anyone with a green thumb will be happy to find some space for your flora, and possibly take better care of them than you would.

Pets

It's not always easy to find someone who will love your pet as much as you do. Your best bet is going to be leaving your canine, feline or fish with a friend or family member, which may involve some carefully chosen endearment opportunities (long-term kennelling is both unkind to your pet and expensive). However, there can be a lot of effort involved in finding a pet-sitter, so think of your pet's most attractive qualities and try to coordinate those with visits from prospective pet guardians. If you have a dog who can catch a Frisbee, play catch with the friend who would find that most appealing. If the pet is cute and friendly and successfully helps you line up dates, let your desperate friend see this in action. If it cuddles up on your bed and keeps you warm, ring your pals with poor heating. If it's sweet, but looks menacing, perhaps some security-minded woman living alone might find this useful. A creative solution may be in order; think outside the litter box.

Packing

A sk a dozen "packing experts" for a list of what to take and you'll get a dozen different lists. **Packing** is neither an art nor a science; it's a combination of practicality and personal preference. And the only list that really matters is yours. The problem is it will take you a good six months on the road in various conditions to get a solid grasp of what you actually use and what you can do without. Until then, it's better to **bring less** and pick up any additional items you need along the way. This may sound like twisted logic, but throwing things away is actually far more difficult – at least, nobody seems willing to do it. In this chapter, you'll get the lowdown on selecting a backpack, which things you can leave at home, what to do with souvenirs, how to handle your film developing and how to put together your own medical kit.

Why take less

For starters, it's going to be a lot cheaper. And that's not just the cost of the gear itself. As of 2006, airlines began charging crazy fees for **excess baggage** (as much as €45 per kilo) while at the same time lowering the standard baggage weight allowance. (British Airways' limit, for example, dropped from 32kg to 23kg.) The pros of a large pack may seem tempting: you have more stuff you might need, more clothes for the right occasion, plenty of toothpaste, and a few creature comforts from home. The cons are perhaps less obvious, but very much worth noting:

- A bigger risk of getting robbed – you're easier to spot, have more stuff to steal, and it's harder to run away.
- Bigger locker fees – it's harder to walk around with a large pack so you're more desperate to find a place to leave all your stuff, and you'll need a bigger, more expensive locker each time.

www.roughguides.com

What travellers are carrying

In the middle of the summer, I spent a few days walking around Stockholm's central train station with a notepad and a scale to see what (and how much) backpackers take with them. I spoke to every traveller I managed to stop, and weighed their packs. The average weight was just over 20kg. Some of the heaviest packs (over 25kg) belonged to women who weighed less than 55kg. It looked like they were going to be crushed at any second, Wile E. Coyote-like, under their packs. Everyone I asked had something they wished they hadn't brought. I asked several of them to open up their packs so I could peek inside. If you're wondering what people with huge packs are carrying around, here's what's taking up about seventy percent of their load: shoes, a sleeping bag, souvenirs and a full load of dirty laundry.

Least used items: formal shoes for going out, textbooks and extra novels

Most used items: sandals and rain jacket

- Big sweat stains – the more odour you emit, the more often you have to wash. Spend five minutes walking in summer weather with an eight-kilo pack on your back and five minutes with a twenty-kilo pack and you can see for yourself.

- Transport problems – it's more difficult to run for a train or bus (and you will have to run at some point), and it's harder to lift the pack over your head into a luggage rack without disturbing the people around you.

- More gear to lose or forget to pack, and more time spent packing things up each day.

Picking a pack

A standard suitcase or duffel bag won't serve you well for a journey with this much carrying involved, unless you're up for the challenge or don't mind having your arms lengthened to the point that your knuckles drag on the ground. A **rolling suitcase** is a popular option for many, but those little wheels weren't built to contend with European cobblestones. You can, of course, roll them in some places, but there are just as many where you can't. And in most airports (where they work best) you can find free trolleys. There are now a number of packs that have both wheels and backpacking straps. For urban travel, these can work extremely well. If you're planning on doing a good deal of hiking, however, the extra weight of the wheels coupled with a less flexible plastic suspension isn't worth it. At the risk of sounding like a drill sergeant, if you can't carry it, you don't need it.

Newton's law for **backpacks** would have read something like this: no matter what size pack you bring along, you'll always manage to fill it. No one travels with a half empty pack. At least, I've never seen a traveller with a partially empty pack. Therefore, the single best thing you can do is start by buying a small rucksack: 40–55 litres – slightly bigger than your average day bag. Once you do this, it's pretty hard to go wrong. The stuff you don't need simply won't fit in. I managed for nine years with that size just fine, and thousands of others have as well.

But be forewarned: that's not likely to be the advice you'll get from the travel shop assistants. Just remember where they're coming from: the bigger the pack, the more it costs and the more stuff they can sell you to put in it.

A pack is not the place to try to save money. Take an internal-frame model for support. Couple that with a major brand name (you don't want it coming apart at the seams) and you're looking at prices in the range of €75–150. There are a few bells and whistles that are nice to have, but be selective. If you're going to forego the wheeled pack, your best bet is likely to be the rucksacks used by climbers. They keep the gear closer to your torso for a fuller range of motion and better balance.

- You'd do well to skip the zip-off daypack; they don't make the best bags and, when attached, tend to unbalance the main pack and keep your valuables furthest from your body.
- Packs that extend wide with side pockets make it extremely difficult when you're getting on and off trains and buses.

▲ Liverpool Street Station, London

The backpack test

- You should be able to pack it in five minutes.

- You should be able easily to lift it over your head and you should be able to wear it for two hours without suffering minor back spasms.

- Someone (maybe even you) is going to sit on your pack, step on it or drop it at some point, so toss it across the room and then step on it – you may as well get it over and done with now.

- Don't pack breakables – or make sure you pack them well.

- Even if the odds are that your pack won't get stolen, prepare as if it will – leave your mother's pearls, your snakeskin cowboy boots and your collector's-edition silver-plated backgammon set at home.

- Packs that extend straight back (such as those with attached packs) force you to lean forward to counter the weight.

- There should be some kind of alternative opening that allows you quick access to the inside or bottom of the pack for things like a rain jacket or first-aid kit.

- Make sure there are compression straps on the outside (usually, the sides) to keep the stuff inside from jiggling about while you walk and to make the pack smaller.

- Look for a top compartment that's completely detachable, because if you can raise and lower that you can stuff things under it more easily, like a rain jacket during a hike or a damp towel on the way back from the beach. If you need to carry a bag of souvenirs to the post office, for example, the pack can "grow" to accommodate the extra gear temporarily. Also, you could detach it completely, clip on a camera strap, and you've got a shoulder bag that makes an ideal daypack.

The most important feature is that it **fits comfortably**. This is not something you should buy over the internet, unless you've tried it on first. The waist strap should not dig into your hips and the straps should be easily adjustable when you're on the move. Sometimes, there's one strap that's meant to be sized to the wearer, and it's not that simple to find or adjust. Have the salesperson do it for you. Every pack feels great when there's nothing in it. Drop something heavy in before you try it out. (Good shops have weighted inserts for this very purpose.) There are now a number of special packs for women that are worth checking out, especially if you have a more curvy or petite body type. These packs feature narrower shoulder straps, a shorter frame, more cant on the waist strap and a pack mounted lower on the frame.

Organizing your pack

To facilitate the almost daily **packing ritual**, make things easier to find and minimize the damage of a sudden rain shower or a broken shampoo bottle on the rest of your gear, keep things in separate bags, one for each of the following: clothes, toiletries, first aid, miscellaneous items, plus an extra plastic bag for wet clothes.

All of your **clothes**, minus what you need to wear, should fit nicely into a compression sack; one that holds a midweight sleeping bag will do nicely. With a few yanks on the cords, your clothes will be compressed to the size of a rugby ball. Crumpling is unavoidable unless the clothes are wrinkleproof, and even then they won't look perfect. To minimize creases, try rolling your clothes first.

Clothes

If you've gone on a short family vacation to a resort with white beaches or ski slopes, you're familiar with the luggage situation: bring as much as you feel like. Two suitcases the size of Japanese import cars aren't an issue. They only have to be dragged into and out of the airport – and there are people around to help with even this. The problem, you're thinking, is that it was difficult enough to figure out how to get a week's worth of stuff into just two enormous suitcases. How on earth are you going to get several weeks' or months' worth into a single tiny backpack?

To customize your packing list, there's one important question you need to ask. What clothes do I need to survive a day (not just any day, though: a day in which you go from swimming in the ocean to tanning on the beach to a cool evening walk in the rain to a moderately nice dinner at a place where there's casual dancing), and be able to wash it all in the sink afterwards, and let it dry without ironing?

Just one outfit?

There are two basic approaches to **dressing**: stay in the same town and change clothes every day, or wear the same clothes and just change towns. When you travel, you just have to accept that your general standard of cleanliness is going to be lower than you're used to. Also, you're going to have to wash your clothes daily, or tri-weekly – if you try doing it monthly, you're in for some strange looks, not to mention rashes.

Once you get the hang of this, you'll see you don't need more than one set of clothes. If you wash the clothes before you go to bed, hanging them on a clothes line outside, they'll be dry by morning. If you wash the clothes before taking a siesta in the afternoon and hang them in the sun, they'll be dry in about forty minutes.

www.roughguides.com

Once you've got the clothes for such a day, consider if there is anything you could replace with a similar item which would better serve multiple functions.

Let's start with the **swimsuit**. For guys (and possibly ladies), make sure it's quick-drying and has pockets you trust enough to put car keys in while you swim – probably some kind of zipper–Velcro combination that'll foil pickpockets as well. The shorts should cover your legs modestly so they can also be used for city exploring – they're the only shorts you have along. For women, it doesn't matter if it's a bikini or a one-piece. You'll also want a **beach towel**. It should be fairly thin, but long enough to stretch out on comfortably and wrap yourself in modestly (there are special travel towels that work a treat). Later in the day, you'll want a **hat** and **T-shirt** to help ward off additional sunburn after your stint on the beach, and to cover yourself when you run over to a café for a snack.

For a cool evening walk, you can get by with **sandals**. You've got long, comfortable **walking trousers**. They should have deep front

---

Clothes pack list

- 1 T-shirt – if it's a little longer, women can double it as a nightshirt.
- 1 long-sleeve polypro shirt.
- 1 micro-fleece – keep it smart and it can be worn as a pullover in a nice restaurant.
- 1 rain jacket – even expensive Gore-Tex and similar high-tech rainwear won't help much when it pours for hours, and cheaper versions are less likely to get stolen.
- 1 plastic poncho – this covers your pack as well.
- 1 thin beach towel or sarong – an XL special travel towel is ideal.
- 1 swimsuit – doubles as walking shorts for men.
- 1 pair of trousers – not black (because dirt shows), but a good, dark, dirt-hiding colour is ideal. Also, make sure they're lightweight, wrinkle-free, comfortable, fairly stylish and easily washable, with good deep pockets.
- 1 wrinkle-free travel shirt – short- or long-sleeve is fine.
- 1 pair of socks – for cool overnight bus rides and cold hostel floors.
- 2–4 sets of underwear – special travel underwear dries quicker and lasts longer.
- 1 pair of sports sandals. You don't want to skimp on these. They should be reasonably stylish (smart enough for a decent restaurant), have good support on off-road terrain, stay on during a swim, not rot when they get out of the water and allow you to run for a train. You can even use them in the hostel shower.
- 1 collapsible hat.
- 1 bandanna – soak it with water to keep you cool on warm nights. Cover your mouth with it to protect your lungs from dust. Use it to dry off in the shower when you don't have time to let your towel dry.
- 1 wrinkle-free travel skirt, mid-calf in length (women).
- 1 pair of shorts (women).

pockets that will deter thieves and not spill your valuables if you need to make a pit stop in the woods (front pockets, like the type found on jeans, tend to work the best). On top you've got a long-sleeved polypropylene **shirt** that wicks away sweat, a micro-fleece **pullover** (not cotton) and a nylon **rain jacket** and a **cap** or **bandanna**. You're carrying your **plastic poncho** in your small daypack in case it really starts to pour.

For dinner, you can still get by in sandals, especially if they're black or solid earthy colours. You've got a smart, short-sleeved or long-sleeved lightweight, wrinkle-free **shirt/blouse**. If it's still a little chilly inside, the **micro-fleece** should be stylish enough to wear. For men, walking trousers will suffice, provided they're not the "adventure travel" type with more zippered pockets and removable bits than a 1980s breakdancer. They should be dark enough to hide any dirt you might have picked up on your walk. Women might also elect to go with a long wrinkle-free mid-calf-length skirt. For day two, wash and repeat.

If you're heading to Europe in the winter, you'll want, of course, warm shoes, wool socks (or "smart wool"), a good jacket, hat and gloves. If you find you need long underwear, you can pick that up once you arrive.

Sleeping items

Brace yourself: for summer travel in Europe, you don't need to take a sleeping bag. Yes, many people take them and find occasion to use them, but not necessarily because they need to. Nearly every hostel can produce a blanket for you as long as you have a **sleepsheet** (which you do need). And in budget digs where air conditioning is typically not included, you'll rarely need more than a sheet. Beyond that, if you layer on all your clothes for a chilly night on a train or bus, you should be fine. In a worst-case scenario, if the weather does get a bit cold and there is no blanket available, you can always pick up a cheap secondhand one or move on to a hostel that does offer blankets.

The previously mentioned sleepsheet is – well, just that – a sheet in the form of a sleeping bag. You can sew one yourself from a queen-size flat sheet or buy a premade model. The nicest are silk, which cost a fortune, but can be worth it, as they keep the occasional bed bug out better than the others.

Leave your **pillow** at home. Instead, use the ones provided at the hostels, hotels and pensions. You can bring a pillowcase, but it's a better use of space to simply use your T-shirt or micro-fleece as a pillowcase.

If no pillow is available, stuff your towel and micro-fleece and a few other items into your T-shirt and use that. On train rides, if you put your towel in your micro-fleece and gently tie it around your neck, you'll get the same effect as one of those inflatable neck pillows, which can also be left at home.

Toiletries

Start out by buying a **toiletry bag** with a built-in mirror and hanger, since you can't count on much counter space in the bathroom or having an unfogged mirror surface. Many travellers find that a short haircut makes both the grooming and reduced need for hair-products more convenient for travel. There are two odour-related steps: 1) transfer your perfume/cologne from the heavy, breakable, chic bottle to a small sturdy glass one with a tight, screw-on lid (or get a tester vial instead); 2) bring a foot file to help shed dead skin common with extended sandal-wearing so people don't smell you before they see you.

Major-brand **contact lens** fluid can be found at supermarkets, opticians and pharmacists, so there's no need to bring enough to last an entire journey. Bring a pair of **glasses** along just in case, plus your prescription in case something happens to your glasses. Pity to travel the world, then have to check your photos back home to see what it looked like in focus.

Again, only buy the miniature travel containers and restock as you go. Local toothpaste is especially interesting to sample and – there's at least one traveller doing this – collect.

For women, **tampons** and **pads** are no harder to find in Western Europe than they are at home. On remote Greek islands and in countries like Romania, Hungary and the ones that comprise

---

Toiletry packing list

(Mini-sizes only)

- Toothpaste
- Toothbrush
- Dental floss
- Cologne/perfume
- Foot file
- Contact lens fluid (if needed)
- Lip balm
- Comb/brush
- Face and body lotion

- Razor (not electric)
- Sunscreen
- Mosquito repellent with DEET
- Mirror
- All-purpose soap
- Conditioner (if needed)
- Deodorant
- Condoms

former Yugoslavia, they may be slightly more difficult to come by, so make sure you have what you need, especially if you'll be out in the countryside. Another alternative (for those with a higher yucky tolerance) is the Mooncup, a reusable diaphragm-like device made from soft silicon.

Miscellaneous gear

There are a few tiny items that, when you need them, you need them immediately. And they're not always easy to find. Pick your requirements from this list and keep in a separate bag:

- Earplugs – don't leave home without them. Hostels have a nasty habit of occupying the space above nightclubs and next to busy streets. Plus, every dormitory seems to come with at least one snoring champion.
- Pocket calculator – helpful for when you're bargaining in markets (though most vendors have them for this purpose) and calculating exchange rates.
- Media storage device – mini hard disc, USB keychain, or iPod to back up photos, video or audio.
- Permanent marker – for making hitchhiking signs and other notices.
- Superglue – this fixes just about everything (keep it in its own plastic bag).
- Duct tape – this fixes nearly everything the superglue doesn't (wrap it around the marker to save space).
- Guitar string/wire – fixes whatever's left.
- Sewing kit – OK, that's a lie. *This* fixes whatever's left.
- Padlock – many hostels have lockers.
- Lighter – you don't need a €50 lighter that works on top of Mount Everest, just something to light candles, camping stoves and certain Dutch coffeehouse products.
- Power adaptors (if needed) – the Brits have one bulky kind, the rest of Europe uses another. You can pick up a double adaptor at major airports when you land, or before leaving (see ⓦwww .kropla.com for country requirements).
- Pocket knife – you can leave the Rambo survival blade at home, but make sure yours has a can opener and corkscrew to assist with budget picnics. (You might want to wait until you get to Europe to pick up your knife, as you're unlikely to be able to take one onboard your flight. On the way back, you'll likely be checking in a bag with souvenirs, anyway.)

- Spoon – just grab one for free on your first flight. It comes in handy for supermarket-food dining.
- Clothes line – you'll need about 10m of nylon cord. The slightly more expensive version found beside the climbing rope at outdoor shops tangles less.
- Water bottle – for the cheapest version just reuse a water bottle you buy while travelling. Tap water is fine for drinking even if it doesn't always taste great.
- Sink plug – make your own with a piece of duct tape stuck over the drain or chop the top third off a racquetball and you've got one.
- Plastic bag – for wet clothes.

Optional extras

Here are a few extras that you might want to bring along.

- Small travel games: backgammon, chess, Uno and cards are the most popular. They can keep you sane on an overnight train ride, and can be a nice way to meet locals.
- Instrument: OK, it's a cliché, but a guitar can be worth the effort, especially if you're good and plan to earn money playing it on the street or in bars. A harmonica is better suited for transport and not as likely to make people cringe when you take it out.
- Frisbee: doubles as a plate and soup bowl.

First aid

Most prepackaged **first-aid kits** sold in outdoor stores are border-line worthless. And those nylon sacks don't keep your bandages and pills from getting wet or crushed. Make your own. Start out with a Tupperware container large enough to hold about four muffins. You should be able to resupply all you need – see the box opposite – on the road.

A lot of travellers like to take **antibiotics** along. And if you're whacking your way through a rainforest for weeks, it's probably not a bad idea. But in Europe you're never that far from a local doctor or hospital. If you get sick enough to require antibiotics, you should visit a doctor who can prescribe the best ones for your condition. Plus, many antibiotics don't travel well. If you do take antibiotics, take the full course, even if your symptoms abate after just one or two days. Otherwise, the few microbes that don't get killed off tend to mutate and come back stronger.

Medical pack-list

European **pharmacists** have the authority to prescribe many medications that require a doctor's note in North America, and you'll find any medication you might need in Western Europe. Since you usually won't be more than a short hop from a pharmacy (most have a neon-green cross above the door), few items are really that essential. It's nice to have a small kit, though, just in case. You don't need much medicine for a few weeks or months of travel. A few pills of each will usually do the trick. Make sure you bring the directions for consumption, and label the pills if you don't bring the entire packet.

- Elastic wrap bandage – if you or a fellow traveller has a major accident, this is the most important thing to have within arm's reach. Vital for twists and big cuts.
- Anti-diarrhoea medicine – few forget to bring these.
- Laxatives – few remember to bring these; especially useful for those who don't like dirty bathrooms.
- Antihistamines – you never know what will spark an allergic reaction.
- Hydrocortisone cream – cures most rashes and skin irritations.
- Aspirin/paracetamol – for minor aches and major hangovers.
- Compeed – modern science has created the wonder blister cure.
- Band-aids – put them into a clear plastic sleeve that holds photos or credit cards.
- Iodine – for sterilizing cuts and purifying particularly spooky-looking water (5 drops per litre clear water, 10 drops for cloudy water, then let stand for 30 minutes). If you can't deal with the taste, then water purification tablets or drink mixes are a good idea.
- Rehydration packet – one is enough to get you started (in a crisis, make your own mix: 1 litre water, 1 teaspoon of salt, 8 tablespoons sugar, dash of juice if available).
- Melatonin/arnica – helps with jet lag.
- Motion sickness pills – curvy roads and stale air on bus rides make a lethal combo, not to mention stormy ferry rides.

Medical extras

If these don't fit in your first-aid container, toss them in the gear bag:

- Tweezers – find a good pair with a sharp point for removing splinters.
- Vaseline – prevents chafing and blisters during long hikes.
- Sports tape – it's mostly for blister prevention, but helps hold band-aids on.
- Antiseptic wet wipes – a great refresher for when you're stuck in a hot bus seat for hours, trying to clean up before a meal, or helping dab a wound.
- Tiger balm – the all-purpose sports cream that also clears up clogged sinuses and soothes headaches.

Daypack

Even a relatively small, internal-frame pack is not a joy to lug around the entire day while you explore ruins, museums and cities. A **daypack** is a more sensible way to carry the few necessities you'll need.

Most travellers opt for small backpacks, such as the detachable ones that come with packs. To avoid quick-handed thieves and (for women) groping hands in crowds, wearing the daypack on your front is an excellent idea. While it's on your back, though, it can be hard to protect. Some prefer the comfort of a waist pack, but this, too, is something of a thief magnet and looks awfully odd when worn in front. A better idea is a **shoulder bag**. It's easy to tuck under your arm to protect from pickpockets, can be accessed more quickly while you're on the move and doesn't peg you as a tourist, especially in bars and nightclubs. If the top compartment of your backpack detaches, a camera or guitar strap can turn it into a decent shoulder bag. If not, a collapsible one with zipper/Velcro closure is fine.

What to keep in your daypack

- Guidebook – you can lighten the load by ripping out unneeded sections.
- Sunglasses – shades without UV protection allow your pupils to widen and expose your eyes to more damaging rays. You'll want a hard case to keep them in one piece.
- Journal/address book and pen – a necessity. Some photos of home and friends are also nice to include for letter-writing inspiration.
- Something to read – for more info on how many books to bring and how swapping books works, see p.148.
- Pocket knife (but not on flights) – you don't need the Swiss Army knife with all fifty functions.
- Flashlight – the little LCD key-chain ones work well, the LCD headlamp with retractable band even better for cooking in badly lit areas.
- Pocket camera – you can get a good one for under €75. See "Documenting your trip" (p.209) for advice on which type of camera to bring.
- Mobile phone and charger (optional) – a tri-band phone works almost everywhere these days and, even if you keep it off, it can be worth it in the one emergency you need it. See p.171 for more.

Camping gear

If you already have **camping equipment**, using it can save you money, but will more than double the size and weight of your rucksack, so think twice before carting it along. It's really only sensible for those planning to camp the entire time. If you're not sure, leave the gear at home. Even if you only thought about camping a little, you'll be happier with less stuff and a few extra nights in a hostel. Yes, it is legal to "free-camp" in Sweden, and it is possible to pitch a tent after dark on the edge of small towns elsewhere – if you're sneaky about it – but in most decent campgrounds near popular cities, it's not all that cheap and you'll be spending more time and money on local transport getting in and out of town. And you may worry about your belongings when your tent is unattended. If you do decide not to bring camping gear but change your mind later, you can always buy excellent stuff in Europe, and will likely pick up good secondhand gear from other travellers selling theirs on hostel notice boards.

Checklist

- Light, rainproof tent
- Cooking stove
- Pot with lid
- Cooking utensils
- Sleeping bag
- Sleeping pad
- Headlamp (when you need a light, you usually need your hands as well)
- Tarpaulin to lay under tent
- Water-purifying tablets (iodine works) or small water-purifier pump (don't forget drink mix to add to chemically treated water to improve taste).

What you don't need and why

- Shoes – this may come as a shocker, but if you're travelling in May to September in Europe with a decent pair of sandals, you can get by without shoes. If you find you're going out clubbing regularly, need shoes for work or if it's just getting too cold, buy a cheap pair and ditch them when you're done.
- MP3 player/iPod – this is a great way to tune out and relax. However, you're also cutting yourself off from the sounds of the country which, though often annoying, are part of the experience. More importantly, it discourages locals from making contact with you. Besides, it's something else that can break or get stolen. Unless you need it for digital photo storage, either leave at home or use sparingly. Read a book instead.
- Electronic language translator – just try to have a conversation with one of these! I have yet to see someone pull it off. The most common words and phrases can be looked up in nearly all guidebooks. Better still, take twenty minutes and learn a few words and phrases before you arrive.

- Currency converter – your primary school maths skills or a pocket calculator should get you by nicely.
- Pro-camera setup – if you're a serious amateur or professional photographer, bring what you need. If not, this is probably not the time to start. Forget the SLR, lenses and tripod. Stick with a pocket camera and you'll get more use out of it.
- GPS – if you're charting new territory, fine. If not, leave it at home.
- Jeans – resist the temptation to pack your favourite pair, no matter how good you may look in them. They're too warm in hot weather, too difficult to wash by hand and take too long to dry.
- Sweatshirt – the comfort is alluring, but it will take up far too much room, offer no warmth when wet, and require about two days to dry on its own. A micro-fleece (or some petrochemical equivalent) is the way to go. Besides, they're more culturally sensitive than sweatshirts sporting giant university or fraternity logos.
- Water filter – the water in Europe isn't going to kill you. It's easier and more affordable to drink from the tap; just buy bottled water in extreme situations.
- Compass – the sun rises in the east and sets in the west. That knowledge should get you by. At least, if you're not in Scandinavia, where the summer sun never seems to set. If you feel better having a compass along, take a tiny key-chain model. If you set off without a compass, and regret it, you can always buy it along the way.
- Mosquito net – there are mosquitoes in Europe, but such measures aren't typically necessary.
- Mini "travel towel" – the beach-towel-size ones are great. The mini ones preferred by Olympic divers and car washers aren't as practical for the traveller.
- Hair dryer – if you find you must have one, buy a tiny one in Europe so no adapter is needed.
- Full make-up kit.

Resupply on the road

There may not be toilet paper in every stall or ice in the drinks, but you can get sweaters, T-shirts, socks, toothpaste, soap, band-aids, contact lens fluid, superglue, all kinds of film, sport sandals, trendy clothes, hats – nearly everything – almost everywhere you go. If 700 million Europeans can survive with the supplies they have, there's a good chance you'll find what you need to get by for a couple of months. Just start out with the smallest tubes and bottles, plan on buying supplements, and stop at an internet café and special-order something to your next destination if you simply can't find it. If you're taking medication, bring what you need or bring along your prescription for a refill.

Sending gear ahead

If you're going to be trekking in the Alps or Pyrenees, or hiking national parks every other week of your trip, bring your favourite **hiking boots**. If not, they're going to take up thirty percent of your pack and make the other seventy percent smell. Tying them to the outside of your pack may be even worse: the dangling-ornament look makes it tricky to run for departing transport, knocks people in the head as you enter and leave trains, and creates a stench that circles you like the moons of Saturn. Better to use the postal service to get your boots to the place you'll need them (and send them back when finished). Or simply rent boots when you get there. All major trekking centres have boot rental and cheap secondhand ones for sale, but make sure you give yourself a day or two to wear them in before taking off on a serious hike.

Our souvenir habit

Consider the alchemy: the exuberance of travel mixed with the excitement of shopping. It shouldn't come as any surprise that people have a hard time restraining themselves. It's common to want to bring home little pieces of your journey – no problem there – but why buy things that have nothing to do with your trip other than that they were the items available at some kiosk along the way? Either that, or I must have missed the hotel that requires guests to don Dutch clogs and orange windmill hats.

For some reason setting foot in a country (or continent) seems to give a few people carte blanche either to decorate their living rooms with traditional trinkets which others would consider bad taste, or wear an Oxford sweatshirt when the only affiliation they have with the university is having a beer once at Oxford train station. Perhaps, like overzealous mobile phone use, we simply haven't got around to establishing the social etiquette for souvenirs.

Having said that, I must confess, I've got two travel items around the house. One is an automated Japanese toilet seat with a remote control, the other is a Thai bicycle rickshaw I use to pedal my kids to daycare. Admittedly, both items are a little over the top and the rickshaw certainly looks out of its element, but I use them daily, they're experiential, and they provide me with that little taste of travel at home. The mementos that mean the most are the ones I gathered for free – a label from a beer bottle I stuck in my journal, a photo of the travellers I met while on an overnight train journey to Madrid. The rest of the things I bought along the way are all sitting in a box in the basement. They looked so irresistibly cool in the shops I found them in, and the bargaining processes and subsequent mailing experience at the post office were memorable, but I just couldn't find a way to display them that didn't feel forced. When I see that box, it just reminds me I should have spent more time and money travelling and less time shopping.

Doug Lansky

www.roughguides.com

Sending souvenirs home

Many souvenirs get bought, but far fewer make it home in one piece. The best way to make sure your purchases survive the journey home is to **send them back** as you buy them. With almost daily packing and unpacking, plus the normal wear and tear of the road, your souvenirs have a far better chance of getting lost, broken or stolen in your backpack. Check the local postal regulations before you start boxing up your items. Sometimes there's a certain weight or container size that's extremely cheap, and you can divide your purchases into separate parcels accordingly and save a mint. Overland shipping takes a few months but it usually gets there. If you'd rather not take the chance, try registered mail. (Simply request it at the post office and pay the supplemental fee.) Or, if it's of considerable value, look into FedEx, DHL or another reputable courier. If you can wait until your last stop before stocking up on trinkets, simply buy a cheap duffle bag for €5–10 and courier home the items yourself.

Carrying valuables

The euro may have simplified pricing in Europe, but it hasn't made your money any safer from **theft**. With a steady stream of Europeans walking the streets in designer suits and custom-made leather shoes, you may not feel like much of a target. However, with half a glance thieves can see that you're a foreigner and, as such, are probably carrying a bundle of cash, credit cards and a camera. And, with a backpack on, you may not notice their quick hands or be able to give chase if you do. Therefore, you need to handle your valuables with care.

There are several options these days. Passport pouches, also known as **money belts**, come in a variety of styles. Some go around the waist (just under the trousers), some hang around the neck and others fasten to your leg. Choosing which one to wear is a combination of personal preference, how it works with your clothing and how easy it is for thieves to spot (see p.180 for more information on this). Try a few on before you make a purchase, since this is something you'll be wearing round the clock.

Before you leave home, remember to photocopy the contents of your money belt (except the cash!), leave a copy with your parents or trusted friends, and take a copy with you and store it separately from your money belt or with your travel partner. If you're using a service like eKit (see p.174), upload the data into their digital vault. Or, for a slightly less secure method, you could email the info to yourself (but don't label the mail with anything obvious).

Credit cards

Don't leave home without one of these. Two is even better. Visa and MasterCard are the most widely accepted. You should have PIN codes to use both in cash machines and when making purchases (many require the code instead of a signature). If a cash machine can't be found, most banks will still allow you to use credit cards for cash advances. That is, you can go into a bank, let them swipe your card and buy cash (for a fee, of course). This isn't the most economical way to get cash while on the road – a bank card (or debit card) will be a lot cheaper. However, a credit card is a fine way to handle (and track) purchases. Important: you should call your card issuer to activate your credit card for international use when travelling overseas so they don't freeze your account when these charges from numerous countries start rolling in.

The benefits

● You can access emergency funds and cover many daily expenses without carrying a thick bundle of cash.

● You can track your finances easily, even from the road, if you set up an internet account.

● Parents, relatives and friends can send funds to your account, which you can quickly and easily withdraw.

● Cards can be quite easily replaced if stolen or lost.

● You're entitled to additional insurance when you use the card to make purchases or rent cars.

The drawbacks

● Most credit card companies charge a flat fee (usually about €2) for foreign ATM use, as well as a clearing-house surcharge. More recently, they've tacked on "conversion fees" (up to five percent) for cash withdrawals and credit card purchases. Having said that, there are changes in motion within the EU to harmonize fees across the continent, making things clearer – if not necessarily cheaper; check with your card provider for an update.

● You'll have to pay interest (around seventeen percent) on the withdrawn cash until your next bill is paid.

● Hold on; it gets worse. If you buy something with your credit card, find it doesn't work, give it back and get the purchase removed from your credit card bill, it gets reconverted back through the whole process, with the credit card company getting a commission and conversion fee again.

● Merchants who accept credit cards pay a small percentage fee to the credit card company for the right to accept their card. Although they're not supposed to do this, many smaller companies make no secret about passing that percentage on to you (though

www.roughguides.com

paying it is still often cheaper than withdrawing money from a cash machine, especially for one purchase).

Choosing a credit card

- Some credit cards are better than others. It depends on the bank or financial institution behind them and what deals they're offering. When deciding on a credit card, make sure you ask about the surcharges for foreign purchases and cash machine withdrawals. More and more cards are adding a three percent conversion fee (in the US, for example, Capital One may be the only remaining card that doesn't do this). Try to find one that doesn't. If you do, cancel your current card and tell them why.

- Try to boost your spending limit before leaving. Simply call the credit card company and ask if you can get your limit raised. You may have to put more expenses on the card (or cards) than you're used to, and with an emergency purchase, such as a plane ticket or hospital bill, you might be quickly out of funds.

- Many credit cards or bank accounts can be set up for "Auto-pay" ("direct debit"). Each month, your credit card bill (or a minimum payment) will be automatically paid from your cheque or savings account. That way you don't have to worry about missing any payments and getting hit with the high interest rates credit card companies thrive on. Of course, what you may have to worry about is having enough money in your bank account. To be safe, meet with your bank manager before you leave and set up a line of credit (€1000–5000) to cover you in a pinch. If you have internet banking, all this can be easily monitored from any internet café.

Bank cards and debit cards

Try to take along a card that taps directly into your cheque or savings account. Some of these bank-issued cards can be used for purchases ("**debit cards**"), some can't ("**cash cards**"). Both types can be used to withdraw cash, though. You may still be slapped with a withdrawal fee and perhaps a conversion fee, but you won't have to pay interest on the money withdrawn, which makes them better than credit cards for this purpose. For those who don't trust themselves with the spending limit granted on a credit card, this can be a good alternative, but the drawbacks are clear cut: there's no credit, which is no good when you're faced with unexpected, urgent expenses. "Offline" debit cards are generally less secure (they don't require a PIN and it's a few days before the money is taken from your account). "Online" debit cards ("**Chip and PIN**" cards in the UK) require a PIN but have instantaneous processing; if they land in the wrong hands, your money could be as good as gone, especially if the loss is not reported immediately. Check the written policy of the

www.roughguides.com

card: some limit the stolen amount to €50, others €500, depending on how long it takes you to report the theft. If you can't arrange a credit card, or want to use this as a second credit card, you'll need to ring or meet with your bank. To ease transactions, reduce withdrawal fees and quickly remedy any theft problems, it's a good idea to select an international bank with branches across Europe, such as Citibank or HSBC.

Cash machines

Holes in the wall, or **ATM**s, are everywhere, but they're not infallible: they sometimes run out of cash, break down and may even occasionally swallow your card for no good reason. When that happens at home, it's a hassle. Abroad, it can make for a very unpleasant day. With all the fees involved, it can cost as much as €4 to take out as little as €20, so the fewer the withdrawals, the better (though bear in mind that some banks don't charge a fee for international withdrawals, so you may want to shop around). See "Directory", p.347 for ATM locator websites.

Traveller's cheques

For the last decade, the conventional wisdom has been that **traveller's cheques** are defunct, replaced by convenient ATMs. You can certainly get by without them. However, with all the additional ATM fees, traveller's cheques may start making a comeback.

Here's how they work: you buy the cheques (for a small fee) and keep a list of their serial numbers, so if they get stolen or lost you can report exactly which cheques are missing and get the amount refunded. In order to do this, you need to keep the list updated and separate from your unused cheques and hope the bag with the list in it doesn't get stolen or lost as well. Some places accept traveller's cheques as cash, but not the smaller places where budget travellers often hang out. You can easily cash them, and sometimes for free (you can cash American Express cheques at AmEx offices for free, for example – for a list of locations, see ⓦwww .americanexpress .co.uk), but you may not be anywhere near the relevant office. So, in addition to the cost of exchanging the currency, you'll likely pay a fee to convert your cheques into cash. Understandably, some people find this to be a hassle – one that outweighs the security factor.

In general, places that take traveller's cheques also take credit cards (or are not far from a cash machine or bank that allows cash advances). However, if you plan to spend an extended period in a rural area, and have read in your guidebook that cash cards and credit cards are of limited use but that traveller's cheques can be cashed, you can always pick some up in a major city if you're uncomfortable carrying the amount of cash you'll need to get by.

Visa, Thomas Cook and American Express issue the most commonly used traveller's cheques. There are no real advantages in terms of acceptance (though AmEx does allow clients to collect snail mail at some of its offices, and AmEx and Thomas Cook allow two people to sign the cheques). Remember to make sure the assistant watches you countersign the cheques. Don't let them walk off while you're busy scribbling your name, or the whole thing may be void.

AmEx also has a "travellers' cheque card" that works like a bank card: you can load it up with money, then use to withdraw funds from bank machines. When it's empty, simply toss away the card. However, if you've got a cash card from your bank or a debit card, this seems unnecessary: you don't need both.

Cash

Of course, you'll want to carry **cash** as well. The question is how much. For starters, you should try to keep a €250–450 emergency stash on you at all times because … well, you never know – a bank's computer system is down, you get fined by a conductor for failing to make a reservation on an overnight train, the guy selling the last ticket to a Madonna concert in a stone amphitheatre in Greece will only take cash, and so on. I've had to dip into my emergency fund more times than I care to count. Consider keeping €50–100 of your emergency stash separate from your passport pouch. Perhaps in a pocket in your address book or taped to the inside of your backpack – just enough to spend a night in the hostel, get some food or take transport to the nearest embassy.

If you're using credit cards and bank cards instead of traveller's cheques, it's a better idea to use them for as many purchases as possible. That way, you've got records of your expenses and you can limit the amount of cash

▲ Always have some emergency cash on you

143

you need to carry. You'll still need some pocket change, though, as it's not possible to put every beer, postcard or subway ticket on a card. Minimizing cash withdrawals (ie the cash withdrawal fees) is a huge saving. Finding the balance between curtailing cash withdrawals and not carrying too much money is largely dependent on your comfort level and how much you're spending. Some find €50 is fine for pocket change. Others prefer €250. It may take a week or two to find an amount that works best for you.

Other items for your money belt

Passport

The money belt is, in fact, where you want to keep your passport. To find out how to get a passport, see p.110.

Flight tickets

E-tickets mean, if nothing else, more comfort for the traveller. If you have **paper tickets**, write down the vital information on a piece of paper (or email it to yourself) which you can access easily, then remove the bulky folder and cover them in plastic wrap or a small zip-lock bag. A little water or sweat is all it takes to render the tickets virtually illegible.

Train/bus pass

For a long trip, you may want to protect these with a bit of plastic wrap or a zip-lock bag as well.

Driver's licence

It's helpful to have an official **photo ID** besides your passport, especially since there's a chance you'll end up driving a car at some point. There's little need to get an International Driving Permit (which essentially makes it easier for the police to write you a ticket), but it is "recommended" in Austria, Germany, Greece, Italy, Portugal, Spain and Eastern Europe – to find out exactly where it's required, see the updated list at ⓦwww.theaa .com. They are easy to get (see "Directory" chapter, p.344 for a list of automobile associations) and cost €10–15. Should you decide to pick one up, be warned: the document won't easily fit in your money belt.

Student ID card/under-26 youth card/ teacher card

If you qualify for one of these, probably best to keep it close by. It's not as valuable as the other items in your money belt, but its size makes it easy to lose. For more information on these cards, see p.72.

Hostel cards

If you plan to get a Hostelling International card or VIP Backpackers card, remember they need to be purchased before you leave home. For more info on both cards, see p.73.

The decoy wallet

Most thieves want nothing more from you than your money. They're not interested in your novel or sandals or designer toiletry bag. They don't want to hurt you, either. You should always be cooperative, just in case. Nothing in your pocket is worth your life. But before you hand over everything you've got (or let a clever pickpocket nick it), consider carrying a **fake wallet**. That is, a cheap wallet with an old library card, some used airline ticket stubs, an expired credit card, and about €10 in change. This gives you something to hand over (or a more obvious target for pickpockets) to thieves who may not study the contents until they've made their getaway.

Six extra passport photos

This seems like a lot, but when you apply for visas and such you often need three photos just for one application. Local transport cards sometimes require them as well. Better to take a few extra than have to wander off looking for a place to get a snapshot in a hurry. If this is expensive to arrange at home, pick them up once in Europe. Photo booths can be found in virtually every major train station.

Insurance card

If you've got insurance, carry the card. If you're just issued a large piece of paper, make your own card with your account number and emergency telephone number and laminate it. See p.114 for more on insurance.

Phone card

These cards list the local access numbers you'll need (available online if you misplace the card), so you have them handy in case of an emergency. You can get them free from the phone service you plan to use.

Other licences

If you're a trained scuba diver or pilot, or hold other such licences that easily fit into a money belt, bring them along. You never know when you might need them.

One anti-diarrhoea pill

It's hard to predict when dysentery is going to strike. Inevitably, it'll happen while you're out wandering around town or on a long bus ride with your medical kit stored in the luggage hold below. Best to keep one pill handy for such emergencies.

A small pen

Always comes in handy. Pico-pad (Ⓦwww.picopad.com) makes a pen and pad of paper that is the size of a credit card.

www.roughguides.com

145

10

Guidebooks and other reading

This is precisely where you might expect to find a few sentences of Rough Guide propaganda. Happily, you won't. Not much, anyway. Naturally, the editors and writers at Rough Guides are proud of the guidebooks they produce, but they also understand it comes down to individual taste, trust, and how you like your information gathered and presented.

Besides Rough Guides, **guidebook publishers** aimed at the independent traveller include Fielding's, Footprint's Handbook series, Let's Go, Lonely Planet, Time Out city guides and (for French speakers) Le Guide du Routard. For more mainstream travel, there's also Frommer's, Fodor's, the design-intense Eyewitness guides by Dorling Kindersley and Rick Steves's self-guided tours.

You'll want to bring some pure **pleasure reading** as well. This chapter will explain how many books you'll need to cart along on your trip, no matter how many weeks or months you'll be spending on the road.

How to pick a guidebook

The best thing is to "test-drive" a few different guides in your home town or on your next short trip and see **which one suits you**. At the very least, you should go to a bookstore and pick up a few guides on the same country and compare a few paragraphs on the same topic. Start with a city or town you're particularly interested in. Is the layout and writing easy to follow? Are the maps clear? Also take a look at the author bio' – you'll want someone (or several people) who has spent considerable time in the country they're writing about. It's always helpful if they speak the language and have been able to get information by conversing with the locals.

How to use your guidebook

If this trip to Europe will be your first time using a guidebook, you'll be amazed. **Guidebooks** have everything you need to know to get around: where to stay, where to eat and what to do while you're there. However, this does more than just provide incredible help; it removes some of the adventure. Moreover, it sends everyone to the same places; not just the same towns, but the same cafés, hostels, bars and scenic overlooks. Ask nearly any guidebook author and they'll tell you their book is best used as a **reference**, not a bible or substitute tour guide. The little maps are great for helping you navigate your way from the train station to a hostel at 3am, or finding a vegetarian restaurant in Scandinavia, but your best guide is still your own nose. Seek out for yourself those undiscovered restaurants and lodgings, and you'll likely have a much more memorable experience.

Here's another common misuse. The temptation is to sit on the bus or train approaching the city and scrutinize the hostel descriptions. Then, you compare your favourites over and over until you get them into your head, and before you know it you've got the experience largely mapped out before you've even done it. Save yourself the effort; it's not worth it. There's not that much difference between four recommended hostels (the first few on the list are usually the most popular). And if you don't like it you can move out the next day once you've had a chance to look around, or just crash there at night and spend your waking hours elsewhere in town (or lounging in the lobby of a four-star hotel, if you prefer).

You'll eventually find a system that works for you, but mine is something like this: if I'm tired out or staying somewhere a bit longer, I'll pick a place further from the centre. If I'm just staying a day or two and feeling fresh, I'll go for the best-rated of the fleapits in the centre. If I'm not feeling well, I'll go for the cheapest room with an attached bathroom. If there are a few decent choices in any of these categories, I'll typically go for the ones that are the easiest to get to and within walking distance from the centre. But, whatever the case, I won't spend more than five or ten minutes deciding. However, if I want to splurge on someplace special for a night, I'll spend a day in town first and ask around at the tourist office, looking at a few brochures before I decide.

How many guidebooks to bring

Here's some good news. Just because you're planning to hit twelve European countries doesn't mean you need to pack twelve guidebooks. You'll get by just fine with a single, double-Bible-thick **Europe book**: just rip out the pages of the places you've already been to or definitely won't be visiting, to lighten the load.

However, if you're going to be spending considerably more time in one city or country, a **country-** or **city-specific book** is well worth the money. If you're not sure in advance how much time you'll be spending in each spot (or if you simply prefer more background information), then you can easily pick these up once you arrive, from hostels, hotels, bookstores and airports – virtually everywhere. There's usually an English-language bookstore somewhere in town. Ideally, you'll be able to find someone who's heading in the direction you just came from and make a straight swap. If you're trading with a hostel or secondhand bookstore, you may have to throw in some money or a novel to complete the deal.

Another type of guide worth considering, either locally or before you leave, is a **special-interest guide**: hiking routes, architecture, great restaurants, bicycle trails and so on. Books bought locally are often more comprehensive but may not be as professional as those found in your own bookstore back home.

What to read along the way

One of the very best ways to add richness to your trip and bring the locales to life is to read up on them. This entails putting aside the iPod, getting beyond the brief guidebook descriptions and finding stories that explore cultural nuances and history easily missed while searching for your hostel or a better exchange rate. The **Travelers Tales series** (see p.350) offers diverse and well-crafted anthologies on popular destinations that do just this, and has most European countries (and many of the cities) covered. If you can find room for (or manage to lift) James Michener's *Iberia* or *Poland* tomes, you're in for a treat, with folklore and fiction woven into the countries named in the title. But it would be a pity to miss out on some of the **classics**, especially in the regions where they are set. Reading books like *Ulysses* in Ireland, *Crime and Punishment* in Russia or *Death in the Afternoon* in Spain is not just one of the great joys of travel, it's a snap. The classics are among the most popular titles read along the appropriate routes and can be bought or traded quite easily. Even the popular modern travel books, such as Bill Bryson's *Neither Here Nor There: Travels in Europe* or Adam Gopnik's charming bestseller *Paris to the Moon*, are easy to find. So, when you're starting out, one paperback will do. Fiction authors like Dan Brown and Danielle

Steel tend to serve as the strongest currency, but start with something you like and let your continuous swaps serve as a literary adventure that runs parallel to your trip.

If you plan to ignore our advice about electronic gadgets being best left at home, bear in mind that there's also a growing supply of **e-books** and digital maps for PDAs or computers, as well as **podcasts** and **audiobooks** for mp3 players at sites such as ⓦwww.statravel.co.uk, ⓦwww.roughguides.com and ⓦwww.audible.com.

How to pick a map

You can pick up local **maps** for free or for a small charge in every city you visit. The problem: most of them stink. They're either too small, too big, too cluttered with ads, or simply impossible to fold without a PhD in origami.

For larger cities where you plan to spend more than a day or two, it's often worth buying a decent map from local bookstores, tourist shops, or at the tourist information offices when you arrive. You can also try to trade them as you go, but it's not that easy, since most get damaged during the folding process. Maps are also a matter of preference: some prefer the more discreet book-style ones that contain blown-up sections of each part of the city on a different page; others like something they can spread out on the table back at the hostel when looking over the ground covered or the following day's route.

Whichever you choose, you'll probably want to avoid anything that folds out like a picnic blanket and has enough detail to conduct a geographical survey. Look instead for easy folding (if any) and for paper that will survive some rough treatment. Rough Guides has – brace yourself for a dose of propaganda – a line of weatherproof, tearproof maps that combine the book and fold-out formats for those who aren't on the very tightest of budgets. Others worth considering are Insight fleximaps, Hallwag City Flash maps and Artwise/Streetwise maps.

11

When you arrive

Take one step off the plane into the cultural mystery of Europe and – bam! – everything is still in English. Most of the major **European gateways** provide soft landings in this respect. There are free luggage carts and easy-to-use automated ticket machines (with English directions) that accept credit cards. High-speed rail links whisk you to the city centre. Tourist information booths provide enough brochures to fill a small library, and the person behind the desk will answer any question you can think of, probably in no fewer than three languages.

Some people like to book a room for a few nights in advance. That's fine. You can let your travel agent do it or you can find a hotel/hostel on the web. Others prefer to begin honing their room-finding skills right off the bat. That's not a bad idea, either. After consulting your guidebook, you might book a room from the airport through a tourist office. Or take a train or bus into the centre of the city and book via a tourist office there. Alternatively, you might buy a local phone card in the airport and make a few calls to see who has space. Or simply use public transport to get to an area with several hostels and walk from one to the next to check them out on your own.

OK, you've found a place to stay and put your pack down. Now it's time to see some of Europe's sights, right? Sure, but don't forget that you're already travelling. The subway ride to the hostel, asking directions, finding a bite to eat en route…that's all part of the experience. Travelling is just as much about getting there as arriving, or maybe even more.

Points of confusion

- Cities aren't always spelt the same way in their native language. For example, Cologne is Köln, Copenhagen is København, Florence is Firenze, Geneva is Genève, Munich is München, Prague is Praha, Venice is Venezia and Vienna is Wien.

- Nor are countries: Austria is Österreich, Croatia is Republika Hrvatska, Finland is Suomi, Germany is Deutschland, Hungary is Magyar Köztársaság, Italy is Italia, Norway is Norge, Spain is España, Sweden is Sverige, Switzerland is Schweiz or Suisse, and Turkey is Türkyie.

- Often the countries have abbreviations, commonly seen on vehicle licence plates or as a sticker. Some are less than obvious. For instance, BIH is Bosnia and Herzegovina, CH is Switzerland, D is Germany, E is Spain, FL is Liechtenstein and GB is the United Kingdom.

- A comma is used instead of a period or full stop in prices. €3.50 is often written €3,50.

- The date is typically written day/month/year.

- Time is posted military style when written – 0900 is 9am, 1400 is 2pm, 2300 is 11pm. Verbally, the am/pm system (ie "meet you for dinner at seven") is used.

- A road sign of a town's silhouette with a slash through it means you're leaving the town and can resume the speed limit at which you were driving before you had to slow down to pass through the town.

- European banks often close at 3pm, and at midday on a Saturday, if they're open during the weekend at all.

- Many stores in rural areas close for lunch.

One of the best ways to take advantage of your time on the road is to vary the way you travel down it. How you get around, whether it be on water, in the air, on wheels or on the back of an animal, will shape the memories you bring home. And that doesn't just apply to transport. You can be adventurous or timid in your choice of accommodation, what you eat, even the bathrooms you decide to use. It's always going to be easier to travel in the style you are accustomed to at home, but making the choice (often several times a day) to try the local alternatives will ultimately enrich your trip. This chapter will provide you with a little taste of what lies ahead.

Transport

Take as diverse a range of **transport** as you can. Hail a black cab in London, jump on a tram in Vienna, ride a bike in Amsterdam, and hop on every subway you come across. If you have the chance, skip the air-conditioned bus and try . . . well, anything. Here's a guide to getting yourself around. To find the transport that best fits your schedule and budget, see the "Getting there and around" chapter (p.38).

Planes

Confirm your flights by phone or email 72 hours in advance. You won't be automatically bumped if you neglect to do this, but it's nice insurance and more important in some places than others. Most carriers will have English speakers manning the phones, but have the hostel receptionist or tourist office help out if you experience a language barrier. And remember to confirm your in-flight meals if you have any special dietary considerations.

With the **budget carriers**, you may not experience the sort of service you get on flights at home (if, indeed, you get such service at home). If you're nervous about flying with budget companies, that's normal, but remind yourself that they have a strong safety record and it's statistically safer than other modes of transport, including walking. Flying during daylight may help with some of your worries.

Bicycle rickshaws

Some cities offer a sporadic **bicycle rickshaw** service, including a new battery-assisted aerodynamic model. But they are essentially for tourists and, as such, overpriced, especially compared to India, Thailand or wherever the concept was imported from. There's no meter, so always fix the price before you depart.

Bicycle

Bikes can be **rented** nearly everywhere. And where they can't be rented you can pick up a low-tech, used model for €32–65. Take advantage of this. It's an ideal way to get to know an area, particularly those set up to accommodate bicycles: you can stop whenever you get the urge, yet you're more inclined to venture further off the main tourist routes, which will afford you some of the most interesting views. Some cities, like Vienna and Copenhagen, lend out free bikes, though they aren't quite as nice as a rental.

Buses

Long-distance **buses** are convenient and well air-conditioned. Try to get a window seat near the front to help avoid nausea on curvy roads. Sit on the side that's not getting direct sunlight (take a moment to figure this out before you step onto the bus – heading south in the afternoon, you'll want to be on the east side, the side to the right when entering; that way, you can keep the window shade open and get a nice view). For safety, keep a few rows between you and the front to cushion any collision. (For Busabout and Eurolines information, see p.51.)

Canoe

Paddle your way around parts of Iceland, Scotland or France. You can find places to **canoe** just about everywhere, as well as places that will rent you canoes. Pick up a good map, some local tips and a few trash bags to waterproof your backpack, and you're ready to go.

Car

See p.52 for general information on transport, and buying, selling and renting cars as you travel.

Cruise ship

This doesn't fit the traditional traveller image. The cabins aren't conducive to drying hand-washed laundry, the staff don't appreciate people walking down the corridors in just a towel, and body art and piercing may frighten some of the other passengers. But this can be a way to connect certain legs of your trip at a decent price. Especially if you hop aboard an **EasyCruise** (Ⓦwww.easycruise.com), which is relatively inexpensive and full of young, independent travellers.

Ferry

Many of these are nearly as luxurious as their cruise-ship cousins, with hot tubs, saunas, movie theatres and discos, and are more expensive if you try to bring along a car.

Horse

Equestrian travel can be incredibly romantic and exciting. You can take a **horseback tour** on the coasts of Ireland or Spain or in the forests of Germany. But in the words of Ian Fleming, "A horse is dangerous at both ends and uncomfortable in the middle." Make certain, therefore, that you get a little practice before you head out on a longer journey, and spend some time getting to know your steed's signals before you need to interpret them in an emergency.

Motorcycles

There are probably two hundred safer ways to navigate your way around Europe, but few that offer the opportunity to do so in leather. **Helmets** and **protective clothing** are a must, as road conditions change around every mountain curve, and European drivers can be . . . well, capricious.

River kayak

These are short and rugged, and they tip over easier than a toddler on Rollerblades, so it's best to take a course when getting started. Because

www.roughguides.com

handling is so sensitive, most serious kayakers prefer their own boats (and helmets). However, on a long trip, you'll probably just have to make do with what's available. If you stick to the main **rafting centres** (Austria, Germany, Slovenia, Czech Republic, Switzerland), you'll find there's good equipment on hand and, depending on your skill level, you may be able to catch free rides with rafting trips, working as a safety kayaker.

Sea kayak

Both the hard-shell and the collapsible variety have their merits, depending largely on how you're able to transport them. They're increasingly available for rent, so enquire before you drag yours halfway around the globe. You'll also need to check with airlines to see what additional fees are involved for taking them on board.

Subway

No matter how little there is to see out of the window, a **subway** is an integral part of any big city's character. Some offer incredibly high-speed and efficient transport, some are overdue for repair and some are simply underground marvels. The lines in Moscow, St Petersburg and London, and some of the stations in Stockholm, are particularly worth a look.

Taxis

At home, you might order a **taxi** or flag one down for a short ride. You can do that on the road as well. From a financial viewpoint, make sure you know what you're getting into. A ten-minute ride in a Swiss taxi might cost you as much as €40. Also know that, possibly as a result of high petrol prices, many taxis wait at designated spots around the city instead of driving around. So it may be far quicker to ask directions to the nearest taxi stand than wait for one to pass by.

Trains

Important: remember to check that the train carriage you are boarding has the name of the city you are going to posted on the side, or at least a city beyond the one you're heading to. If the individual carriage says "Hamburg" on it, that's where it's going. But that doesn't mean the entire train is going to Hamburg. In fact, there's a good chance it isn't. Trains drop off some carriages and pick up others along the route, so you can easily end up someplace you hadn't counted on – and many people do.

It's tempting, especially with rail passes, to save money by spending a few nights on the train. **Overnight trains** aren't the safest form of accommodation or quite the bargain they might seem so see p.75 to learn about supplementing your pass with other cost-effective travel.

France's TGV is the world's fastest train on rails (Shanghai's new Maglev train is the fastest "floating" train). There are several other high-speed services in Europe: Germany's Inter-City Express (ICE), the Netherlands' and Belgium's Thalys, Eurostar, Spain's Alta Velocidad España (AVE) and Italy's Pendolino. It hardly feels like you're moving, never mind travelling. Until, that is, you catch the blur out of the window. When **high-speed trains** are involved, it's almost always cheaper to get some type of rail pass. (It may even be cheaper to fly.) There's a monopoly on the food, so plastic-wrapped sandwiches are priced like Michelin-star entrées; fortunately, though, the rides don't last that long, so a few pack-along snacks should see you through.

Water taxis/buses

Water taxis are found in several cities, from Venice to Stockholm, and are usually priced for vacationing millionaires, so make sure it's a special occasion before you flag one down. **Water-buses**, or vaporetti and traghetti as they're known in Venice, are quite reasonable and good for getting around. Vaporetti travel on fixed routes (€3.50–5 per journey) and traghetti are flagged down, but cost just 40 cents to take you the other side of the Canal Grande. It's the gondolas that require a wallet the size of a life jacket.

Accommodation

Barcelona is a little too far to travel to stay at the *Hilton*. And your budget is likely to suffer from even one night's plush rest. It may take some time to get used to staying in **budget digs**, but it's more rewarding than it might initially seem. There's a sense of camaraderie that you simply won't find at the *Ritz*. You can swap tales at breakfast, make dinner together, play backgammon – it's a nomadic commune of sorts. The atmosphere changes from place to place, even from day to day if enough new travellers pull in. You can also seek more interesting places from time to time: a hostel in a cave, a bed in a backyard tree house, an ice hotel. Even if these unconventional digs cost a little more, it's usually worth the experience.

Camping

Traveller camping falls into two categories: **free camping**, which is usually illegal but pretty easy to do outside of big cities; and **paid camping**, at designated campgrounds with bathrooms and other amenities. If you plan to go down the free-camp route, you'll

155

probably need to give big cities a miss. Many of the city parks are too dangerous to sleep in, or too likely to be patrolled by police. In smaller towns, you can usually find a field, perhaps even a remote part of a park, if you're discreet. Some designated campgrounds are quite extravagant, with a restaurant, supermarket and pool, but even the smaller ones can be surprisingly expensive. For just a little more, you can often rent a walk-in tent with a "real" bed. Sweden and Norway allow you to put up tents legally, even on private property (if 100–150m from the nearest residence and you don't stay more than two nights; as a matter of etiquette, ask the permission of the owner if possible), which makes these ordinarily expensive destinations a good deal cheaper.

Farmstays

The name conveys the gist. You stay on a **working farm** where the family has made a few rooms available to those who are willing to pay for the experience. It's a bit like a B&B with animals. There's a significant range in comfort and price, but many of them dip well into the budget range (€25, including breakfast). Some offer courses in riding

▲ Camping in the Alps near Mont Blanc

or gardening, many provide family-style meals, and you can sample everything from grape-growing to feeding pigs to making cheese to horseback riding. For lists of farmstays all over Europe, visit Ⓦwww .agrisport.com/europa.htm.

Guesthouses, pensions & B&Bs

These are typically private homes or apartments with a few spare rooms or bungalows. They're often run by older people whose children have moved out, and who are looking to earn a little extra money by letting travellers into their private living space. This means showing a little more respect and courtesy than you might at a hostel. Even if these places are rather lacking in services, keep in mind you're living in someone's home.

Couchsurfing

One of the best ways to save money on accommodation and meet the locals to boot is to **couchsurf**; see p.79 for more information.

Independent hostels

Independent hostels come in as many different shapes and sizes as rocks, which, coincidentally, is what some of them seem to stuff their mattresses with. You'll find some setups extremely professional, and others lacking. Some have great bar scenes with cheap food and people dancing on the tables in the evenings; others feel like giant, anaesthetized dormitory-type buildings with concierges who could easily double for nurses in *One Flew over the Cuckoo's Nest*. Others are blissfully charming and serene with hammocks and sofas. Some are even housed in converted boats moored to the pier or in disused trains permanently parked near the train station. They can be both centrally located and fiendishly remote, with little commonality other than being the cheapest digs in town.

For general **hostel bookings** around Europe, try Ⓦwww.hostels .com, Ⓦwww.hostelworld.com or Ⓦwww.eurotrip.com. Also, Ⓦwww .hostelz.com offers reviews. For other travellers' opinions go to Ⓦwww .tripadvisor.com.

International youth hostels

You don't have to be a certain age to stay at a youth hostel. Being young at heart is enough. With all the senior travellers around, some hostels even seem more like retirement communities. Official **Hostelling International** (**HI**) **hostels** are part of an organization, which means there are certain standards, although it doesn't mean the standards are terribly high. Nearly all of these are well cleaned, some practically sterile, with dormitory-style rooms and separate quarters for men and women, self-service kitchens, common rooms, lockers and a cost of €8–24 per night if you're avoiding any of their "luxury" rooms. Some are equipped with pools, hot tubs and barbecues, while others are about as basic as their tree-and-hut logo. There are some notable exceptions, but official HI hostels don't usually earn many points in the architecture, cosiness or roaring-social-life departments. Most are located a little way out of the centre of town and a few come with a curfew or kick you out during the day for cleaning. There are almost always budget alternatives, but if this sounds like your cup of dis-counted tea, pick up the **membership card**. Without the card, you're still welcome, but you will pay slightly more. Try to book in advance if you know when you're arriving, especially in high season. (See p.72 for more info on discount cards.)

- **Hostelling International** ⓦwww.hihostels.com. A not-for-profit association (and brand name) of hostels (over 4000) around the world, with discounts for members.
- **European Alliance of YMCAs** ⓦwww.eay.org. Similar in atmosphere to the HI hostels, the YMCA also offers health club facilities and fairly inexpensive accommodation for members.

Hotels

These are still often judged on a "**star**" **ranking system**, and it's often hard to know who's doing the officiating. But typically, one star denotes low budget, sometimes without maid service. Two stars usu-ally has daily maid service. Three stars is supposed to be a moderately priced (for the region) middle-class operation, sometimes with a pool and in-room internet access. Four stars is an expensive, top-tier hotel with luxury services. And five stars is the ultimate in luxury – just park your private jet at the front and the staff will offload your polo ponies for you.

Sleeping rough

Ah, the last resort of the traveller, the safety net that leaves your back out of alignment, the experience that will help you overcome whatever was annoying you about hostels. At some point, it's possible you'll be spending the night on a park bench or in a train station or airport lounge. There are obviously risks associated with **sleeping rough**. In particular, it's not a good idea for single women travellers, especially in (or just outside) a train station – in fact, train stations are best avoided by all, really. And a secluded park bench at night is even riskier.

McDonald's

On one hand, there's simply too much wonderful food out there to justify a trip to
the Golden Arches. On the other, **McDonald's** has some rather interesting (albeit
processed and chemically enhanced) dishes in addition to the old classics. Italy (some
argue you should be shot for entering a *McDonald's* while in Italy) has a Caprese salad
with mozzarella and tomatoes; Germany has a shrimp lemon burger and beer to wash
it down; Greece has a Chicken Mythic burger with Monterey Jack cheese; Spain has
gazpacho; and Turkey has the Köfte Burger, a spiced patty inside a bun enriched with
yoghurt mix. Poland even tried a McKielbasa that flopped. The point is, if you absolutely
must get your McFix while you're on the road (and these places are packed with
travellers), you can at least give yourself a push by trying something you haven't seen or
can't pronounce.

But if you do find yourself having to sleep rough, bear in mind the
following **tips**. Firstly, you probably won't be the only one doing it,
so when it looks inevitable start trying to secure a good spot. What's
a good spot? You'll know it when you see it (if there is one). Not too
hidden, not where people have to step over you, not right under bright
lights. Corners are usually quite nice, and frequently coveted. You may
be inadvertently borrowing the resting place of a "regular" – so be
forewarned that they may not take too kindly to this. Look for newspaper or cardboard to place under you; a cold marble floor will drain your
body heat and make it difficult to rest. If you've got a travel partner,
take turns staying awake. If not, make sure you're bear-hugging your
backpack while you sleep. Alternatively, look for an all-night snack shop
or bar and sip tea or coffee until the sun creeps up, then find a more
comfortable place to sleep at a park or beach.

Eating

No matter what level of comfort you choose to travel in, you don't
want to circle the globe without sampling the **local cuisine**. Check
out the produce, meat and fish markets, or follow your nose into a tiny
restaurant and discover hand-rolled pastas in Sicily or fresh tapas in
Seville. There's no need to be paranoid about what passes your lips. If it
looks truly vile (like greenish drinking water, for example), you might
want to give it a miss. Otherwise, eat, drink, be merry, and see p.196 for
lightning-fast cures for diarrhoea.

Hostels

They know the budget of their customers better than anyone. They
also take advantage of traveller physics: a traveller not yet packed tends
to stay that way for a while. Once in "hangout" mode, it's tempting

www.roughguides.com

159

to stick around the hostel. Many hostels offer extremely cheap stews, sandwiches and plates of pasta. The ones that don't may offer **cooking facilities**. Team up with another traveller, or an entire group, head to the supermarket and make a meal together.

Restaurants

Eating at **restaurants** can run up your expenses quicker than Imelda Marcos with an hour to kill in Milan, so choose where you eat with care. As comforting as it may be to dine with other travellers, you'll often get a better deal ditching the guidebook, heading to the poorer parts of town and checking out the places (normally packed with locals) that don't take credit cards.

Street vendors

Don't believe the intestine-quivering rumours. Not every **street snack** leads to a week in bathroom solitude. In fact, buying food from street vendors is a wonderful way to supplement your diet: some travellers manage to exist entirely on these budget snacks. As a tip, when possible pick the vendors who prepare the food right in front of you.

Personal hygiene

Staying clean on the road is a challenge at times. It becomes particularly rough during the back-to-back long-transit stretches (an overnight train ride followed by a day walking around a hot city followed by another overnight train ride). If you encounter some intimidating toilets, that can be a problem as well. Either way, relief can be found.

Airports and buses

Many **airports** now have showers available for a small fee (€1–3). Some have a sauna and gym as well. You may have to hunt around a little, as they're not as well situated as the duty-free items and postcards. Even if you have to put your yet-unwashed clothes back on, a refreshing shower can be an enormous boost. And you'll probably have some spare coins to get rid of anyway. If you don't take the opportunity during a long haul, the smell is only going to get worse. The budget route, of course, is simply to wash up in the restroom, perhaps with a damp paper-towel "shower", and swing by the duty-free and take a squirt of perfume before the next leg of your journey.

On nicer **bus rides**, particularly around Eastern Europe and Turkey, don't be surprised if an attendant comes by and offers you

Hot hammams

Galatasaray Hammam

Built by Sultan Beyazit in 1481, now an upscale classic more popular with visitors than locals. €35 with full treatment – including massage and abrasive sponge scrub-down; 24 Turnacibasi Sk, İstanbul, Turkey; ☎0212 252 4242, ⊛www.galatasarayhamami.com.

Gellert Baths and Spa

Budapest has some of the planet's top Turkish baths, some complete with Ottoman architecture. €13 entry fee; Kelenhegyi út 4. Budapest, Hungary; ☎ (36-1) 466 6166, ⊛www.gellertbath.com.

Les Bains du Marais

Elegant upscale hammam and sauna, with a restaurant and hair salon as well. €35 entry fee; 31–33 rue des blancs Manteaux, Paris, France; ☎1 44 61 02 02, ⊛www.lesbainsdumarais.com.

Paris Mosque baths

Marble baths built in 1922. Moorish courtyards with gardens for relaxing afterwards with a cup of mint tea. €15 entry fee; 39 rue Geoffroy St Hilaire, Paris, France; ☎1 43 31 38 20, ⊛www.la-mosquee.com.

Portobello Centre

An old restored bathhouse at a good price. €7 entry fee; 57 The Promenade, Edinburgh, Scotland; ☎0131 669 6888, ⊛www.edinburghleisure.co.uk.

The Royal Baths

England's most famous Turkish baths. €21 peak, €14.50 off-peak (Tues) Royal Baths Assembly Rooms, Crescent Road, Harrogate, England ☎01423 556746, ⊛www.harrogate.gov.uk/turkishbaths.

Sturebadet

Upscale, luxury bathhouse in the city centre. €45 Mon–Thurs; €55 Fri–Sun; Sturegallarian 36, Stockholm, Sweden; ☎08 545 01500, ⊛www.sturebadet.se.

a splash of unisex perfume or some fragranced towellettes. They're not as pleasant as the warm washcloths distributed by many airlines, particularly considering they have the olfactory properties of toilet-bowl cleaner, but it's still better than being trapped beside someone with nuclear BO. The individually wrapped moist tissues function better, since they also remove the dirt and odour rather than simply masking it. Bring some of your own just in case.

Turkish baths

You'll find some classics in Turkey but also in other cities around Europe, like Paris, Stockholm and London. Look for the word "**hammam**". They're a perfect remedy for travel grime – the accumulated film that covers your body after weeks of low-pressure showers. These medieval bathhouses are mild steamrooms with washbasins, and most offer, for an additional fee, a joint-cracking, back-popping, skin-blasting

Turkish baths for women

Traditional Turkish bathing rituals are a little complex, but I kept reminding myself: how many mistakes can you make when you are naked? Well, after visiting numerous *hammams* across Turkey, I came up with my eight rules for women:

1. Wear nylon panties. (Just because it's a bathhouse doesn't mean they're really prepared to see you naked.)
2. Carry travel-sized soap and shampoo.
3. If you want to bring a razor, put it with the soap and shampoo in a small plastic bag.
4. Never put anything in the washing basins, but your dipping bowl. No soap, razor, washcloth or anything. The basin needs to stay perfectly clean. Never use another person's basin unless invited.
5. Do not take a single step without your bath slippers on. (You're provided with a pair when you enter.)
6. Always have a massage (personal rule).
7. Bring a bottle of water to drink.
8. Put five to ten million Turkish lira (€2.50–5) in the bathhouse jar if you enjoyed your bath.

Justine Merrill
Ⓦ www.justinetravel.com

"massage" that will leave you feeling like a boneless chicken. Upon exiting, you can cool down wrapped in towels with a refreshing yoghurt drink.

Toilets

To find out how to sidestep **pay toilets** see p.82, and to keep from having to visit too often, see p.196. Meanwhile, here's a look at what you may end up facing.

There aren't too many **squatters** left in Europe, but you may stumble across one. The trick is not to stumble while you use it. Place your feet on the small foot-size platforms provided and align your bottom with the hole in the floor, which usually means facing the way you came in as you would on a Western toilet. There's rarely anything to hold on to, or anything you'd *want* to hold on to, so beyond the obvious danger of tipping over, the position causes your trouser pockets to become somewhat inverted, so your valuables may go sliding irretrievably down the hole. And if this doesn't sound challenging enough, remember you may have to hold a flashlight in your mouth, since these lavatories often don't have any lighting. How to flush the hole is not entirely apparent. There's no little handle to push. No knob to turn. You have to fill up the plastic bowl a few times and dump the water into the hole and let water displacement take care of the rest.

More commonly, you'll happen upon loos that look like Western models, but which were installed by someone who may not have fully understood the directions that came with the assembly kit. Or who lacked the necessary tools. If so, notice the seat has usually been secured by something with the equivalent strength of chewing gum, so if you don't sit down exactly straight, the seat detaches and you slide right off the porcelain rim, which – take it from me – can be pretty painful. Sometimes, the plastic seat is missing altogether. This means that you're squatting again; only now it's more difficult than a standard squatter, because you have to do a "standing squat" to clear the rim of the toilet. This usually entails bracing yourself with one hand on the wall behind you, which is highly exhausting for your arm and leg muscles and often makes them cramp painfully.

When using a toilet on a train, remember that some of the older trains will empty directly onto the tracks, so try to refrain from going while at a station.

A few of these bathrooms do come equipped with paper, but it's rarely the cottonsoft kind. So, while you're sitting there (or semi-squatting), use your time wisely by crumpling and uncrumpling a piece of paper (from an unused section of your guidebook if necessary) until it's almost tolerable. This takes about five minutes (twenty with the glossy stuff), so you may want to start working on it before you actually get to the toilet. Important: if there's a little waste bin beside the toilet, put your used paper there. Don't even think of throwing it into the toilet. Though they may look vaguely like the loos you have at home, they can have a violent reaction to toilet paper: just one square of paper can clog it beyond repair.

In other words, whatever the road sends your way, don't shy away from it. It's all part of the travel experience.

12

Culture shock

I t may sound like what happens when Britney Spears visits the opera, but **culture shock** is simply a dramatic way of saying that things aren't quite the way they are at home. When you change everything you eat, say, do, smell and hear at the same time, the effect can be jolting, especially if amplified by sadness or apprehension about leaving home, fatigue from the journey or illness. The natural tendency is to return home immediately. But if you give yourself time the bout of anxiety or despair will almost certainly pass.

▲ Tapas menu, Madrid

Four stages of culture shock

Anthropologist Kalfery Oberg first introduced the term in 1960 and defined it as a state precipitated by the anxiety that results from losing all our familiar signs and symbols of social intercourse. Everyone has slightly different reactions, the speed of the process varies and many people go through different phases more than once, so this may not provide a complete blueprint for your adaptation.

1 Honeymoon
Cultural differences are intriguing and new sights fascinating. You are still comforted by the close memory of your home culture.

2 Crisis
After some time abroad, differences begin to affect you. Differences in language, concepts and values begin to create feelings of confusion and anxiety. This is normal – it's a sign you're reconnecting with your own cultural values.

3 Recovery
You begin to accept the differences and feel comfortable in new situations. Often the crisis dissipates as lingual skills improve.

4 Adjustment
Despite occasional bouts of strain, you're enjoying the new culture and able to make choices based on preferences and values.

Combating culture shock

On the face of it, Europe, especially its larger cities, may not be all that different from the way of life you're accustomed to. There are a few more cobblestones, the architecture's more impressive, the clothing more stylish and there are more tiny cars with drivers who seem to be trying out for the Formula One circuit. But the closer you get, the more differences you'll see. To help people cope, researchers Furnham and Bochner developed the idea in the 1970s and 1980s that the individual traveller didn't need to embrace all or even most aspects of the society, just some key features to be able to operate within the culture. By reading this and simply being aware of the phenomenon, you're already a step ahead.

Here are several practical things you can do to minimize culture shock:

● Recognize it for what it is: a reaction to sensory overload and unfamiliar surroundings ("Oh, that's just a bout of culture shock – I'll be fine soon"). Look at the upside of what it represents: you're having new experiences, new insights and a new perspective. How bad is that?

● Start your journey in countries similar to your own. The UK is ideal in this respect.

● Read up on the place before you arrive. You're going there to experience what that country has to offer, but a little knowledge can decrease the number of cultural surprises. It can be enough

www.roughguides.com

165

Finding the real Europe

Everything seems so new and exciting when you first arrive that it's possible to overlook the tourist infrastructure that surrounds you. But as with bad toupees, once you notice, you'll wonder how it ever eluded you. A well-decorated Greek restaurant in Paris with an overpriced menu (in six languages) on a touristy street may seem exotic, but it couldn't be less authentic, even with Greek waiters and a Greek owner and food imported from Greece. You may be used to these things in your own country (a Texas Steakhouse in Vancouver with waiters wearing cowboy hats, for example), but in Europe, where you've come to see the culture of the places you're visiting, it seems somehow painfully false. There may be an excellent Greek restaurant tucked away in an immigrant area, but that's a different story. As a rule of thumb, if you're the only traveller in the place, you've stumbled into somewhere **authentic**.

Naturally, in your hostel, you'll be surrounded by other travellers, as you will be at all the major attractions, on popular beaches and along the most famous shopping streets. You're not likely to escape this bubble by travelling longer or further or faster. Instead, **go deeper**. Hang out in places where the tourists don't go. Learn a language, communicate with the locals, spend time with them (a lot of time), and form your own first-hand perspective.

One of the best ways to do this is to **work** for them or alongside them. **Volunteering** is another excellent path (see p.102). Joining a local sports club or choir will also create inroads. Since there's no membrane on this bubble, it's impossible to say when you've burst it. But there are a few signs. Can you describe the character of the local people to someone back home? Do you have the phone numbers and addresses of local friends you've made? Have you been invited over for dinner? Have you invited others to visit you back home? These are certainly more worthy things to strive for on your trip than passport stamps.

for some just to buy the guidebook a day before departure and start reading background information, but reading a novel set in that country will do far more to get you in the mood.

- Jet lag gets your trip off to a poor start (see p.197), so get some sleep on the plane.
- If you're making a large cultural jump early in your trip, you can do a number of things to ease into your new location. Start by staying in a Western-style hotel for a day or two, and looking for cheaper, local digs after you've had a chance to acclimatize. Or simply spend some time just relaxing in a nice hotel lobby free of charge and don't return to your hostel until you're ready to examine the back of your eyelids.
- Speak to other travellers and compare observations.
- Keep a journal.
- Allow yourself to get excited about your trip. It's natural to be a little nervous about what's ahead, but focus on converting that into positive energy.

Your travel philosophy

What you take with you on your trip will, to a large extent, determine the experience you take away from it. And in this case, I'm not referring to the dual-current hairdryer that you should probably leave at home. I'm talking about your **travel philosophy**; your approach to dealing with the cultures you encounter.

You'll face this the moment you begin your journey. The locals you meet in more out-of-the-way places will tend to be more genuine, as they haven't been hardened by years of loud tour groups and tough-bargaining backpackers. Likewise, the travellers you run into off the main routes are likely to be a bit more interesting and into their trips. If you're passing through small towns not plagued with tourists, you're in a more culturally fragile environment and should thus move about and interact with care.

Getting away from it all

But why are we so seduced by the idea of getting away from it all? Maybe it's a reaction to the travel industry telling us where to go (cruise brochures lure us into "escaping" but then stick us in living conditions with a higher population density than the urban slums of Bangladesh). Some of us simply want the opposite.

The last time I tried to seek out solitude was during a two-week layover. My wife and I were hoping for some cultural decompression before heading home after a long trip, a chance to scrape off six months of accumulated travel grime, and find a little spinal realignment after countless overnight bus rides. We ended up at a backpacker-style beach compound on a beach that seemed well suited for our needs. After a few days of delightfully brainless hammock testing, we began to wonder where the other travellers were going during the day. Most, we learned, were heading to a remote beach several kilometres away: there was a beach right in front of our little cottage, but that was evidently not remote enough. The one on the other side was obviously whiter, the water clearer, and had trees that jutted out like the horticultural equivalent of dislocated shoulders.

So we dutifully trudged off to find this isolated nirvana. After an hour's hike, we arrived at a postcard-perfect beach. The shin-deep water made it too shallow for swimming, but it felt like Mother Nature might cast down a few lightning bolts if such critiques were going muttered aloud. Upon closer inspection, we could see there were many other travellers hanging out here as well. There we all were, trying to get away from everything . . . together – trapped on the backpacker equivalent of a cruise ship.

The thing is, even if you do succeed in getting away from it all, as I've done on a few occasions, you may come to the conclusion that there's no one there for a good reason. Sure a dose of serenity can be wonderful, but it's hard to summon mutative thoughts while being blasted with horizontal freezing rain on the west coast of Ireland. I guess it just never feels quite as glamorous as it's portrayed on the postcards or in the advertisements.

Besides, as Benjamin Franklin pointed out, "the trouble with doing nothing is not knowing when you're finished".

Doug Lansky

Tourism impact

With good reason, travel publications have long asserted that mass tourism destroys the very things – quaintness, genuine hospitality, serenity, unique culture – that attracted visitors in the first place. There are still thousands of small, picturesque towns and villages around Europe that haven't found their way into guidebooks and are yours to discover. But it doesn't take long before they've got parking lots to handle dozens of tour buses; view-blocking, shadow-casting luxury hotels right on the beach; colourful costumes for evening cultural dance programs; light shows with multilingual recorded voiceovers; and air-conditioned restaurants serving food the locals would never touch. Truth be known, we independent budget travellers contribute to this as well, probably more than we'd care to admit. Simply by being aware of your impact, though, you'll probably make more thoughtful decisions about where you spend your money and how you interact with people.

Here are a few concepts to keep in mind:

● You are a (uninvited) guest in a foreign country. Be gracious. Travel with an open mind and a desire to learn.
● Familiarize yourself with local customs and make an effort to learn at least a few words of the local language. Your efforts will make an impression on those you meet. (How would you react to someone who came to your country and asked you for directions in another language, then spoke louder and slower when you didn't understand?)
● Be a sensitive photographer. Be discreet or ask permission before you take someone's picture. And consider the long-term implications before paying someone in cash or confectionery to take their photograph.
● Resolve conflicts with a smile.
● Look beyond the tourist streets and resorts. Here's a worthy goal: meet and spend time with at least one local who is not trying to sell you any goods or services.
● Pay attention to what the locals are wearing. Shorts, vest tops and other revealing items often aren't appropriate. Better to choose styles and colours that help you blend in rather than display the latest fashions from your own country.
● Try to refrain from beginning sentences with "back home … ".
● Do not litter.
● Get used to secondhand smoke. In Europe, smokers are not treated like crack dealers.

13

Staying in touch

Just twenty years ago, **staying in touch** from Europe meant dealing with fickle overseas operators while you pumped a pocket full of coins into a payphone that would, like an Italian Vespa driver, cut you off at will.

Today, perhaps the best setup is emailing at internet cafés, using Skype, MSN's Messenger, or another cheap/free VoiP program to make phone calls from internet cafés. (Tip: buy your coffee and snacks outside the café, where they're likely be cheaper.) For emergencies (or local use with a local SIM card), a mobile phone is an easy way to stay connected and a list of collect-call numbers is a smart backup.

Email

With time zones and long-distance charges, **email** is going to be your best ally for almost-immediate contact. You can knock off one letter and send it in bulk, or alter it for specific people with a little cutting and pasting and save yourself (not to mention your metacarpal ligaments) the hassle. Unless you're writing a novel along the way, there's no reason to bring a laptop.

Overconnected

One of the sad developments of the social media age is that hostels have become less a gathering point to meet fellow travellers from around the world and more a place to update friends and family back home by blog, twitter, SMS, skype and the like. Instead of people talking, everyone has their face glued to their mobile phone or laptop. Give it a rest. This is your big chance to meet the international people around you.

Doug Lansky

www.roughguides.com

169

▲ Internet café, Paris

You can get internet access virtually anywhere. And by anywhere, I really mean anywhere. Nearly all hostels are now equipped with a connection, and if they're not you shouldn't have to walk more than ten minutes to find an **internet café**. Expect to pay anything from €0.40 to €2 for fifteen minutes, although libraries, universities and many hotels offer free access. Just make sure you're set up with an account you can check from the web. If the email account you currently use can only be accessed from your work or school workstation, consider getting a free account. There are many to choose from, but Hotmail (Ⓦwww.hotmail.com), Yahoo! (Ⓦwww.yahoo.com) and Gmail (Ⓦwww.google.com) are among the most popular. If you have a digital camera, you can easily **upload photos** as you go. Some internet cafés are equipped with a scanner, so developed film can be sent for a slight additional cost. (For other photo options, see p.209.)

If you need a safe way to keep track of all your online passwords, try Ⓦwww.passwordsafe.com or Ⓦbriefcase.yahoo.com.

Phone

There are several ways to place a call, and making the right choice can save you over €10 on a single five-minute overseas conversation.

Cheapest calls

VoIP (**Voice over Internet Protocol**) currently offers the best deals. It's hard to beat a free call (computer to computer) or about €0.02 per minute (to the US or Australia) when calling from a computer to a regular phone or mobile phone back home. Skype (Ⓦwww.skype .com), MSN's Messenger (Ⓦwww. msn.com) and other such programs are free to download and should be available at most internet cafés. That means you just need to set up an account (free) and bring along a headset (USB types cost a bit more – about US$40 – but will be the easiest to plug in).

If you're bringing your own laptop or a smartphone with wi-fi, look for wi-fi hotspots at Ⓦv4.jiwire.com.

Mobile phones

Carrying a **mobile phone** is a decision worth thinking about, but if you're coming from the US, chances are the phone you bring with you will be about as effective as a refrigerator magnet (see below), so it's important to get the right model and service plan. In that one emergency situation, a mobile phone could save you, or at least make your life much easier. But it may feel like an expensive and obtrusive umbilical cord. One simple solution is to leave it turned off and have the calls diverted to your voicemail service or a family member, or simply leave a message instructing people to email or text you. Europe has extensive mobile phone **coverage**, but be careful not to use your phone as a crutch when venturing, say, up into the mountains. You can get yourself into serious trouble thinking that a rescue team is just a call away. Coverage is especially patchy in rough and remote terrain, so that helicopter ride out may take longer to arrange than you think. Better to go in prepared with the right equipment and solid backup plans, as if you had no phone with you at all.

Choosing the right phone and service plan

Most of the world uses 900/1800 GSM, but the US and Canada use 1900 GSM and there's no way a 1900 GMS phone is going to work with an 1800 network. So, if you want something that will work well in both places, you'll need a **tri-band phone**. These start at around €100, not including monthly fees, rising to €450 for the top-end models with a camera – more important, though, is that it operates on 110–240V and has a lithium-ion battery.

If you opt for a tri-band phone and stick with your subscription back home, remember that each local call you make in Europe will be "international" – calling one *quartier* of Paris from another, for example, will use a US network, so you'll end up getting fleeced on both ends. Furthermore, you'll have to pay surcharges for accepting incoming calls as well. To put it another way, if you use your phone for anything but emergencies, the bill will be frightening.

There is a (sort of) solution for people who want to make more practical use of their phone. If you plan to stay somewhere for a while and want to use your mobile phone locally, **buying a local SIM card** makes the most sense. These cost €8–25, can be topped up easily and, best of all, incoming calls are free and local calls cost €0.20–0.80 a minute, instead of a few euros. And, for international calls, you can simply use the local card to ring eKit or another callback service and make a cheap call (double-check to see that the service will call back to a mobile phone first, though). Only one small problem: many US service providers "lock" in your subscription SIM card, stopping you from switching networks. At the moment, only T-Mobile (in the US) lets you switch (you have to wait fourteen days after purchasing before putting in a request).

You could, of course, buy a used 900/1800 GSM phone once you arrive in Europe (for about €35), and buy a SIM card in every country (which you could keep loaded up as needed), but after about three countries those cards are going to really add up. So, if you're travelling through many countries, consider a **roaming SIM card** which enables you to stick with the same phone number. Telestial (ⓦwww.telestial .com) has several plans, but figure on about €55 for the SIM card and €0.35 per minute to call. As long as you keep funds in your prepaid account, you can make and receive calls. Yes, it's pricey, but if you want to use it in ten or more countries over the summer, it's probably the cheapest option for semi-regular use. And if you decide to stay in one country for a month or so, you can just slap in a local SIM card. You can use it with both a US/Canadian tri-band phone or a European dual-band.

Of course, there are **mobile phone rentals**, as you'll no doubt see in the airport, but after more than a week or two of travel they make these other options seem like bargains.

Satellite phone

Maybe you've heard about this and conjured up some notion that it's exactly what the doctor ordered for overseas travel. Well, for field researchers on a corporate account it might be (Globalstar makes a 7oz model that uses 48 orbiting satellites), but for budget-minded travellers, price (€600+), weight (heavier than normal phones) and rates (relatively high per minute) make it impractical at best. Besides, it doesn't work indoors.

Making direct calls

To make a **direct-dial call from Europe** (that is, one from a private phone, hotel phone, or phone booth with coins or a locally purchased calling card), dial 00 plus the country code and number. So, to dial Australia, ring 0061 plus the number; for Canada and the US, it's 001 plus the number; for South Africa, it's 09 plus the number; and for New Zealand, it's 0064 plus the number. See below for how to dial the UK.

Calling Europe

Calling Europe is just as easy. To call from Australia, Canada or the US, dial 011, then the country code and number. To call from New Zealand, dial 00 then the country code and number. If the European number you're calling starts with a zero or has it wrapped in parentheses like this "(0)" after the country number, you typically don't dial it when calling from overseas. So, if calling England from the US, and the number is written "+44 (0)70 222 2222", you would dial 011 44 70 222 2222.

In case you want to make some pre-trip plans, here's a list of **country codes**:

Country	Code	Country	Code
Austria	43	Latvia	371
Belgium	32	Lithuania	370
Britain	44	Luxembourg	352
Bulgaria	359	The Netherlands	31
Croatia	385	Norway	47
Czech Republic	420	Poland	48
Denmark	45	Portugal	352
Estonia	372	Romania	40
Finland	358	Russia	7
France	33	Slovakia	421
Germany	49	Slovenia	386
Greece	30	Spain	34
Hungary	36	Sweden	46
Ireland	353	Switzerland	41
Italy	39	Turkey	90

Collect calls

Calling collect is a nice back-up plan, but too expensive to be your main source of contact. Many major national phone companies in your country have set up special numbers abroad so you can be connected directly with an operator back home (and so they can keep your money!). This enables you to reverse charges (or use a calling card account number you have with that phone company), all while speaking with an operator who shares your language. For example, to call the US from Belgium using a public phone, you'd dial 001 800 100 10 to reach an AT&T operator. After entering or saying the area code and local number you're calling, you get a voice prompt, at which point you can either enter your calling card account number or wait for an operator and request a collect call. The other option is to use a local operator to reverse the charges. The directions for that are often on the payphone itself or in your guidebook. Collect calls are convenient but not cheap, best in emergencies or when people back home won't mind paying the obscene charges.

Time zones

Britain, Ireland and Portugal
Five hours ahead of New York, eight hours ahead of Vancouver, eleven hours behind Sydney.

Austria, Belgium, Croatia, Czech Republic, Denmark, France, Germany, Hungary, Italy, Luxembourg, the Netherlands, Norway, Poland, Slovakia, Slovenia, Spain, Sweden, Switzerland and Turkey
Six hours ahead of New York, nine hours ahead of Vancouver, ten hours behind Sydney.

Bulgaria, Estonia, Finland, Greece, Latvia, Lithuania and Romania
Seven hours ahead of New York, ten hours ahead of Vancouver, nine hours behind Sydney.

Phone cards

Phone cards are the best option for local calls and sometimes prove a great deal for international calls. They look like flimsy credit cards and can be found both in your home country and at newspaper stands and grocery stores across Europe. They are either inserted directly into the public phone, with the units ticking by as you talk or (as with some international cards) the card's number and special code are dialled first to access a special account that lets you call overseas. Before you buy any card, ask if it works internationally, how many minutes you get and if it has an expiration date (some become invalid after one to three months). If you want to keep things simple, pick up local cards as and when you need them. If you prefer to arrive with one in your pocket, you can buy similar cards at special websites (such as ⓦ www.besttelephonerates.com) before leaving home or set up an account with eKit (ⓦ www.ekit .com), which will also give you access to their online vault for valuable documents.

Know the rates

Example: Sweden to the US, four-minute call

* Skype, MSN Messenger or other computer-to-computer call: free

* SkypeOut (from computer to regular phone): €0.07

* Private Swedish phone: €0.35

International prepaid card bought in Sweden: €3

* Budget phone card (eKit): €0.85

* Mobile phone with account at home: €4

* Hotel room phone (with hotel charges): €6

* AT&T World Traveler ($5.99 a month fee): €5

Local phones

You're still going to encounter the coin-eating dinosaur phone, but they're heading towards extinction and it's much more likely you'll be using a phone card that can be inserted into the phone. Sometimes there are special overseas phones that offer better rates; your guidebook should advise you on that.

Snail mail

Sadly, **letter writing** is becoming a lost art. There's still nothing quite as nice as receiving an actual letter from abroad: the stamps, the smell and knowing it had to travel across oceans and continents to get to you. The proliferation of email simply makes the occasional postcard or letter all that much more special. It's easy to forget this while you're on the road hopping from one internet café to the next, but it's worth the effort and is likely to strengthen friendships and ensure you'll be getting mail from your travelling friends in years ahead. Bear in mind that most letters take five to ten days to arrive.

Sending packages – know the local weight cutoffs

There are a few tricks you can use to simplify the process, but they all revolve around the same concept: **scout out the requirements** before you try to mail something. In many European countries, there are special postal boxes you can buy that will speed up the shipping process and bring down the costs. More often, there are package weight limits in various price categories (it's a drag to show up with your carefully wrapped package, only to learn you're 20g over a price cutoff, which will cost you an additional €10). Sometimes you can get good bargains within a lower weight range, so if you divide up a larger package you can actually save money. Consult your guidebook for local tips.

Surface mail

Surface mail from almost everywhere in Europe is cheap and slower than a worm with a hangover. It's perfect for sending home items you realize you no longer need (or never did), inexpensive souvenirs, worn-out clothing you simply couldn't part with, and so on. Just about the time you've forgotten you sent it, it'll arrive, prodded and shaken by countless customs officers, like a gift from the heavens.

Registered mail and major couriers

If you're sending anything of value, such as jewellery you purchased, a filled diary or film, it's better to be safe than sorry. Spend the extra money for **registered mail** to make sure it arrives. Or go straight for a private **delivery company**, such as DHL or FedEx.

Receiving mail and packages

If you're organized enough to make an itinerary, you could send it off to your friends and relatives with a note trying to encourage some letter writing. Mail and packages can be sent to you marked with the city, country, and the words "Poste Restante, Central Post Office". If you

Secure web surfing

Surfing on the road is not like surfing at home. The connection may be fine, but you need to be aware of a new breed of pickpocket – the kind that watches you type in your various passwords or logs on to your machine after you're gone and accesses your private accounts with the info that you've unknowingly left in the far reaches of the computer's memory. There are a few things you need to do to adjust the browser settings every time you sit down at a terminal. You'll want to do it for any **online shopping** and **banking** especially, but to keep them from getting your email access info you'll probably want to do it every time you go online. Practise getting the settings switched quickly so it doesn't tie up your paid minutes at the internet café.

1. With Internet Explorer (it's similar with Firefox) click on "Tools", then scroll to "Internet Options". Set "Days to keep pages in history" to zero.
2. Also under "Tools/Internet Options", click on "Security" and then "Custom Level" and disable both "Download unsigned ActiveX controls" and "Initialize and script ActiveX controls not marked safe for scripting". Set "Java Permissions" to "High Safety"; set "Software Channel Permissions" to "High Safety", and disable the following: "Meta Refresh", "Launching programs and files in an IFRAME", "Userdata Persistence", "Active Scripting", "Allow paste operations via script" and "Scripting of Java applets".
3. Back under "Tool/Internet Options" menu, click "Advanced" and look under the "Security" heading. Untick "Enable Profile Assistant". Then tick "do not save encrypted pages to disk" and tick "Empty Temporary Internet files folder when browser is closed".
4. Click "Control Panel", then "Network", and check that file and printer sharing are disabled. (An internet café controller can access what you're doing from another terminal.)
5. Accept session cookies but not stored cookies. Never, never allow Windows to save any of your passwords.
6. Finally, make sure there's no one peeking over your shoulder.

have an American Express Card or at least one AmEx traveller's cheque, you can pick up your mail at their global offices found in nearly every major city, though it's better to shoot the individual office an email before you get sent anything of real value, as some don't have space for packages or have specific guidelines for handling them. Addresses can be found on the web at ⓦ www.americanexpress.com. Note that most AmEx offices do not accept parcels, just letters, and only hold them for thirty days. If you don't have an AmEx card or traveller's cheques, and don't trust the main post office with a valuable delivery, you could, for a small fee (or perhaps nothing, if you find a kind clerk), make a delivery arrangement at a top-end hotel.

Forwarded mail

Check with your national mail carrier to see if your post can be forwarded for free or an additional charge. In **Australia**, a year of forwarded mail costs Aus$393 to Asia Pacific, Aus$550 to the rest of the world; mail holding rates are Aus$12 for the first week and Aus$4.50

for each additional week (ⓦwww.auspost.com.au). **Canada Post** (ⓦwww.canadapost.ca) offers international redirection for Can$69 for three months and Can$23 per month thereafter. Holding mail services cost Can$15 for the first ten business days and Can$7.50 per additional week. **New Zealand Post** (ⓦwww.nzpost .co.nz) will redirect internationally for NZ$80 for up to two months, and hold mail for up to twelve weeks for NZ$5 per week. In the **UK**, overseas redirection from the Royal Mail (ⓦwww.royalmail.com) is £15.50 for one month, £33.75 for three months, and £52.05 for six months. For up to 66 days, they'll hold your mail for £29.40. In the **US**, they'll only hold your mail for up to thirty days, but won't charge for it (ⓦwww.usps.com). Best, of course, is if you can have a friend or relative filter out the junk mail and send the rest along.

Keeping up with current events

When you're in travel mode, **current events** can feel as distant as some of the relatives you've been meeting. Shelling out for a newspaper at newsstand prices seems like museum, souvenir and beer money put to bad use. Some distance can be wonderful, but keeping an eye on things can also keep you safe. You don't want to unwittingly walk into a strike (which in France or Italy is a monthly occurrence). Don't neglect the local press, provided you can read the language; besides, there's often an English edition. These are usually the cheapest newspapers and magazines and the ones most likely to tell you about local security issues as well as events, shopping sales and performances you may not want to miss. For a taste of home, you'll be able to find most major international newspapers in big cities. They're expensive, but sometimes provided for free in nice hotel lobbies. And there's always the internet. Check out your hometown paper on the web from time to time, too; there are usually things going on that your family and friends forget to tell you about.

14

Security

Europe is, for the most part, no more **dangerous** than your local health food store. However, though violent crime is rare, Europe is hardly devoid of thieves. Your rental car and pockets are at risk virtually everywhere if you're not on your toes. To find out how to avoid becoming a victim, read on.

Is my destination safe?

If there's no G8 or World Bank summit in town, your first guess can be "yes". Europe is wonderfully low on homicidal maniacs and civil wars. Nearly all the major guides have good **security information**, but even recently updated ones can't stay up to the minute with security issues. So get the official position of state departments; just keep in mind that a country can be very safe but for a single border dispute or town. Consider London, for example. There are places you wouldn't want to wander in at night, but that doesn't mean the entire city or country should be put on a warning list. The UK Foreign Office website (ⓦwww.fco.gov.uk) is more likely than others to specify the volatile area when they place an entire country on warning; cross-check with Canada's Consular Affairs Department (ⓦwww.voyage.gc.ca), Australia's Department of Foreign Affairs (ⓦwww.dfat.gov.au) or the US State Department (ⓦtravel.state.gov).

If you're still uncertain, surf the web for **tourist bureaus** (ⓦwww .towd.com). You can almost always find an email address of a specific office within that country. The people who staff the counters meet travellers all day and generally have a good feel for travel conditions. Tell them your nationality, when you're planning to travel and roughly where you hope to go. Ask if there are any security issues you should be concerned about. Lastly, check with other travellers. Visit internet chat sites so you can hear directly from travellers who've been there in recent weeks, or are still in the country: try Let's Go's Forum (🌐www.letsgo.com) or Lonely Planet's Thorn Tree (🌐thorntree.lonelyplanet.com).

If the **political conditions** take a turn for the worse, you probably don't want to stick around, no matter how exciting it may seem. And if you're American you probably don't want to go to the US embassy either (often a prime target, so it shuts its doors when the going gets rough). The Australian embassy, Canadian embassy, New Zealand embassy, UK embassy and others should be fine – even for American citizens. The other option is to get out of town immediately (it's rarely a country-wide riot). If you hadn't picked up some discreet local clothes yet, now would be the time. Keep an eye on the local news, and head to an internet café, if necessary, to find English updates.

How to avoid being robbed

The basic trick here is to **blend in**, keep out of areas where you're likely to become a target, stay alert, carry your valuables securely and provide yourself with a quick exit when you need one.

Start by removing all jewellery (if necessary covering a wedding or engagement ring with a band-aid or tape). Wear a cheap digital watch or no watch at all. Keep your camera well concealed. Then you'll want to wear clothing that blends in, the more discreet (earth tones, inexpensive and not ironed) the better. A little tip: safari pants with zip-off legs and a photojournalist vest are generally not what the locals are wearing.

Show that you don't have much to steal – or that you have less than other potential targets. With just a backpack and no carry-on bag, you have both your hands free and can remain mobile for a quick getaway or to give pursuit, so robbing you looks like more of a challenge. If you're travelling with a partner,

Stay alert

I've never had anything stolen in a war zone, but my track record isn't nearly as impressive in developed countries. You're on vacation, your guard is down, and you're thinking, "Hey, I'm a tourist, there's a cop, nothing to worry about." That's when I always get nailed. Heading for a tour of the Vatican, I parked and locked all my possessions in the trunk of my rental car. When I returned, everything was gone except a few rolls of film on the trunk floor.

You have to remember that just like everyone else in civilized countries, Europe's criminals go to work every day. They feast off the herds of roaming tourists, showing up in droves at the same place and same time every year. The crooks get away with it because they use kids for the theft, and keep it mostly nonviolent – so as far as the police are concerned, it's a catch and release sport.

Robert Young Pelton,
Author, *The World's Most Dangerous Places*
🌐www.comebackalive.com

▲ How not to protect your pack while sleeping

make sure one person isn't carrying all the cash and valuables. And at ATMs, have one stand back a bit to guard against someone who might grab and dash. And remember: put nothing (you can't afford to lose) in the overhead compartment on overnight trains. Your pack is your pillow (or at least spoon with it).

Packing for safety

- Keep your money and passport in a **secure travel pouch**, not a handbag or daypack. A money belt (see p.139) under the waistline of your trousers is effective, and similar pouches that hang around your neck (under the shirt) or fasten to your ankle are also available.

- Don't access your pouch in busy areas like train stations and markets. Walk over to a quieter spot (if you have a travel companion, you can make a privacy shield if you stand between them and a wall so that your actions are hidden).

- Use a fake wallet; that is, a cheap wallet with some old cards and some pocket change in it (see p.145). This can prevent a pickpocket from getting at your real valuables and provide you with something to hand over should you ever come face to face with a mugger.

- To protect your slightly-less-valuables, wear your backpack on your front in crowded places and don't use a backpack for a day bag. Better still, use a shoulder bag and keep it tucked tight under your arm in crowded places. Try to find a model with Velcro flaps, which are difficult to open without you noticing, or a double-entry system (eg a zipper plus a clasp). "Bum bags" (waist packs) are thief magnets and as such are best avoided – at least refrain from keeping your valuables there.

- Don't keep all your money in one place. Stash some emergency funds (€50–100) in the secret compartment of a belt, in a dirty sock that few would dare to go near, or tape some (in a small plastic bag) to the inside of your backpack.

Avoiding dangerous areas

Just because Europe is a safe continent doesn't mean every street is safe 24 hours a day. Often, 100m can be the difference between a harmless street and a dangerous one. And these boundaries may change when it gets dark. Ask your hotel clerk or tourist office to mark any danger-ous areas on your map (both day and night). Be particularly aware at night. Muggers can easily hide in doorways, so the closer you are to the street, the less chance they have to surprise you. If you spot one or more suspicious characters in a doorway up ahead, cross the street. Or hop in a taxi if you've got a bad feeling about the area. **Trust your instincts** and always keep enough change ready to pay for a short cab ride. For less than €5, you can quickly get yourself back to a safer area. Otherwise, walk with confidence. When you're in an area you're not sure of, resist the temptation to pull out your map on a street corner. Keep up a brisk pace and duck inside a coffee shop or store to study the map or ask directions.

Accommodation safety

It's not just local thieves – travellers steal as well. Sad, but true. There's little threat to your dirty laundry, but your **valuables** still need to be guarded. And travellers know the value of a brand-name Gore-Tex jacket no matter how crumpled it may look. At night, cameras and such are better left at the reception desk in a safe, in a hostel locker, or behind the counter, but only if there's someone keeping an eye on it and the hostel staff don't appear too shady. Some places also offer the reception safe to travellers who need a place to keep their money belt while at the beach – which is better than taking it along. Otherwise, treat your money belt like your spleen: don't remove it when you go to bed and take it along when you shower – you can hang the pouch on the hook, just under your towel *inside* the shower stall.

Some hotels require your passport for a few hours to gather informa-tion. They should not require it any longer than that. Ask for it back as soon as they're done.

If you're particularly concerned about safety while you sleep, request a room that's not on the ground floor or on the roof, where burglars have easiest access. And don't book a room higher than the seventh floor – the highest ladders on fire trucks stop about there.

Rental car safety

Rental cars are popular targets for thieves, especially at night. There are a few things you can do to make yours less appealing to them. Start by taking the rental sticker off. That's like putting up a neon welcome sign, and thieves may cross the parking lot just to check it out. Take off the face of the radio (most have this feature) and store it out of sight. Empty the car of virtually everything, especially valuables (iPod, camera, etc). Leave the glove compartment open so they can see there's nothing in it and, if there's some sort of screen in the back of a hatchback/wagon, leave that open so they can see the car is empty. If you must leave items in it during the daytime, put them in the boot (trunk). And always ask your hotel receptionist for a safe place to park.

What to do if you have everything stolen

Even if you do lose the lot, it's not the end of the world and you shouldn't let it ruin your trip. It's happened to enough people that a good system is largely in place, so it's not the hassle it used to be. You could very well have everything you need – credit cards, passport and cash – in one to ten days. But **act immediately** to get the process started. Your first job is to file a police report. Go to the nearest police station, report the robbery and ask for a numbered copy of the report. Presenting this at your embassy will expedite the issuance of a new passport. Your insurance company will also want a copy.

You may be waiting a while at the police station for the forms to be processed, so use this time to make phone calls. Try a guidebook, local operator or take a peek at the back page of the *International Herald Tribune* for collect-call numbers. Start with a call to your **travel insurance company** (assuming you have one). A good insurer takes collect calls and keeps you on the line while they cancel your credit cards and have new ones issued. Otherwise, you'll have to cancel them yourself by phone or email. If your insurance or credit card provider doesn't supply **emergency cash**, Western Union (Ⓦ www.westernunion.com) or MoneyGram (Ⓦ www.moneygram.com) can assist, as long as you have someone at the other end to put money in. (Without ID, you can claim money by using a code word given to you by the person sending you funds.) Expect to pay a fee of four to seven percent, depending on location, so sending €1000 will cost around €50.

If you're not going to have copies of your **documents** stored in an online vault (see p.174), you should scan and leave copies of your credit cards, passport, tickets, ID cards, a list of the contents of your backpack with photos of any expensive items (camera, laptop, tent) and insurance papers with your parents and/or trusted friends. Give it to them in a FedEx (or similar) envelope that can be dropped in the mail in an instant or on a disk that can be emailed. Sending documents by email is not secure, but if you decide to do it give the attached file a vague name (for example, "travel stuff"). Do not label it "Visa card" or "Passport number" or include any of that info within the email. At the very least, work out a private code on the phone for a special "dingbat" font or number system.

Then call your **embassy**, tell them what happened and that you'll be on your way over as soon as you get the report. Ask for an appointment or a specific name you can request at the gate to help bypass any queue. If you can, try to get a few passport photos before you show up at the embassy. If you have no copies of your documents or any cash, throw yourself at the mercy of your embassy. If you're travelling with another citizen from your country who has a valid passport, have them come along and vouch for you. And have your friends or parents fax any documents they have (old photo ID, pictures, birth certificate, etc) directly to the embassy.

How to avoid sexual harassment

Most harassers are triggered by appearance, so let's start there. Women travelling alone, especially in southern Europe, should **dress conservatively**. Even if your clothes aren't racy by your own standards, they might send out the wrong signals. Shorts, short skirts, long hair, tank tops and tight-fitting clothes are popular in Europe, as elsewhere. But to avoid getting the attention of the wrong sort of admirer, try to find a modest alternative.

To help fend off would-be suitors, you can always pick up a cheap, simple **ring** when you arrive. You'll need a story to go with it – something about your husband coming to meet you in a day or two. Talk of children can also be off-putting.

For information on hitchhiking safety, see p.57.

That should take care of much of the harassment, but don't be too surprised by the occasional rude remark, catcall or quick pinch in a crowded public place. Do your best to ignore them and keep walking. Or, alternatively, react with clarity and confidence and tell them you don't like it. If you get followed, head into a nearby busy shop and tell the manager.

If you're alone and see a crowded or well-lit area in sight, consider running (but make sure you have shoes that allow you to run). If the harasser chases or grabs you, scream for help. This is, in fact, how most women escape rape. Pleading and stalling are not very effective. Kick in the knees or groin and don't think twice about jabbing him in the eyes. Feel free to use any objects nearby to aid your fight: pen, car aerial, rock or camera.

How to avoid scams

The best trick, really, is just to learn some of the most **common scams**. Con artists are hatching new plans all the time, but they tend to be slightly mutated versions of the ones you'll read about here. Keep your guard up, but not too high. Not all foreigners are out to scam you. Many of their gestures, although odd, are genuine acts of hospitality that you wouldn't likely experience at home. You'll have to learn to trust your instincts.

Cardboard scam

You're walking from one ancient architectural treasure to the next in Rome when a group of kids approaches you, one carrying a big piece of cardboard. The seemingly innocent kids in torn clothes swarm around you while one holds the piece of cardboard to your chest much like you might hold a map (it might even be a map they're showing you). While you're trying to give them a few coins, explain you don't understand, or even back away, the other kids have picked your pockets under the cover of the cardboard. Some aren't even subtle about it, but what are you going to do: push or kick a small child?

How to beat it: when you see them coming, keep a firm hand on your belongings and head quickly in another direction. Throw in a firm "Go away!" if they start to follow.

Local "assistance"

Having trouble with a subway ticket machine, train station locker or ATM? If someone starts offering help before you've had any problems, beware. They get a free look into your wallet or chance to guide you to a locker that they have rigged.

How to beat it: thank them, but refuse help. Look around for someone to ask; chances are you'll find a good Samaritan happy to help within a few seconds.

Credit card scam

A store owner takes your credit card to a back room to swipe it, then swipes it again for another price. You sign one, then he forges your signature on the other.

How to beat it: keep a close eye on your credit card and ask the person to run it through the machine in front of you. Take a business card from the shop when you make any purchases so you can better alert the credit card company in case you later learn you were robbed.

Football moves scam

A friendly guy on the street offers to show you a cool football move. It results in you being knocked over and mugged.

How to beat it: decline any offers for demonstrations of contact sports and walk away immediately.

"Drug-buy" scam

Especially common for those heading over to Morocco for a quick visit: you buy a small amount of hashish from a local dealer, then he tips off his buddy, the police officer, who comes knocking at your door to demand a fee for not taking you to prison.

How to beat it: it's a dangerous game of chicken. You can pay the fine, try to bargain a little, or call their bluff and tell them you have no money, you were set up and that you're happy to go to police headquarters and explain it. Best just to avoid buying the drugs in the first place. If you absolutely must, make sure other travellers have bought from the person previously.

Taxi dash scam

You've paid your taxi and the driver leaves before you can get your bag out of the boot.

How to beat it: leave your door open or don't pay up until you've got your bag.

"Fake travel agent" scam

You buy a ticket from a travel agency you found on the web in your own country or even in Europe (most likely in London). The ticket never arrives, and when you try to call you find out the place has gone out of business.

How to beat it: make sure you're signing up with an accredited agency. In Australia, check with the Australian Federation of Travel Agents (Ⓦwww.afta.com.au); in Canada, the Association of Canadian

Travel Agencies (@www.acta.ca); in the UK, the Travel Association (@www.abta.com); and in the US, the American Society of Travel Agents (@www.asta.org). And pay with a credit card so you can stop payment, if necessary.

Help from your embassy or consulate

If you think of your government's embassies, consulates and high commissions as a **safety net**, you're liable to slip through one of the holes. They can't do much if you've been arrested for violating local laws, and they won't help send you home or give you a place to sleep if you run out of money. They can, however, help you in the event of a lost or stolen passport. They can also provide contact information during emergencies; give you the latest travel advice; allow you to register your travel plans if you're heading into areas for risky adventures (don't forget to check back in); and assist with overseas marriage and birth documents. And most of them make excellent cocktails, should you manage to attend one of their functions – consider swinging by if you're in the neighbourhood during a national holiday.

15

Health

urope is hardly a Petri dish of virulent microkillers waiting to pounce on unsuspecting travellers. In fact, many of the vaccinations and precautions suggested below are also recommended to European travellers heading to your country. The things you should concern yourself with are actually quite basic: get your pre-trip health details in order before you leave (including any necessary immunizations); take some fundamental precautions; keep an eye out for specific symptoms, and get yourself to a doctor if you encounter any of them. Despite the tales you may have heard, many of the common illnesses are avoidable or easily curable with some of the basic information you'll find in this chapter. If you want more details, get hold of a copy of *The Rough Guide to Travel Health*.

Health warnings for Europe

According to the Centers for Disease Control and Prevention (CDC), **diarrhoea** is the top illness among travellers in Europe and motor vehicle crashes the leading cause of injury. There's risk of salmonella, cholera (in Eastern Europe only, and only where there are public warnings), hepatitis, *E. coli*-associated diarrhoea, tick-borne encephalitis (certain areas) and Lyme disease (certain areas). Read on to see which vaccinations you need.

Pre-departure checkup

Far too many travellers neglect basic **pre-trip medical arrangements** and suffer needlessly as a consequence. Your first order of business is a **checkup**. Don't make the common mistake of putting this off till the last minute. A month or two before departure is a more sensible time to schedule an appointment (though some vaccinations require

⑮

▲ Traveller's tummy is one of the most common travel ailments

more time before they start working). If the doctor finds something during the checkup and wants you to come back for a second consultation, your next-day flight is buggered. Besides, you'll want to get your checkup before you start getting your vaccinations. Some vaccinations should not be given if you have so much as a cold, or if you're taking other medications. Make sure to ask for a copy of your clean bill of health to take along so you don't have to pay for one again if you end up working or volunteering for an organization that requires such a document.

Schedule a visit to the **dentist** as well. It would be a serious setback to get a gnawing tooth problem while you're in a country like Romania or Turkey, which are not exactly world-renowned epicentres of dentistry. Needless to say, getting this taken care of beforehand is a lot cheaper than flying home to do it.

If you wear glasses or contacts, you'll want to swing by the **optician**. Make sure you have enough contacts and fluid to keep you going (you can always send some lenses ahead as well). Glasses are important backups, even if you never wear them at home – you may find yourself in dusty environments where contacts don't function well. If you're trying to decide between two frames for your glasses, take the most durable, even if they're not the most flattering. Make sure you bring along a copy of your prescription and your optician's telephone number in case you need emergency replacements on the road or ordered from home.

Vaccinations

Once you decide the jabs you want (visit the CDC's website, ⓦwww .cdc.gov, or its European equivalent at ⓦecdc.europa.eu, for updated info), call around to make sure you get a good price. A full course of shots might set you back around €200 in the US. If your country has a national health plan, a number of the shots (such as hepatitis A and polio) may fall under that policy and can be received free from your GP.

Confirm the information you get from the CDC with the doctor or clinic administering the shots, and be sure to inform them of any medical conditions (even allergies) and medications (including the contraceptive pill) you're taking. Also, explain where you'll be staying and how long you'll be there.

Some vaccinations, such as hepatitis B, require a **course of shots** over six months to take effect, so don't leave it until the last minute, or even the last month. If you're getting several jabs, bear in mind that you may not be able to get them all on the same day. They may conflict with one another, require more than one injection or take time to become effective. However, if you're not entirely sure where you're headed, you don't need to get every needle in the cabinet. Vaccinations are all available on the road. Just make sure the clinic looks clean and professionally run, and that it uses sterile needles. If you have the option, try to get this taken care of in more developed countries.

Get a **vaccination record card** and keep it with your passport while travelling. It's nice to have it to hand. With all these mega-syllabic names, it's hard to remember what you got, what you didn't want to get but got anyway, and what you were going to get but decided not to get at the last moment.

Update your basic vaccinations

Start by dusting off your medical records to see which boosters you're going to need.

Diphtheria

You'll definitely want to make sure you're vaccinated against this bacterial illness. It's passed person to person quicker than an email chain letter, and typical unpleasantness includes fever, chills and a sore throat. Eventually, it can cause heart failure and paralysis. Be aware that if someone you know has it, they're highly infectious for ten days. Seek medical help if you suspect it; a quick throat swab can determine if you've got it or not.

> ### What if I don't get any shots?
>
> No one says you have to. You'll still get into Europe just as immuno-under equipped as you are now. And you'll most likely do just fine. European travellers don't always follow the advice of getting a Hep A shot when going to the US (or bringing a bulletproof vest) and still make it home alive. The idea is that a little inconvenience now will help prevent a major hassle later. It's like giving your car a tune-up, oil change and new air filter before a big road trip. Only, when it's your motor that's at risk, and not the car's, the stakes are substantially higher.

Tetanus

You've probably been vaccinated against this already. However, you may be due for your ten-year update. Check your records to be sure the **booster** is taken care of. With tetanus, spores enter the body through open wounds as small as a pinprick, and can be picked up through contact with dirt, manure and – the classic – rusty nails. You won't get the symptoms for five to twenty days, but the one that should get your attention (and any doctor's) are spasms of the jaw muscle. Those will spread across your face and into your torso, and that's when things get really nasty. It is potentially fatal, so if you recognize these symptoms yourself, get thee to a hospital immediately.

Other possible vaccinations

Cholera

Only found in parts of Eastern Europe during outbreaks, this particularly unpleasant diarrhoeal disease is caused by consumption of contaminated water or shellfish. When you hear warnings about it (it seems to follow natural disasters and wars), avoid the area if possible and be very careful what you eat (no ice, only bottled water; no raw food unless peeled). There's no vaccination recommended by the CDC for this, but two relatively new oral vaccines (Dukoral and Mutacol) have proven effective (85–90 percent immunity within six months of taking the vaccination, decreasing to 62 percent immunity after three years) and should be considered if you're heading to areas where outbreaks are occurring. Because the vaccine is new, it may not be available everywhere.

Hepatitis A

This is a shot I'd get. It'll come in handy if you're planning on eating seafood (particularly shellfish) in southern Europe, where high temperatures and dodgy refrigeration can provide ideal breeding grounds for the disease. Contaminated water and people (who don't wash their hands well) also pass this bowel blaster along. Good news: there's a vaccination. One jab of a Havrix vaccine will last a year. Follow it up with a second injection six to twelve months later and you're good to go for a decade. The downside is it takes nearly a month after the first dose to take effect. The more traditional gamma globulin shot works right away, and provides protection for three to six months. There is also a Hep A and Hep B combination called Twinrix, which will also give you ten years of immunity. It

Where medications are listed, you'll only find the generic medical name. These are known by various commercial names in different countries. Simply check the label or consult your pharmacist or doctor.

Travelling with immunodeficiency

If you have special health considerations that render you immuno-compromised, keep in mind that the bacteria and bugs that affect all travellers may have a more profound effect on you. Less developed countries in particular pose significant risks for exposure to opportunistic pathogens. Your consulate or the International Association of Medical Assistance to Travellers (Ⓦ www.iamat.org) can provide trained English-speaking physicians in Europe.

Vaccinations

The CDC currently recommends that "killed vaccines" such as diphtheria, tetanus and hepatitis A are OK for "healthy" HIV-infected travellers. However, the degree of immunity after a vaccination may vary with the degree of immunodeficiency caused by the HIV. For more information, visit Ⓦ www.cdc.gov

Medications

Discussing an emergency plan with your doctor prior to departure is an excellent idea. The CDC advises all HIV-infected travellers heading to Bulgaria, Romania and Turkey to bring an antimicrobial such as ciprofloxacin (500mg twice a day for three to seven days) for empirical therapy for diarrhoea, although alternatives (such as TMP-SMX) should be discussed with a doctor. If the diarrhoea does not respond to this treatment, there is blood in the stools, fever and shaking chills, or dehydration, get to a doctor.

Going through customs

If you are carrying a full array of HIV drugs, or just the virus, be aware that some European countries have vague restrictions preventing those with "communicable diseases" from entering. So, faced with an inquisitive customs officer holding your medications, you might offer other half-truths about the things you're suffering from first (such as liver/heart/kidney problems), and delay mentioning HIV. If you're staying for an extended period to work or study, you may face a serological screen in many countries. Check out the unofficial list compiled by the US State Department at Ⓦ www.travel.state .gov/travel/HIVtestingreqs.html

normally takes six months to get all three shots taken care of, but you can ask for an accelerated schedule that will do the job in 21 days. If you opt for this, you'll need a booster shot after a year. Or ask your doctor about Hepatyrix, fifteen-year protection against Hep A and typhoid in one stab.

Hepatitis B

This vaccine is recommended for healthcare professionals, but it's transmitted through sexual contact and needles, so if you're planning on some heavy romance or heavy knitting (in the vicinity of drug users), it's probably worth the extra jab. Even if you're just considering a tattoo, it's not a bad idea. The vaccination is a bit of a drag – three jabs over seven months – but well worth it for a long trip. For those who put it off to the last minute, it's possible to get three jabs in three weeks with an additional booster, but this is slightly less effective. As previously noted, there's also the Hep A and Hep B combination jab Twinrix to consider, which will give you ten years of immunity.

Vaccination roundup

Cholera

Full course Two oral doses
Booster One week apart ("killed vaccine") or one single oral dose ("live vaccine")
Comments Eighty-five to ninety percent protection for six months after two doses of killed vaccine; 62 percent after three years. Considered for people going to endemic areas. Should be taken at least three weeks (one week for live vaccine) before departure. Avoid antibiotics and malaria prophylaxis with proguanil one week before and one week after cholera vaccine.
Time before effective immunity One week after final dose

Hepatitis A

Full course Single dose
Booster After 6–12 months
Comments Gives good protection for at least twelve months; booster protection lasts more than ten years
Time before effective immunity One month

Hepatitis A (immunoglobin type)

Full course Single dose
Booster Only gives protection for 2–6 months, depending on dose
Comments Needs to be given close to departure
Time before effective immunity Immediately

Hepatitis B (optional)

Full course Two doses one month apart, plus a third dose six months later
Booster Provides protection for at least ten years; booster dose is not recommended for adults with intact immune system
Comments More rapid three-week courses are available if you're close to departure, but this gives lower immunity and requires a booster after twelve months
Time before effective immunity One month after final dose

Rabies (optional)

Full course Three doses over one month
Booster After 2–3 years
Comments Pre-exposure immunization gives greater protection but does not eliminate the need for prompt treatment if bitten by a rabid animal
Time before effective immunity Two weeks after completed course

Tetanus

Full course Three doses: leave four to eight weeks between first and second doses; third dose six to twelve months after second. Usually given with diphtheria
Booster Every ten years
Comments Full course usually given in childhood. If pressed for time before departure, only first and second dose can be given
Time before effective immunity A few days after third – or second, if only two can be given – dose

Tick-borne encephalitis

Full course Two doses over a month
Booster After 1–3 years
Comments Fever a common side effect after first dose. Not needed for children under 7. Get in Europe once you arrive, if necessary
Time before effective immunity Ten days after final dose

Rabies

The CDC recommends this one, but a lot of people survive in Europe without it. If you steer clear of packs of wild dogs in Istanbul and strays in rural areas, you'll probably be fine. Always enquire about a dog's biting habits before petting – it's cheaper than getting the vaccine (three shots over a month, plus another two if bitten, scratched or even licked by a rabid animal), but possibly not as effective. Without the vaccine, you're looking at nearly twice as many shots – although no longer the nasty ones in the stomach. If you have an encounter with an animal that puts you at risk, get tested immediately.

Tick-borne encephalitis

This viral infection of the central nervous system comes from tick bites and is untreatable. The CDC says it exists in Central and Western Europe, but that doesn't mean it's everywhere. For example, if you're going to Stockholm, you're not at risk. But if you're planning a kayaking trip down the east coast of Sweden, where you'll be camping in the forest, you are. Some Stockholmers who live in these tick-infested areas in the woods get the vaccination. Others chance it. Removing the tick doesn't work – if you find one, you may be too late. But just one tick bite is very unlikely to bring on the virus, and only one in 250 who get infected develop the symptoms. For those who do, it starts out like flu, and then causes dizziness, tremors and paralysis. The risk is seasonal, occurring when ticks are out and about: May to September.

What you can't get vaccinated against

These are the ones you'll have to watch out for, and may just get anyway. Some maladies are more common than others and some more severe, so read through the descriptions to get acquainted with the symptoms and dangers you may face.

AIDS/HIV

You've probably heard an earful about this already, but it can be caught in Europe as well – something to consider before you have unprotected sex or share a needle.

Allergies

If you experience allergies at home, you'll probably encounter them on the road. Watery eyes, a runny nose, sneezing . . . you know how it goes. Pack an **antihistamine** (chlorpheniramine or loratadine) to relieve the symptoms. If these don't help, visit a doctor.

For a list of basic medical supplies you should take with you, see p.133.

Altitude sickness

This is more dangerous than most people believe, especially when those who don't have it are egging you on to keep going up. "High altitude" is considered 2438–3658m; "very high altitude" is 3658–5487m. If your head feels like it's about to implode or you're dizzier than a wino trapped on a Ferris wheel, then head down the mountain. It doesn't mean making a beeline for the bottom (unless it has reached a critical stage), but **descent** of some kind is vital. Usually, the symptoms will abate after just a small drop in altitude, and you may even be able to continue once your body has adjusted at its own pace.

Fitness is only one factor: you could be a champion triathlete or an Olympian on performance-enhancing drugs and still get a case of altitude sickness worse than the couch potato with a liver condition hiking beside you. Follow a careful **acclimatization** plan and, most importantly, listen to your body. Diamox (acetazolamide) is most useful as a high-altitude sickness preventative, but will require a doctor's prescription. Take 125mg (half a tablet) twice a day for two days at sea level a few weeks before the trip. If your body accepts the drug without side effects, take the same dose for three days just before heading to 3500m and continue taking it for two or three days until you feel acclimatized. Do not take it for more than five days.

Bed bugs

These aren't merely bedtime-story myths. They're out there, typically in the cheapest hotels, and they do bite. The bites aren't serious, but they seriously itch. And you'd have a better chance spotting Elvis than some of these critters (they hide during daylight, though you might be able to spot small black or brown spots of dried insect excrement). Your best defence is a good **sleepsheet**: make sure it's big enough to cover the pillow as well. A tight weave should keep most of them out. Failing that, they hate light so you could always sleep with the light on if that's an option. The bites look like two or three little red dots in a row. Treat with hydrocortisone or antihistamine cream and – easier said than done – refrain from scratching. Also, wash all your clothes and sleep sheet in hot water (60°C) if you suspect you may have been exposed.

Cold sores

Don't kiss people with lip sores or blisters. Don't share water bottles with them either. There's really nothing cold about these sores, which are actually herpes picked up by **oral contact** (fellatio and cunnilingus included). If you get one, you've got a recurring menace for life, often triggered by too much direct sunlight. To keep the sores at bay, keep your lips well glossed while exposed to the sun and apply aciclovir cream (may require prescription) as soon as you feel the tingling sensation coming on (apply five times a day for five days). Once the sore breaks open, the medicine won't help.

Constipation

Travellers get all worked up over diarrhoea, but forget about an opposite ailment that is nearly as uncomfortable and troublesome. Travellers who are new to the trail and spending time in Eastern and southeastern Europe are especially susceptible. They take one look at a squat toilet (or even an unsanitary Western version) and suddenly they don't need to go any more. A few days later, the mental block has become an intestinal one. This can often be solved by trying some natural **laxatives** (coffee, prune juice, psyllium seed). Better yet, make yourself go when you have the urge, no matter what the loo looks like. And a little diet altering won't hurt: more fruit, bran and fluids.

Dehydration

The trick here is to **drink before you get thirsty**. For a full day of walking in, say, Rome, you should be drinking about four litres of water. In the Alps, you'll need even more, and wind masks the amount you're sweating away. Once you're dehydrated, you'll experience a dry mouth, dark urine, headache and, in extreme cases, fainting. Find some shade, take it easy and mix your water with a rehydration

Gastro-intestinally challenged

You can travel the world and never get a single bout of dysentery. For that matter, you can also find a customer service representative who actually cares about your two-hour flight delay.

When I started travelling, there weren't many more fearful eaters than me. I followed the conventional wisdom of "cook it, boil it, peel it or forget it". And when that wasn't possible, I sought refuge under the wrapper of a Big Mac or – as a last resort – in an all-beer diet.

My first gastro-intestinal challenge (still not sure what caused it) lasted about a week and made me even more meticulous about what passed my lips: no ice in my bottled drinks, only reputable restaurants, no street food. Like many other travellers, I was far more willing to bungy jump, mountain climb and white-water raft than eat a fried grasshopper.

After a few months, another traveller set me straight, "Whatever you do, don't try to ride it out. Get tested. Immediately." It may be the best travel advice I've ever received, acting as a sort of insurance for gastronomic experimentation.

Armed with this knowledge, the only reason you should be spending a week in an uncomfortable squatting position is if you decide to circumnavigate Europe on budget airlines.

The most noticeable side effects of this were huge savings (less bottled water, much more cheap street food) and an enriching culinary journey that ran parallel to my trip. In every town, I began to make an effort to seek out the local dishes and snacks. What I had dismissed as foolish risk-taking was now one of the highlights of my travels.

Doug Lansky

www.roughguides.com

solution so you get your salt balance back, and if fluid can't be taken orally get to a hospital for an IV.

Diarrhoea

The good news is that it's most often treatable and the troublesome symptoms can be cured in less than a day. The following advice may save you a week of traumatic toilet dashes and, as such, this book will have paid for itself a few times over. You'll meet numerous travellers suffering from diarrhoea for days or weeks. The typical reason is that they're trying to ride it out. You want to do exactly the opposite.

The moment you start to "go liquid", drink a bottle of water mixed with a packet of rehydration mix that you should be carrying in your first-aid kit. And keep drinking. The biggest danger with diarrhoea is **dehydration**. The next biggest risk is that you sit by the toilet for days waiting for the diarrhoea to abate. As soon as possible, bring a little plastic film canister (or something similar) and put a **stool sample** in it. Either take the sample to a nearby clinic yourself or have a trusted fellow traveller do it for you if you can't risk leaving a toilet for that long. With a quick look under the microscope, a doctor will most often be able to identify the cause. If so, they'll write a prescription on the spot, which will likely include the pharmaceutical equivalent of a cork. Less than a day after you start taking the medicine, you may feel back to normal, or at least better. While recovering, stick to simple, unspiced foods like rice for a day or two just in case. Little tip: carry an anti-diarrhoea pill (such as Loperamide) in your money belt. If you're on a long bus ride with your pack in the baggage bin underneath or you're walking around town, it will come in handy more than you can imagine. Women travellers should be aware that diarrhoea can reduce the effectiveness of the contraceptive pill.

E. coli diarrhoea (aka food poisoning)

You may hear this name tossed about. It also goes by its given name of *Escherichia coli*, and it is about the most common type of diarrhoea, though it comes in several different strains. It's about as nice to contract as it is to spell. Often picked up from eating undercooked, contaminated ground beef, it can also be passed from person to person. Drinking raw milk and swimming in or drinking sewage-contaminated water may also do the trick. The infection makes itself known with bloody diarrhoea. Hang out with people who wash their hands carefully.

Hepatitis C

Less common than Hep A and Hep B (but with no vaccination), to catch this one requires contact with contaminated blood, which means stay alert where any needles are concerned. It can be spread by sexual activity, but this is rare. Symptoms include dark urine, nausea, jaundice, abdominal pain and loss of appetite.

Hiking blisters

The face of Mont Blanc is not the ideal place to try out a new pair of hiking boots. If you buy or rent some, give yourself at least a day or two for your feet to adjust (especially with new boots). For serious treks, make sure you bring Compeed (a skin-like blister cover), sport tape, Vaseline, or a silicon spray and a needle (with antiseptic to sterilize) to drain **blisters**. Always make sure to puncture the blister in the centre, not on the sides where the skin is more sensitive. Also, give them as much time to dry out as possible before taping them up again. Some people have success with a needle and thread, leaving the thread in the opening for better drainage. Tape can be applied in advance to trouble spots, then sprayed with silicon. Two pairs of socks are advisable, neither of them cotton. Polypropylene or silk (next to the skin) and wool (or Smartwool) make an excellent combination.

Infected cuts and scrapes

In humid coastal environments, cuts don't tend to heal that fast. They're easily infected and can actually grow in size. So if you pick up some scooter road rash around the Med, head up to the Alps where it can more easily dry and heal. Visit a doctor if you're unable to stop the growth of the wound on your own.

Jet lag

It's a fancy way of saying you spent your flight over watching a B-movie or glued to a book instead of getting much-needed sleep. An alarming number of travellers don't take simple steps to combat jet lag, and are then plagued by fatigue for days (typically, one day per time zone crossed), starting off their trip on the wrong foot. If you can **sleep** on the plane and get a good night's sleep the first night in the new time zone, you're not going to experience much, if any, jet lag. Sleeping on the plane, if you're not naturally gifted at the art, can be achieved with an over-the-counter or prescribed sleeping pill.

According to studies, drinking **alcohol** is exactly the wrong approach. The next worst thing you can do is stay up late. There's no reason to eat dinner at 11pm, then watch a movie at midnight simply because you're at 30,000ft. Eat a meal in the airport, pop the sleeping pill when the plane leaves the ground and drink plenty of water when you wake up. Once you've arrived, refrain from naps (this is a great chance to try some of that strong European coffee) until bedtime (when the locals sleep), and take another sleeping pill if you wake up during that first night, or pop a Melatonin tablet (available by prescription only in the UK and NZ) before bed to ensure you sleep a little longer. Arnica tablets are also reputed to alleviate jet lag.

www.roughguides.com

Lyme disease

Ticks carrying the disease are found in the forest, long grass and trees, waiting for a host animal (typically deer, but humans will suffice) to pass by. The ticks need around 24 hours attached to your body to transfer the disease, so, if you give yourself a good check a few times daily, you'll spot them in time. You'll have to check in hard-to-view places, though, including the hair on your head as well. If you miss it at the time then you'll notice a few days or weeks later, when the classic "bull's eye" appears at the bite site. It can affect the nervous system, joints and heart, and can become very serious if not treated (with amoxycillin or doxycycline).

Motion sickness

It's not serious, but it's bad enough to ruin a day or two of your trip. On a winding bus ride, try to sit near the front and next to a window or air vent (motion sickness is also related to breathing exhaust fumes). Make sure you get out to stretch your legs whenever the bus stops. On a boat, stay above deck and try looking at the horizon. Take deep, relaxing breaths or simply try to stay busy. And, in any event, have a motion sickness pill or a skin patch (such as Hyoscine or Scopolamin) ready just in case. It takes at least an hour before the effects of these pills are noticeable, so you may need to take them in advance of boarding.

Rashes

You'll be encountering plants, fruits and bugs that your skin has never been exposed to before. It's common for travellers to experience a host of new body art. Try applying topical antihistamine, calamine lotion or steroid creams (hydrocortisone) to the area. If it persists, visit a local doctor.

Salmonella

This is the one most commonly associated with eating undercooked chicken. Or when the cooks forget to wash their hands after a trip to the toilet. The food gets contaminated from animal (or human) faeces. And here's the scary part: you won't be able to smell or taste infected food. Most of those who get salmonella develop diarrhoea, fever and abdominal cramps 12 to 72 hours after infection. That's the bad news. The upside is that most people recover without treatment (four to seven days). However, if the person becomes severely dehydrated (see p.195) or the infection spreads from the intestine, it should be treated promptly with antibiotics (such as ampicillin or gentamicin).

STDs

Just because you're choosy about whom you have sex with, doesn't mean *they* were. And once is all it takes to wake up with syphilis (which is resurging), gonorrhoea, chlamydia, chancroid, trichomoniasis or herpes. **Symptoms** include: a rash on the palms, unusual vaginal or penile discharge, pain when passing urine, itching, abnormal vaginal bleeding and genital ulceration. There's only one thing to do if you get any of these: go to a doctor. With chlamydia, it's a little trickier. Most women don't know they have it. Some never find out. Some only learn of it at an infertility clinic while trying to find out why they can't get pregnant. A condom is your best defence.

Sunburn

Sunscreen keeps you from burning, but it also keeps people out in the sun longer with more UV exposure, and the long-term effects of this are yet to be determined. Still, burning is bad. So get in the habit of using **sun block** (minimum SPF 25) and reapplying it frequently. For those on medications, note that some reduce your skin's ability to fend off the sun's powerful rays: ciprofloxacin, tetracycline group antibiotics, sulphonylurea (taken for diabetes) and thiazide (taken for high blood pressure).

Vaginal thrush

Warm climates, tight nylon underwear and increased sexual activity are among the factors that lead to a higher incidence of yeast infections on the travel circuit. Men who carry the fungus rarely show any signs of it. For women, soreness, discomfort during sex, pain while urinating, and passing a white or yellowish discharge are among the symptoms. It's easily treated by an antifungal preparation that should be straightforward to find in most countries, but you may want to carry one just in case. In a jam, try applying regular plain yoghurt and altering your diet briefly: no sugars, breads, beer, wine, mushrooms, Vegemite or other yeast-containing or yeast-encouraging foods.

If you do get sick

Here's the basic approach: with a high fever, loose stools or vomiting – anything very painful or unusual – **get to a doctor** and have blood and/or stool tests conducted. It's generally quick and cheap and far better than trying to weather it. With a quick diagnosis and the right medicine, you could be feeling fine within a day or so.

This is also a great time to check into a decent **hotel** with a private toilet and phone. You owe it to yourself and your fellow travellers. Hostel dormitories are not meant as recovery wards (beyond temporary alcohol-related afflictions). When you check in, tell the desk clerk that you're not feeling well and see if they have a doctor who can pay you a visit. You can always ring for an ambulance or taxi if things take a turn for the worse.

If things seem serious, **don't take chances**. Get yourself to a hospital and contact your family and travel insurance company. If you're in a remote area, get to a major city immediately.

16

Travellers with special considerations

For many, just navigating your way around Europe – or even just one large city – with transport strikes, spaceship-like pay toilets and incomprehensible menus is challenge enough. But there are some groups who must also cope with a number of issues, from a medical condition to sexual-preference discrimination. If you fall into one of these groups, this chapter focuses on the concerns you might face and offers a few tips that will hopefully smooth out your journey.

Senior travellers

Retirement can be a perfect time in your life to travel, and you don't need to be in outstanding physical condition, as long as you plan your trip well and stay prepared. There are a number of speciality items available these days – from lightweight canes that can be collapsed and stored in a handbag to inflatable back-support rests – that can make a mild trip comfortable and a rough ride tolerable.

Health

When planning your itinerary, consider the **medical facilities** of the country you're visiting. The Netherlands or Denmark, for example, will have a more modern healthcare system than Bulgaria or Estonia.

Consider the **temperature** of the places you're headed. Even if you've experienced such sweltering heat before, it can be another thing entirely if you're out walking in it most of the day or staying in places without air conditioning. And air-con in Europe is less common than it is in the US or Australia.

If you're concerned about **pre-existing ailments**, discuss them with your doctor before leaving and come up with a game plan if you spot symptoms en route. Depending on your case, it may not be a bad idea to bring a copy of your medical file along, or at least the relevant pages. Check your medical insurance for travel coverage and supplement it with any special travel insurance you may need (see p.114).

Medications

Bring your **prescriptions** if you want to get refills, but ask your doctor to include the generic name, since some brand-name prescriptions are not available abroad. Keep medicines in their original labelled container to avoid problems at customs and have the prescriptions handy; the label on the plastic bottle is not always enough, especially if you're transporting stronger pain medications, which may require a special permit obtained at the pharmacy. If you need medication refilled in an emergency, a good travel **insurance plan** will assist. And keep the phone number of your doctor and pharmacist with you for backup.

Security

Europe is a very safe place to travel. Perhaps as safe as or even safer than where you live. However, seniors are especially vulnerable to **theft** while travelling. It is perceived that your guard is down more often, you're more likely to be carrying valuables and are less likely to give chase or fight back. To combat this, take special notice of the tips in the "Security" chapter (see p.178). As always, you can best avoid putting yourself at risk by carrying very little and disguising what you do have. Then take special care when and where you wander. Get good information from the reception clerk on which areas are dangerous and which to avoid after dark.

Discounts

There's enough material to write an entire book on **senior discounts**. In fact, someone has. Actually, several have. One of the things that seems to get better with age is the number of rebates available. Seniors might get anything up to fifty percent off museums and other sites, and local transport. Look for notices at ticket windows, check your guidebook, and get into the habit of asking.

Flights

On airlines, the magic discount age is usually 60 or 62. Rates vary, but you can typically get ten percent off "the lowest published fare" (and that's exactly how you should phrase it when you ring a travel agent). Not only that, but you're often allowed to bring someone of any age along at the same rate. Several struggling airlines have cut back senior discounts lately, but it never hurts to ask since they are still available, if only for select destinations or times.

Accommodation

There's nothing that says you have to be a youth to stay in a **youth hostel**. In fact, in many of the calmer hostels, senior travellers far out-number the youths. International Youth Hostel cards for seniors cost just €10–15 if you've turned 55. There are also special organizations, such as the non-profit-making Elderhostel (ⓦwww.elderhostel.org), which run trips around the world for those aged 55 and older. For roughly €90 a day, you get a room, food, educational classes on a variety of subjects and the chance to meet plenty of like-minded, interesting people. Seniors may also be offered ten to fifty percent off normal rates at major hotels (and some minor ones) across Europe. Always enquire when you book.

Travel agents

- **50+ Expeditions** Adventure trips for the over-50 set ready to hit the road. ⓦwww.50plusexpeditions.com
- **CARP** Not the most inviting acronym, CARP is an online community for Canadians over 50, with its own travel agency. ⓦwww.50plus.com/travel
- **Saga** Guided tours, cruises and adventure holidays for "today's over 50s". ⓦwww.saga.co.uk/travel
- **Senior Women's Travel** They bury the "old lady" image for the 50+ set with a thirst for active travel. ⓦwww.poshnosh.com
- **Wired Seniors** Under "Travel guide", they have lists of "senior-friendly" travel agents and hotels. ⓦwww.wiredseniors.com

Travellers with disabilities

If you can get to the store to pick up this book, don't let anybody tell you that you're not physically able to get to Europe. There's going to be more planning than an able-bodied person may face, more hassles, and you may have to give up more independence than you'd prefer at times, but if you're prepared to accept this the rewards are immeasurable.

Some parts of Europe will be better suited to deal with your disability than others. But no matter how much planning you manage, you'll still need to **prepare yourself for the unexpected**: unstable or missing handrails, faulty ramps, narrow passages, and assigned assistants with little training and even less enthusiasm. Greet them with good humour and look for ways to solve the problems on the spot.

What you can do to prepare

Much depends on your degree of disability, and no one has a better grasp of that than you. Stay in control of your options. An activity that may not be a possibility for someone else could be fine for you. But if a travel agent or tour operator hears that you're disabled first, they may decide which things are suitable and present you with an inappropriately limited selection. In other words, look into things you'd like to do, then ask questions to find out if you can be accommodated. Don't simply look for "disabled activities".

Before you begin your trip, whether you're joining a tour or doing it alone, think about ways to enhance the experience of travel and **remove potential obstacles**. For example, a deaf person may wish to purchase a rail pass in advance to avoid the hassle of buying individual tickets at a station counter, and a vision-impaired traveller might pick up souvenir replicas of the famous monuments once they arrive to help get a better feel of the structures they're standing in front of. Consider activities that can be done on an equal level. For those in a wheelchair, a cultural show, botanical gardens and recommended restaurant should take minimal preparation beyond confirming that they can accommodate you where stairs and doorways are concerned.

What you'll face

In most European countries, **accessibility** will range from excellent to completely nonexistent. However, there should be a fundamental infrastructure in place and your requests for assistance will often find an experienced ear. In less developed countries, expect to find little infrastructure, if any at all. What you may experience, however, is a refreshing abundance of helpers with an enlightened indifference toward disability. On the other hand, you may feel like a novelty act at times. If so, keep in mind that you may be one of the first independent disabled people that locals have seen. And even if it doesn't seem appreciated at the time, the inspiring tale of seeing you will likely find its way to those locals with disabilities who need to hear it most.

Most of Europe's great attractions are accessible to all. A few aren't or are at least extremely difficult for manoeuvring, like the tower of

Notre-Dame. At such times, you'll either have to content yourself with a view from afar, have a travelling companion record it on a camcorder and replay it on the spot, or seek alternative activities.

It's not impossible to find accessible toilets, but it may not be easy everywhere you go. Make sure there's one at your hotel. These websites should prove useful:

- **Mobility International USA** Sponsors international exchange programs for people with disabilities, and sells books and even a DVD/video (All Abroad) to help those with disabilities cope on the road. ⓦwww.miusa.org
- **The Society for Accessible Travel and Hospitality** A nonprofit organization with membership and a magazine and special deals for seniors and students. ⓦwww.sath.org
- **Britain's Royal Association for Disability and Rehabilitation** Publishes a guide for disabled people in Britain and Ireland, with over 1400 places to stay in the UK and Ireland. ⓦwww.radar.org.uk

Getting around

Around Europe, **trains** may just be the best of your options. The Thomas Cook Timetable or individual country rail websites (see the country profiles for these) detail which trains are specially equipped to handle wheelchairs.

Next in this somewhat sorry selection is **air travel**. The toilets may be impossibly narrow and the seats painfully uncomfortable, but at least it's generally the quickest option. Always call the airline well in advance if you need any special assistance. If you have a wheelchair, let them know which kind and be prepared for a transfer to a special aisle-sized chair. At All Go Here (ⓦwww.allgohere.com), there's a list of airlines that cater for those with disabilities, with detailed information on what they do.

Taxis are usually the most convenient and most comfortable option for getting around a city, but also the most expensive. In some enlightened cities (Stockholm, for example), there are elevators that take wheelchairs down to the subway at every station (though most underground transit systems are ill-equipped) and buses that dip down and provide space to roll on.

With assistance, the transport possibilities are as limitless as your imagination. If you need some inspiration, pick up Patrick Simpson's book *Wheelchair Around the World*.

If you're not ready to go it alone, there are **tour agencies** for the disabled:

- **Accessible Europe** Has a collection of European travel agents and tour operators who specialize in disabled travel. ⓦwww .accessibleurope.com
- **Flying Wheels Travel** Specialize in escorted and disabled tours. ⓦwww.flyingwheelstravel.com

Where to stay

Not all hotels and hostels have special facilities, but many do. Often, the local tourist bureau is well versed with this information. Find them at ⓦwww.towd.com.

Access-Able (ⓦwww.access-able.com) has a database of hotels that accommodate those with disabilities, plus listings of places where you can rent special medical equipment and get it repaired.

- **Hostelling International** Has a listing on its website of the hostels that can accommodate disabled guests. ⓦwww.hiusa.org
- **Independent Living's Accessible Vacation Home Exchange** Helps those with disabilities swap homes with similarly disabled Europeans. ⓦwww.independentliving.org/vacaswap.html

Gay travellers

It's certainly much easier now for gay people to travel openly than it was twenty years ago, with scores of guidebooks, travel publications and websites devoted to gay travel (for example, *Spartacus International Gay Guides*, *OutTraveler Magazine*, ⓦwww.gaytravel.com, ⓦwww.gay.com). And Europe offers numerous social scenes, depending on what you're looking for.

Europe is about as enlightened as a continent gets, but that doesn't mean that **public affection** is welcomed in all settings. Holding hands won't land you in jail, but it can do more than turn a few heads, even in socially liberal cities like Amsterdam. Just make sure you look around and enquire about any potential risks before you make an active protest against an intolerant rural community. If you're not sure, simply avoid public affection, which is often frowned upon no matter who's doing it.

Vegetarian travellers

It's one thing to organize your diet at home, and quite another to maintain your eating habits in a new setting every day. But it can be done. And it doesn't even have to be stressful. Naturally, your chosen destinations are a major factor. Knowing where to look is another. A number of supermarkets, restaurants, resorts and B&Bs around Europe

The reluctant family traveller

There are a few things I never thought I'd do, and buying a charter trip for my family was one of them. I'd spent nearly a decade regarding tour groups with the sort of suspicion normally reserved for unsolicited email from Nigerian bankers. But as I repeated the mantra, "I'm an independent traveller", my fingers – the same ones that had once crumpled torn pages from guidebooks into emergency loo paper – clicked the online purchase button for a week-long trip.

This was no doubt an overreaction to my previous attempts not to let a child change my ways. When our daughter first arrived, we kept packing her along for transatlantic journeys without much of a thought. As she got older and more fidgety, it became more of a challenge, but we were determined to remain backpackers. When she was older – old enough to carry her own mini-rucksack – her bladder wasn't quite prepared to go four hours on a rustic Dominican Republic bus. And, on several occasions, we crammed her into budget accommodation so tight we had to fold ourselves into a family lotus position to squeeze onto the single bed. Nothing that required professional counselling, mind you, but if this continued, how would I avoid a lifetime of resentment from the very person I was trying to "educate" with real experiences?

Maybe the charter trip would lighten things up.

I knew I had crossed over to the Dark Side when the plane touched down in Gran Canaria and I saw a woman with our hotel's logo embroidered on her shirt pocket standing there with a little clipboard, directing people onto numbered buses. I was no longer finding my way through the maze of public transport to some obscure dwelling; I had simply become human luggage. There would be no encounters with actual local people on this trip. Sure, there was plenty for kids to do and it was child-proof, plus there was enough space at the complex for a cargo plane to airdrop all the kiddy gear we'd hauled along (note to self: actually airdrop it next time), but I had strayed too far into the cultural void.

The trick, I now realize, is to find the middle ground between flea-bag hostels and generic hotel complexes.

The antidote, if there is such a thing, is going to vary from family to family, but there are at least two key ingredients for a successful journey. 1: Other kids. Consider a family-stay or farmstay where the host family has kids of roughly the same age so you know the place is kid-proof: the children will likely get an instant "cultural" connection and the adults will have something in common. 2: It doesn't have to be exclusively kid-oriented. You shouldn't have to "put up with" your own travels. Remember: happy parents, happy kids. Or perhaps that's what Prozac is for.

Doug Lansky

cater specifically to **vegetarians**. Produce markets offer an incredible variety of fresh fruit and vegetables.

Bear in mind some European chefs have a different idea of what vegetarian means. You can repeat "no meat" eight times, but your dinner will come drenched in beef-stock soup or topped with bacon. Many seem to think it only applies to the main ingredient, so you need to be specific in this regard when enquiring.

Scandinavia doesn't offer much of a vegetarian selection outside of major metropolitan areas, but delicious non-meat Italian pastas and pizzas can be easily found, not just in Italy but all across Europe. Salad bars are becoming more and more common; large supermarkets are increasingly well stocked with vegetarian food; and the produce in southern Europe is outstanding (Italian tomatoes alone might convert thousands of meat-eaters).

To pinpoint **vegetarian restaurants** everywhere you go, check your guidebook. For a more complete listing, you might pick up a book such as *Vegetarian Europe* by Alex Bourke, which lists three hundred vegetarian and vegan restaurants. Or search the web for each specific city at Ⓦ www.happycow.net, where you can also find some short reviews and helpful translations on how to explain your dietary requirements.

Eating veggie as you travel

Start by booking a vegetarian meal when you arrange your flight, then confirm it when you check your luggage. It's that easy. If you forgot, you can usually request the meal up to 48 hours before departure. Some veggie meals receive better reviews than their carnivore counterparts, while others are dire. See Ⓦ www.vegparadise.com/airline.html for airline contact information, and to view the different vegetarian menus.

Trains, ferries and buses have captive audiences. Your best shot at feeding yourself a decent vegetarian meal during the trip is if you buy one at a supermarket before boarding. Doing this is also a great money-saver, so you're helping your wallet as much as your digestive tract.

17

Documenting your trip

For many, the time spent travelling will provide some of the most vivid memories of their lives. However, memories fade. Even travelling with your best friend, or an entire overland group, doesn't mean you're going to collectively remember everything. When you're going solo, it's even harder. A journal, camera, tape recorder, camcorder, colour pencils, paints and watercolour set are the most common tools for **recording your journey** and its impact on you. Taking along all these is overkill, but keeping some record of your trip is an excellent idea and will help keep the experience fresh in your mind long after your return.

Capturing the moment

Eating alone can be especially depressing. But with a journal you feel like you're reporting, even conspiring. And it lets you focus on the little things in front of you. I like a medium-sized journal with non-lined paper in case I want to doodle. I'm not particularly gifted artistically, but I want to draw if I'm in the mood. That's part of the beauty of a journal: it's more personal, more private. With pictures you often take them for other people. The journal is my trip, just for me.

John Hoult,
Producer, Savvy Traveller Radio

Keeping a journal

Many travellers say this is the single best thing they brought on their trip (or bought when they arrived – you certainly don't need leather-bound hand-pressed paper to record your thoughts, but it makes for a nice souvenir). If you've kept a **journal** before, you'll be bringing one anyway. If not, this is the perfect time to start. It's

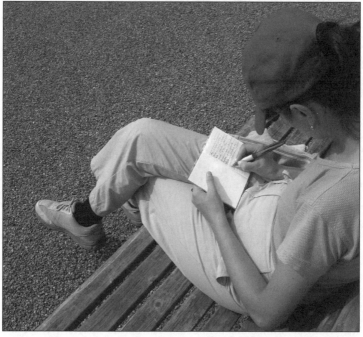

▲ A journal is an essential travel companion

not easy to process, or even remember, all the places and people and stories, but simply putting your thoughts down on paper can have a soothing, therapeutic effect. It can be a friend when you're alone or provide structure for your day. If you have some artistic skill, spend a little more and get paper that will soak up your watercolours or hold ink better.

Taking photographs

Bringing along a camera is pretty obvious. Which kind – and how to use it – isn't. The temptation for many is to get a "good camera" – that is, one above their level of expertise. If you're a professional or exceptional amateur, bring what you need. Just be aware of the security risk of carrying valuable gear. Remove the brand names from the bags, try to select a case that doesn't look like a camera case, and minimize your lenses and accessories. If you're not a pro, go for an inexpensive **digital pocket camera**. No amount of features can make up for poor photo composition. Plus, SLRs are bulky, expensive and more likely to get

> **Need a zoom?**
>
> The most cost-effective answer is to **skip the zoom** feature altogether and just take a few steps forward or backward – you'll get better results that way. With digital cameras, go for the optical zoom. A digital zoom is a lower-end feature.

stolen. If you're really no-frills or need to slim your pack, you could just get by with your camera phone.

Because you can keep a pocket camera handy in a day bag (if it's really small, even a pocket) and pull it out quickly without attracting much attention, you're much more likely to use it. And – here's one of the oldest photography tricks in the book – the more photos you take, the more likely you'll get a great photo.

If you already have a pocket camera that takes decent pictures, you'll be fine, and sticking with what you've got is likely to be the most budget-wise move. If you're starting from scratch, skip the zoom. It jacks up the price, runs down the battery, brings down the quality, and is not very powerful. If you take one to three steps forward, you'll get the same effect for free. Plus, if the moving zoom parts get so much as a grain of sand in them, kiss the camera goodbye for a month or two while it gets sent back to the manufacturer.

Digital cameras eat up batteries like a starving sumo wrestler, and you may run out of memory before you can upload images if you don't splurge on an extra memory card or **backup storage device** like a mini hard disc, USB keychain flash drive or iPod. Uploading images onto one of these means you can hold out until you find a high-speed, cheap (or free) web connection.

Turning your digital images into prints

You might consider uploading them to an **online developer** (see opposite) so your friends and family can easily view them and even have prints made if they want to, but bear in mind it will take a while, even with a high-speed connection, so you will have extra internet café costs to consider (many cafés will copy images to a CD for you, though).

How to get the best from a pocket camera

Postcard photographers use the best equipment, know the best vantage points and wait until the lighting is perfect. For monuments and panorama shots, chances are slim you're going to do better yourself. If you want a great shot of the city or a favourite attraction for your album back home, just buy the postcard. Besides, nothing will put your friends and family back home asleep quicker than endless landscape shots.

Online developers and printers

Winkflash ⓦ www.winkflash.com
Developing: No developing, just digital uploads
4″ x 6″ print: €0.6
Comments: Free hosting of images online, with unlimited storage. Also does books, albums and posters. Photos can be ordered at 4″ x 5.3″, the size used by most digital cameras, if you'd rather not risk distortion by stretching the shot to fit the traditional 4″ x 6″ parameters.
Ofoto ⓦ www.kodakgallery.com
Developing: No developing, just digital uploads
4″ x 6″ print: €0.12
Comments: Good online editing tools (photos can be cropped and red-eye removed), but it's not as cheap as its competitors. Registration is free and you can store and share your pics for up to a year without buying anything. Ships internationally.
Shutterfly ⓦ www.shutterfly.com
Developing: No developing, just digital uploads
4″ x 6″ print: €0.11
Comments: Visitors don't need to register to view your online album, so sharing your pics is more convenient. Membership is free and you get unlimited storage and discounts on large orders.
Snapfish ⓦ www.snapfish.com
Developing: €2.15 per roll, includes set of prints (plus €1.40 per roll for shipping and handling)
4″ x 6″ print: €0.09
Comments: Easy to use. The only site that enables digital photographers (and Photoshop users) to upload their non-JPEG images. You can also email your pics in if you're not comfortable with uploading.

Instead, **photograph things that show your life on the road**. It takes some effort to remember to photograph them (doorways, weird meals, freaky buses, scary toilets, charismatic taxi drivers and so on), and it may feel odd taking out your camera in the middle of the restaurant and snapping a picture of the meal, but those are the shots that'll spark your memory the most back home. Also, resist the urge to photograph your travel companions posing. Catch them off guard and you'll get a more honest, interesting photo.

With **scenery**, and often even with people, try to compose the photo so there's something very close, something mid-range and something in the distance. If you want to photograph someone standing in front of a waterfall, for example, try positioning yourself just behind a texture-rich tree branch and allow it to appear in a third of the picture.

Despite the fact that things seem brighter, midday **sunlight** actually flattens images and makes for unappealing photos. For people, animals and objects, you want overcast skies or indirect light. A cloudy day is the perfect time to get great pictures. If you must shoot people in the middle of a sunny day, use your flash to eliminate unattractive shadows or have your subjects step into a shaded area.

www.roughguides.com

211

When not to take photos

There's a reason it's called taking a picture: rarely is permission requested. It may be your camera, but it's their image and privacy and that trumps whatever you've got in your hand, even if it's a Nikon with a Zeiss lens. The path to pictorial enlightenment involves respecting local bans on photography and asking all subjects for the right to snap their photo. Everything else – including the temptingly easy zoom-lens sniper approach – is **nicking pictures**. That sounds a bit dramatic, but for many travellers photography is their only interaction with locals, and it's a relationship largely based on selfishness and insensitivity (the author has been guilty of this as well at times). For some, our swinging lenses can feel as intrusive as if someone walked up and took your picture while you were lying on the beach half-naked or stuffing your face at a restaurant. To get those great portraits you see on guidebook covers and in magazines, simply **ask permission**. Or go one better and try to initiate conversation. Make a few friends or even a small connection and it will add another dimension to the picture. Then, if you can, get an address and send them a copy. Or bring along a disposable camera that creates instant photos and take one with that. Giving photos has a much nicer ring than taking them.

For film cameras, 100–400 ISO film is pretty versatile for action, both indoor and outdoor, and it's available everywhere. Special professional films, conversely, are not always easy to come by in smaller towns, so make sure you pack enough.

Recording sound

If you think the **sounds** of Europe – French chatter in a trendy café, Italian Vespas zipping by, Big Ben bonging, an animated story told by a drunk German in an old beer hall – will conjure stronger memories than photos, or if you'd prefer to dictate your journal or record directions when you can't find pen and paper, mini-cassettes and mini-discs are both options, but the digital models are handier. Even your iPod can easily be transformed into one. An added bonus with digitized format is that you can upload sound clips and attach them to emails at internet cafés. Consider what you'll be using it for when you select a **microphone**. For voices, go for a unidirectional mic. For ambient sounds, you'll want a wider spread. Some of the better microphones are equipped with both, and you can toggle between them with a simple switch.

Shooting video footage

Many of today's smallest digital **camcorders** can slip into a jacket as easily as a pocket camera. Plus, they record sounds and make still images. The downside is that they cost €800–2000, don't take digital stills as well as most regular digital cameras (this bit seems to be improving in recent models, though), and don't have great versatility for sound recording (though you can fix this with an additional microphone).

Like photography, video has spawned stacks of books on method and technique. If you're going to shoot, here are two simple **tips**: first, hold the camera very steady, even if it's equipped with an electronic stabilizer. That may mean leaning against a tree or lamppost. Better, however, is to bring a simple tripod – nothing induces headaches and screams "amateur" like shaky footage. The second tip is to resist letting the camera follow your natural head or eye movement all the time. For example, allow someone to walk across the field of vision – entering on one side and disappearing on the other. This will make editing much easier once you return home.

Drawing and painting

No one will see Europe quite the way you do. To personalize the visual impact, you might consider toting along watercolours, colour pencils or sketching charcoal – all relatively cheap and extremely easy to transport. Even if you don't have much artistic skill, or much that you're aware of, this is an ideal time to give it a shot. It's a nice alternative to reading or writing when you're stuck somewhere for a long time, which, invariably, you will be at some point.

Blogging your trip

Memories fade, surprisingly quickly. After a few days back home on the sofa in your old pair of jeans, the entire experience can feel like it never actually occurred. Best to jot things down while they're still fresh in your mind.

One way is to create an **online scrapbook** with a photo service such as My Yahoo! (it will basically happen on its own if you use one of the online photo developers listed on p.211). Just make sure you don't forget to label the photos with names and places as you go. It may seem obvious at the time, but several months down the road, when you finally return and get around to assembling the photos, it's not going to be quite as clear. (If you're getting film processed along the way, remember to write names and places on the back of the prints.)

There are loads of online services that will help you keep an online **blog** of your trip, including ⓦ www.roughguides.com. Others include:

ⓦ www.traveljournals.net
ⓦ www.travelpod.com
ⓦ www.travelpost.com
ⓦ www.travellerspoint.com
ⓦ www.traveleor.com

www.roughguides.com

213

Flatpack souvenirs

One of the best things you can do aside from taking photos or painting is to collect small, flat items that catch your eye and evoke a memory: concert and train tickets, a beer label, a fortune-cookie prediction. Send it home with your film or wedge it into your journal for safe transport.

What to do with souvenirs

Send them home. That Venetian lace tablecloth, stolen gelato spoon and Mona Lisa bottle opener will make nice mementos, provided you get them back. Dragging your souvenirs around Europe in your backpack is a great way to get them ruined, lost or stolen, but is not as effective as the postal service for actual delivery to the final destination.

No matter how small, lightweight and space-saving the items may seem individually, they can take over your pack like Dutch elm disease.

Foto frenzy

Cameras elicit odd behaviour. They turn many of us into trophy collectors of sorts. I've been guilty of this. Who, after all, would travel around the world and not bring back any proof? Dopey smile of me in front of the Eiffel Tower? Check. At the Spanish Steps in Rome? Check. Next to the statue of David in Florence? Check. Beside a prostitute in Amsterdam? Nope. But I did spot a family taking a picture of their grandmother.

There's no need to stand in front of things. It's like shopping at the supermarket. See something that catches your attention, just snap a picture; it's in the bag; you can take it home with you. Cameras barely capture the image in focus with decent lighting, yet they're expected to somehow preserve the entire moment for later enjoyment.

When travel becomes exhilarating, often the only outlet is that little button on the camera. It's great to take pictures, but don't forget to put your camera away now and then and just enjoy the experience of being there.

Doug Lansky

The obvious exception is waiting until the tail end of your trip for a big shopping splurge.

Naturally, there are several levels of security available (as well as private couriers) at a range of prices. Consider the reliability of the postal service (are you in Denmark or Russia?), the weight of the package and the value of what you're sending, before you ship. There's no magic formula, but it's not uncommon to pay more for postage than the actual item enclosed. Keep that in mind when you're about to buy that set of terracotta roof tiles in Spain.

Another thing to remember is that not everything you buy may be allowed back into your country, and that's not just a veiled reference to the popular agricultural products in Amsterdam. All plants, seeds and items made from wild animals may be removed by customs officials. You won't be reimbursed, but you may get fined.

18

Returning home

E
xcept perhaps for getting your gums scraped, nothing seems less appealing during your trip planning process or the trip itself than taking a moment to work out your **return details**. But this information may affect your planning, so best that it's addressed, at least briefly, now. Let's assume you've conquered Europe. You've picked up six languages, run with the bulls, bungy-jumped off the Eiffel Tower, foiled pickpockets, fallen in love, fended off dysentery and learned the difference between a Châteauneuf du Pape and a Châteaupape du Neuf. All you have left is to return home.

But here's where things can get problematic. With a comfortable bed and a fresh set of clothes in sight, it's tempting to lower your guard. Instead, you're going to need to brace yourself for a potentially rough re-entry.

Re-entry shock

Even if Europe is similar in many ways to your own culture, many people coming home from a long trip still experience a **shock** – it's often bigger on their return than when they first went abroad, and at a time when they're least prepared for it. It's a lifestyle shift as much as a cultural one. On the bright side, there are a few simple things you can do to turn the experience into a smooth landing, and the most important of these is learning what to expect.

The **stages of re-entry** mirror those of culture shock: honeymoon, crisis, recovery and adjustment. The honeymoon is the initial exhilaration of returning home, and is precisely what most are expecting. The

www.roughguides.com

surprise left hook is the "**reverse culture shock**", which lasts until you acclimatize to your home surroundings and eventually return to your old self (with a bit more wisdom and experience).

The degree of the reverse culture shock you experience largely depends upon how integrated you became into foreign cultures during your journey, and how different they are from your own. Upon returning, you may miss the regular and close social interaction you had with your foreign community and other travellers. You may find yourself revolted by the TV commercials and telemarketers you had previously learned to ignore. More likely, you may feel a distance has come between you and your friends and family because they can no longer relate to your "new" well-travelled persona – one that has grown and been shaped by your range of different experiences. Instead, they're treating you the same way and don't have the patience to hear the thirty hours of stories required to bring them up to speed. And if you're returning to a job, you may notice reduced responsibilities and little acknowledgement of your overseas accomplishments.

This is compounded by **The Questions**. If you've ever broken your leg and had to explain what happened to everyone you met for a month, you already have a good understanding of what it's like to be a human recording. But when you're trying to sum up a few incredible weeks or months of life-changing experiences in one or two cute lines, it's even more frustrating. The Questions tend to be the same worldwide. They'll start with "How was the trip?", move on to "What was your favourite?" and quickly get to "So what are you going to do now?"

Coping strategies

Scuba diving and cultural immersion are similar in at least this one respect: a little **decompression** is a good idea. Before you return home, try to build in a little stop for mental refuelling. It needn't be a month of silence at a

Coming home

If we hadn't prepared for our return, if we had just done the usual routine and taken the same ride from the airport to our flat and walked in to face ten months' worth of junk mail, I think we would have had to buy a shotgun and kiss life goodbye. OK, that's a bit dramatic, but it would have been rough.

Fortunately, we built a transition period into the trip. Instead of travelling abroad for eleven months, we decided to return earlier and spend a month travelling around our own country, visiting friends and hanging out with fellow travellers around England. There was no pressure to find work right away, face the flat, or take care of bills.

The toughest part was just fielding the questions. If I had a pound for every time someone asked me my favourite place, I'd have enough to head back out on the road. It's good we spent at least some of that month with fellow travellers because the others don't quite understand how your life has been defined by your travels.

Adrian Lee

monastery; a beach will do fine. You just need a place with minimal stimulus. It can take a while to process the lifetime of experiences that you've just crammed into a ridiculously short period. And, more important still, you need to begin to engage the concept of returning home. You're going to have enough to think about when you get back, so try to work out a game plan in advance – where you're going to stay when your plane touches down, who you plan to visit, and so on.

Brace others for your arrival

The best single thing you can do in this respect is keep your friends and family up to speed during your trip with short, regular dispatches from the road. The easiest way to do this is with a **group email**. Let them know where you are and what you're up to. In general, people will have more patience to read about your experiences in bite-size chunks than to listen to them all in one go.

Write that last dispatch from the road

When you're just about to head home, take some time to **sum up your trip** in your last email or letter. Answer the questions they're likely to ask. Tell them what your favourite places are, if in fact you have any. Tell them what your plans are. Those around you will want to get that extra dose of info when they see you in person. Help them out. Give them something they can ask about. You might say, "For a beer, I'll be happy to fill in the details on the time I was gored in the backside by a bull. But the time I had a few shots of vodka and woke up in a Siberian prison camp is worth at least two." Some people will be more interested to see your photos than others. Prepare them for it with a bit of humour and the option to back out of the full seventeen-roll photo presentation. You might try something like: "I'll be carrying around a very small selection of photos in case you're curious to see some of the things I've been writing about. If there aren't clean sheets on the bed when I visit, I'll be forced to show you all 824 photos."

Stay in touch with people you met

Keep in contact with the friends you made on your trip. It improves the chance you'll see them again, gives you a free place to stay (and a cultural guide) when you head back to Europe next time, and gives you a free support network.

Keep involved with the places

Study that **language** you were dying to speak at the time but couldn't. **Read** fiction or non-fiction books on the subject. If you do eventually head back to any of those places, you'll be able to appreciate them on another level.

www.roughguides.com

Seek out travellers in your area

There's probably a **hostel** in your area filled with Europeans (and Aussies and Kiwis and Americans and Canadians, if that's who you miss). Spending time with travellers, visiting students or an immigrant crowd can be just enough of a dose to remind you that you're sane after all.

View your own city as a tourist

Chances are you've only done a fraction of the things most travellers do when they arrive in your city. Check out the **museums**, attend a **sporting event** you haven't been to before or **take pictures**.

Find your patience

It's common to feel **superior** to those around you who haven't had such international experiences. Suddenly, their views may seem pedestrian and insular and you feel the continued need to "set them straight". Just remember: your own views may not be that popular, either. Time outside your own country tends to highlight its faults, and you may come off sounding like a born-again critic. Take heart. You will have enlightened perspectives, but don't expect others to come around easily.

Revive the memories

If you need a **quick fix**, you might try escaping back into your travels for a brief tour. This is where a good scrapbook and well-kept journal come in handy (see p.208). Using your notes and images, it can often be helpful to write about your experiences more fully. Who knows? This may be the chance to release that budding travel writer within.

Get busy

If you have the possibility to arrange your work/study schedule before returning, keep this in mind: a little downtime at home is wonderful, but too much can be self-defeating. Finding that right **balance** is up to you, but in general the less, the better. One or two weeks is usually sufficient.

Start travelling again

If all else fails (except your finances), **hit the road again**. It doesn't have to be a long trip, or even a European one. Just taking some trains and buses, packing up your rucksack, sleeping in a few ratty hostels and meeting some other travellers can be enough.

First-Time Europe

Where to go

- Austria 221
- The Baltic States 225
- Belgium and Luxembourg 230
- Britain 235
- Bulgaria 241
- Croatia 245
- The Czech and Slovak republics 249
- Denmark 254
- Finland 258
- France 262
- Germany 267
- Greece 272
- Hungary 276
- Ireland 280
- Italy 285
- Montenegro 290
- Morocco 292
- The Netherlands 293
- Norway 298
- Poland 303
- Portugal 307
- Romania 311
- Russia 315
- Slovenia 320
- Spain 324
- Sweden 329
- Switzerland 333
- Turkey 337

Austria

Capital Vienna
Population 8,192,880
Language German
Currency Euro (€)
When to go Mid-December to
March for skiing, July and August
for hiking, or June, when the

Alps are in full bloom, crowds are
manageable and prices have yet to
hit their peak
When not to go Many theatres and
performance centres close during
July and August
Minimum daily budget €37

As the homeland of personalities as
diverse as Mozart, Hitler, Schwarzenegger
and Freud, you could say Austria brings
out the best and worst in people. It's one
of the world's richest and most stable
democracies, and has plenty of the Alps
thrown in for those who enjoy risking life
and limb. Fantastic skiing and hiking in
western Austria draw the outdoor adrenaline nuts, while there is enough grand
imperial art and architecture in Vienna
to leave the culture vultures gasping for
air. What the kleptomaniac Habsburgs
couldn't steal from their vassal states,
they commissioned themselves, leaving
the Kunsthistorisches Museum with one
of the four largest art collections in the
world. There's a lot of Egyptian, Greek
and Roman antiquities, but also enough
of Ye Olde Masters to fill entire rooms.

If your taste leans to the less dusty
side of culture, Austria has a bubbling
electronic music scene, too. It might

not be the zaniest of countries, but
it's making strides in that direction.
Traditionally pork-loving Austrians are
even warming to such unheard-of
concepts as vegetarian dining. What will
they embrace next?

Main attractions

● **The Austrian Alps** Hundreds of
3000-metre-plus peaks will take care of
your climbing needs. If you prefer the
assistance of a ski lift to get you up the
mountain, every self-respecting village
has at least a dozen.

● **Eisriesenwelt caves** A walk-in
refrigerator of gigantic proportions,
with over 40km of frozen waterfalls and
weird-looking ice sculptures. They're
easily accessible from the town of
Werfen, south of Salzburg, and are open
between May and October. Even in the

Average daily temperatures (°C) and monthly rainfall (mm) in Austria											
	Jan	Feb	Mar	Apr	May	June	July	Aug	Sept	Oct	Nov	Dec
Vienna												
max °C	2	4	9	14	19	22	25	25	21	14	7	4
min °C	-3	-2	2	5	9	13	15	15	12	6	2	-1
rainfall mm	38	42	41	51	61	74	63	58	45	41	50	43

www.roughguides.com

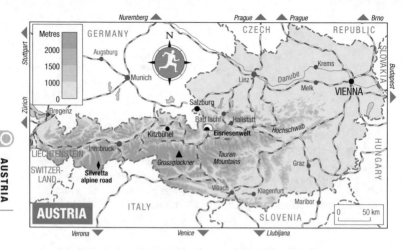

summertime, the temperature hovers around freezing point, so bring a fleece.

● **The KunstHausWien, Vienna** The modern exhibitions are upstaged by the museum itself, which was completed in 1991. Once inside, the walls twist, floors undulate and trees grow out of third-storey windows. The architect, Friedensreich Hundertwasser, ranks as one of the most original architects of the twentieth century.

● **Mozart's Salzburg** This famous border town is not only worth a visit to pay homage to the man, but also has churches so cute you want to pinch them, plus plenty of art, city squares and chocolate galore.

● **MuseumsQuartier, Vienna** The shape of things to come, within the world of a museum building. The Viennese complex houses, among other things, the Leopold Museum (Austrian Art), the Kunsthalle Wien, the ZOOM Children's Museum and the Tanzquartier Wien (the New Centre for Contemporary Dance). A total floor area of 60,000 square metres makes this one of the most impressive mega-museums in the world.

● **Schönbrunn, Vienna** If you find the Habsburg Palace in downtown Vienna

confusing and gridlocked, this 1685 "summer cottage" commissioned by Emperor Leopold I gives you a much better idea of how Viennese royalty spent the taxpayers' money. When crowds arrive, head outside – the park out the back is bigger than Monaco.

Also recommended

● **Cruise the Austrian Alps on a motorbike** Long and winding Alpine roads offer unparalleled two-wheel riding. Classic tours include the Grossglockner mountain, the Silvretta high-Alpine road, the Tauern mountains and the tour around the Hochschwab.

● **Ski the Hahnenkammrennen, Kitzbühel** Let's face it – your chances of competing in the actual race are about as slim as Kate Moss. But you can always do a couple of practice runs to test your mettle. The start is at 1665m, the finish at 802m, and the total course spans 3.3km. You might want to ratchet up your insurance first, though.

● **Bring the hills alive on a *Sound of Music* tour** Plenty of tours follow in the dance steps of the von Trapp family, but

Panorama Tours (@www.panoramatours
.com/salzburg-Original-Sound-of-Music
-Tour.aspx) had the backing of Fräulein
Maria herself. Trips centre on the city of
Salzburg but also include the palaces of
Frohenburg and Leopoldskron. The whole
wonderfully (or painfully) kitsch experience
is typically tackled with a bus tour that
can be arranged anywhere in town.

● **Take a yodelling course** When in
the Alps, strike a blow for non-verbal
throat noises and make lots of alternative
friends at the same time. Just don't use
your new-found vocal skills in downtown
Vienna. To get a little warm-up, try
@www.jodelkurs.com.

Costs

Don't be put off by Austria's well-heeled
surrounds; it's not as forbiddingly expensive as it seems at first glance. You can
eke out an existence on €37 a day, but
you may not get much of a feeling for
the country that way. Plan to spend
closer to €50, which will give you the
occasional private room and restaurant
meal, especially once you learn to spot
the money-magnet cafés that will gladly
relieve you of half your daily budget for a
Sachertorte and a cup of coffee. Just as
in the rest of the Germanic world, cash is
king, so avoid embarrassing situations by
not relying solely on your credit card.

Accommodation

Paying for a place to stay is likely to be
a major post in your budget. For €38–50
you will get a double room in a mid-range
pension; an extra €18 will make your
temporary home just that little bit nicer. If
you're willing to slum it, you can squeeze
under €16 for a bed in a hostel.

Eating and drinking

When Austrian xenophobes ask what
immigrants have ever done for Austria,
the rest of the country answers, "Cheap
food!" All the usual suspects can be
found, especially in student areas in the
larger cities. You can tank up your gut for
around €4. For a hearty Austrian sit-down
meal, figure on €16. Coffee is particularly
expensive, so make every cup last.

Transport

Austria is as well equipped as any
other environment-conscious Western
democracy when it comes to public
transport. The rail network is not the
fastest in Europe, but it is punctual and
clean and the views are often incredible. Where rail services terminate, the
Bahnbus and Postbus systems will take
you farther. The former is run by the
ÖBB (who operate the trains as well)
and hence they leave from train stations,
while the Postbus service departs from
post offices. Both are usually cheaper
but slower than the train. Their prime
functions are delivering mail and shuttling
kids to school, though there are a few
late-night services that can bring you
home after a night on the town.

In Vienna, the Vienna Card (@www
.wienkarte.at) is worth looking into.
For €18.50, you get 72 hours of
unlimited free travel by underground, bus
and tram, and discounts to nearly
all museums, concerts and restaurants.
You can pick up the card in almost any
hotel or department store around the city.

By train

Austrian Rail Pass Any three days of
travel in fifteen days US$213 (first class)
and US$148 (second class). Additional
travel days cost US$28–32 (first class)
and US$20–24 (second class).
Eurail Austria-Switzerland Pass
Any four days of travel in two months
US$389 (first class), US$275 (youth,
second class). Additional travel days cost

▲ Skiing in the Austrian Alps

US$40–46 (first class) and US$30 (youth, second class).

European East Pass (also valid in the Czech and Slovak republics, Hungary and Poland) Any five days of travel in one month US$299 (first class) and US$209 (second class). Additional travel days cost US$36 (first class) and US$28 (second class).

InterRail Austria Pass Ranges from any three days of travel in one month – €157 (first class), €116 (second class) and €75 (youth, second class) – to any eight days of travel in one month €329 (first class), €244 (second class) and €159 (youth, second class).

For Europe-wide **Eurail** and **InterRail** passes, see p.50. For tips and tricks on maximizing your rail pass, see p.75.

By bus

Busabout (see p.52) allows some travel in Austria. For internal bus prices, see Ⓦwww.bahnbus.at. For buses to other countries, see Ⓦwww.eurolines.at.

Events

The Imperial Ball, Vienna The Imperial Ball (Kaiserball) at the Hofburg on New Year's Eve kicks off the traditional ballroom season in Vienna, and it's not as hard a party to get into as you might think – just expensive (€60–560). Even if you miss it, there are plenty of other opportunities later in the year to waltz until the end. Dec 31; Ⓦwww.hofburg.com.

Salzburg Festival If classical music floats your boat, try this five-week extravaganza. Mozart is a natural focal point, but there are plenty of international stars performing other works, too. July–Aug; Ⓦwww.salzburgfestival.at.

ImPulsTanz, Vienna Dancing, or something that looks vaguely like it, is nonstop during this month-long celebration of rhythmic movement in Vienna. World-famous choreographers and dance companies perform all over the city, and there are courses and workshops if you want to get in on the action yourself. Early July–early Aug; Ⓦwww.impulstanz.com.

Austria online

Country info Ⓦwww.austria-tourism.at
Rail Ⓦwww.oebb.at
Bus Ⓦwww.bahnbus.at
Vienna info Ⓦwww.aboutvienna.org

The Baltic States

Estonia
Capital Tallinn
Population 1,324,333
Languages Estonian (also Finnish, Russian and Ukrainian)
Currency Estonian kroon (EEK)
Minimum daily budget €24

Latvia
Capital Riga
Population 2,274,735
Language Latvian
Currency Latvian lat (Ls)
Minimum daily budget €24

Lithuania
Capital Vilnius
Population 3,585,906
Language Lithuanian
Currency Lithuanian litas (Lt)
Minimum daily budget €22

When to go May–August for the best weather and outdoor café scene
When not to go September, when rain is heaviest. December–March can be severe, with icy-cold temperatures and few daylight hours

Estonia, Latvia and Lithuania have clearly gone to great lengths to maintain their independence and defined borders after breaking away from the Soviet empire, yet the three of them continue to be grouped under a heading that sounds like a 1970s heavy metal band. There are several nations bordering the Baltic Sea that could have also landed this rather unfortunate moniker, but for these three it stuck.

One of the best reasons to visit this region is precisely because you're not familiar with it. Few are. And that means far fewer tourists and far more cultural insight (and value for money). Estonia's blood sausages aren't the big draw, anyway. Nor are Latvia's bogs. Or the Frank Zappa statue in Lithuania.

The people, prices and the notion of untrampled lands attract a different breed of traveller – ones who are less interested in a checklist of "must-sees" and more interested in finding a path of their own. That said, the Baltics are booming, at least compared to other former Soviet nations. You'll see designer brands and BMWs everywhere you go, and all three capital cities are vying to become the area's economic and cultural hub.

Main attractions

● **Pärnu, Estonia** You won't find many foreigners taking a beach vacation in Estonia, but this resort is a big draw locally. The white sandy beaches attract thousands, and those who want to get away from the crowds head for the nearby dunes and mud baths.

● **Riga Castle** Now home to Latvia's president, Riga Castle has sat for nearly 700 years on the bank of the Daugava River, though only the Tower of the

www.roughguides.com

225

Holy Ghost remains from the original. Its southern part houses the Foreign Art Museum, the Rainis Museum of Literature and Art History, and the Latvian History Museum.

● **Tallinn's old town** Often compared to Prague, Estonia's capital is an up-and-comer on the budget travel scene, as is its burgeoning nightlife. It turns out that Soviet rule was a sort of backward blessing for this old city (except the part when the Soviets bombed the old quarter one day in 1944 and flattened ten percent of it). The economic stagnation kept development to a minimum, so Tallinn's old city has remained largely intact. Check out the area round Toompea Hill, where the aristocracy and clergy once lived.

● **Toomkirik, Tallinn** The Cathedral of St Mary the Virgin, Estonia's oldest church, was built in 1223 and remains the burial site of German and Swedish noblemen. It was founded by the Danes, and houses the largest organ in the country.

Average daily temperatures (°C) and monthly rainfall (mm)

	Jan	Feb	Mar	Apr	May	June	July	Aug	Sept	Oct	Nov	Dec
Estonia (Tallinn)												
max °C	-2	-3	2	7	14	18	20	19	13	8	3	-1
min °C	-6	-7	-4	1	6	10	13	12	8	3	-1	-4
rainfall mm	33	23	25	30	38	51	66	71	71	58	53	43
Latvia (Riga)												
max °C	-2	-2	3	9	16	19	21	20	15	10	4	0
min °C	-6	-6	-2	2	7	11	13	13	9	5	1	-4
rainfall mm	33	23	25	36	43	58	71	69	66	53	51	38
Lithuania (Vilnius)												
max °C	-3	-2	2	10	18	21	22	21	16	10	3	-1
min °C	-8	-8	-4	1	7	10	12	11	8	3	-1	-5
rainfall mm	43	33	38	48	51	76	84	69	66	56	51	53

Also recommended

● **Explore Lahemaa Park** Estonia's largest national park, Lahemaa combines dense forest, coastal bluffs, lakes, waterfalls and eighteenth-century manor houses. Situated in the north of the country, the park encompasses the Koljaku–Oandu and Laukasoo reserves, a wet sea forest and – brace yourself – 7000-year-old bog respectively.

● **Visit Hiiumaa (aka Dagö)** If you're looking for ecotourism, consider this sparsely populated Estonian island 22km west of the mainland. There's a concerted effort under way here to protect the 1000-square-kilometre island's lovely stretches of coast from overdevelopment. There's no shortage of wildlife for viewing: elks, red deer, wild boars, foxes, lynxes, black storks, golden eagles and cranes.

● **Relax in Abruka** This tiny Estonian island offers a summer retreat for naturalists. Horse riding and farmhouse accommodation await visitors, as does the big attraction: a botanical-zoological reservation.

● **Climb the Hill of Crosses** Ten kilometres north of the Lithuanian town of Siauliai, this is one of the world's most spectacular cemeteries. Thousands of crosses dot the hillside like wildflowers. Some are memorials, others are devotional, but the wooden and metal crosses make for a moving (if slightly creepy) hike.

● **Canoe Gauja National Park** The Gauja, Salaca and Abava rivers in this Latvian lake region provide some of the best paddling around, and there's plenty of flora and fauna to keep you and your camera occupied. This unique Baltic Sea environment allows northern–southern and western–eastern vegetation to flourish side by side. See Ⓦwww.gnp.gov.lv for information on the park.

Costs

Lithuania is the cheapest of the Baltic States, but within Estonia and Latvia there's a range from great deals to rip-offs. At the upper end, Latvia and Estonia compare to Western Europe, but on the budget end it's easier to dig

www.roughguides.com

for bargains. If you're using traveller's cheques, remember to change them in the larger towns or you may not get much use out of them.

Accommodation

Outside of Lithuania (where hostels cost around €8), this is likely to be your biggest expense. Figure on more than €25 for a shared room with a bathroom. However, breakfast is often included with the deal. Look for campground cabins, which can be as low as €7.50 a night.

Eating and drinking

It's not difficult to find a nice meal for €25, but dining is where you're likely to save the most. A simple meal, for example, can be had for under €4, even in Latvia and Estonia. Pep yourself up for pork and potatoes, soup and sausage, and smoked fish. In summer, you can skip the blood pancakes if you please, but don't miss the fresh berries. If you want to drink something extra special (and extra revolting) in Latvia, try the Riga Black Balsam, a brake-fluid-like 45-percent-proof concoction. The syrupy, sweet Vana Tallinn liqueur is also a palate challenger, whether you add it to coffee or champagne.

Transport

Getting around the Baltic States is still quite cheap (and slow). No regional rail passes cover the area, nor do Eurail or InterRail, but there is a local rail service, running two types of train: "passenger" and "fast". Both are slow, but inexpensive. Busabout doesn't operate in the region either, but for buses to other countries, see ⓦwww.eurolines.ee (Estonia), ⓦwww.eurolines.lv (Latvia) or ⓦwww.eurolines.lt (Lithuania).

In the capital cities, there's a comprehensive network of trams, trolleys and buses, but these can get very crowded. Save money by buying a ticket before boarding, or better, buy a ten-ticket pack.

Events

● **Jazzkaar, Tallinn** It can't be easy getting the big names to make a trip to the Baltics, but that's exactly what the Jazzkaar festival has managed to do over the years. Acts have become increasingly international, with artists gathered from France, Portugal, Cuba, Brazil, Japan and the US and UK performing across the city. April; ⓦwww.jazzkaar.ee.

● **Martini Festival** Not to be confused with 007's favourite cocktail, this is an ancient festival that marks the start of winter in Lativa. There are, however, Martini balls – non-alcoholic wads of beans, peas, potatoes and hemp. It also marks the start of the masquerade season. Nov 10.

● **Midsummer** People flee to the countryside when the summer solstice arrives. Special foods (cheeses and pies) are made for the occasion, while flower-and-grass wreaths are strung up. Usually June 21.

● **Ollesummer, Tallinn** The largest beer festival of the Nordic countries, Estonia's Ollesummer has over 100 different brews on hand to lure nearly 100,000 thirsty visitors. Music and food stalls keep you busy while you drink. Early July; ⓦwww.ollesummer.ee.

● **Vilnius Jazz Festival** Jazz junkies turn up en masse for this East–West music fusion, while Lithuania's Russian Drama Theatre comes alive for the three days the acts come to town. Mid-Sept; ⓦwww.vilniusjazz.lt.

Baltic States online

Estonia info www.visitestonia.com
Rail www.edel.ee
Tallinn info www.tallinn.ee

Latvia info www.latviatourism.lv
Rail www.ldz.lv
Riga info www.virtualriga.com
Lithuania info www.visitlithuania.net
Bus www.eurolines.lt
Vilnius info www.vilnius.lt

THE BALTIC STATES

www.roughguides.com

Belgium and Luxembourg

BELGIUM
Capital Brussels
Population 10,379,067
Languages Flemish, French and German
Currency Euro (€)

LUXEMBOURG
Capital Luxembourg City
Population 474,413
Languages Luxembourgish (national language), French and German (administrative languages)

Currency Euro (€)
When to go May–September, when the weather's at its warmest. Fortunately, the crowds aren't much of an issue, outside of Bruges (Belgium)
When not to go Overcast skies, raincoats and umbrellas are prevalent year-round, but November–March provides the strongest dose of misery from above
Minimum daily budget €28

Belgium's cultural diversity belies its reputation among travellers as merely a great country to pass through. The EU's central administrative offices here may have added to the diversity, but the notorious bureaucracy that comes with the influx of Eurocrats has been a difficult image issue to overcome.

Belgium has three official languages. The French-speaking Walloons in the south make up about forty percent, the Flemish speakers up north account for nearly sixty percent, and there are small pockets of German speakers on the eastern border who barely show up on the lingual radar screen. The effect

Average daily temperatures (°C) and monthly rainfall (mm) in Belgium and Luxembourg

	Jan	Feb	Mar	Apr	May	June	July	Aug	Sept	Oct	Nov	Dec
Brussels												
max °C	14	14	16	18	22	27	30	30	27	23	18	15
min °C	6	6	8	9	13	17	19	19	17	14	9	7
rainfall mm	53	53	46	36	25	10	3	10	30	58	56	53
Luxembourg City												
max °C	3	4	10	14	18	21	23	22	19	13	7	4
min °C	-1	-1	1	4	8	11	13	12	10	6	3	0
rainfall mm	61	65	42	47	64	64	60	84	72	53	67	51

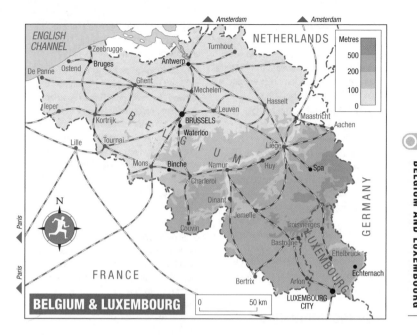

ENGLISH CHANNEL

NETHERLANDS

Amsterdam   Amsterdam

Zeebrugge   Turnhout

De Panne Ostend Bruges Antwerp

Ghent   Mechelen

Ieper   Hasselt

Kortrijk   Leuven   Maastricht

Lille Tournai   BRUSSELS   Aachen

Waterloo   Liège

Mons Binche   Namur   Huy   Spa

Charleroi

Dinant

Couvin   Jemelle   Troisvierges

Bastogne   Ettelbruck

Echternach

Bertrix   Arlon

LUXEMBOURG CITY

FRANCE

Paris

BELGIUM

LUXEMBOURG

GERMANY

Metres
500
200
100
0

BELGIUM & LUXEMBOURG   0   50 km

is a divided country (and incredible gourmet beer and rectangular waffles). Luxembourg, though just barely large enough to be found on a hand-held map of Europe, is a fairy tale of villages and woodlands that, unlike Belgium, clings fiercely to its identity. In the north of the country, there's skiing, hiking and rock climbing, waterfalls and fast-flowing rivers, and towering castles. The south has a history of wine-making, and you can reach just about any spot in the country from the capital within an hour.

Main attractions

● **The Bock casemates, Luxembourg City** In 963 AD, Sigefroi, Count of Ardennes, laid the cornerstone of Luxembourg City on a rocky outcrop now called "the Bock". The most impressive remains of this high fortress are the labyrinthine casemates – built in

1644 – which sheltered 35,000 people when the city was bombed during World War II. There are 17km of this damp maze of subterranean passageways open to the public.

● **Bruges** The most popular tourist attraction in Belgium is this entire town, the best-preserved medieval city in Europe. On some streets you feel as if you're wandering through a museum's thirteenth-century installation.

● **Grand Place, Brussels** Unfolding like a personal discovery as you enter from one of the many narrow side streets, the Belgian capital's twelfth-century central square is a popular place to sip coffee or eat an intimate meal while gazing at some of the finest Baroque guildhalls in the country. The Hôtel de Ville is the only building that survived King Louis XIV's bombing in 1695 and is open for tours.

● **Waterloo, Belgium** In 1815, the Duke of Wellington drafted a message

www.roughguides.com

in this town announcing the defeat of Napoleon. The Battle of Waterloo (which was mostly fought in nearby Braine-l'Alleud) is commemorated with the Butte du Lion (Lion's Mound) monument and a platinum-selling song by Abba.

● **Manneken Pis, Brussels** This tiny statue of a urinating boy, sculpted in bronze by Jerôme Duquesnoy in 1619, has an undefined history (some say he extinguished a fire with his you-know-what), yet the city has embraced this rather unorthodox landmark, sometimes dressing up the boy in one of his many hundreds of costumes (which allow for simulated urination). And, thanks to the tourist industry, you can take home a "urinating boy" key chain or bottle opener to help rekindle the feeling you had when you first laid eyes on him.

Also recommended

● **Play some chess** Head to Le Greenwich, rue Royale 316, an "Old World" café in Brussels known for its top-notch chess matches, and test your skills against one of the local masters.

● **Try the local brew** Belgian beer must, possibly by law, only be served in the glass that was specifically made for it, such is the level of sophistication (and marketing) in this country. Many of the beers have a higher alcohol content than wine and, if you sink a few of those cute little bottles, you may have a difficult time finding your way back to your hostel. But if you only taste one a day, it'll take about a year to try them all.

● **Visit Spa** Not just any old spa, *the* spa. Since Roman times, the Belgian town of Spa in the Ardennes has been known for its curative baths. The rich and famous of the sixteenth century came here, and Victor Hugo was a regular. There are still several spas in this

town you can visit: Pouhon Pierre-le-Grand Spa and Les Thermes de Spa are among the best known.

● **See diamonds being cut** The diamond trade has made its home in Antwerp for centuries. Precious stones may pass through continually, but it's not all that easy for visitors to see what's happening. At Antwerp's Diamond Museum (@www.diamantmuseum.be), you can watch a diamond-cutter at work.

Costs

Luxembourg may have the highest GDP per capita in Europe, but it's not as expensive as Norway or Switzerland. Both Luxembourg and Belgium are priced roughly the same as Germany – bargains aren't easy to come by, but they can be found with careful looking and a willing-ness to wander well off the main routes. Living on €28 a day is possible sleeping in tents and on public-park benches, but €45 a day is going to allow for some cheap restaurant meals, museums and a few lattes to wash down your waffles.

Accommodation

Hostels are cheap here (€13–18 for a dorm), but there's not an abundance of them and most get booked up over the popular summer months. Campgrounds with cabin rentals can be a good option (there's a free booklet you can pick up in the tourist office listing where they are and what they cost), but you'll want to get in the habit of booking ahead.

Eating and drinking

You can find sandwiches for under €5, and there's the usual assortment of kebabs and pizzas, but in general you'll have to choose between your wallet and your palate – one is likely to suffer. A decent meal can be found for under €17. The food in the French part of the country is on a par with the best French cuisine. In the Flemish part, it's much like the food in the Netherlands.

Transport

As compact countries, Belgium and Luxembourg are easy to get around, and the short distances make the fares relatively cheap. There are no domestic flights and even the official tourist website recommends the trains over the inter-city buses. In the major cities, trams and buses are available – the only subway is in Brussels, for which five- and ten-journey tickets are good value if you're in town for more than a day. Check out the multi-mode travel cards for longer visits.

Luxembourg has one main rail route with a few lesser lines that branch off. Buses supplement the other areas. Ask at the train station for special one-day travel cards.

By train

Benelux Tourrail Pass (also valid in Luxembourg and the Netherlands) Any five days of travel in one month US$233 (first class), US$148 (second class) and US$116 (youth pass). Several more rail deals are available through the Belgian rail website (Ⓦwww.railpasshop.com).
Eurail Benelux-Germany Pass (also valid in Germany and the Netherlands) Ranges from any five days of travel in two months – US$429 (first class), US$325 (second class) and US$265 (youth, second class) – to any ten days of travel in two months US$655 (first class), US$495 (second class) and US$395 (youth, second class).
InterRail Benelux Pass Ranges from any three days of travel in one month – €157 (first class), €117 (second class) and €75 (youth, second class) – to any eight days of travel in one month €329

(first class), €244 (second class) and €159 (youth, second class).
Weekend Ticket You get fifty percent off rail fares if you leave after 7pm on Friday and return by the Sunday of the same weekend. It's also possible to leave and return the same day. The catch is that tickets are not transferable, change-able or refundable. Visit Ⓦwww.b-rail.be for more information.

For Europe-wide Eurail and InterRail passes, see p.50. For tips and tricks on maximizing your rail pass, see p.75.

By bus

A Busabout pass (see p.52) allows some travel in Belgium. Because so much of Belgium is accessible by train, buses are only used for short distances and parts of the Ardennes with few rail lines. For internal bus prices, see Ⓦwww.delijn.be. In Luxembourg, domestic buses can be found at Ⓦwww.autobus.lu. For buses from Belgium to other countries, see Ⓦwww.eurolines.be.

Events

● **Binche carnival, Belgium** Binche hosts the famed orange-throwing parade (don't throw them back; they're good luck) when dozens of Gilles march with what appears to be John Lennon masks and giant ostrich-feather hats. This multi-day carnival fest is one of the oldest in Europe. Feb (Shrove Tues); Ⓦwww.carnavaldebinche.be.

● **Dancing Procession of St Willibrord, Echternach** There are probably several ways to purge your sins, but since the death of St Willibrord in 739, pilgrims in Echternach have been shaking a leg while shaking loose the evil spirits. People come from across Europe to dance to the sound of the sixteenth-century bell in the town's abbey. May (Whit Tues); Ⓦwww.willibrord.lu.

www.roughguides.com

- **National Day, Luxembourg**
National Day is June 23, but for more action than the traditional cathedral Te Deum song and military parade, show up the evening before for a torchlight parade, fireworks and a huge party. Several other towns around the country have celebrations, complete with pyrotechnics. June 22–23.

- **Ommegang pageant** Brussels' Grand Place gets invaded by 3000 spectators (including the royal family) for the Ommegang, a procession of nobles in period costume as well as craftsmen and soldiers. To view the pageant, book in advance with the tourist office (Ⓦwww.ommegang.be). Try the town of Mechelen if the one in Brussels is sold out. First Tues & Thurs of July.

Belgium and Luxembourg online

Belgium info Ⓦwww.visitbelgium.com
Rail Ⓦwww.b-rail.be
Bus Ⓦwww.delijn.be
Brussels info Ⓦwww.brusselsinternational.be
Luxembourg info Ⓦwww.ont.lu
Rail Ⓦwww.cfl.lu
Bus Ⓦwww.autobus.lu

Britain

Capitals London (England), Edinburgh (Scotland) and Cardiff (Wales)
Population 60,609,153
Languages English (also Welsh and Scottish Gaelic)
Currency British pound (GBP)
When to go May–September, when the weather should be lovely (if it's not raining and there's no heat wave), but with so much to do inside (museums, pubs, getting lost on the Underground), you can get by just fine if the weather turns miserable
When not to go July and August are crowded at the best budget accommodations, while October–March is seriously cold and rainy, and makes seeing London by foot rather unpleasant
Minimum daily budget €46

A famous headline that ran in the British press read: "Fog in the Channel, Continent Cut Off". There's now an underground umbilical cord of sorts, but in the minds of the Brits there's little question who the parent in the relationship is. That is to say, there's a strong sense of cultural independence. The Brits are profoundly British and only European by default. Moreover, the nation has developed the sort of pride one can only acquire as the power centre of a colonial empire. Never mind the state of the empire today; the rich history and left-over architecture seems to be enough. Yet, with common immigration issues, flourishing trade, and quicker (and cheaper) international transport, Britain finds itself becoming increasingly closer to mainland Europe.

Average daily temperatures (°C) and monthly rainfall (mm) in Britain

	Jan	Feb	Mar	Apr	May	June	July	Aug	Sept	Oct	Nov	Dec
Edinburgh												
max °C	6	7	8	11	14	17	19	18	16	12	9	7
min °C	1	1	2	3	6	9	11	11	8	5	3	2
rainfall mm	56	41	48	38	51	51	64	69	64	61	64	63
London												
max °C	7	7	9	12	16	19	22	22	18	14	10	7
min °C	3	3	4	5	7	10	12	12	10	8	5	4
rainfall mm	64	51	51	48	56	56	66	76	64	74	69	69
Cardiff												
max °C	8	8	11	13	17	19	22	21	18	15	11	9
min °C	2	2	4	5	8	10	12	12	10	7	4	3
rainfall mm	119	91	89	65	65	66	61	90	104	117	117	128

www.roughguides.com

235

The nations of Wales and Scotland, each with proud cultures and rich histories of their own, are politically connected to England via the central government in London. The names get a bit confusing from here on. The official name of the country is the United Kingdom of Great Britain and Northern Ireland. When people speak about the UK, they're referring to this: the political grouping of England, Scotland, Wales and Northern Ireland. When they say "Great Britain" or "Britain", they're excluding Northern Ireland (but sometimes they don't mean

to). That's the confusing part for most visitors. England, Scotland and Wales (and Northern Ireland) each try to qualify a team for the football World Cup and European Championships, but only the United Kingdom sends a team to the Olympics (under the banner of "Great Britain and Northern Ireland"). Go figure.

The hamlets and towns in the countryside resemble scenes out of Frodo's Shire, while the cities are a maze of thriving, bustling commerce and fashion (and near misses, as tourists forget to look right as they cross the street).

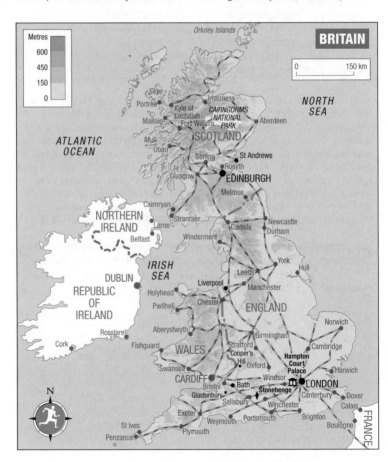

There are far more famous sites than your wallet and schedule will allow, but the cheap international air tickets and language combine to make London an excellent starting point for many travellers, so you won't be the only one trying to get your footing on the travel trail.

Main attractions

- **Hampton Court Palace, Greater London** For nearly 200 years, Hampton Court was the centre of England's royal and political history. The State Apartments of Henry VIII, whose Great Hall features a double hammerbeam ceiling, are among the most popular attractions, though some time should be saved for exploring the extensive gardens, plus one of the most vexing hedge mazes you'll encounter. It's 35 minutes from London by train from Waterloo station. Ⓦwww.hrp.org.uk.

- **Houses of Parliament, London** The original building can be traced back to the eleventh century and is today home of the House of Commons (elected) and House of Lords (if you own more than ten polo ponies or a Gulfstream jet). It's mostly known for Big Ben, which is not the clock, but the 13.8-tonne bell inside. For reasonably good entertainment, view the House of Commons from the gallery when the Prime Minister fields (sometimes ruthless) questions. See Ⓦwww.parliament.uk for parliamentary session times.

- **Westminster Abbey, London** Every Coronation since 1066 has taken place in this architectural masterpiece. There are also over 3000 people buried here, including Geoffrey Chaucer, Charles Dickens, Charles Darwin, Isaac Newton, Laurence Olivier and Ben Jonson, an Elizabethan poet who was buried standing up.

- **British Museum, London** When a colonial superpower decides to bring home souvenirs, it doesn't mess about. Many of the world's treasures can be found under this one (impressive) roof, with free admission. See p.26 for more.

- **Tower of London** The Tower of London isn't much of a tower, but it is the best-preserved medieval castle in any European capital. It's been the royal living quarters, a prison for notorious traitors and, once, even housed lions and bears. Today, it's best known as the only place you can get nearly as close to the royal jewels as Camilla. See Ⓦwww.hrp.org.uk for opening times and prices.

- **Bath** Here you'll find the Royal Crescent, a majestic half-ring of buildings designed by John Wood in 1767. There's also Bath Abbey, with arching stained-glass windows and ornate spires. But the big pull (with a price to match) is the Roman Baths (Ⓦwww.romanbaths .co.uk), built approximately 2000 years ago over a hot spring that spits up over a million litres of 46.5ºC water a day.

Edinburgh Castle This castle looks like it's dropped straight out of *The Lord of the Rings*. Occupying the top half of a rocky hill in the centre of the city, this ancient castle and current UNESCO treasure gets over one million visitors a year and seems to sell as many postcards. See Ⓦwww.edinburghcastle .biz for tour times and prices.

- **London Eye** If you tire of things designed and built by dead people, take a spin in the world's largest Ferris wheel (138m), which takes 3.75 million visitors per year. Pre-book tickets online to avoid the queues, Ⓦwww.londoneye.com.

Also recommended

- **Join in the Summer Solstice at Stonehenge, England** The most

www.roughguides.com

interesting time to visit this ancient enigma is during the longest day of the year, when about 30,000 people show up. What's the big deal about this pile of rocks? Stonehenge is believed to have been built by the Druids, but how they moved these four-tonne stones from 400km away (in the Preseli mountains in Wales) in 2000 BC, a time when hydraulic fork-lift operators were hard to find, is something of an engineering marvel.

● **See a play at Shakespeare's Globe** A reconstruction of the original open-air playhouse, the Globe Theatre in London is Shakespeare's backyard. The season runs from May to September; see ⓦwww.shakespeares-globe.org for play schedules and prices.

● **Hike or ski Cairngorms National Park, Scotland** It may be a relatively new park (created in 2003) but its 3800 square kilometres contain the UK's largest arctic mountain landscape (including four out of five of Scotland's highest mountains), plus a quarter of Britain's threatened birds, mammals and plants. Loaded with forests, lochs and glens, there's enough variety to suit any avid hiker or skier. ⓦwww.cairngorms.co.uk.

● **Play golf at St Andrews, Scotland** The Royal and Ancient Golf Club of St Andrews is unlikely to accept you as a member, but that doesn't mean you can't play a round on the 600-year-old Old Course, the world's first golf course. The bunkers are the size of squash courts, the wind is typically hovering just around gale force and the thick gorse bushes can eat golf balls by the twelve-pack, if the €153 green fee doesn't eat your wallet first. See ⓦwww.standrews.org.uk for course information and bookings.

Costs

Britain's a cheap place to fly to and from, but that's where the bargains start and

end. London, in particular, can put a hole in your budget, largely because of all the perceived "must-sees", many with a horrific admission fee. In London, figure on €46 a day as a minimum, more if you plan to see a few things and sample the odd pint of lager. With a full day of sight-seeing, a public transport travel card and a pit stop at the pub, don't be surprised if you're closer to €55 a day. The London Pass (ⓦwww.londonpass.com) gives you access to a fistful of museums and tours for €39 per day, or €46 if you throw in free public transport.

Accommodation

In London, there's no such thing as a cheap place to stay unless you're taking a nap in the park and partying all night. There is plenty of budget accommodation – even in high season – but it's hard to find anything for under €16. Single rooms at hostels can be found for €35–50; expect to pay higher in London. To find a room, ⓦwww .londontown.com offers some great discounts.

Eating and drinking

There are loads of fantastic inexpensive treats, especially the Indian offerings at the local curry house and a selection of trendy sandwich delis and hip gastro-pubs. Still, a portion of hot chips (French fries) with salt and vinegar is hard to beat (about €1.50). Much of the traditional pub food doesn't seem all that fresh or appetizing, especially since they seem to think it's a selling point to announce that there's blood in some of the items. Black pudding (made with pig's blood and eaten at breakfast), for example, sounds more like something you'd expect to find in Transylvania. Restaurants can be budget killers, but there's plenty of non-*McDonald's* fast food to keep your palate busy.

BRITAIN

www.roughguides.com

▲ British Museum, London

Transport

Britain has the unique distinction of being home to Europe's most expensive rail service, and without getting any prizes for efficiency, speed or comfort. Neither Eurail nor InterRail passes cover Britain, though numerous regional rail passes do – for all the options, see Ⓦwww .britrail.com. The bus (or coach as the long-distance variety is usually called) is a very popular option in Britain, especially for single trips. It takes a bit longer, but unless you book your train tickets in advance, there are significant savings to be had. A trip from London to Edinburgh, for example, costs €164 (less with advance purchase) and takes about 4hr 30min by train; it's €42 by coach, but takes nearly twice as long.

As much fun as London is to traverse by foot, it's somewhat easier and much faster by Underground (aka "the Tube"). The cheapest single ticket costs around €4.70; for more than a short trip, a Travelcard (also valid on buses) is the way to go: a one-day pass for travel in zones one and two costs €6.60 (€8.50 peak), a three-day Travelcard is €21.75. If you're staying for longer than a day,

buy an Oyster card, see Ⓦwww.tfl.gov .uk for more details, which gives reductions on all fares.

Car drivers shouldn't forget the €9.45 congestion charge to drive into London (see Ⓦwww.cclondon.com).

London River Services runs public transport on the Thames from Embankment to Woolwich. Many operators offer a 33 percent discount if you have a Travelcard or Oyster card.

By train

BritRail Consecutive Pass Ranges from any three days – US$305 (first class), US$159 (youth, second class) – to a month of travel US$1195 (first class), US$635 (youth, second class). **BritRail Flexi Pass** Any three days of travel in two months US$375 (first class), US$255 (second class) and US$205 (youth, second class). Any eight days of travel in two months US$679 (first class), US$459 (second class) and US$365 (youth, second class). Any fifteen days of travel in two months US$1025 (first class), US$689 (second class) and US$555 (youth, second class). Note: This one needs to be booked from home six months in advance. Can be

239

combined with a Eurail pass if you're between 16 and 25, which shrinks the price by fifty percent.

Britrail Scottish Freedom Pass Any four days of travel in eight days US$235 (second class). Any eight days of travel in fifteen days US$315 (second class).

By bus

A Busabout pass (see p.52) connects London with Paris and mainland Europe. For internal bus prices, see Ⓦwww.nationalexpress.com. For buses to other countries, see Ⓦwww.eurolines.co.uk.

Events

- **Grand National, Aintree** You might call it "the Ironman Triathlon for horses". Four and a half miles long with thirty wicked fences – many riders are happy if they can just hold on until the finish. There's a statue on hand at the Aintree racecourse in Liverpool so you can pay homage to Red Rum, the Grand National's greatest champion. April; Ⓦwww.aintree.co.uk.

- **Chelsea Flower Show, London** Even if you don't have the greenest of fingers, or know a fern from a Ficus, the Chelsea Flower Show is likely to impress. At the end of spring, the eleven-acre site at the Royal Hospital becomes a blooming wonderland of colour with more fragrances than an airport duty-free shop. May; Ⓦwww.rhs.org.uk/chelsea.

- **Glastonbury Festival, Somerset** The open-air music festival of all open-air music festivals (much of it spent under a tent). The perimeter of the Worthy Farm venue stretches for more than 10km, and you'll find more diversity here than Darwin found in the Galapagos Islands, not to mention some of the world's top music acts. June; Ⓦwww.glastonburyfestivals.co.uk.

- **Wimbledon Championships, London** The world's greatest tennis tournament is set on a stage that most people associate more with golf. Tennis aficionados, celebrities and long queues of fans turn out to see who will hold the jug trophy (men) and the oversized hors d'oeuvre plate trophy (women) over their head at the end of the two-week contest. End June–beginning July; Ⓦwww.wimbledon.org.

- **Edinburgh Fringe Festival** August in Edinburgh means one thing: The Festival, and the Fringe forms just one major part of it. From near and far, high and low, come the world's jugglers, fire eaters, comedians, singers, dancers, prancers … Over a million tickets get sold for this eclectic performing-arts bash. Aug; Ⓦwww.edfringe.com.

- **Notting Hill Carnival, London** Each summer, the streets of Notting Hill in west London fill with technicolour floats, costumed dancers and half a million spectators (Europe's largest street fest) as the spleen-shaking sound systems fill the air. Last weekend in Aug; Ⓦwww.nottinghillcarnival.biz.

- **Bonfire Night** (Guy Fawkes' Night) On November 5, 1605, the Gunpowder Plot, a conspiracy to blow up the English Parliament and King James I, was under way. Someone leaked the plot to Lord Monteagle, word spread, and it failed. The foiling of this rebellious deed has become a national pastime, celebrated nationwide with fireworks and bonfires, during which effigies of the conspirator, Guy Fawkes, are burned.

Britain online

Country info Ⓦwww.visitbritain.com
Rail Ⓦwww.nationalrail.co.uk
Coach Ⓦwww.nationalexpress.co.uk
London info Ⓦwww.visitlondon.com
Edinburgh info Ⓦwww.edinburgh.org
Cardiff info Ⓦwww.visitcardiff.com

www.roughguides.com

Bulgaria

Capital Sofia
Population 7,385,367
Language Bulgarian
Currency Lev (Lv)
When to go Mid-April to mid-September, when the weather is warm. If snowfall is plentiful, you can ski from just before Christmas until April
When not to go October– February, when there's little relief for non-skiers
Minimum daily budget €19

Tucked away in the southeastern corner of Europe, Bulgaria calls itself the "Jewel of the Balkans", but that may be overstating things just a tad. It has come a long way since it threw off the choke-hold of the Ottoman Empire in 1870, but there are far fewer sights and accommodation choices than most European countries offer – though fewer tourists, less Western influence and lower prices as well. Independent travel isn't common, but the traditional towns, romantic architecture and mountain scenery provide enough to sculpt an interesting itinerary.

There's a strong Russian influence here (Cyrillic alphabet included), partly out of gratitude to the 200,000 Russian casualties suffered while liberating Bulgaria from the Turks in 1878. Today, only 85 percent of the country's inhabitants are Bulgarian. Besides almost a million Turks, there are smaller minorities of Macedonians and Roma (Gypsy).

Finding Bulgaria on the map isn't the only thing that trips up some travellers; nodding up and down means "no" and shaking your head from side to side means "yes".

Main attractions

- **Valley of the Roses** Roses have been grown in the fertile valley east of Sofia since the Phoenicians were the hottest act in town. You won't find a more all-encompassing celebration of their beauty anywhere in the world.

- **The Black Sea Riviera** Arguably Bulgaria's greatest asset, the beaches of the Black Sea rightfully fill up during the summer holidays. The best ones can be found northeast of Varna. If you

Average daily temperatures (°C) and monthly rainfall (mm) in Bulgaria											
	Jan	Feb	Mar	Apr	May	June	July	Aug	Sept	Oct	Nov	Dec
Sofia												
max °C	2	4	9	14	19	23	26	26	22	16	8	3
min °C	-4	-3	1	5	9	12	14	14	11	6	1	-2
rainfall mm	33	36	38	53	69	79	56	43	41	36	51	43

www.roughguides.com

241

need a day in the shade, the cliff-caves which form Aladzha Monastery are 7km southwest of Golden Sands.

● **Nesebâr** This former Byzantine trading hub is at least 2500 years old, and you can't swing a cat in it without hitting a medieval church. It's all about adorable little squares, cobbled streets and a crumbling city wall – impressively jammed together on a tiny peninsula shooting out into the Black Sea.

Also recommended

● **Ski on the cheap** The alpine skiing World Cup hasn't raced in Bulgaria for twenty years, but there's good skiing to be had if you're not too picky about amenities. Aim for Borovets, Bansko or the Rhodope

mountains. See Ⓦwww.bulgariaski .com for resort information.

● **Take a holy hike** Over the ages, God-fearing Bulgarians have built monasteries with a vengeance (many of them well and truly off the beaten track), so there are plenty of pleasant, calorie-burning vistas for the visitor. Rila Monastery, 120km south of Sofia, is where Bulgarian culture was nursed during the five centuries of Turkish rule, and it can be reached after a few days on foot from Borovets.

● **Sip some water** Mineral water, that is. The Bulgarian stuff has been world famous in the Balkans since the pre-tap-water days. There are 1600 wells to choose from, but if you only have time to fill your water bottle in one or two spots, try Hissar in the middle of the country, and Pomorie (🖰www.pomorie.com) outside Burgas. If you've previously been abusing your liver, get the stuff with sulphate in it, said to get that organ back into shape.

Costs

Bulgaria is about as cheap as Europe gets. You can probably find ways to scrape by on pocket change, but allow for €19 per day at the very least. Double that to rub some comfort on it.

Accommodation

This is the one area where the Bulgarian tourist industry slaps you with special tourist prices, so don't expect accommodation to be as comparatively cheap as other Bulgarian prices. Upper-end hotels charge €45, but if you shop around, you can find a bed with a roof over it for under €10.

Eating and drinking

Bulgarians keep full with meals of meat, potatoes, beans and salads. These, plus the precarious liquors (rakia and mastika) used to toss it back, are going to be your cheapest feed. Breakfast is a nice bread-based snack on the run picked up at most hole-in-the-wall kiosks and washed down with boza, a gluggy millet drink loved by those who've managed to acquire a taste for it. Lunch is the main meal of the day and offers the best value. A late dinner – which you should be able to find for less than €7 – signals the switch from aperitifs to serious drinking.

Transport

Due to the Balkan mountain range, travelling east–west is going to be faster and easier than any north–south routes. You can get across the country by train

in first class for under €15 (worth it, if you have long legs). The buses are slow, but the trains are even slower.

Sofia has a well-organized public transport system of buses, trams and trolleybuses. And the roughly 25-cent fare is extremely reasonable. The trick is getting good information, as the signs (sometimes just a rusted pole) leave a lot to the imagination. Don't forget to buy an extra ticket for your rucksack and punch both tickets when you get on – or face a stiff (€2) fine.

By train

Eurail Bulgaria Pass Any three days of travel in one month US$109 (first class). **Balkans Flexi Pass** (also valid in Greece, Romania, Serbia, Montenegro, Macedonia and Turkey). Any five days of travel in one month US$256 (adult) and US$153 (youth). Any ten days in one month US$447 (adult) and US$268 (youth). Any fifteen days in one month US$539 (adult) and US$324 (youth).

For Europe-wide InterRail and Eurail passes, see p.50. For tips and tricks on maximizing your rail pass, see p.75.

By bus

Busabout doesn't operate in Bulgaria. For internal bus prices, see 🖰www .biomet.bg and 🖰etapgroup.com /etap. For buses to other countries, see 🖰www.eurolines.bg.

Events

● **Trifon Zarezan** This wine festival takes place on "Vinegrowers' Day" and is a blessing of the grape harvest. Its roots (no pun intended) go all the way back to the Thracians, an illiterate group of ancients who nevertheless enjoyed the odd cup of tinto. Feb 1 or 14.

● **Ladouvane** The name means "Singing to Rings", but this festival is

www.roughguides.com

243

all about unmarried women looking for husbands. Confusingly enough, it's celebrated on opposite ends of the year in different parts of the country – either New Year's Eve or Midsummer's Day – so if you're a lovelorn man, make sure you're in the right place at the right time.

● **Festival of Roses, Kazanlûk** With over seventy percent of the world's production, Bulgaria has long cornered the market on rose oil. Not as lucrative as petroleum, alas, but still a matter of some national pride. In early summer, homage is paid to this symbol of youth and beauty. First Sun in June.

● **Fake Christmas** Under communism, Bulgarians weren't allowed to celebrate Christmas. Solution: make up a new, non-religious holiday the day after. And guess what? It looks an awful lot like Christmas. Today, they celebrate both. Dec 26.

Bulgaria online

Country info Ⓦwww.bulgariatravel.org
Rail Ⓦwww.bdz.bg
Bus Ⓦwww.biomet.bg and Ⓦetapgroup .com/etap

Croatia

Capital Zagreb
Population 4,494,749
Language Croatian
Currency Kuna (Kn)
When to go May–June and
September are good for beating
crowds on the Adriatic

When not to go July and August
are hot, expensive and jam-packed
with tourists. Best avoided unless
you're going for the classical music
of Zagreb's Summer Festival, in
which case you have no choice
Minimum daily budget €34

The Croatians managed to keep their
glorious coastline from the limelight
thanks to communism and the Yugoslav
Wars. Now that it's safe to go, travellers have realized that just across the
water from the overdeveloped Italian
coast is the even nicer Croatian one.
And it's cheaper. Cities such as Solin,
Rab, Rovinj and Pula, and islands like
Korčula and Mljet, have become the new
playgrounds of those who appreciate
the pristine. Well, comparatively pristine.
The best way to enjoy it is from the deck
of a yacht, but if you can afford one of
those, chances are you won't be holding
this book.

Many rock climbers come to Croatia,
and there are even a few inland
ski resorts – though the Croatians
themselves go to neighbouring Slovenia
or Austria to ski. Only a few areas, in
eastern Croatia, display the ravages

of war, but regular tourism won't take
you near them; all the attractions
are either in the capital or along the
coast. The extreme southeast is also
a good jumping-off point into the even
less explored Montenegro, and we've
included a mini-profile of Montenegro
on p.290.

Main attractions

- **Dubrovnik** Situated near the
southern border with Serbia, this
1300-year-old architectural city gem has
been lovingly rebuilt, stone by stone,
since the intense shelling in 1991, and is
looking better than ever.

- **Diocletian's Palace, Split** You'd
think that Italy would have all the best
Roman ruins in the world, but these
rock piles in the southern city of Split

Average daily temperatures (°C) and monthly rainfall (mm) in Croatia

	Jan	Feb	Mar	Apr	May	June	July	Aug	Sept	Oct	Nov	Dec
Zagreb												
max °C	3	5	11	16	21	24	27	26	22	16	8	4
min °C	-4	-3	1	5	9	13	14	14	11	6	2	-1
rainfall mm	52	48	56	68	83	95	79	79	79	93	86	66

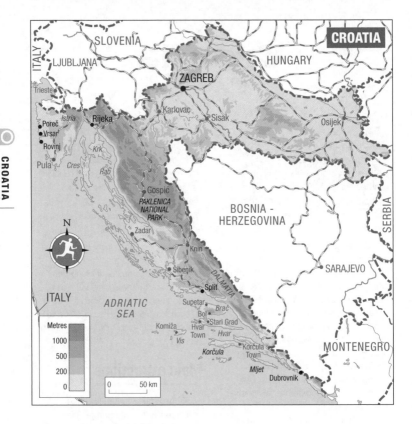

must make it into the Top 10 at least. The ruins are what are left of the retirement home of the Roman Emperor Diocletian.

● **Lotrščak Tower, Zagreb** The medieval centre of Croatia's capital is a treat for the eyes, and no place will give you a better view than this old watchtower at the southern gate of the inner city. Among the sights is the Cathedral of the Assumption of the Blessed Virgin Mary.

● **Korčula** This Dalmatian island south of Split claims to be the birthplace of Marco Polo. Whether or not it's true, it's captivating enough to merit a visit – imagine the Greek islands before tourists

started outnumbering locals and you've got Korčula. If you can, try and catch the Morecka (performances held weekly May–Sept), a twelfth-century sword dance.

Also recommended

● **Skinny-dip in the Adriatic Sea** Croatia has a claim to fame as the first European country to open its arms to nude bathers – or naturists, to use the rather eco-sounding euphemism. Rab Island is where the bare-bum tradition started back in the 1930s, but the sites to head for today are Valalta outside Rovinj, Koversada near Vrsar, and Porei on the Istrian peninsula. Note: single men aren't welcome without a member card from the International Naturist Federation (Ⓦwww.inffni.org). Not to worry – there are plenty of non-official nudie beaches, too. Just to be on the safe side, make sure you're not the first naked person on the beach.

● **Dive off Mljet Island** Even though the cool Adriatic offers less exotic diving than tropical waters, French scuba-gear inventor Jacques Cousteau called the waters around Mljet Island (near Dubrovnik) "one of the most beautiful diving locations in the world". It may be just a matter of time before the place fills up with divers and you have to float in line to get a glimpse of the corals. See Ⓦwww.diving.hr for more information.

● **Climb Aniia Kuk** The innards of Croatia are as rocky as the coast is flat, making it great for climbing. Good routes are accessible from big cities such as Zagreb and Split, but for the truly hair-raising stuff, head for Paklenica (between Rijeka and Split), and take on the 350-metre-high face of Aniia Kuk. See Ⓦwww.climb-croatia.com for route information.

Costs

Communist Yugoslavia was cheap for Western travellers, but those days are all but gone. Prices have steadily risen in recent years, though Croatia is by no means challenging Switzerland or Norway. Be prepared to spend €34 a day as a minimum. Add an extra €20 to sweeten the deal. By the time you reach €75 a day, you're living in style. As always, big cities and tourist spots will charge you more for just about everything.

You'll notice most tourist prices will be displayed in euros but rejigged to kunas according to the day's rate when it comes time to pay.

Accommodation

It's not as cheap as it used to be, but with a smart eye and some patience you can squeeze by on €15–18 a day in living expenses. Ask the tourist office about private rooms in Croatian homes – abundant, reasonably priced and even fun if you're lucky. There are also scores of inexpensive campgrounds along the coast.

Eating and drinking

Figure on at least €10 a day to ward off undernourishment and scurvy. You can save money by grabbing at least one meal a day from a street vendor. Inexpensive cheese-stuffed pastries (*burek*) will keep you going for a few hours. Supermarkets can set you up with the basics, but if you aim for a market instead, like the Dolac market in Zagreb, you'll get a cultural experience thrown in for free.

Transport

Trains are a good deal, with a greater network found in the north and the east, though there is no coastal service, and your Eurail pass won't work here (an InterRail pass that includes Zone D will). The buses are more common transport along the coast (and thus should be booked in advance in the summer). Busabout doesn't cover Croatia but Eurolines (Ⓦwww.autotrans .hr) does; however, if you're coast-hopping and not in a hurry, ferries offer a nice alternative.

In Zagreb, bus and tram tickets cost approximately €1.40 if bought from the driver or by SMS (send "ZG" to 8585); and €1.10 at newsstands; a day pass is around €3.50. In Dubrovnik, a city bus

www.roughguides.com

247

ticket costs roughly €1.40 from the driver and €1.10 at newsstands.

For Europe-wide InterRail and Eurail passes, see p.50. For tips and tricks on maximizing your rail pass, see p.75.

Events

Rijeka Carnival The advent of spring (well, at least the thought of it getting nearer) has been turning things upside down here for over a hundred years. Costumed inhabitants parade through the streets, scare off evil spirits, celebrate their escape from Turkish invasion and generally have a blast. Jan–Feb; ⓦwww .ri-karneval.com.hr.

Split Summer Festival The Croatian National Theatre has been putting on a big show since 1954, and every summer season sees a variety of concerts, dance shows, operas and exhibitions from both Croatian and international performers.

Mid-July to mid-Aug; ⓦwww .splitsko-ljeto.hr.

International Puppet Festival, Zagreb Either you love 'em or they freak you out. Puppets are all the rage in Zagreb as summer winds down. When you're not taking in a show, you can check out a puppet exhibition or learn how to make your own puppet. All performances are judged by two juries – one made up of experts and one of kids. Aug–Sept; ⓦpublic.carnet.hr /pif-festival.

Croatia online

Country info ⓦwww.croatia.hr
Rail ⓦwww.hznet.hr
Bus ⓦwww.zet.hr
Zagreb info ⓦwww.zagreb.hr
Dubrovnik info ⓦwww.dubrovnik -online.com

The Czech and Slovak republics

Czech republic
Capital Prague
Population 10,235,455
Language Czech
Currency Czech crown (CZk)

Slovak republic
Capital Bratislava
Population 5,439,448
Languages Slovak (also Hungarian)
Currency Slovak crown (Sk)

When to go May–June and
September–October, when the sightseeing is at its best (good climate,
fewer visitors). May–October for hiking
When not to go July and August
(for Prague), when it can be hard
to see the cobblestones for all the
tourists standing on them. Outside of
Prague, many castles and museums
close down October–April
Minimum daily budget €18

In 1989, Czechoslovakia divided itself into the Czech Republic (Czechia) and the Slovak Republic (Slovakia) without a shot being fired. This impressive separation, a testament to the liberal, global-minded citizens on both sides, became known as the "Velvet Revolution". The Czech Republic has emerged as one of the star economic engines and tourist attractions of Eastern Europe and keeps raising the bar for its neighbours, though it's no doubt experiencing the growing pains of a young nation. The most famous Czechs fall into two categories: in one, there's Franz Kafka, Milan Kundera and playwright-turned-dissident-turned-president Václav Havel; and on the other side of the rink, Jaromir Jagr and Dominik Hasek. But when you arrive, the literary and ice-hockey powers are overshadowed by the country's wealth of architects. Situated in the middle of Europe, the Czech Republic has been a natural trading centre for centuries, a geographic advantage that has worked against it as well, since more powerful nations have been anxious to march in and take the country for themselves when the opportunity presented itself. Miraculously, Maticka Praha ("little mother Prague") emerged largely unscathed from World War II.

The modern travel hippies making jewellery and playing *Stairway to Heaven* may be limited to the streets of Prague, but the knock-your-socks-off architecture isn't. Several towns, such as Cheb, Kutná Hora and Loket, can boast striking Renaissance and Baroque facades. With hiking, spas and mountain biking, there's also plenty to do once your neck tires of staring at all the soaring spires.

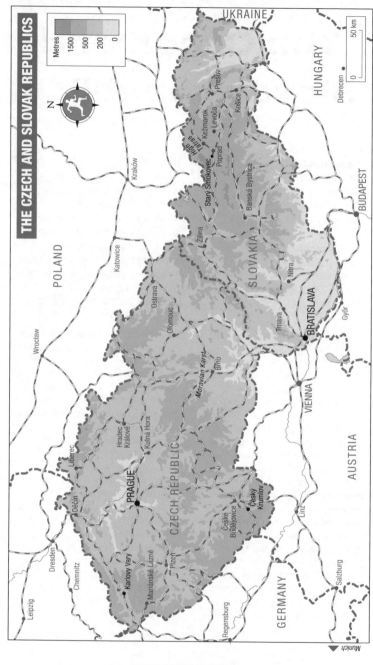

THE CZECH AND SLOVAK REPUBLICS

Metres
1500
500
200
0

N

UKRAINE

HUNGARY

50 km

0

Debrecen

POLAND

Kraków

Katowice

Wrocław

SLOVAKIA

Prešov

Kežmarok

Levoča

Košice

High Tatras

Poprad

Starý Smokovec

Banská Bystrica

Žilina

Nitra

BRATISLAVA

Trnava

Győr

BUDAPEST

VIENNA

AUSTRIA

Linz

Salzburg

Ostrava

Olomouc

Moravian Karst

Brno

CZECH REPUBLIC

Hradec Králové

Kutná Hora

Liberec

Děčín

PRAGUE

Karlovy Vary

Mariánské Lázně

Plzeň

České Budějovice

Český Krumlov

GERMANY

Dresden

Chemnitz

Leipzig

Regensburg

Munich

Slovakia was left holding the less glamorous (or rather, more industrial) end of the stick (but the better skiing facilities) when the countries separated, and is attempting to rebuild without the magnetic draw of a city such as Prague. What that means is there are fewer tourists, cheaper prices and the folk traditions are more intact. There are also plenty of castles and rugged terrain to keep cultural buffs and hiking enthusiasts busy.

Main attractions

● **Staromrstské námrstí (Old Town Square), Prague** You can probably count on one hand the number of people who've visited Prague and never seen the Old Town Square. This 17,000-square-metre centrepiece is the heart of the city, and has been since the tenth century. Today, cafés, buskers and horse-drawn carriages compete for your attention, but this commercial circus still can't hide the beauty of the square. If you follow the flow of human traffic, you'll make the short, cobblestoned stroll to the 600-year-old Charles Bridge, lined with Baroque statues.

● **Prague Castle** On the other side of the river from the Old Town Square, the 1000-year-old walled-in castle peers down on the city from its cliff-top perch. There's plenty of room in the compound for visitors (it's the most popular attraction in Prague) to view the seat of the Czech government since Prince Borivoj.

● **Josefov (Jewish Quarter), Prague** Prague's Jewish cemetery, plus a half-dozen old synagogues and a ceremonial hall, were disturbingly saved by Nazi leaders as an "Exotic Museum of an Extinct Race". Instead, this former Jewish ghetto has survived as a memorial to hundreds of years of oppression.

● **Bratislava** Old City torture chambers, a museum of wine, and the Primate's Palace can all be found in the Old Town centre. The castle hovering above the River Danube was part of the Roman Empire for 400 years and offers great views of the city plus a folk museum.

Also recommended

● **Cleanse your soul at Karlovy Vary** World-famous (in certain circles, anyway) for its regenerative waters, Karlovy Vary, southwest of Prague, is the oldest of the Bohemian spas. The Victorian atmosphere and elegant colonnades may aid the healing process; if not, the surrounding parks with wooded hills should. See ⓦwww.karlovyvary.cz for spa price info.

Average daily temperatures (°C) and monthly rainfall (mm)

	Jan	Feb	Mar	Apr	May	June	July	Aug	Sept	Oct	Nov	Dec
Czech Republic (Prague)												
max °C	1	2	8	12	18	21	22	23	18	12	5	3
min °C	-4	-4	0	2	7	11	12	12	9	4	0	-2
rainfall mm	20	18	25	36	58	69	66	64	41	30	28	23
Slovakia (Bratislava)												
max °C	2	4	11	16	21	24	26	26	22	15	7	3
min °C	-3	-2	2	4	9	13	14	14	11	6	1	-1
rainfall mm	36	41	38	36	56	71	63	61	38	41	53	-1

- **Enjoy "Prague" without the crowds** Český Krumlov is one of Bohemia's most striking towns, and is deservingly on UNESCO's World Heritage list. The charming city centre is car-free and the city's castle (the second largest in the country) rests, almost picture-postcard-like, on a hill overlooking a bend in the Vltava River.

- **Go canyoning and caving around the Moravský kras** The heavily wooded and hilly region of the Moravský kras (Moravian Karst) is home to caves and canyons, several with evidence of prehistoric human inhabitants. You can boat on the underground river or abseil through waterfalls in Rudice. Check out Ⓦwww.cavemk.cz for more info on the region.

- **Hike the Vysoké Tatry** The narrow peaks of the Vysoké Tatry (High Tatras) tower over glacial valleys with dizzying cliff faces, and, down at lower elevation, thick forests cover the hillsides. With a hundred glacial lakes and gurgling streams neatly packed into a small area with trails, it couldn't be better suited for hiking. The end of August is a good time to go, and Starý Smokovec is perhaps the best starting point. For details of hiking and where to stay in the area go to Ⓦwww.tatry.net.

Costs

Outside of Prague and the famous spas, costs can easily be kept to a minimum. The problem for most is that Prague is unmissable and Prague's prices, at least for accommodation, are on a par with those found in Europe's biggest cities. With stand-up dining and hostel dorms, you can survive on around €18 a day, but €28 will give you some breathing room. If you share a decent double room with bath in a mid-range hotel or pension and eat out

at inexpensive restaurants, figure on €38 a day. In Slovakia, things remain a bit cheaper; perhaps €4–5 cheaper per day, slightly more if you're comparing to Prague. ATMs aren't common outside major towns.

Accommodation

This is the most expensive part of travelling here. Private rooms, which a decade ago cost a pittance, are already competitively priced in some areas and, in Prague, exceed the bargains long associated with Eastern Europe. Campgrounds aren't as fancy as some of the multi-star complexes in Western Europe, but there are "chalets" for rent, and a shared double may very well beat whatever deals you can find in the city centre. Around Slovakia, you should be able to find accommodation for less than €15.

Eating and drinking

Normally you can't count beer as a meal, but in this part of the world some travellers seem to be doing just that. And with beer this good (and cheap), it's hard to fault them. Plus, all that communist isolation didn't do much for the development of the cuisine, other than condition people to not pay too much for it. Check out some of the "wine cellars" outside of Prague for a stylish meal. And expect lots of soups, pork and beef, with the occasional goose or wild boar. A nice meal can be found for under €10.

Transport

The region has a comprehensive rail network that's reasonably cheap, clean and mostly dependable. There are some internal flights, but the short distances don't allow you to shave many minutes off the journey. Bus connections for longer routes are often more frequent than the trains (even if a bit slower), and can be especially useful for visiting more remote locations.

By train

InterRail Slovakia Pass Ranges from any three days of travel in one month – €71 (first class), €53 (second class) and €34 (youth, second class) – to any eight days of travel in one month €171 (first class), €128 (second class) and €83 (youth, second class).

InterRail Czech Republic Pass Three days of travel in one month – €71 (first class), €53 (second class) and €34 (youth, second class) – to any eight days of travel in one month €171 (first class), €128 (second class) and €83 (youth, second class).

For European East Pass prices, see p.224.

For Europe-wide InterRail and Eurail passes, see p.50. For tips and tricks on maximizing your rail pass, see p.75.

By bus

A Busabout pass (see p.52) allows some travel in the Czech Republic but does not operate in Slovakia. For internal bus prices, see ⓦwww.vlak-bus .cz (Czech Republic) and ⓦwww.cp.sk (Slovakia). For buses to other countries, see ⓦwww.bei.cz (Czech Republic) and ⓦwww.slovaklines.sk (Slovakia).

Events

● **Burning of the Witches, Prague** This pre-Christian festival for warding off evil has been politically corrected with the burning of bonfires in Prague, mostly at all-night parties. April 30.

● **Khamoro World Gypsy Festival** The itinerant Roma (Gypsies) steer their show on the road into Prague for a gathering to showcase their classical music, jazz, film, theatre, dance, painting and photography. May; ⓦwww.khamoro.cz.

● **Prague Spring International Music Festival** Early summer brings great musicians from around the world to Prague, the international stars complemented by impressive home-grown soloists and orchestras. Venues include Smetana Hall and Rudolfinum, as well as Prague Cathedral. Mid-May to beginning of June; ⓦwww.festival.cz.

● **Bratislava Jazz Days** The first international star appeared here in 1982. Since then, the likes of Bill Evans, Herbie Hancock, Bobby McFerrin and Wynton Marsalis have played this festival. Sept; ⓦwww.bjd.sk.

Czech and Slovak republics online

Czech Republic country info ⓦwww.czechtourism.com
Czech Republic rail ⓦwww.cdrail.cz
Czech Republic bus ⓦwww.vlak -bus.cz
Prague info ⓦwww.prague.cz
Slovakia country info ⓦwww .slovakia.org
Slovakia rail ⓦwww.zsr.sk
Slovakia bus ⓦwww.cp.sk
Bratislava info ⓦwww.bratislava.sk

Denmark

Capital Copenhagen
Population 5,450,661
Languages Danish (also Faroese and Greenlandic)
Currency Danish krone (DKK)
When to go May–August, when the days are long enough to enjoy the frequent spurts of good weather that come your way
When not to go Mid-October to March the gloom is filled with far more freezing drizzle than snow
Minimum daily budget €37

Denmark is full of surprises. An unaccomplished singer and ballet dancer who goes on to become one of the world's great storytellers (Hans Christian Andersen), for example; or the north of the country being home to Europe's largest desert. Denmark may be the smallest Scandinavian nation, but it's no easier to pin down than a Greco-Roman wrestler. It shares social policies with Sweden and Norway and alcohol prices and perceptions with the rest of Europe. And, as such, neatly bridges the gap between its northern neighbours and the centre of the EU.

The three landmasses that comprise the bulk of the country (Zealand, Funen and Jutland, the peninsula that's connected to Germany) each have their own sensibilities. Zealand is perhaps the most distinct, with green hills and undulating heathlands. The northwest part of the peninsula has incredible beaches, some of which are wide and compact enough to drive and bike on.

Copenhagen, Scandinavia's largest and most affordable capital is (like the rest of the country) best conquered by bike. The only thing more stunning than the architecture is the people. As Bill Bryson wrote in *Neither Here Nor There*, "Everyone, without exception, is youthful, fresh-scrubbed, healthy, blond and immensely good-looking. You could cast a Pepsi commercial in Copenhagen in fifteen seconds."

Main attractions

- **Legoland** The little plastic snap-together blocks have got a good deal more sophisticated than they once were, but their simplicity is still their strength,

Average daily temperatures (°C) and monthly rainfall (mm) in Denmark												
Copenhagen	Jan	Feb	Mar	Apr	May	June	July	Aug	Sept	Oct	Nov	Dec
max °C	3	2	5	9	16	19	21	21	16	12	7	4
min °C	-1	-2	0	2	7	11	13	12	10	7	3	0
rainfall mm	43	25	36	41	43	53	66	74	51	53	53	52

and a visit to their Danish birthplace should cap off any lingering childhood fantasies about an entire Lilliputian Lego city. ⓦwww.legoland.dk

● **Ribe** You don't need to be a history buff to be charmed by the oldest town in Scandinavia. The 700 AD market town almost looks its age, partially because it was spared from modernization due to economic decline. If Ribe itself doesn't feel enough like a museum, try its Vikinger (Viking Centre) just south of town.

● **Kronborg Castle, Helsingør** This castle was made famous by Shakespeare when he penned *Hamlet*

and set his play in Elsinore (Helsingør in Danish). Never mind that the real Hamlet was the son of a Zealand pirate and lived on the island of Mors; the story makes for better tourism. And the castle, situated on a promontory jutting into the sea, is impressive enough.

● **The Little Mermaid, Copenhagen** Perhaps the most petite of Denmark's attractions, the statue sitting atop a small rock a few metres from shore at the entrance to Copenhagen's harbour attracts an astounding number of visitors (and graces possibly even more postcards). The mermaid was made famous as Hans Christian Andersen's heroine, but the statue, despite losing its head on a number of occasions, has taken on a following of her own.

Also recommended

● **Dip your feet in the "Marriage of the Waters"** On the northernmost part of Denmark, in the artist's community of Skagen, you can rent a bike and pedal 4km north to the Grenen lighthouse and stand on the very tip of the country, with one foot in the Kattegat Sea and the other in the Skagerrak Sea, and peer out at a faintly visible line where the two seas meet.

● **Take a bike tour around Funen** Stay in farmhouses and castles and, after a long day in the saddle (and if your budget allows), sample one or more of the famous gourmet restaurants in the area. See Ⓦwww .fyn.dk for more info.

● **Windsurf Denmark** Few tourists get blown away by Denmark's wind, but there's good reason to take advantage of it. Just ask Danish World Champion windsurfer Bjorn Dunkerbeck. The sheltered coastal inlets are perfect for beginners and the open sea offers ideal conditions for advanced surfers. And, with over 7300km of coastline, there are plenty of locations to choose from.

Costs

Denmark may be the cheapest of the Scandinavian countries, but that's not saying much, especially since free camping is common in Sweden and Norway, which typically cuts costs by sixty percent. What is inexpensive, compared to its Nordic neighbours, is alcohol. If you're camping (often for free) and preparing your own food, you might squeak by on €19–25 a day. Figure on a minimum of €37 a day with hostel dorms, and €55–65 with cheap rooms and inexpensive restaurants.

▲ Cafés on Nyhavn, Copenhagen

Accommodation

Hostels are a few euros cheaper, on average, than Sweden, but that mainly applies to dorm rooms, which cost €20–25. A private room for two in a hostel with your own bathroom costs €75. Looking for rooms on the side of the road (the sign for a room rental is *rum* or *zimmer*) may be your best bet. You can also find cosy farmhouses that charge less.

Eating and drinking

You'll find most places you stay will set you up with a filling breakfast, included with the accommodation. If not, it's probably available for a relative bargain. Lunch deals for under €8 can be found easily. For dinner, your hostel may provide the best option, even if that's just a kitchen where you can make it yourself. A decent meal in a restaurant isn't going to cost less than €17.

Transport

Denmark is covered by trains, and the few parts that aren't have good bus services. In Copenhagen, you can rent a bike for a small fee at your hostel. If you're going to use public transport a lot, a Copenhagen Card (€30.20 for 24 hours, €60.45 for 72 hours) will save you money, and also gets you into sixty museums for free.

By train

Eurail Denmark Pass Any three days of travel in one month US$136 (first class), $90 (second class) and US$68 (youth, second class). Any seven days of travel in one month US$213 (first class), $140 (second class) and US$105 (youth, second class).

Eurail Scandinavia Pass (also valid in Finland, Norway and Sweden) Any four days of travel in two months US$335 (second class) and US$255 (youth, second class). Any ten days of travel in two months US$525 (second class) and US$395 (youth, second class).

For Europe-wide Eurail and InterRail passes, see p.50. For tips and tricks on maximizing this rail pass, see p.75.

By bus

Busabout doesn't operate in Denmark. For internal bus prices, see Ⓦwww .xbus.dk. For buses to other countries, see Ⓦwww.eurolines.dk.

Events

● **Roskilde festival** Every year, Denmark's (and northern Europe's) biggest rock concert (30min by train from Copenhagen) ignites a pilgrimage stretching to all corners of the continent. The week-long festival kicks off with a bang and doesn't stop no matter how much it rains. Free camping (and mud-pit sliding) included with ticket. Late June or early July; Ⓦwww.roskilde-festival.dk.

● **Copenhagen Jazz Festival** For ten days every summer, many of the world's greatest jazz musicians congregate in the nation's capital and turn it on its head. Early July; Ⓦfestival.jazz.dk.

● **Århus festival** Jesters, jugglers, archers, thespians, jousters and thousands of visitors invade Århus for nine days of cheer and tomfoolery. First Sat in Sept; Ⓦwww.aarhusfestuge.dk.

Denmark online

Country info Ⓦwww.visitdenmark.com
Rail Ⓦwww.dsb.dk
Bus Ⓦwww.xbus.dk
Copenhagen info Ⓦwww.visit copenhagen.dk

www.roughguides.com

Finland

Capital Helsinki
Population 5,231,372
Languages Finnish (also Swedish along the southwestern coast)
Currency Euro (€)
When to go July–August for the warmest weather and midnight sun; late January–May for world-class cross-country skiing
When not to go November–March, unless you love skiing or plunging into a hole in the ice after a sauna
Minimum daily budget €38

Once the Finns were able to get the occupying Swedes and Russians out of their hair (independence was gained in 1917), they could get back to their national pastime: sitting in a sauna and coaxing the vodka out of their systems with a birch branch. Skiing and hiking in Europe's largest preserved wilderness is also popular. This unique combination may explain why Finns believe that 75ºC in a sauna is chilly, but 25ºC outside is hot. For those who'd rather take a more cosmopolitan approach to this Nordic climate, Helsinki offers art and architecture in abundance. The former capital, Turku, is the country's oldest city.

Many travellers use Finland as a gateway to Russia – it's just a short train or ferry ride from Helsinki to St Petersburg – but be careful you don't zip by too quickly. The country is worthy of a trip all on its own.

Main attractions

• **Kiasma Museum of Contemporary Art, Helsinki** This building in downtown Helsinki is so striking (with its gleaming steel exoskeleton) it will surely lure you inside. The high-tech interior alone may be worth the price of admission, even if the experiential installations sometimes aren't. See Ⓦ www.kiasma.fi for visitor information.

• **The North Pole** Rovaniemi may be a few thousand kilometres from the North Pole, but don't tell Santa, who has set up shop in the North Pole Shopping Centre (where else!) and has a team of elves that take photos and answer children's letters. With European flights dropping off passengers all winter for an intimate chat with the multilingual Santa, this is as close as you'll get to the real

Average daily temperatures (°C) and monthly rainfall (mm) in Finland											
	Jan	Feb	Mar	Apr	May	June	July	Aug	Sept	Oct	Nov	Dec
Helsinki												
max °C	-3	-3	1	2	7	15	21	19	13	8	2	1
min °C	-9	-9	-5	-1	5	9	12	11	6	2	2	7
rainfall mm	46	36	36	38	43	46	61	74	66	69	66	56

FINLAND

thing. See Ⓦwww.santaclauslive.com to find out about getting some face time with St Nick.

● **Stockmann Department Store, Helsinki** You can't miss it. It's Europe's largest department store, selling everything you need and even more that you don't.

● **Helsinki Train Station** This 1914 industrial-looking terminal is believed to be architect Eliel Saarinen's finest work.

● **Uspenski Cathedral, Helsinki** The green turnip domes of this Russian Orthodox cathedral create the most striking of sights when approaching Helsinki from the water. Inside, there's a cornucopia of icons and incense-burners, and Slavonic choirs set the mood.

Also recommended

● **Try an ice dive** If you like to dive, you might like this: cutting a hole in the ice and slipping below the bluish surface into the freezing water (with excellent visibility). When it's really cold (by Finnish standards, that's around minus 20ºC), you need to have a sauna nearby. Not so much to warm up, but to get your scuba gear off in. It will literally freeze to your body.

www.roughguides.com

259

● **Take a walk in Lemmenjoki National Park** This Finnish national park deserves more than a day's stroll. Some of the best trekking in Lapland – rivers, Arctic landscapes, waterfalls – awaits, though getting there may take more effort than the walking. A postbus leaving from Inari will suffice, or grab a river taxi from Kultala.

● **Watch a reindeer race** Fearless Finns don't actually drive reindeer to the North Pole, but they do race them chariot style. Standing on downhill skis just behind the reindeer with short reins, they shout and whip them into a sprint and compete side by side in an Arctic *Ben Hur*. In winter, races are held all over Finland, often through the closed-off streets of small towns.

● **Take a snowshoe or snowmobile safari through Lapland** If you're heading to Finland in wintertime, you might as well embrace it. Strap some high-tech tennis rackets to your feet, or hold on tight as you speed over frozen rivers and through snow-covered woods on a snowmobile. For more information on tours go to Ⓦwww.arcticsafaris.fi or Ⓦwww.laplandsafaris.fi.

Costs

Nothing in the Nordic lands is cheap, and Finland is no exception. If you're arriving from Russia, the price of almost everything may be a shock. Otherwise, you'll be used to it by the time you pass through Denmark and Sweden. The one thing that may catch you off guard is that accommodation prices buck the trend and can actually go up out of season, which can make that €38 daily budget even more challenging.

Accommodation
Finding a cheap place to stay can be a challenge. The Finncheque program (Ⓦwww.finncheque.fi) allows you to

purchase vouchers – €50 per person in a double room, breakfast included (category I) or €41 per person in a double room, breakfast included (category II) – and use them to stay in 110 participating hotels. There's a €27 surcharge for single occupancy. Also, you need to buy these Finncheques before arriving, and you can't make reservations more than three months in advance. There are 150 hostels in Finland, most starting at €19 for a dorm. There are plenty of campgrounds (two people sharing a spot €10–12), but to take advantage of them, you'll need a Camping Card Scandinavia (€7), which you can use in twenty European countries (Ⓦwww.camping.fi).

Eating and drinking
You'll need to figure on €6–8 for fast food, €12–22 for a decent meal and over €40 for fine dining. As in the rest of Scandinavia, sticking to falafels, pizza, hot dogs and supermarket food is a matter of budget survival.

Transport

Regular train travel is quite reasonable and covers the country particularly well on north–south routes. And if you can find two or more other travellers heading to the same place, you can book a group ticket at the train station and get about twenty percent off. Buses take care of east–west travel and connect well with the trains.

Helsinki transport isn't exactly a bargain. A single ride on the metro costs €2, or €2.50 if you buy from a tram or bus driver, so you're better off buying a Tourist Card, which covers all city transport for €6.80 (one day), €13.60 (two days) or €20.40 (three days). Or go for a Helsinki Card (Ⓦwww.helsinkicard.fi; one day €30, two days €42; three days €52), which allows unlimited travel on all public transportation as well as free entry to several museums and some discounted theatre tickets. You even get a free sightseeing tour thrown in.

True to the high-tech nature of the country that brought us Nokia, you can buy public transport tickets by mobile phone. Just SMS "A1" to the number 16355, make sure you receive an answer SMS before you board the train, then show the answer to the ticket inspector. The charge will be added to your phone bill.

By train

Eurail Finland Pass Any three days of travel in one month US$275 (first class), US$189 (second class). Any five days in one month US$369 (first class), US$245 (second class). Any ten days in one month US$499 (first class), US$335 (second class).

See p.257 for Eurail Scandinavia Pass costs.

For Europe-wide Eurail and InterRail passes, see p.50 and Ⓦwww.raileurope.com. For tips and tricks on maximizing your rail pass, see p.75.

By bus

Busabout doesn't operate in Finland. For buses to other countries, see Ⓦwww.expressbus.com.

Events

● **Midsummer Day** The biggest event of the year is a private one, and to truly experience it you need to meet a Finn and get invited along. Most flee the cities for summer cottages, welcoming the longest day with bonfires and overzealous alcohol consumption. Mid-June.

● **Savonlinna Opera Festival** Finland's most famous festival is held at the ambience-rich medieval Olavinlinna Castle. The operatic blowout lasts a month. Early July; Ⓦwww.operafestival.fi.

● **Wife-Carrying Championships, Sonkajärvi** Finland's most media-savvy event is the annual wife-carrying championships. Strapping Finns carry their wives over a 253.5-metre obstacle course, competing for the fastest time. The winner receives his wife's weight in beer. New rules state that "cohabitants living in a marriage-like relationship" may also compete. Early July; Ⓦwww.sonkajarvi.fi.

● **Pori Jazz Festival** This annual festival attracts top-end acts to the old factory buildings that line the banks of the Kokemäenjoki River. There are over 100 concerts at this week-long jam, and you'll have to vie for a spot among the 130,000 revellers. Late July; Ⓦwww.porijazz.fi.

Finland online

Country info Ⓦwww.visitfinland.com
Rail Ⓦwww.vr.fi
Helsinki info Ⓦwww.hel.fi

FINLAND

www.roughguides.com

France

Capital Paris
Population 60,876,136
Languages French (also Alsatian, Basque, Breton, Catalan, Corsican, Flemish and Provençal)
Currency Euro (€)
When to go March–May and September–October, when the weather is great and the tourists are fewer; June–August for the Mediterranean (but also its busiest time); November–March, when it's ski season in the Alps and Pyrenees
When not to go Mid-July to August, when most of the French take their holidays – everything closes and the transport system feels the strain
Minimum daily budget €36

France still carries a certain mystique, preserved in part by the wickedly decadent pastries served up in boulangeries, the tiny shops that regularly stock no less than twenty types of goat's cheese, doctors who still prescribe red wine for common ailments, small doggies with couture outfits that leave even smaller landmines on the pavement for you to navigate, and zippy cars that take on roundabouts at Mach 3. In other words, France is still French enough to fulfil the high expectations of most travellers. But brace yourself also for *McDonald's* and *7-Elevens* and neighbourhoods with far more North African cuisine than baguettes and foie gras. As long as you don't expect an artisan crêpe maker with a beret juggling Grand Marnier on every street corner, France will not disappoint. The country that brought the world the Yellow Leader's jersey, the croissant, Debussy and champagne still has much to offer. In Paris, you'll have a hard time walking ten minutes without bumping into a building you've seen on a postcard. In Chamonix, you'll pull a neck muscle taking in all the vistas. In Lyon, you can find enough Michelin-starred chefs to fill a rugby team, with plenty left over to cheer. There's a

Average daily temperatures (°C) and monthly rainfall (mm) in France

	Jan	Feb	Mar	Apr	May	June	July	Aug	Sept	Oct	Nov	Dec
Paris												
max °C	7.5	7	10	16	17	23	25	26	21	17	12	8
min °C	1	1	3	6	9	12	14	14	11	8	4	2
rainfall mm	54	46	54	46	63	58	54	52	54	56	56	56
Marseille												
max °C	11	12	14	17	21	26	29	28	25	20	14	12
min °C	3	3	6	8	12	16	19	18	16	11	7	3
rainfall mm	48	41	46	46	46	25	15	25	64	94	76	58

good reason France is the world's most popular tourist destination.

Main attractions

● **The Louvre, Paris** This museum could eat most sports stadiums for breakfast and still have space left over to confuse the most directionally gifted art connoisseur. It first opened in 1793 and was immediately stuffed full of stolen goods pillaged by Napoleon's armies. Courtesy of architect I.M. Pei, it now sports a snazzy glass-pyramid entryway with a reflective pool that helps calm the impatiently waiting crowds. The world record for seeing the *Mona Lisa*, *Winged Victory* and *Venus de Milo* and getting back out of the front door is something like two hours.

● **Palace of Versailles** Louis Quatorze certainly knew how to live. Or so it would seem. There's the grand entrance, room enough to properly house an entire class of illegitimate children, endless gardens that require an army of trimmers and pruners, and a hall with more mirrors than a Las Vegas magic act. It's good to be king.

● **Eiffel Tower, Paris** Built for the International Exhibition of Paris in 1889, this giant phallic radio antenna has

become not just the urban icon for Paris but for all Europe. It didn't win over the French right away: many petitioned to have it torn down. You can still ride the elevator or you could make the world's most famous stair climb and earn the spectacular view.

● **Mont St-Michel** This outcropping town on the north coast of France with its eighth-century abbey and jumble of Gothic buildings looks like a sandcastle come to life. The tide once rolled in and turned Mont St-Michel into an island for half the day. However, because of canals and polderized coastal flats, the water began to stop short. In 2006, a 150-million-euro project was approved to build a hydraulic dam to bring back the water and make it a mystical island once again (by 2012).

● **The French Alps** In the winter, it's a skiers', snowboarders' and ice-climbers' paradise. In the summer, the hikers, mountain bikers and rock climbers take over. Either way, you can't lose. The soaring jagged peaks seem fresh off the pages of a fairy tale.

● **Notre-Dame, Paris** The lady with the stone flying buttresses sits on the Île de la Cité in the middle of Paris. In fact, stand out in front of the main entrance and you'll find a spot in the cobblestones that marks the very centre of the city.

Also recommended

● **Skate through Paris** At 10pm on Friday, at the base of the Montparnasse tower, about 15,000 in-line skaters congregate to commence their three-hour (30km) tour of Paris. In 1994, the Paris Roller Club turned the once ragtag gathering into an established event that now consumes the city. It runs all year long, unless it's raining or the streets are wet.

● **Taste wine in Bordeaux** Even if you fancy yourself as a beerophile, a tasting tour of the greatest vineyards on the planet is a remarkable experience. The hardest part may be spitting the wine out (on a long day of tasting, the idea is to keep yourself from slipping under the table).

● **Cycle in Corsica** Corsica lives up to its billing as the île de beauté (the island of beauty); roads wind by cliffs and beaches as they circle this unlikely piece of French property off the southeastern coast. The capital, Ajaccio, is as well known for its cuisine as it is for being the birthplace of its most famous son, Napoleon.

● **Shop at the Clignancourt Market, Paris** It doesn't really matter what you're looking for, or even if you buy anything, the market will keep your eyes and nostrils on full alert. There are elaborate antiques – and mass-produced fakes that will fool people back home for a fraction of the price – and every street food vendor worth his salt (and cayenne pepper) seems to have a stall.

● **Barge through Bordeaux** Thomas Jefferson wrote of barging, "Of all the methods of travelling I have ever tried, this is the pleasantest", and you can actually float all the way from the Atlantic coast to the Mediterranean. Just head up the Garonne to the Dordogne – which will bring you to Toulouse – then take the Canal Lateral to the Canal du Midi. Travellers tend to pony up for week-long rides on lavishly renovated models with full catering and scheduled pit stops at wineries.

● **Sample cheese in the Savoie** Each region of France is famous for its own particular type of cheese, and you'd fare well following your own taste buds. However, if you're not sure which of the 265 kinds to try, head to the Savoie, the region that packs in the most cheese diversity.

- **Watch the Tour de France go by**
Join the 15 million people who line the roads each year to watch the 189 riders and 1600 support vehicles zip by in a few eye-blinks. In some of the more popular spots along the big climbs in the Alps and Pyrenees, you may have to camp out to get a good view; in other places, five minutes ahead of time will suffice. The route changes each year. To find out when it's passing by, see Ⓦwww.letour.fr.

- **Browse for perfume in Grasse**
Centuries of gardening and perfume mixing in Grasse have seen it blossom into the olfactory epicentre of Europe. Master sniffers (called nez, or "noses") train for years to recognize thousands of scents. If you're not interested in a tour of the perfumeries, a garden stroll will still delight the senses.

Costs

France is one of the most expensive countries in Europe for the budget traveller, mostly because the low-end accommodation is comparatively high. On the tightest budget, €36 a day can be a challenge. In addition to the expense of Paris, be particularly wary when heading to the Riviera. The haves and have-yachts aren't anxious to see scores of budget travellers marching their streets and have priced things accordingly to keep them at bay.

Accommodation
Even the cheapest rooms aren't that cheap. A dorm bed in a Parisian hostel costs between €25 and €32; a single room will set you back €50–75 – about the same as a hotel if you book ahead on the web. A double room is €60–80. Outside the capital, prices drop, though not as much as you'd expect.

Eating and drinking
In most towns, you'll be able to find restaurants offering a basic three-course meal for €13, and it won't cost you more than €1 to pick up a warm baguette. Wine is cheap (even more so if you buy it at a store). If you're whipping up your own meal, any wine vendor can recommend the vintage that best accompanies your food – and it shouldn't cost more than €5.

Transport

France has the world's fastest train – the expensive, double-decker TGV – and one of the best rail networks on the planet. The bus system isn't quite so comprehensive. The cheapest way of getting round Paris is to buy a Paris Visite Ticket (Ⓦwww.ratp.fr), which is valid on the metro, bus, RER and the Montmartre funicular. Prices range from €8.80 for a one-day ticket covering Zones 1–3 to €48.40 for a five-day ticket covering Zones 1–6. For information on Paris transport go to Ⓦwww.ratp.fr.

By train
Francerail Pass Any three days of travel in one month US$293 (first class), US$250 (second class) and US$217/US$186 (youth, first class/second class). Additional days US$45 (first class), US$37 (second class) and US$33/28 (youth, first class/second class).
France-Italy Pass Any four days of travel in two months US$372 (first class), US$325 (second class) and US$246 (youth, second class).
France-Spain Pass Any four days of travel in two months US$372 (first class), US$325 (second class) and US$246 (youth, second class).
France-Switzerland Pass Any four days of travel in two months US$398 (first class) and US$281 (second class

and youth). Additional days US$45 (first class) and US$31 (second class and youth, second class).

For Europe-wide Eurail and InterRail passes, see p.50. For tips and tricks on maximizing your rail pass, see p.75.

By bus

A Busabout pass (see p.52) allows you to travel throughout France. For buses to other countries, see ⓦ www.eurolines.fr.

Events

● **Nice Carnival** A million spectators take in the parade, music and fireworks, while papier mâché figures are danced down the street on giant floats. "Fat Tuesday" following Lent; ⓦ www .nicecarnaval.com.

● **Monaco Grand Prix** The glam stop on the Formula One circuit, with cars racing through the pretzelled roads that comprise James Bond's stomping ground. May; ⓦ www.visitmonaco.com.

● **Paris Grand Steeplechase** The most prominent horseracing event on the French calendar. Watch fantastic leaps over the Hippodrome d'Auteuil's carefully clipped hedges and precariously placed ditches. May 30; ⓦ www.france-galop.com.

● **Biarritz Surf Festival** Dude, it's not just one of Europe's biggest surfing events: as world-class riders rip up the waves, Biarritz gets inundated with surfing enthusiasts who jump-start the beach party. July 10–18; ⓦ www .aspeurope.com.

● **Le Mans 24-Hour Race** Endurance, skill and auto mechanics come together in this gruelling, legendary car race. June; ⓦ www.lemans.org.

● **French Open Tennis Championships, Paris** The world's elite players duke it out on the famously unforgiving red-clay courts of Stade Roland Garros. Last week in May to first week in June; ⓦ www .rolandgarros.com.

● **International Kite Festival, Dieppe** The world's best gather to show their piloting skills at Europe's biggest kite festival. Early Sept; ⓦ www.dieppe -cerf-volant.org.

France online

France info ⓦ www.franceguide.com
French rail ⓦ www.sncf.fr
Paris info ⓦ www.paris-info.com

Germany

Capital Berlin
Population 82,422,299
Language German
Currency Euro (€)
When to go The weather's at its finest March–September, while March–May and September–October provide the best combination: nice climate, few tourists

When not to go The Dark Rainy Miserable Season (possibly the actual name) is November–February. If you're heading to popular attractions, July and August are packed with people trying to do exactly the same thing
Minimum daily budget €37

You can leave your stereotypes (that Germany is a robotic industrial power-house that favours rules over creativity and hockey haircuts over fashion) behind with your 2000-watt hairdryer. OK, maybe there's a dash of truth in there, but Germany today is a modern, multicultural patchwork of regional and international identities that are as diverse as its open fields, thick forests and mountain terrain. Its large cities are throbbing with haute couture shops, and its beer gardens continue to serve up some of the world's best brew.

The shadow of World War II still lingers for many who visit, but new generations of Germans have moved beyond carrying this heavy inherited burden with them 24/7. The reunification of the country in 1990 has been a far greater issue, and bridging the forty-year divide is a work in progress.

For the traveller, Western Europe's largest and most populous nation is extremely accessible. Smaller festivals can be found almost year-round and getting to them with public transport couldn't be easier (unless you speak German).

Main attractions

- **Heidelberg** A picturesque town featuring picturesque Heidelberg Castle and picturesque postcards. It couldn't be more … well, scenic. Visitors rarely miss a stroll along the Hauptstrasse through the old town.

Average daily temperatures (°C) and monthly rainfall (mm) in Germany											
	Jan	Feb	Mar	Apr	May	June	July	Aug	Sept	Oct	Nov	Dec
Berlin												
max °C	2	4	8	12	18	21	23	23	19	13	7	3
min °C	-3	-3	1	3	7	12	13	13	10	6	2	-1
rainfall mm	43	37	38	42	55	71	53	65	46	36	50	55

www.roughguides.com

267

● **Reichstag, Berlin** Germany's past and future are represented in a unique building. Construction started in 1884, and a decade later it was the parliament for Bismarck's German Empire. After the collapse of the Berlin Wall in 1989, British architect Sir Norman Foster's glass dome has capped off the Hitler-tainted building's rebirth as a symbol of united democracy. Visitors can walk right up to the dome and even have a meal there.

● **Cologne Cathedral** The *dom* is a positively enormous thirteenth-century Gothic cathedral in the centre of the city (a few steps from the central train station) that makes a trip to Cologne worthwhile on its own.

● **The Marienplatz glockenspiel, Munich** This hyperactive cuckoo clock in central Munich forms part of the town hall's Gothic facade. Time your visit for 11am, noon or 5pm and you'll get to see

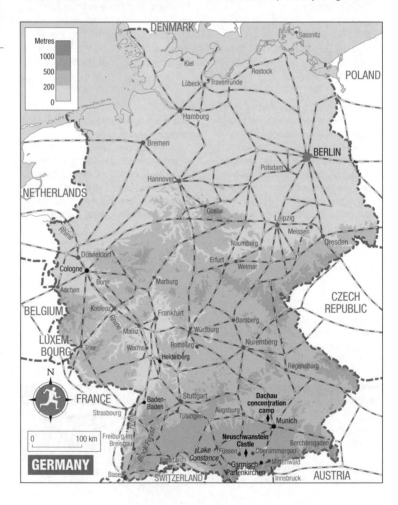

the re-enactment of Duke William V's
wedding to Renata von Lothringen.

- **Neuschwanstein** If you're one of
those picky travellers who'd rather see
the original than be satisfied with the
Disney replication, you'll need to brave
the crowds and make a pilgrimage to
this famous "Sleeping Beauty" castle.
(Extra kitsch bonus: there's also the
Musical Theatre Neuschwanstein, a
nightly performance based on King
Ludwig II's tragic life.)

- **Dachau concentration camp** No
matter what you've read or how many
movies you've seen on the subject,
it's hard to appreciate what happened
under Hitler's regime without a trip to a
concentration camp memorial. Dachau
wasn't the largest such death machine
but it was the first to be built, and a few
hours of wandering the grounds will
leave a powerful imprint on your soul.

Also recommended

- **Have a soak in Baden-Baden**
Germany's most famous spa lies in the
heart of the Black Forest. Its famed
curative mineral waters bubble up
from thermal springs at temperatures
over 68°C. The Therme of Caracalla
is popular with families, but for a more
upscale (and less clothed) experience, try
Friedrichsbad.

- **Cycle along the Danube** The cycle
path that runs along the Danube River
passes monasteries, castles, meadows
and forests on a route that is littered with
UNESCO World Heritage Sites. If you
get hooked, you can continue all the way
down to Vienna and Bratislava.

- **Windsurf Lake Constance** Near
the Swiss border, the winds of Lake
Constance lure German windsurfers by
the dozen. Rent a board at Strandbad
Eichwald. If your arms get tired, you

can also fish the lake (with a permit) for
pike, perch and eel. Or head to Lindau,
rent a bike, and circle the water on two
wheels. Alternatively, just take a dip; the
surrounding mountains provide a magical
backdrop for a swim.

- **Mountain bike the Black Forest**
The Black Forest Bike Park has the
largest network of mountain-bike trails
in the world – about 1400km worth,
and with routes for all levels. There are
several places to access the trails: the
Elz and Simonswälder valleys, Triberg,
Schonach, Schönwald, Furtwangen,
St Georgen, Hardt, Lauterbach,
Schramberg and Tennenbronn.

Costs

Germany's prices are just about the
average for all of Europe, which means
stretching your €37 daily budget in
Germany isn't that easy, but it won't
be as fiscally painful as the northern
countries or around the French Riviera.

Accommodation

You'll see plenty of Zimmer signs adver-
tising rooms in private homes, which
go for about €22 for a single and €30
for a double (more in cities). The prolific
HI hostels are clean but often booked
with giant school groups, so check the
web for bookings as far in advance as
possible. Prices are €12–15 at the low
end, and €5 for a campground spot.

Eating and drinking

German cuisine doesn't get the sort of
fanfare that welcomes Italian and French
culinary arts, and for good reason. It is,
however, nice and filling in a meat-and-
potatoes and deep-fried-anything sort
of way. The bread is excellent and you'll
find plenty of puffy pastries, but these
German street snacks aren't especially
cheap. For the very tightly budgeted,

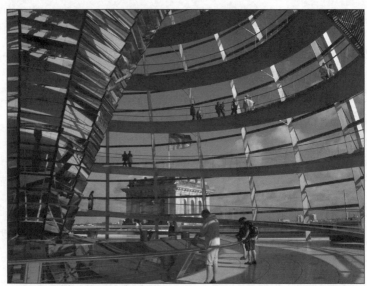

▲ Reichstag, Berlin

supermarket shopping and Turkish food (Germany has a large Turkish population) is the key. The beer isn't ridiculously priced for the amount you get. The problem, budget wise, is that this delicious swill comes in sizes you could use to put out a fire. Figure on €8–12 for a meal.

Transport

German transport is clean, fast, comfortable and reliable, but not particularly cheap; figure on about €12 per 100km in slow trains and €25 per 100km on fast ICE (InterCityExpress) trains. The buses are mostly owned by Deutsche Bahn and run in conjunction with the trains, which makes for convenient connections, but monopolize pricing. Within the larger cities, you'll most likely want a strip card (multiple use) or day card if you plan to hop on the city transit subways (U-Bahns and S-Bahns) for more than three rides.

By train

German Pass Any four days of travel in one month US$340 (first class), US$260 (second class) and US$216 (youth, second class). Additional days US$46 (first class), US$29–32 (second class) and US$15–18 (youth, second class).

For Eurail Germany-Benelux Pass prices, see p.233.

InterRail Germany Pass Any three days of travel in one month – €272 (first class), €202 (second class) and €134 (youth, second class) – to any eight days of travel in one month €430 (first class), €319 (second class) and €207 (youth, second class).

For Europe-wide **Eurail** and **InterRail** passes, see p.50. For tips and tricks on maximizing your rail pass, see p.75.

Bahn Card This comes in three flavours. The BahnCard 25 (€114 in first class, €57 in second class) gives a 25 percent discount, the BahnCard 50 (€450 in first class, €225 in second class) gives a fifty percent discount, and the BahnCard

100, which is wickedly expensive and not useful for budget-minded folk. Students between 18 and 25 can buy the BahnCard 50 for half the price. If you plan to spend more than €200 (roughly the cost of a return ticket from Frankfurt to Munich), this is a good way to save.

By bus
Busabout barely operates in Germany, merely serving Berlin, Dresden, Munich and Stuttgart. For internal bus prices, see Ⓦwww.berlinlinienbus.de. For buses to other countries, see Ⓦwww .eurolines.de.

Events

● **Cologne Carnival** Germany's biggest pre-Ash Wednesday blowout bash is in Cologne, where the 178-year-old event is called Fasnacht. The second of the three-day event is Rose Monday, and if you're there, it's hard to miss the giant parade through town, with political-themed floats and a bizarre collection of costumes. If you want to dress up, the only guideline is "brighter is better". Late Feb/early March.

● **Rhine in Flames** On five selected dates between spring and autumn, pyrotechnics from decorated barges cruising the Rhine River fill the night sky with colour, while blue flares (known as "Bengal fires") light up the castles and palaces. May, July, Aug & Sept; Ⓦwww .germany-tourism.co.uk.

● **The Love Parade** (see p.00) and **Munich's Oktoberfest** are Germany's two largest events. One is the biggest street party in the Western world, the other is the biggest beer party in the Western world. Both encourage participation and get wonderfully out of hand. July & Sept respectively.

● **New Year's Day ski jumping in Garmisch-Partenkirchen.** Of all the good arguments for not getting into ski jumping, the best one is that you have to stay sober every New Year's Eve. Why? Because the sadistic competition organizers at Garmisch-Partenkirchen insist on hosting the world's most prestigious competition on January 1st. Pick a favourite and get in on the cheering, or choose a spot to nurse your hangover. When nearby Zugspitze (Germany's highest mountain at 2692m) comes into focus again, you'll know you're sober.

Germany online

Country info Ⓦwww.germany-tourism.de
Rail Ⓦwww.bahn.de
Bus Ⓦwww.berlinlinienbus.de
Berlin info Ⓦwww.berlin.de
Munich info Ⓦwww.muenchen.de

www.roughguides.com

Greece

Capital Athens **Population** 10,688,058 **Language** Greek **Currency** Euro (€) **When to go** Mid-April to mid-June and September to mid-October, when the attractions are less crowded, the temperature is pleasant, and accommodation easy to find	**When not to go** In the heart of summer (mid-June to August), when the heat is searing, and the winter months (November–February), when the tourist infrastructure goes into lock-down mode **Minimum daily budget** €32

For the backpacker, Greece has traditionally been about island hopping, ouzo drinking and plate smashing. But this country has far more to offer than most ever realize. The land that gave the world the Olympics, Socrates, drama, democracy, an enormous chunk of our vocabulary and the inspiration for toga parties deserves more than a cursory glance. From the recently renovated Athens with its Acropolis views to riding a mule up the cliffs of Santorini or farmers that are happy to have you taste their just-pressed olive oil, the Greek gods seem to have blessed the country with ample sights and activities.

Before heading out to explore the country's 2000-island archipelago, where you can easily lose yourself for years, you might head up the mainland or down to the Peloponnesian peninsula, where many of the most outstanding archeological sites and monuments can be found.

Main attractions

- **Acropolis, Athens** You may not get above the *nefos* (smog), but the views are still stunning from this ancient site, often called the "Sacred Rock" of Athens. Four masterpieces are assembled on this rocky hill: the Parthenon, the Propylaea, the Erechtheum and the Temple of Athena Nike.

- **Medieval city of Rhodes** Perched at the northern tip of the island of the same name, this is one of the most festive UNESCO World Heritage Sites

Average daily temperatures (°C) and monthly rainfall (mm) in Greece

	Jan	Feb	Mar	Apr	May	June	July	Aug	Sept	Oct	Nov	Dec
Athens												
max °C	13	13	16	19	23	28	32	31	28	23	18	14
min °C	7	7	8	11	15	19	23	22	19	15	12	8
rainfall mm	48	41	41	23	18	8	5	8	10	53	56	63

www.roughguides.com

you'll come across. Bustling bars and restaurants now occupy this walled city that was previously run by the Order of St John of Jerusalem (1309 to 1523), Turks and Italians. You can sit on the beach just outside the walls and look out to the Turkish coast.

● **Delphi** One of Greece's greatest cultural treasures, Delphi lies just 150km northwest of Athens, harbouring the Temple of Apollo, Castalian Spring and Corycian Cave in its hillside complex. It's not just another collection of ruins, though; according to mythology, Delphi was the "navel of the Earth" (centre of the world).

● **Olympia** The site of the first Olympic Games (776 BC), Olympia still houses some of Greece's most important monuments: the Temple of Zeus, the Temple of Hera, the Stadium, the Bouleuterion, the Gymnasium and the Prytaneion (site of the eternal flame).

● **Knossos' Royal Palace, Crete** According to legend, King Minos's wife give birth to the half-bull, half-man Minotaur at Knossos on the island of Crete. The labyrinth-like West Court is where the Minotaur caught his victims, and where Daedalus and his son, Icarus, were imprisoned and created wings of wax for their ill-fated escape.

Also recommended

● **Row into the Melissáni Cave** "Cave" may be a loose definition for this geological wonder on the island of Kefalloniá, since part of the roof collapsed thousands of years ago, leaving most of the football-pitch-sized submersed area in daylight. What you won't be able to see from a rowboat is that a series of subterranean passages connects the cave to the other side of the island, 28km away.

● **Climb the cliff-top monasteries of Metéora** James Bond climbed the walls to one of these monasteries using only his shoelaces in *For Your Eyes Only*, but it was a favourite spot among travellers long before that. The agile ninth-century hermits who first settled in the caves and rock fissures would descend every Sunday for Mass.

● **Visit the gods of Mount Olympus** Mount Olympus, Greece's highest peak, served as a sort of Melrose Place for the Greek gods. Today, it's Greece's oldest and most carefully protected national park. Staying at refuges along the way, visitors can trek among the peaks, stopping at the Plateau of the Muses to see the peak of Stefani (the throne of Zeus), and look down on the world like the gods once did.

● **Kayak around the Ionian Islands** In the waters between Greece and Italy, you'll find a calm and clear passageway, sheltered from the prevailing northeastern winds. Kayak between famous islands and uninhabited little jewels. Sightings of loggerhead turtles, monk seals and dolphins are common.

● **Attend a show at Epidaurus** Throughout the summer (on Fridays and Saturdays), the well-preserved Ancient Theatre of Epidaurus takes a step back in time to put on classical Greek dramas. The acoustics are excellent but the tickets are hard to get; ⓦ wwwgreekfestival.gr.

Costs

Greece is one of those countries that was dirt-cheap not so long ago, and if you run into an ageing budget traveller, you'll get an earful of how great it all was before you arrived. Figure on €32 per day for a bare-bones budget, with hitching, supermarket food and minimal island hopping. For ferries, and eating out at a few restaurants, it rises to €45–50.

Accommodation
Travel out of peak season (mid-June through August) and you'll save a small fortune on hotels, which typically drop their rate by over 25 percent.

Eating and drinking
A nice restaurant meal costs about €13, but you can snack your way to a full meal for less than that. Small kebabs and cheese pies are delicious and cheap. You can find oven-baked mousaka and tzatziki (yoghurt, garlic and cucumber dip) everywhere.

Transport

Mainland Greece is an easy place to travel around by a combination of buses and trains. The rail lines are cheap (€12–15 for a 6hr journey) but somewhat limited, while the buses reach even the smallest villages. Eleven ferry companies serve the islands domestically, but are not terribly punctual, and erratic services to some islands make scheduling difficult. High-speed ferries go twice as fast for twice the price. For three times the price, you can fly. One of the most charming ways to island hop is by tagging a lift on a private yacht or by taking one of the colourful wooden skiffs, called kaikia or caiques. On the islands, bikes and scooters are popular to rent, but be warned: Greece has the second-highest traffic fatality rate (after Portugal) in Europe.

By train

Greek Pass Any three days of travel in one month US$145 (first class), US$129 (youth, first class). Any ten days in one month US$449; US$ 399 (youth, first class).

See p.243 for Balkans Flexi Pass prices.

For Europe-wide InterRail and Eurail passes, see p.50. For tips and tricks on maximizing your rail pass, see p.75.

By bus

Busabout (see p.52) has recently moved into Greece, with a four-island Flexi-Hopper pass covering Mykonos, Paros, Ios and Santorini for €249 (adults) or €235 (students) For internal bus prices, see Ⓦwww.ktel.org (only in Greek).

By ferry

Greece is often best accessed by boat. To check times and book tickets, visit Ⓦwww.hellasferries.gr or Ⓦwww .minoan.gr.

Events

● **Easter** Easter is the biggest holiday in Greece, with celebrations across the country. In central Macedonia, villagers walk barefoot across hot coals. In Lerissos, there's line dancing. In Agios Nikolaos, you'll see the Burning of Judas; in Corfu, jar smashing. Greek Orthodox Easter, however, does not always fall on the same Sunday as the Catholic and Protestant Easter, since it's calculated with a different calendar.

● **Rockwave, Athens** The capital's premier rock concert brings in headliners such as Mötley Crüe, W.A.S.P, Guns 'n Roses and Franz Ferdinand to keep the 50,000-plus visitors entertained for three days of live music. July; Ⓦwww .rockwavefestival.gr.

Greece online

Country info Ⓦwww.gnto.gr
Rail Ⓦwww.ose.gr
Bus Ⓦwww.ktel.org
Ferry Ⓦwww.ferries.gr
Athens info Ⓦwww.cityofathens.gr

Hungary

Capital Budapest
Population 9,981,334
Language Hungarian
Currency Forint (HUF)
When to go March–May is ideal, but be prepared for spring showers; June–August is warm and sunny, but can be crowded in parts around July and August;
September and October are also pleasant
When not to go November means cold rain, and after that it's just cold; August is called "the cucumber-growing season" because there's not much else happening with so many Hungarians on holiday
Minimum daily budget €25

When most travellers head to Hungary, they bring few of the preconceptions that typically get carted along with them to France, Italy or England. And, for many, Hungary feels like one of those surprise foreign films that you never realized you'd enjoy so much. Make no mistake, Budapest doesn't pack the architectural punch of Paris, but there's plenty of Magyar magic in this town, and without any of that Parisian pretence. The country's history reads like a James Clavell novel. As recently as 1999, Hungary joined NATO. Before that, János Kádár's 1970s reforms, a "goulash communism" that was slightly more consumer-oriented, helped make this the richest, most liberal country in the region. When the fence along its border with Austria came down in 1989,

the country held its first free elections in forty years. So be careful when you lump Hungary together with the rest of the Balkans – you might get an earful from a local. Keep in mind the ballpoint pen, match, Rubik's cube and helicopter were all invented by Hungarians.

If you want the charm, luxury and tree-lined walkways of Western Europe and the prices of Eastern Europe, Hungary offers a nice compromise. The language may be an enigma, but there's no mystery about the rich wines and elegant thermal spas. The lakes are lined with resorts and there's a lively – though not frenetic – café scene. Budapest straddles the River Danube with Buda to the west, rising dramatically from the banks, and Pest sitting on the edge of the eastern Great Plain.

Average daily temperatures (°C) and monthly rainfall (mm) in Hungary

	Jan	Feb	Mar	Apr	May	June	July	Aug	Sept	Oct	Nov	Dec
Budapest												
max °C	2	4	11	16	21	24	26	26	22	15	7	3
min °C	-4	-3	2	5	11	13	15	15	11	1	1	-2
rainfall mm	41	38	34	41	61	68	45	55	39	34	59	48

Main attractions

- **Castle Hill, Budapest** Castle Hill beckons to travellers when they arrive. It's the "What's that?!" up on the hill that holds Budapest's most important museums and monuments. Make the trip over the river and up and you'll find both the Old Town and Royal Palace within this walled area. Plus, some of the best views in town.

- **Lake Balaton** Just 100km outside Budapest, this lake is one of Europe's largest. The south shore has most of the glitz and hotels (specifically the town of Siófok), while the north shore has the hiking trails and historical sights. Balantonfüred, once a writers' colony and political retreat, seems to bridge the gap.

- **Gellért Hill, Budapest** When your legs have recharged after Castle Hill, the next panoramic climb is to the Citadella, a fortress atop Gellért Hill that also serves as Budapest's unofficial symbol. On the way down, stop at the

Gellért Hotel, an old-world lodging with a remarkable spa that feels as if you're swimming in a half-submerged church.

- **Royal Palace, Budapest** The Royal Palace has been rebuilt more times than Michael Schumacher's car. It now houses the Hungarian National Gallery, the National Széchényi Library and the Budapest History Museum; allow plenty of time.

Also recommended

- **Take a bath** Taking a dip in the warm thermal and cool mineral springs that bubble under Budapest is the perfect antidote to the tired legs and traveller grime you get from sightseeing, though some of the baths are architectural wonders themselves. Two baths (Palatinus and Hajos) are located on Margaret Island, just between Buda and Pest. The Király baths – sitting just on the Buda side, with four pools and a sixteenth-century sky-lit dome – are flanked by the Lukács baths to the north and the Rác, Rudas and Gellért baths to the south.

www.roughguides.com

277

- **Row down the Danube** Rowing and kayaking are possible on the Danube. In Budapest, you can hire boats, kayaks or canoes on Margaret Island or along the Romai River Bank.

- **Head underground** The Mátyás Caves can be found right under Budapest, formed by thermal waters gushing through thousands of years ago. The tiny passageways don't make for a leisurely stroll; you may spend more time on your belly than your feet. Helmets, overalls and headlamps are the way to go. Trips can be arranged through several of the hostels in town, such as Backpackers Ⓦwww .backpackers.hu.

- **Take a day-trip to Veszprém** A few hours by bus or train out of Budapest is one of Hungary's most impressive sights: the walled-in castle district of Veszprém, resting atop a plateau. Formerly a royal residence, it now serves as a museum of Baroque art and architecture.

Costs

The relatively low costs are one of Hungary's biggest draws, but it's not exactly dirt-cheap. Figure on €22, with some real scrimping, or €25 with basic frugality. You can live well for under €50, but as you move up in quality the tipping also goes up – Hungary is tip-conscious, though ten percent is the norm.

Accommodation
Hostels and, in the summer, university dormitories are less than €15. But don't rule out B&B-style private homes, which can be arranged through the tourist office for €10–20. For a three-star hotel, rates start just under €50. Campground bungalows will be your cheapest roofed option in many parts

of the country, and the quality of the bungalows ranges from "fully operational kitchen" to "at least the roof isn't leaking too much".

Eating and drinking
There are slim pickings for vegetarians in this farmhouse-style meat-and-potatoes-based cuisine. Goulash soup doesn't get everyone excited, but it's worth a try while you're here. A traditional three-course meal can be had for less than €10, and a simple, filling meal for less than €4. A beer in a trendy bar starts around €1 and in a regular bar is just 80 cents. Which all means it's a fine place to treat yourself.

Transport

You won't break any speed records on the Hungarian public transport, but it'll get you around. The toughest part might just be getting information without access to the web at every train and bus stop. The trains are dependable, although also dependably late. You'll probably have better luck buying tickets at a MAV office than the train station. (A reservation is cheap and avoids standing for hours on the train.) Eurail and InterRail passes cover Hungary, but buses can be quicker between many of the destinations, and cost just €6–8 per 100km.

In Budapest, a block of ten single tickets costs €9.25, a one-day travel card is €5.30 and a three-day card is around €13. A two-day Budapest Card costs €22 (€26 for a three-day card) and gets you into museums, gives you discounts on restaurants and spas, and entitles you to free transport. (Don't forget to punch each metro ticket you use in the machines provided on every bus, tram, trolleybus and at each metro station entrance, however.)

By train

Eurail Hungary Pass Any five days of travel in fifteen days US$109 (first class). Any ten days of travel in one month US$149 (first class).

Eurail Romania-Hungary Pass Any five days in two months US$269 (first class) and US$189 (youth, second class) to any ten days in two months US$405 (first class) and US$285 (youth, second class).

For European East Pass prices, see p.224.

For Europe-wide Eurail and InterRail passes, see p.50. For tips and tricks on maximizing your rail pass, see p.75.

By bus

For domestic bus prices, see ⓦwww .volanbusz.hu. For buses to other countries, see ⓦwww.eurolines.com.

Events

● **Budapest Spring Festival** The onset of spring signals the start of Hungary's biggest annual cultural event. There are chamber concerts, opera, jazz, dance, film screenings and more scattered at venues throughout Budapest. You'll see the best Hungarian performers, in addition to international artists. Last two weeks March; ⓦwww .fesztivalvaros.hu.

● **Danube Water Carnival** The Danube Water Carnival is one of the most stunning sights in Budapest. It includes stunt-plane flying, parachuting, a rowing regatta, a parade of illuminated yachts and a water show by fire-service boats. There's also a fireworks display from the Chain Bridge. Third Sat in June; ⓦwww.karneval.hu.

● **Budapest Parade** Over fifty carnival floats prance across Budapest from Roosevelt Square to Hero's Square. Wild costumes and revelling accompany the floats until the fireworks kick off to signal the start of the "real" party, as clubs open their doors for the post-parade bashes. Don't forget to wear something that looks good when completely covered in foam. Fourth Sat in Aug; ⓦwww.sziget.hu.

● **International Guitar Festival, Balatonfüred** During a week in mid-June, you can listen free to the plucking and strumming of top-end guitar music on the shore of Lake Balaton. There are even master classes on offer for skilled student players; ⓦwww.balaton-guitar.com.

Hungary online

Country info ⓦwww.hungary.com
Rail ⓦwww.elvira.hu
Bus ⓦwww.volanbusz.hu
Budapest info ⓦwww.budapestinfo.hu

Ireland

THE REPUBLIC OF IRELAND
Capital Dublin
Population 4,062,235
Languages English (also Gaelic, spoken mainly on the western seaboard)
Currency Euro (€)
Minimum daily budget €34

NORTHERN IRELAND
Capital Belfast
Population 1,685,000
Language English

Currency Pound sterling (GBP)
Minimum daily budget €37

When to go April–May and September are ideal. June–August is (with a bit of Irish luck) lovely, even if crowded
When not to go Prices go up in the summer, and the miserable winter weather chases so many away that many small hotels and restaurants outside the main cities shut from October to the end of March

The Irish landscape has an enchanting and mystical nature that's nearly as disarming as the Irish themselves. Despite the hypersaturated weather conditions ("horizontal rain" is common in some parts) and lack of leprechauns, few leave without being touched by the country's green charm.

For all the years of strife between the Republic and Northern Ireland, we've thrust them together for the sake of the traveller, who is not confined by boundaries or history. Both countries share the same landmass, and even many of the same bus and rail connections. They also share green, rolling hills; wild, rugged coastlines; and people with an uncanny ability to strike up conversation. As the expression goes in Ireland, "It never rains inside a pub." And they're not just a shelter from the elements; the pub is a social engine that powers the

Average daily temperatures (°C) and monthly rainfall (mm) in Ireland and Northern Ireland

	Jan	Feb	Mar	Apr	May	June	July	Aug	Sept	Oct	Nov	Dec
Belfast												
max °C	7	7	9	11	14	16	17	17	15	11	8	7
min °C	4	5	6	7	9	12	13	13	11	8	6	6
rainfall mm	86	58	67	53	60	63	64	80	85	88	78	78
Dublin												
max °C	8	8	9	11	14	17	19	18	16	13	10	6
min °C	3	3	4	5	7	10	12	12	10	8	5	4
rainfall mm	15	10	10	8	15	36	48	46	25	20	18	20

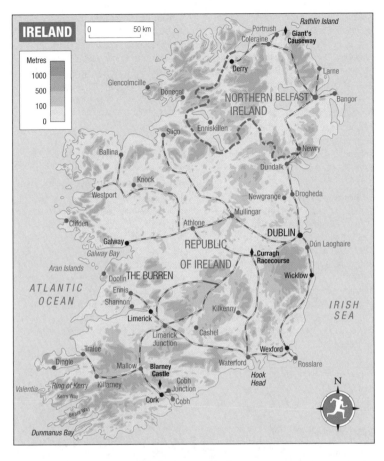

IRELAND

0   50 km

Metres
1000
500
100
0

Rathlin Island
Portrush   Giant's
Coleraine   Causeway
Derry   Larne
Glencolmcille
Donegal   NORTHERN   BELFAST   Bangor
IRELAND
Sligo   Enniskillen
Ballina   Newry
Dundalk
Knock
Westport   Newgrange   Drogheda
Mullingar
Clifden   Athlone
Galway   DUBLIN   Dún Laoghaire
Galway Bay   REPUBLIC
Aran Islands   OF IRELAND   Curragh
Racecourse
Doolin   THE BURREN   Wicklow
ATLANTIC   Ennis
OCEAN   Shannon   Kilkenny   IRISH
Limerick   SEA
Limerick   Cashel
Junction
Tralee   Wexford
Dingle   Mallow   Blarney   Waterford   Rosslare
Castle
Valentia   Cobh   Hook
Ring of Kerry   Killarney   Junction   Head
Kerry Way
Cork   Cobh   N
Beara Way
Dunmanus Bay

IRELAND

www.roughguides.com

country, whether you're tasting traditional Irish stew, listening to folk tunes
on the fiddle, or getting a long, almost-
coherent Guinness-fuelled tale from a
pub regular. In *Ulysses*, Joyce noted:
"A good puzzle would be to cross Dublin
without passing a pub."

Ireland's recent economic upturn may
have fizzled, but the effects can still be
felt. The ebb of Irish seeking fortune
abroad has turned into a flow of tourists,
and the country has become one of
the top destinations in Europe. Things
may seem a bit grey at times, the urban

architecture less impressive than in other
European cities, but if it's the personal
connections that make the strongest
memories, you'll be hard-pressed to find
more welcoming citizens over on the
continent.

Main attractions

● **Guinness Storehouse, Dublin**
Guinness may look like discarded
brake fluid, but this thick stout with a
scientifically measured head of foam is

281

worshipped like a minor deity. And the Guinness Storehouse in Dublin is the high altar. Naturally, you have to suffer a marketing blitz to get to the liquid lunch at the end of the tour. See Ⓦwww .guinness-storehouse.com for tour details.

● **Dublin Castle** One of the best parts of Dublin Castle, built in the thirteenth century by order of King John, is the bit beneath it. Recent flooding has led to excavations, which revealed new finds: the old city walls and a moat.

● **Blarney Stone** Blarney Castle in southwest Ireland holds the famous Blarney Stone – given to Cormac McCarthy by Robert the Bruce in 1314, a time when stones were appropriate gifts – high up in its battlements. To kiss it (and give yourself the gift of the gab – that is, an eternity of yapping) you have to lie down, tilt your head back, get lowered in upside down by a helper and plant your pucker on the stone.

● **Giant's Causeway** The only World Heritage Site in Northern Ireland is a geological phenomenon on the North Antrim coast. Caused by a volcanic eruption sixty million years ago, the rock formations look something like a ceramic plate warehouse, or perhaps the world's largest collection of petrified tortoise shells.

Also recommended

● **Watch Gaelic games** Croke Park in Dublin plays host to the All-Ireland Hurling finals; something between lacrosse and field hockey, this uniquely Irish sport is not for the timid. While you're there, you might check out the Gaelic football finals. It's just like regular football, except there's none of that offside nonsense. And you can use your hands, provided you alternate using your feet as well. And if the ball sails over the goal, you still get a point (if it goes in, you get three). Other than that, just like football.

▲ Giant's Causeway, Antrim

- **Go fishing** Ireland is famous for its fishing, and it's not uncommon for people to show up at the airport with a rod and reel. Permits are mandatory, as is a state national licence, if you're going after salmon or sea trout. There's over 5000km of coastline to cast in for the big one.

- **Take a walk in the country** Believe it or not, walking is one of Ireland's biggest draws. There are several designated walks, such as the Wicklow, Kerry and Beara Way, to help you reach some of the most beautiful sections of the country. Or you can head underground for a walk in The Burren, a series of caverns, springs and chasms just outside Limerick and Galway.

- **Dive the Irish Sea** Ireland is unlikely to be the first place that comes to mind when you want to go scuba diving, but it has some of Europe's best conditions. At Dunmanus Bay near Cork, Bantry Bay around Hook Head and Galway Bay near Wexford, you'll find plenty of dive sites. For a wreck dive, there's the HMS *Drake* off Rathlin Island on the northeast coast.

Costs

Ireland isn't a cheap place to visit. In fact, for most shopping it can be downright expensive. Accommodation is one beacon of budget hope, with reasonable prices by European standards.

Accommodation

Regular rain can make the camping experience fairly unpleasant, but many tough it out. There are plenty of hostels to keep you dry if you prefer to stay indoors. Independent hostels in larger city centres are reasonable (€14–20) and the Irish Youth Hostel Association and Hostelling International Northern Ireland can help find even cheaper

digs, provided you have Hostelling International membership (see p.73). B&Bs are a good option as well. For about €35, you can find a charming place to spend the night.

Eating and drinking

There are more hearty, inexpensive dishes in this country than you can shake a shamrock at. Most can be bought in a pub and few are fit for vegetarians. There's less high-end, gourmet fare, so a typical meal is unlikely to break your budget – €10 is standard for a small feast. For a real treat, try the oysters, one of Ireland's most celebrated catches.

Transport

Rail fares aren't cheap, so many travellers without a rail pass go by bus, bike or thumb.

By train

Irish Explorer Any eight days in fifteen consecutive days €245; valid in Ireland only; allows travel on Bus Èireann as well.

Eurail Ireland Pass Any five days in one month US$215 (second class), US$185 (youth, second class).

For Europe-wide Eurail and InterRail passes (which cover Ireland but not Northern Ireland), see p.50. For tips and tricks on maximizing your rail pass, see p.75. For internal rail prices, see ⓦwww .irishrail.ie (Ireland) and ⓦwww.nirailways .co.uk (Northern Ireland).

Translink Student Discount Card Full-time students can buy a discount card (around €8.25) that gives up to fifteen percent discounts on buses and up to 33 percent discounts on rail travel in Northern Ireland and fifty percent on cross-border services to Ireland. You should be able to make up the cost

www.roughguides.com

of the card with just a few trips. See
Ⓦwww.translink.co.uk.

By bus

Irish Rover Any fifteen days of travel in
thirty days (bus only; valid in Ireland and
Northern Ireland) €234. Ⓦwww
.buseireann.ie.

Busabout doesn't operate in Ireland or
Northern Ireland. For buses to the UK
(from Ireland only), see Ⓦwww.eurolines.ie.

Events

- **St Patrick's Day** Ah, finally, your
chance to dress up like a leprechaun and
drink yourself silly. There's far more than
a parade for this multi-day event. See
p.30 for more.

- **Irish Derby** Each summer, this
enormous equestrian event takes place
at the Curragh (one of the oldest sporting
venues in Europe), and most of the
country tunes in to watch the top horses
speed around the racecourse. June;
Ⓦwww.curragh.ie.

- **Bloomsday, Dublin** Every June,
the work of author James Joyce is
celebrated on the day his masterpiece,
Ulysses, is set, and the literati retrace the
steps of the book's famous character,
Leopold Bloom. June 16; Ⓦwww
.visitdublin.com/bloomsday.

- **Banks of the Foyle Halloween
Carnival, Derry** At the end of October,
Ireland's best Halloween carnival gets
cranked up in Derry as over 35,000
witches, ghouls and a mix of Harry
Potter-types take to the streets.
Fireworks, ghost tours and the like
can be found in this spooktacular fest.
Oct 31; Ⓦwww.derrycity.gov
.uk/halloween.

Ireland online

Ireland info Ⓦwww.discoverireland.ie
Ireland rail Ⓦwww.irishrail.ie
Ireland (and Northern Ireland) bus info
Ⓦwww.buseireann.ie
Dublin info Ⓦwww.visitdublin.com
Northern Ireland info Ⓦwww
.discovernorthernireland.com
Northern Ireland rail Ⓦwww
.nirailways.co.uk
Belfast info Ⓦwww.gotobelfast.com

Italy

Capital Rome
Population 58,133,509
Language Italian
Currency Euro (€)
When to go April–May and
October–November, when the
landscape colours are at their
best, the temperatures are more
moderate and there are relatively
few crowds
When not to go August. Italians
take their vacations then, so many
shops and businesses are shut, and
the tourists are the only ones walking
the searing streets
Minimum daily budget €37

From frescoes to Ferraris, Venice to
Versace, and the Pope to pasta, there's
something in this boot-shaped, football-
world-champion nation for every sort of
traveller. You can take a chilly dip in the
Med at one end of the country or go
skiing at the other. There's fashion on the
streets of Milan and fish in the markets
of the little villages dotted around Sicily.
The rich textile town of Treviso, just north
of Venice, couldn't be more different to
the rougher areas of Naples. At times,
the country seems so diverse, the only
thing holding it together is the national
football team. In other words, a short
visit to Venice, Florence or Rome will
provide little more than a snapshot of
this culturally overflowing land.

Main attractions

● **The Vatican, Rome** OK, technically
this is a city-state, not an attraction
within Italy, but guidebooks have been
guilty of pairing them for decades with
less justification than this. Let your
jaw drop when you enter St Peter's
Cathedral, considered Christianity's most
magnificent Renaissance church. And
get ready to queue for Michelangelo's
Sistine Chapel (or book ahead), though
many find the maps and frescoes on the
way to the chapel even more compelling
than the main draw.

● **Assisi** Perched halfway up
Mount Subasio, overlooking the

Average daily temperatures (°C) and monthly rainfall (mm) in Italy											
	Jan	**Feb**	**Mar**	**Apr**	**May**	**June**	**July**	**Aug**	**Sept**	**Oct**	**Nov**	**Dec**
Rome												
max °C	13	13	15	17	22	25	28	28	26	22	17	14
min °C	4	4	6	8	12	16	19	19	17	13	8	6
rainfall mm	81	71	69	66	51	33	15	25	69	114	112	97
Venice												
max °C	6	8	12	16	21	24	27	27	23	18	11	7
min °C	-1	1	4	8	13	16	18	18	15	10	4	0
rainfall mm	56	53	61	74	69	79	69	79	66	76	89	62

town of Perugia, this walled city with a fourteenth-century fortress (Rocca Maggiore) is the birthplace of St Francis (1182). Work began on his basilica in 1228, two years after his death, and if you can get past all the religious pilgrims, it's one of the most enchanting towns in the country.

● **The Colosseum, Rome** Long before Gladiator was made into a movie and David Beckham put on body armour for Pepsi, the Colosseum in Rome

(completed in 80 AD) was the ultimate arena for public games.

● **Venice** It's sinking (possibly under the weight of all the tourists), and there's a chance the water may be knee-deep in St Mark's Square by the time you visit, but to stroll Venice without crowds (off season, or at sunrise) may top your European visual highlights. There's a reason so many use it for comparison (Stockholm says it's the "Venice of the North", the Okavango Delta calls itself the "Venice of Africa"). There's

▲ The Palio races, Siena

little need for an overpriced gondola ride. A cheap city bus-boat will do just fine. Do yourself a favour while visiting and get lost; put away your map and wander the narrow back-alleys until you need to ask a local for directions.

● **Florence** This city offers more art history per square metre than any other place outside the Louvre. You could spend a year here and not see it all. In fact, several guidebooks far thicker than this book are devoted entirely to Florence. This Renaissance wonderland boasts the Uffizi Gallery, Ponte Vecchio, the Duomo, Michelangelo's *David*, and the Basilica di San Lorenzo, to name but a few.

Also recommended

● **Walk the Cinque Terre** The five postcard-perfect fishing villages of the Cinque Terre (Riomaggiore, Manarola, Monterosso, Vernazza and Corniglia) along the northwest coast are connected by a cliff-side hiking trail that can be completed in one long day or divided up into a few days with hotel stays and good meals.

● **Climb the vie ferrate in the Dolomites** The *vie ferrate* (iron ways) are a magnificent system of steel ladders and fixed cables, originally built during World War I to help Alpine troops move through the mountains. With only modest modifications, they now allow beginner climbers to clip in and safely ascend to incredible heights.

● **Take a wine tour** Brunello di Montalcino is the Rolls-Royce of Italian wines. You can tour Montalcino, Chianti, or try the Cabernet Sauvignon of the Tuscan coast. The choice is limitless; you can taste some of the world's top wines almost everywhere you go.

- **Watch a volcano blow** Check your insurance coverage (see p.114 for more details), then take a ferry from Naples or the north of Sicily to the island of Stromboli, hike a few hours with a guide up to the top of its volcano (you can't miss it), watch the sunset and then stick around for Mother Nature's fireworks as small eruptions send orange molten lava 50–100m up into the air. The actual summit has been closed since March 2007 due to eruptions, so double-check how far you can climb before taking off.

- **Take in a football match** The bigger clubs like AC Milan, Inter Milan and Roma are among the best in the world, but you might find it more culturally enlightening to watch a game at a smaller stadium. Just make sure you're wearing the right colours. Rather, make sure you're not wearing the wrong colours. If you're not sure, bring a bag with a few options so you can adapt to your surroundings.

Costs

Italy may be cheaper than Switzerland and Scandinavia, but between the beckoning gelato, coffee and museums, there's a load more tempting "necessities" you're likely to spend your money on. Prudent backpackers might manage on €37 a day, but cutting costs is extra painful in this country, even if the museum visits are minimized. Comfortable hotels and restaurants with table service will up this to over €80 per day.

Accommodation

Lodging can be found for €16 a night, but it's typically over €20 and, as soon as you get into the genuine hotel range, prices soar. There are a number of luxury campgrounds just outside the cities that provide budget relief (and a pool).

Eating and drinking

Italy may be famous for its cuisine, but if you want to mangiare on the cheap, especially in the tourist areas, you'll likely be underwhelmed by what you get. Pasta may be difficult to mess up, but it's not always easy to find the truly divine dishes. Pizzas come in one size, taste better than average (occasionally amazing), and are relatively cheap. Prices vary around Italy, but generally it's high prices up north and better deals down south. There's a reason you'll see so many people standing at cafés and bars – prices are higher if you grab a seat.

Transport

Major train and bus lines are quick and reliable (when not on strike); even the small village buses are surprisingly timely. And, aside from the high-speed rail, it's quite cheap. Always check the local prices before you use your rail or bus pass; it's better value to pay €10–18 for a short ride than waste a day of your pass.

The Rome public transport system (Metrebus) sells a daily transport pass ticket for €4, a three-day pass for €11 and a seven-day pass for €16. Tickets can be bought at newsstands, hotels and vending machines. For more information, see Ⓦwww.atac.roma.it.

By train

Eurail Italy Pass Any three days within two months US$259 (first class), US$209 (second class) and US$169 (youth). Additional days US$30–36 (first class), US$24–26 (second class) and US$20 (youth).
Eurail France-Italy Pass Any four days of travel in two months US$375 (first class), US$325 (second class) and US$245 (youth, second class).

For Europe-wide Eurail and InterRail passes, see p.50. For tips and tricks on maximizing your rail pass, see p.75.

By bus

A Busabout pass (see p.52) allows you to travel throughout Italy. For internal bus prices, see the Italian-language-only site Ⓦwww.sitabus.it. For buses to other countries, see Ⓦwww.eurolines.it.

Events

● **Alba Truffle Auction** You can call them fungi if you like, or *turber magnatum pico*, if you want to impress. But in Alba, the home of the delicacy found in the ground by trained dogs, they're known as *tartufo bianco* – white truffles. More prized than France's black truffles, top chefs shell out over €1500 per kilo for these "white diamonds", most popular on omelettes, fresh pasta and risotto. Some truffle oils even fall within the price range of normal people. Mid-Sept to Nov.

● **The Italian Job** If you like the film you might want to catch this film-inspired sponsored rally. A train of Mini Coopers speed across the Alps, pick up a load of local wine and then head back to the UK to auction it off for charity. Late Oct–Nov; Ⓦwww.wordserf.co.uk/italianjob.

● **Carnevale, Venice** Perhaps the only thing better than seeing St Mark's Square without tourists is seeing it during Carnevale, which comes alive with theatrical, dance and acrobatic performances. The most famous and traditional aspect of the festival is the traditional masked balls, which feature elaborate eighteenth-century costumes. Feb–March; Ⓦwww.carnevalevenezia.it. See p.30 for more.

● **Verona Opera Festival** Even if you don't like opera, seeing grand performances in Verona's exquisite Roman amphitheatre will stir your emotions. All classes of society come together for this highlight of Italy's summer calendar. June–Aug; Ⓦwww.arena.it.

● **Il Palio, Siena** This madcap medieval horse race in Siena's town square is surrounded by days of rituals and pageantry – nearly all of it just as much fun for visitors as the race itself. See p.31 for more.

● **Regata Storica, Venice** A trial of strength and skill for the city's gondoliers, this floating parade of antique boats and rowers in period dress couldn't be any more photo-friendly if it had been invented by a team of Fuji film executives. Spectators are expected to support the contestants and may even get issued with the appropriate colours. First Sun in Sept.

Italy online

Country info Ⓦwww.italiantourism.com
Rail Ⓦwww.trenitalia.com
Bus Ⓦwww.sitabus.it
Rome info Ⓦwww.romaturismo.com
Florence info Ⓦwww.firenzeturismo.it
Venice info Ⓦwww.veniceonline.it

www.roughguides.com

Montenegro

Capital Podgorica
Language Montenegrin (although more than sixty percent prefer Serbian)
Currency Euro (€)
When to go May–September, when the mountains are perfect for hiking and the 117 beaches are nice and toasty
When not to go November–February, when the entire country is treated to some of the most insistent rain in Europe
Minimum daily budget €26

With 294km of unspoiled coastline along the glittering Adriatic, Montenegro has all the makings of a travel hotspot. The tourist industry has some way to go in repairing the image backlash of the Yugoslav wars, but it's getting there, one shared bathroom at a time. Unfortunately for budget travellers, the official goal is to model the country as an "elite destination", but there are also efforts under way to open up for more hiking, biking and green travel.

Montenegro was the last of the Yugoslav republics to see reason to leave the union. It suffered limited bombing during the NATO campaign of 1999, but has generally had a less confrontational relationship with the West than Serbia. In 1996, for example, it severed diplomatic ties with Serbia and adopted the German Deutschmark as the official currency. Today, it uses the Euro, despite being neither a member of the EU nor the eurozone.

Main attractions

- **Kotor** Named a UNESCO World Heritage Site in 1979, Kotor is Montenegro's only major tourist spot, with tiled roofs and a clear Venetian tilt to its architecture. Not a sunbathing destination, but there's plenty to keep you busy.

- **Durmitor** National Park Durmitor mountain is the country's highest, at 2522m, but it's the surrounding national park that merits an inland detour. Centred around the town of Zabljak, the park encompasses Tara River Canyon which, at 80km, is the second

Average daily temperatures (°C) and monthly rainfall (mm) in Montenegro

	Jan	Feb	Mar	Apr	May	June	July	Aug	Sept	Oct	Nov	Dec
Bar												
max °C	8	9	13	17	22	25	29	29	25	20	14	10
min °C	0	2	4	7	11	14	17	17	14	10	6	2
rainfall mm	172	148	133	122	87	64	43	59	104	146	199	182

longest in the world (after some canyon in Arizona called the Grand).

Also recommended

- **Ride the train** The Belgrade–Bar railway connects the capital of Serbia with the coastal city of Bar in Montenegro, and notches up 254 tunnels and 435 bridges. Most of it runs through Serbia, but the prettiest parts are in hilly Montenegro. Look out for the 200-metre-high Mala Rijeka viaduct outside Podgorica.

Costs

Costs in Montenegro are pretty low, sitting somewhere in the twilight zone between prices in eastern and western Europe.

Accommodation

Hostel dorm beds can go for as low as €7, even in tourist honeypots like Kotor, and you can get a private room for under €15. Hotels start just below €30, although most hover between the €45 and €50.

Eating and drinking

The close proximity of Italy is evident in the Montenegrin diet, with plenty of bread, meat, cheese and wine, while the long-occupying Ottomans contributed dishes such as mousaka and kebabs as well as pitta bread and baklava. Homegrown meals include boiled lamb up north, dried mutton (kastradina) and carp from Lake Skadar in the middle, and seafood is, unsurprisingly, found near the coast.

Locals are proud of their Rakija grape brandy, and the beer to drink is a Niksicko, which will cost anywhere between €1 and €2.50.

Transport

Montenegro's weak spot is its infrastructure, in terms of everything from electricity and clean water to its roads. Huge sums are being poured into developing exclusive marinas along the coast, but unless you're arriving in a luxury yacht, this won't exactly impact much on your trip.

By train

There are few train lines in Montenegro other than the one from Bar on the coast which heads inland to Podgorica and on to the border with Serbia, plus a sideline north to Niksic. As underfunding has compromised safety (in 2006, 47 passengers were killed when a train derailed and fell into a ravine near Podgorica), railway travel in Montenegro is not for the faint-hearted.

By bus

Buses will take you anywhere in the country for no more than €25. See Ⓦwww.blueline-mne.com/bluetraveleng.html for info on routes.

Montenegro online

Country info Ⓦwww.visit-montenegro.com
Rail Ⓦwww.zeljeznica.cg.yu
Bus Ⓦwww.blueline-mne.com/bluetraveleng.html
Podgorica Ⓦwww.podgorica.cg.yu

Morocco

Capital Rabat
Language Arabic
Currency Dirham
When to go September–April along the coast, when the weather is still good but the summer rush has abated; December–February for skiing
When not to go Mid-June and August are crowded along the coast, and winters up north can be wet
Minimum daily budget €18

As a place where Christianity meets Islam head-on, the Spain–Morocco border should in some strategists' minds be a staging ground for a war of civilizations. But the only invading going on is carried out by desperate Moroccans trying to force their way into the Spanish enclaves of Ceuta and Melilla on the north African coast, or attempting to cross by sea and being picked up by the Spanish Coastguard.

Meanwhile, a steady stream of travellers take the opportunity of seeing a slice of Africa while in Spain, and you'll get a distinct feel of a completely new country and continent as soon as you step off the ferry.

Main attractions

● **Fez** Not just the place that named that funny party hat, but also one of the world's oldest medieval cities. Its medina (fortified city), the Fes el-Bali, is the largest car-free urban zone in the world.

● **Marrakesh** The third-largest city in Morocco after Casablanca and Rabat, but probably the most pleasant thanks to it's mild year-round climate. Don't miss the hectic square Djemaa el Fna or the country's largest souk.

● **The Sahara** The mighty sandbox is just around the corner. Even if you're an adventurous type, visit as part of a tour group or bring someone who knows what they're doing. Venturing out on your own is not a good idea.

Also recommended

● **Ski the Atlas** Morocco's ski resort, Oukaimeden, is an unexpected find some 70km south of Marrakesh. Lift passes cost €9.

Costs

A budget meal won't cost more than €5–10, and a bed for the night can be found for €15–20. Note that restaurants outside of tourist areas close for lunch during Ramadan.

Morocco online

Country info Ⓦ www.visitmorocco.org

The Netherlands

Capital Amsterdam
Population 16,491,461
Languages Dutch (also Frisian)
Currency Euro (€)
When to go Mid-March to mid-May, when the tulips and daffodils are in bloom and when you'll get the best views of the country, while missing the crowds

When not to go Late October and November, when there's freezing rain, and December–February, unless you're happy to ice-skate your way around the country.
Minimum daily budget €34

The preconceived images of windmills, wooden clogs and tulips have given way in recent decades to sex, drugs and tulips. Sure, you can buy small amounts of marijuana in coffee shops. And yes, prostitution is legal and regulated. But it's a shame to visit and leave without learning more about the Netherlands than this.

The country is one of Europe's most developed and densely populated, yet the Dutch maintain a charming balance between the fun-loving attitude found along the Mediterranean and the more reserved and regulated philosophy of the Scandinavian countries. Among the many misconceptions is the country's name. It's often called Holland – even by the tourist board, who believe this is an easier name for foreign visitors

to remember – but this is technically incorrect. Holland is one of the most populated regions, and the one where many of this once-great colonial power's sailors came from, but "the Netherlands" is the official name.

Nearly half of this nation is below sea level, and much of it has been physically reclaimed from the sea. The part that does rise above the watermark looks, at least on a topographical profile map, like the chart of a patient who just flatlined. Which is why the country is so popularly navigated by bike. Or by canal, on the barges in the summer or by ice skates in the winter (it's no accident the Dutch bring home Olympic speed-skating medals by the crate). The capital, Amsterdam, is centrally located and

Average daily temperatures (°C) and monthly rainfall (mm) in the Netherlands

	Jan	Feb	Mar	Apr	May	June	July	Aug	Sept	Oct	Nov	Dec
Amsterdam												
max °C	8	6	8	12	17	19	21	21	18	14	9	7
min °C	5	0	3	4	8	12	13	13	11	8	4	3
rainfall mm	78	45	94	37	51	62	73	61	81	106	76	69

www.roughguides.com

rarely missed by those trying to conquer Europe in a summer. You may be lured in by the famous vices and a reputation for budget travel, but you'll often find this visually stunning city serves only as a gateway to a very accessible country largely overlooked by most travellers.

Main attractions

● **Van Gogh Museum, Amsterdam**
The drawings, notebooks and letters of this one-eared Dutch Master come with a chronologically displayed collection of his paintings. Famous works such as the *Potato Eaters* and *Sunflowers* series and the tortured *Wheatfield with Crows* can all be found here. See ⓦwww .vangoghmuseum.nl.

● **Anne Frank House, Amsterdam** In July 1942, Otto and Edith Frank and their daughters, Margo and Anne, went into hiding in this building on Prinsengracht in Amsterdam. Along with a few others,

THE NETHERLANDS

they hid for two years before they were betrayed and deported to Auschwitz. Both sisters died just weeks before their concentration camp was liberated, but Anne's diary survived, and has since been published in more than sixty languages. The house is now a popular museum (965,000 visitors per year by recent count – visit off-peak hours to avoid crowds). See ⓦwww.annefrank.nl for exhibition info.

● **Tulips** It will take some time to tiptoe through them all, but you can rent a bicycle and pedal through fields of them extending to the horizon. Or you can pay to enter the tourist-friendly Keukenhof Gardens (ⓦwww.keukenhof .nl), where they've been impressively arranged in every conceivable manner. The tulips are in bloom from mid-March to mid-May.

● **Amsterdam's Red Light District** Started as a place to "comfort" the returning sailors after long voyages, the district is now mostly a strange sight: bored women in ornate lingerie beckoning passers-by (often tourist families with grandmothers in tow) to come a little closer to their door-sized windows. Innocently snap a picture and you'll likely find the entire roll of film forcefully removed from your camera and tossed in the canal by a human tank in a leather jacket. For all its famed erotica, this area is one of the least arousing places you'll stumble across.

Also recommended

● **Sample some cheese** Cheese is no laughing matter in the Netherlands, where it's been made for over 1600 years and can still be found in round chunks the size of wagon wheels; Gouda, Edam and Leiden are the best-known varieties. At a traditional cheese market, like the one in Alkmaar (Friday: April–Sept 10am–12.30pm), which has been held here since the 1300s, you can see porters in white uniforms carrying sleds of heavy cheese.

● **Go kite skating** With exceptional winds and long stretches of firm beach, kite skating (racing along the beach on a special skateboard with a powerful kite) is perfect for this environment. In IJmuiden, Renesse, Oostvoorne and the Drunen Dunes area, you'll find the best conditions to try this unique sport.

● **In-line skate along the coast** The Netherlands is considered one of the best in-line skating countries in the world. Strap on a daypack and go. Routes have been mapped out to take you along the most beautiful spots on the coast, past dunes, dykes and even along sections of the famed "Eleven-City Skating Tour".

● **Tour the Heineken brewery** The old Heineken brewery, just a stone's throw from the Van Gogh Museum in Amsterdam, may not be churning out beer any more, but it's still serving it at least to the hordes of tourists who pay €10 for the chance to see the old vats and stables. Three beers are included on this walk-through infomercial, as well as a souvenir glass. ⓦwww .heinekenexperience.com.

● **Walk the mud flats** Wadden Sea is the largest continuous nature reserve in Europe and, when the tide is low, it's possible to walk the uncovered mud flats. These are actually sandbanks crisscrossed by channels, leaving a soft footing that makes for a low-impact but strenuous hike.

● **Cycle across the Netherlands** You can easily rent a bike and find your way around Amsterdam, but there's really no reason to stop there. Dedicated signed

www.roughguides.com

trails lead you from town to town. You don't need a dual-suspension mountain bike, either. A simple three-speeder should do the trick.

Costs

The Netherlands is slightly more expensive than your typical European country but, with so many budget travellers hanging out there, it's easy to slip into the frugal lifestyle. You can scrape by on just over €34 a day, but €50 is a more reasonable target for the first few days in Amsterdam, when you're paying admission fees to the various attractions. To live in backpacker budget comfort, figure on €68 a day.

Accommodation

Some of the classic budget digs, like Bob's Youth Hostel (Ⓦwww.bobsyouth-hostel.nl) in Amsterdam, are still up and running. However, they're not the bargains they once were, so for real budget accommodation, you'll need to check into a campground, where you can probably split a cabin with a few others for around €10 each. The cheapest hotels start at round €55, then jump to €85 for a room at a three-star hotel. For information on city campgrounds in the Netherlands go to Ⓦwww.stadscampings.nl.

Eating and drinking

The Dutch aren't famous for their food and, even though you can certainly find excellent top-tier restaurants, this may not be the best place for a big splurge. Fast-food street snacks, especially around the Red Light District in Amsterdam and other nightspots, offer filling cheap eats. There's plenty of Indonesian culinary influence (a former colony), and the noodle dishes are excellent and a good way to keep your

batteries charged. If you eat at hostels, you can find a good meal for around €9, but you should be able to do better than that out on the town or at a supermarket.

Transport

There aren't many places in this country you can't reach by rail, whether it's on the quiet city trams that catch wandering tourists off guard or the high-speed rail links to Brussels and Paris. Dutch Railway has reasonable fares and frequent and modern trains that welcome Eurail and other pass-holders.

For the inner-city trams, you'll want to pick up a strippenkaart (valid throughout the country on buses, trams and subways), which can be purchased anywhere, though it's more expensive to actually buy it on the tram or bus. A basic fifteen-strip card costs €7.30 and will get you a few rides, depending on how far you go (each strip buys you a zone). The other way to go is the I Amsterdam Card, which gives you unlimited transport (and one canal cruise) and free entry to the top museums. It can be bought at tourist offices and comes in three flavours: 24 hours (€38), 48 hours (€48) and 72 hours (€58). Ⓦwww.iamsterdamcard .com. For information on transport around Amsterdam go to Ⓦwww.gvb.nl.

By train

Eurail Benelux-France Pass Any four days in two months US$369 (first class), US$319 (second class) and US$239 (youth, second class). Ten days in two months US$585 (first class), US$539 (second class) and US$415 (youth, second class).

For Benelux Tourrail Pass see p.233. For Eurail Germany-Benelux Pass prices, see p.233.

For Europe-wide Eurail and InterRail passes, see p.50. For tips and tricks on maximizing your rail pass, see p.75.

By bus

Busabout (see p.52) only serves Amsterdam, connecting it with Bruges in Belgium and Berlin in Germany. For internal bus prices, call the contact at Ⓦwww.connexxion.nl (the website is Dutch-only). For buses to other countries, see Ⓦwww.eurolines.nl.

Events

● **Queen's Day, Amsterdam** About a million people descend on Amsterdam for this annual street party on behalf of the previous queen's birthday. On this day, all street trade is unregulated so there's a citywide (and nationwide) rummage sale to the delight of secondhand shoppers. Many are out for more laughs than profit. At night the party continues in the clubs. April 30.

● **Amsterdam Pride Parade** The Amsterdam Pride Parade isn't just one of the biggest gay carnivals in the world, it's also the only one with floats that actually float. The spectacular show moves down Amsterdam's main canals with costumed dancers and probably a few things you (or the other 250,000 visitors) never thought you'd see. Find a spot on a bridge for the best views. Aug; Ⓦwww .amsterdamgaypride.nl.

● **International Nijmegen Four-Day Marches** The four-day, 50km-a-day walking marathon (running is not allowed) is centred on the city of Nijmegen (pronounced nigh-may-gen) and is one of the most gruelling physical challenges in Europe. (There are still Dutch octogenarians who do it every year in wooden clogs. And they will pass you!) To sign up, visit Ⓦwww.vierdaagse .nl. Or just stay downtown and party as seemingly half of the country descends on the city to cheer the walkers on. Third Tuesday of July.

The Netherlands online

Country info Ⓦwww.holland.com
Rail Ⓦwww.ns.nl
Bus Ⓦwww.connexxion.nl
Amsterdam info Ⓦwww .visitamsterdam.com

Norway

Capital Oslo
Population 4,610,820
Languages Bokmal Norwegian and Nynorsk Norwegian
Currency Norwegian krone (NOK)
When to go January–April for some of the world's best cross-country skiing, June–September for hiking, biking and sightseeing

When not to go November and December, when it's dark and freezing cold. January and February aren't much better, but at least winter activities are under way by then
Minimum daily budget €42

Norway offers the most spectacular landscape in Europe and is a country best enjoyed outdoors. The weather isn't always that accommodating, but that doesn't stop the Norwegians. "There's no such thing as bad weather, only bad clothing", goes the popular saying. And if you don't let the occasional rain shower (or freezing rain shower, or blizzard) get in your way, Norway is like a giant playground for the outdoor enthusiast. To Norwegians, fjords and their surrounding mountains are meant to be hiked, biked and skied, not viewed from a cruise-ship deckchair, and the fact that this is how most of the world chooses to see their nature continues to baffle them (possibly just as much as their determination to continue hunting whales in the face of international bans baffles most of the world).

Norwegians' oil reserves have made them one of the richest countries in Europe. The oil has also made Norwegians less worried about trade, which is one of the reasons they voted to stay out of the EU. Besides, as Sweden voted to enter the EU, they had a slight obligation to do the opposite.

The Norwegians have been explorers since the Viking ages. Thor Heyerdahl was the twentieth-century hero of the high seas, conquering them on a boat that looked to the untrained eye like a big bale of hay. Many of today's heroes, however, are cross-country skiers and biathlon competitors – if you see a crowd of burly men hovering around a bar TV in the winter, chances are they're watching one of these two events.

Average daily temperatures (°C) and monthly rainfall (mm) in Norway

	Jan	Feb	Mar	Apr	May	June	July	Aug	Sept	Oct	Nov	Dec
Oslo												
max °C	-1	-2	4	9	17	20	22	21	16	9	4	0
min °C	-7	-7	-3	1	7	11	13	12	7	3	-2	-6
rainfall mm	49	36	47	41	53	65	81	89	90	84	73	55

For the traveller, Norway is one of the most expensive countries in Europe and, with the exception of seafood, has one of the least appealing regional cuisines. A few days in the fjords, however, and this is easily forgotten – in part because of the natural beauty and in part because, if you're camping, you're actually spending less than you would staying in hostels in Spain.

Main attractions

● **Kon-Tiki Museum, Oslo** In 1947, Thor Heyerdahl crossed the Pacific on a balsawood raft to prove that the first Polynesian settlers could have sailed from pre-Inca Peru. This adventure – and the rest of his research – are celebrated in this excellent museum.

● **National Gallery, Oslo** In theory, no one's meant to be able to walk in and rip paintings off the walls during opening hours at the National Gallery, but with less security than your average pet-food store, a pair of crooks did just that with *The Scream*, Edvard Munch's masterpiece. Hopefully, there will still be a few famous paintings left by the time you arrive.

● **"Norway in a Nutshell" Tour** This tour of Sognefjord by train, boat and bus

▲ Lofoten Islands

is an extremely popular (and expensive) day-trip from Oslo and Bergen. As one Norwegian called it, "Fjords for people who can't be bothered to do them." See Ⓦwww.norwaynutshell.com for tour times and prices.

● **Coastal Steamer** In 1893, the Vesteraalens Dampskibsselskap steamship company opened an express shipping route between Trondheim and Hammerfest along the same rocky and treacherous route that was rejected by the larger shipping companies. Today, they carry passengers as well, and the Hurtigruten (Ⓦwww.hurtigruten.com) is now called – at least in all of the tourist propaganda – "the world's most beautiful voyage".

Also recommended

● **See the Northern Lights** You don't need to head up to Hammerfest as Bill Bryson did in his book *Neither Here Nor There*; this celestial show can be viewed across the country (Oct, Feb & March are ideal, the rest of winter is also good). There's no magic winter date to see the psychedelic display, but if you leave the big cities and find some large stretch of flat terrain for a wide-open view (or take a quick drive out of town on a clear night), and give yourself at least a few days, chances are you won't miss it.

● **Hike a glacier** Norway is home to the largest glacier on continental Europe (the Jostedalsbreen), and several tour companies arrange hikes on the ice. One of the better-known spots to try your hand at scaling the slippery slopes is Briksdalsbreen. Ⓦwww .briksdalsbreen.com.

● **Kayak the fjords** A great way to view the fjords is from a sea kayak. The waters are calm, it's hard to get lost, there are small towns along the way with guest rooms and food, and the kayaks can be rented all across Norway.

● **Raft the mountain rivers** In addition to the spectacular scenery, Norway boasts excellent rafting. This can be done in several spots, including the Trysilelva River in Hedmark, and Dagali River in Voss.

● **Fish for salmon in a fjord** You can go fishing just about everywhere, but the best spots require a guide (or a good tip) and, more importantly, a licence, which you can pick up around the country. Many local deep-sea angling associations and tourist information offices organize fishing trips. Typically, the best time for salmon fishing is from mid-July to mid-August, but this can vary a lot from region to region.

Costs

Because of the costs (and logistics), few budget travellers spend much time (or any time at all) in this Nordic land. This means there aren't the typical gaggles of backpackers – even in high season – but few places to save money, either. Tightening the budget belt is a necessity here, no matter which bracket you plan to travel in. Even though it's more expensive in general, there are fewer "must-see" museums and attractions with fees. It's more about the natural beauty of the country, which is free, so you can sneak by on €42 a day. A more realistic goal for budget travel is €55, though you can get

by on €20 or less if you bike, camp and cook for yourself.

Accommodation

Youth hostels go for around €22 for a dorm, €60 for a double room, and that's just for starters. For a single room in an "inexpensive" hotel, paying €80 is not unheard of. Prices go as high as you like once you start looking for luxury.

Eating and drinking

Alcohol is prohibitively expensive and, if you're trying to save money, this is a decent place to cut back on consumption. Even *McDonald's* and the average petrol station hot dog are shockingly pricey, so it's a case of bulk cooking with items at the supermarket if you want to squeak by on a budget. A decent meal isn't going to cost less than €16.

Transport

Norway has relatively few train lines compared to the rest of Europe. A number of them – Oslo to Bergen, Oslo to the airport and Oslo to Lillehammer – are modern and quick. The rest can be painfully slow. This can also be said for the roads – often single lanes with minimal passing opportunities and low speed limits – and the buses that travel along them. The railways have some excellent scenic routes, but the bus network is more extensive and there are plenty of picturesque passages to be viewed from the road. All transport is extremely pricey, so this is the place to use a rail or bus pass.

By train

Eurail Norway Pass Any three days in one month US$275 (second class) and US$209 (youth, second class).

For Eurail Scandinavia Pass prices, see p.257.

For Europe-wide Eurail and InterRail passes, see p.00. For tips and tricks on maximizing your rail pass, see p.00.

By bus

Busabout doesn't operate in Norway. For buses to other countries, see Ⓦwww.eurolines.no.

Events

* **Independence Day** On May 17, 1814, Norway declared independence from Denmark and established its own constitutional government. To celebrate this day, many Norwegians dress up in traditional costume of regionally decorated and handmade colourful *bunad* to march down the street of their local town. Some of the more sports-oriented take to the high-elevation glacial tracks on skis.

* **Pagan bonfires** On the longest day of the year in Norway (Sankt Hans), the sun doesn't set in many parts of the country. Even in the south, it barely dips below the horizon. To celebrate the ancient Pagan ritual of the summer solstice, huge bonfires are lit all over Norway.

* **The ExxonMobil Bislett Games, Oslo** One of the biggest track and field meets of the year takes place in June or July at this classic old stadium in the centre of Oslo. The track is notoriously fast, so many top athletes time their peak condition with this event to go after world records. See Ⓦwww.bislettgames.com for info on the games.

Norway online

Country info Ⓦwww.visitnorway.com
Rail Ⓦwww.nsb.no
Bus Ⓦwww.nor-way.no
Oslo info Ⓦwww.visitoslo.com

Poland

Capital Warsaw
Population 38,536,869
Language Polish
Currency Zloty (zl)
When to go Mid-May to June and September to mid-October, when the weather's decent and you'll miss the (relative) crowds

When not to go July and August, when the walking trails, lakes and beaches get swamped with people, and November–February, when it's cold and dark, and many hostels are closed
Minimum daily budget €25

Long tucked away in the economic doldrums between the Soviet Union and Western Europe, Poland has been sliced up by conquering nations in more ways than a bag of onions. Today, however, Poland is emerging as a diverse and vibrant state. The exciting part is that it's still in its capitalist infancy, trying to figure out the road ahead – there are Coke billboards and chic cafés in the cities and horse-drawn wagons kicking up dust on country roads.

Poland offers a slightly more rugged experience than countries in Western Europe, but it's far easier on the wallet. You can find the luxury living, but there's also all the sports and outdoor pursuits you're likely to ever want, from horseback riding to sailing or scuba diving; the challenge is just carving out enough time

to do them. There are beaches on the Baltic, craggy mountains in the south, and lakes and green rolling hills; there's also a long tradition of Slavic hospitality, with feast-like meals for even casual visitors. As the Polish saying goes: "a guest in the house is God in the house." The trick, of course, is getting invited through the front door.

Main attractions

- **Kraków** This southern city emerged from World War II relatively unscathed, making it one of UNESCO's twelve greatest historic cities in the world and an architectural treasure trove. The church spires and old, cobbled square provide the ideal backdrop for lounging in cafés and people-watching; it may

www.roughguides.com

Average daily temperatures (°C) and monthly rainfall (mm) in Poland

	Jan	Feb	Mar	Apr	May	June	July	Aug	Sept	Oct	Nov	Dec
Warsaw												
max °C	1	1	7	12	18	21	23	23	18	12	6	2
min °C	-4	-4	0	3	8	11	13	12	8	4	1	-6
rainfall mm	28	25	30	38	51	66	76	71	46	41	38	30

look like a history lesson, but the city is very much alive and buzzing.

● **Oświęcim** Most know this industrial town 60km west of Kraków by its German name: Auschwitz. The largest of the concentration camps, much of it was destroyed as the Nazis retreated in 1945, but there's still plenty to get a sense of the magnitude of this death factory. Four million people were killed here (and at the nearby linked camp Birkenau) during the Holocaust. It's hard to forget a trip to this haunting memorial.

● **Royal Castle, Warsaw** Like much of Warsaw, the Royal Castle has been rebuilt (1971–77). The Baroque lines seen at a distance give way to Gothic traits once inside – tapestries, paintings, even the furniture are crafted into place in each room, and it makes for an inspiring visit.

Also recommended

● **Pay homage to Copernicus** Nicolaus Copernicus, the famous astronomer who "stopped the sun and moved the earth", was born in Toruń. The town itself, with soaring Gothic buildings, is worth a visit anyway, but Toruń's planetarium packs extra meaning to the journey.

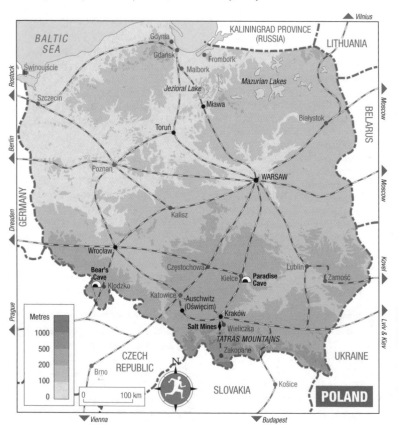

- **Hike the Tatras** Poland's outdoor life is often overlooked by visitors, but head into the Tatra mountains and you'll get a taste of the Poland the locals enjoy. The Pieniny, Bieszczady and Karkonosze mountains will all do as well.

- **Sail across the Mazurian lakes** Few would put "Poland" and "sailing" in the same sentence, but the Mazurian lakes are packed with hundreds of boats in summer. Sailors also head for Jeziorak lake near Mlawa. In winter, the sailing continues on ice, with championships held in the Mazurian region.

- **Head underground** Caving is common near Kraków and in the Tatra mountains. There are literally thousands of caverns to choose from, but just a handful are ready for commercial visitors without experience. The most famous are the Bear's Cave near Klodzko and the Paradise Cave near Kielce.

- **Salt of the earth** Fifteen kilometres outside of Kraków are the salt mines at Wieliczka. Since medieval times, creative miners with time on their hands have carved incredibly elaborate (mostly religious) sculptures from the salt. There's even a seventeenth-century chapel with decorations made out of the stuff. It's been listed by UNESCO World Heritage since 1978. ⓦwww.kopalnia.pl.

Costs

At the upper end, you can certainly spend in Warsaw what you would in most of the world's big cities. If you're travelling cheap, though, this is an excellent place to do it. You can get a hotel room, restaurant meal with drinks, entry to a museum and a latte for the price of a dorm-room bed and supermarket snacks in the more expensive European countries.

Accommodation
You shouldn't need to pay more than €19 for budget accommodation anywhere in Poland. In some places, like university hostels in the summer, you might be able to survive on less than €8 a night, but figure on €10 to be safe. Even private rooms – that is, a room in a private home – shouldn't be more than €15 outside of Warsaw and Kraków. Camping doesn't offer the same sort of savings it does elsewhere, though.

Eating and drinking
The best place to fill up is a "Milk Bar", which is open from early morning until 6pm and offers traditional Polish snacks for prices well under the syllable count on the items you're ordering. Soups are an integral part of the meal, or even a meal unto themselves. The main dishes often don't look haute cuisine (there's only so much you can do with stewed cabbage), but you'll find several that agree with your palate and even more that are at least wallet-friendly. A decent restaurant meal will cost about €6, and a good one can be had for €9.

Transport

Trains are moderately efficient (provided you're not stuck on a "normal service" train that stops at every third mound of dirt) and well priced – it's difficult to pay more than €25 for a single-day trip. A second-class sleeper for a long journey is under €16. See ⓦwww.polrail.com for info on passes. In rural areas, the bus is probably faster than the train. The national bus carrier, PKS, specializes in cramped and slow service. Polski Express, a private company, is better, but most useful out of Warsaw.

In Warsaw, a 24-hour transport ticket costs just €2 (€1 with student card), and a three-day ticket is €3.55 (€1.75 with

www.roughguides.com

student card). The Warsaw Card costs €7.75, covers transport for 24 hours and also gets you into 28 museums (including all the big ones) either free or at a discount. Kraków is very accessible on foot, but if you're hitting loads of museums and want to save energy by taking buses and trams in between, try the Kraków Tourist Card (Ⓦwww .krakowcard.com). The two-day (€11) or three-day (€14.40) card entitles the holder to free travel on city buses and trams and to free entry in up to thirty museums. It even includes airport transport on a local bus.

By train

Polish Railway Pass The one-week pass allows travel on seven consecutive days for €140 (first class) and €100 (second class).

Eurail Poland Pass Five days within one month for US$169 (first class), US$129 (second class) and US$89 (youth, second class).

For European East Pass prices, see p.224.

For Europe-wide InterRail and Eurail passes, see p.50. For tips and tricks on maximizing your rail pass, see p.75.

By bus

Busabout doesn't operate in Poland. For internal bus prices, see Ⓦwww.pks .poznan.pl and Ⓦwww.polskiexpress .pl. For buses to other countries, see Ⓦwww.eurolinespolska.pl.

Events

● **Music in Old Kraków Festival**
Established by the early-music ensemble Capella Cracoviensis in the 1970s, this annual event continues to grow. It's now a seventeen-day happening with concerts filling venues across the city. Aug; Ⓦwww.krakow.pl.

● **Wratislavia Cantans, Wroclaw**
Every year, 2000 performers and 25,000 spectators flood into the thousand-year-old city of Wroclaw for a cultural jamboree: classical concerts, ballet performances, films and art exhibitions. Sept; Ⓦwww.wratislavia.art.pl.

● **Warsaw Autumn Festival**
Organizers pack twenty concerts into nine days in this premier event, which was started in 1956. The audience can expect to hear Schönberg and Webern, as well as avant-garde, experimental performances. Third week in Sept.

Poland online

Country info Ⓦwww.polandtour.org
Rail Ⓦwww.polrail.com
Bus Ⓦwww.pks.poznan.pl and Ⓦwww.polskiexpress.pl
Warsaw info Ⓦwww.warsawtour.pl
Kraków info Ⓦwww.krakow.pl

Portugal

Capital Lisbon
Population 10,605,870
Languages Portuguese (also Mirandese)
Currency Euro (€)
When to go March–October for the south, May–September for Lisbon and the north

When not to go November–February, when the weather's chilly, even in the Algarve. June–August is best avoided if you're not partial to crowds
Minimum daily budget €25

Neatly tucked away on the "other" side of Spain, this century-long gateway to Africa and the Americas is often missed by travellers who start heading west across Europe, then get caught up in Spain's attractions and run out of time. Those who do make it to the far end of Iberia typically make a pit stop in Lisbon before beelining it to the Algarve for a glimpse of the poster-pin-up beaches, leaving the many small-town and countryside gems largely undiscovered.

The Portuguese take life slowly (unless behind the wheel of a car) and savour the little things: folk festivals, fish, fruit, flowers and food drenched in olive oil. The ethos of the nation is very much tied to the sea: Vasco da Gama is more than a historical seafarer in Portugal; he embodies the spirit of the country.

The nation is cut tidily in half by the River Tagus. To the south, where the Moors and Romans once had strongholds, you'll find darker-skinned people and a more Mediterranean lifestyle. To the north, you'll find a more Celtic and Germanic sort.

Main attractions

● **Lagos** The spectacular combination of cliffs and white beaches in Lagos sells plenty of postcards and even more beer; the beach scene in this Algarve town is a party stop on the travel circuit, though it's steadily pricing itself out of most people's range. Renting a bike, moped or even a horse will make beach exploration easier.

● **Évora** This walled town has seemingly been dropped into a field of

Average daily temperatures (°C) and monthly rainfall (mm) in Portugal											
	Jan	Feb	Mar	Apr	May	June	July	Aug	Sept	Oct	Nov	Dec
Lisbon												
max °C	14	15	17	18	21	25	28	28	27	21	17	14
min °C	7	8	9	11	12	15	17	18	17	14	11	9
rainfall mm	110	111	69	64	39	21	5	6	26	80	114	108

vineyards, olive trees and flowers. The cathedral and Roman temple provide popular focal points, but the ossuary chapel, made from thousands of human skulls and bones, is too bizarre to miss.

- **The Rossio, Lisbon** The actual name of this plaza is Praça D. Pedro IV, but if you want to sound like a local (or just want to be able to pronounce it), go with "Rossio". Benefiting from a well-earned face-lift, the plaza looks better than ever, and still acts as the heart of Lisbon.

- **The ruins of St George's Castle, Lisbon** Used to defeat the Moorish invaders, St George's offers the classic panoramic overlook of Lisbon, with a great view of Santuario do Cristo Rei, the 34-metre replica of Rio de Janeiro's *Christ the Redeemer* statue, and the remains of a cathedral destroyed in the 1755 earthquake.

Also recommended

- **Hike Madeira** The volcanic island of Madeira is a little over 50km wide, but it has been providing shelter to transatlantic travellers since 1420.

Mountain trails make for azure panoramas, while wild flowers and lush landscape take care of the rest. It's a 90min flight from Lisbon.

● **Test some port** With its low lighting, squidgy sofas and soft music, the Institute of Port Wine in Lisbon (a short tram-ride uphill from Praca dos Restauradores) is a great place to while away the hours with friends. A glass of the national snifter costs anywhere between €1 and €25 and goes best with Serra – a viscous cheese scooped up with crackers. Better yet, tour the wineries and get a shot for free at the end of the historic walkabout.

● **Eat a meal to the sound of Fado** Fado is the traditional music of Portugal, and in a Fado-themed restaurant, classic Portuguese food is served while guitar players and singers perform their lament. For a list of Fado restaurants in Lisbon, see Ⓦwww.visitlisboa.com.

● **Surf the Atlantic coast** Portugal's waves aren't in the same league as Hawaii's, but there are enough breakers around the country to keep most beginner and intermediate surfers happy. Peniche, just outside of Lisbon, is one of the top spots. Surfing's also popular in Lagos and Sagres on the Algarve, and Sines, just between Lisbon and the Algarve.

● **Pick up a bargain at the Alfama market, Lisbon** Originally named Fiera da Ladra, or "Thief"s Market", the Alfama has been selling tschoskes to bargain hunters for over a hundred years. Hand-painted pottery and lace are among the most popular items, but you can find loads of deals on rugs, glassware, jewellery, books, old sailing gear and art. Tues and Sat 5am–1pm.

● **See fish get tanked** When Lisbon hosted the World Expo in 1998, this modern aquarium served as a centrepiece. Located, appropriately enough, right next to the harbour, the Oceanário de Lisboa offers environmental soundscapes and interactive media, in addition to a vibrant array of sea life. Ⓦwww.oceanario.pt.

Costs

Portugal is one of the cheaper countries in Europe, but not so cheap that you can comfortably release the grip on your wallet. However, with a bit of restraint you can stretch your funds a long way.

Accommodation
There are plenty of cheap hostels around Portugal, but far fewer in the resort towns along the Algarve, where you're more likely to pay the sort of rates you would in Paris or Barcelona. If you feel like a bit of a splurge, you might try a *pousada* (Ⓦwww.pousadas.pt), which are converted castles, fortresses or historical sites.

Eating and drinking
You'll find some of Europe's best seafood in Portugal, and it's decently priced. Add to this some vinho verde (green wine – so-called because it should be consumed before the wine has aged) and you've got one of the best meals you'll find on your trip for under €12.

Transport

Train prices are reasonable (about €9 per 100km), so any journey less than two hours is not going to be worth using a day of your Eurail pass. Buses cover many of the same routes as trains, in less time, and for competitive prices.

www.roughguides.com

Since many also leave from the central station, it's easy to compare if you're buying tickets individually. If you're thinking of renting a car or scooter, be warned: Portugal has the highest traffic fatality rate in Europe.

Look into a Lisboa Card (Ⓦwww .askmelisboa.com) if you're just in the capital for a day or two and are trying to hit every attraction. Prices are €16 (one-day), €27 (two-day) and €33.50 (three-day), and include free transport and up to fifty percent off entry to museums and monuments.

By train

Portugal Pass Any three days of travel in one month US$145 (first class). **Eurail Spain-Portugal Pass** Three days of travel in two months US$315 (first class). Additional travel days are US$40–44 per day.

For Europe-wide Eurail and InterRail passes, see p.50. For tips and tricks on maximizing your rail pass, see p.75.

By bus

Busabout doesn't operate in Portugal. For internal bus prices, see Ⓦwww .rede-expressos.pt and Ⓦwww .eva-bus.com.

Events

● **Funchal Carnival** If you're in Portugal during Carnival, consider heading to the island of Madeira to celebrate this pre-Lenten event. The capital, Funchal, is overrun with party-goers, as a parade of floats takes to the streets, and comes alive to the sound of samba troupes. Late Feb.

● **Festa do Colete Encarnado, Vila Franca de Xira** Portugal's answer to the running of the bulls, where the macho and the mad dodge bulls let loose on the streets. During the daily Portuguese-style bullfights, the bull is wrestled, but not killed, which is more impressive and less gruesome than the Spanish version. First Fri of July.

● **Alta Estremadura Jazz Festival** Four towns two hours north of Lisbon (Pombal, Leiria, Marinha Grande and São Pedro de Muel) host this talent-heavy jazz festival. Sept–Oct.

Portugal online

Country info Ⓦwww.visitportugal.pt
Rail Ⓦwww.cp.pt
Bus Ⓦwww.rede-expressos.pt
Lisbon info Ⓦwww.atl-turismolisboa.pt

Romania

Capital Bucharest
Population 22,303,552
Languages Romanian (also Hungarian and German)
Currency Leu (L)
When to go May–August, when the weather's best (crowds aren't much of an issue). September and October have decent weather as well

When not to go July and August, when it's crowded along the Black Sea and at the Painted Monasteries of southern Bucovina. November–February is normally too cold for sightseeing
Minimum daily budget €21

Romania's main export, other than Olympic gymnasts, seems to be Dracula. And neither of these are large income-producers, especially with Hollywood reluctant to cough up name-use fees. So the country has to rely on an industry of textiles, auto assembly, mining, timber, food processing, petroleum refining and football stars. The problem is that these don't bring in much income either (except Gheorghe Hagi). But big change is under way as Romania pulls itself into the capitalist arena. You might call it the "Wild West of the Eastern Bloc"; the dichotomy shows itself in myriad forms: horse-drawn carts steered by drivers with one hand and the other on their mobile phone, or a traditional craftsman beside a businessman in the latest Hugo Boss suit. It's no secret that the new

money is leaving many behind on the journey towards development, but other nations in the region share a similar path.

One of the old-style customs that's still found in abundance, though, is hospitality. Romanians welcome you into their unassuming homes and feed you to bursting capacity. Then they sink their sharp teeth into your neck, or so the tourist bureau would have you believe with all the Dracula hype. Medieval towns, stately castles and excellent hiking trails await, and for about half the price (and a fraction of the tourists) of Western Europe's flagship cities.

Main attractions

- **Bran Castle** Also known as "Dracula's Castle", the popular castle

Average daily temperatures (°C) and monthly rainfall (mm) in Romania

	Jan	Feb	Mar	Apr	May	June	July	Aug	Sept	Oct	Nov	Dec
Bucharest												
max °C	2	4	10	17	22	26	28	28	24	17	8	3
min °C	-5	-4	1	6	11	14	16	15	11	6	1	-3
rainfall mm	43	38	36	46	66	86	56	56	36	28	46	43

actually has no ties to Vlad Tepeş, the medieval prince associated with the vampire extraordinaire. It doesn't look so ominous either, but what did they expect with white walls and Disney-style towers? None of this seems to prevent the tourists from coming, though.

● **Sighişoara** This atmospheric Saxon medieval town in Transylvania is another destination on the Dracula trail. Vlad Tepeş was born within the citadel's walls, in the "Dracula House", which is now – surprise! surprise! – a bar and restaurant.

● **Palace of Parliament, Bucharest** It's the second-largest building in the world (after the Pentagon), but Ceauşescu ploughed over 7000 homes and 26 churches to build it in the 1980s, so there's understandably less pride in this engineering achievement than there otherwise might be.

● **Painted Monasteries of southern Bucovina** These frescoed monasteries near Suceava in Romania's northeast corner are UNESCO treasures – the Voronet church is known as the "Sistine Chapel of the East". Despite their remote location, the sites do get crowded in high season.

Also recommended

● **Twitch for birds in the Danube Delta** From late spring to mid-autumn, the Danube Delta is home to hundreds of species of birds. Binoculars are a good idea, but you don't need a licence or any other equipment. If you'd rather not birdwatch on your own, tour operators will happily guide you to the best spots. With a bit of luck, you might even see a black pelican colony.

ROMANIA

- **Go skiing** Romania may not be the first place that comes to mind when you plan a ski trip, but don't rule out this bargain vacation. Cross-country skiing, snowboarding and tubing are also possible, with peaks around 3000m. The major ski resorts are Poiana Brasov, Sinaia and Predeal. See ⓦwww .skiresorts.ro for season info and lift-pass prices.

- **Track wolves in the Carpathian mountains** The forested slopes of Romania's Carpathian mountains help shelter the grey wolf, and Zărneşti, at the southern tip, makes the best base for setting out on their trail. See ⓦwww .cntours.ro for details of guided trips.

Costs

Even though Romania may be the cheapest country in Europe, not everything is priced for the budget traveller and there aren't always great savings where you might expect them. But with a bit of looking (and limiting your time in Bucharest), there are plenty of insanely cheap deals reminiscent of the prices grey-haired backpackers still wax on about. ATMs are increasingly common, as well as vendors who accept credit cards.

Accommodation

The best deals are private accommodation outside Bucharest (for guesthouses in rural areas, see ⓦwww.antrec.ro), where you can get a room and breakfast for under €10. In the capital, things can cost fifty percent more, though you can get a double for €22 if you find another traveller to split the cost. For under €45, you can stay in a nice hotel.

Eating and drinking

Because most Romanians can't afford to eat out, many restaurants cater to wealthy foreign visitors and up their prices accordingly. Finding a local hangout with local rates may take some looking, especially around Bucharest and the more touristy areas. Outside of these places, you can easily dine for less than €5 and pick up a bottle of Romanian wine for under €2 to wash it down with. However, this is beer country, and it's as cheap as any you'll find in Europe.

Transport

Romania has an impressive railway infrastructure that covers the entire country. Trains are the best way to get around; they're cheap and tend to arrive on time. Local trains are a bargain but stop at every other telephone pole. The Express trains only sound fast, but with €6 taking you approximately 100km, they are inexpensive. The fastest inter-city trains cost a bit more. There are several bus companies offering connections between Romania's main cities, but they typically aren't as cheap or quick as the trains. Several bus companies provide daily service to İstanbul (700km) for under €20. Bucharest's trolley-buses and trams cost €0.30 per ride, and tickets can be purchased from almost any street kiosk. Day passes are just under €2 and week passes cost €4. A one-day metro card is around €1.15 and a ten-trip carnet is €1.90. The city's "express buses" are roughly double the standard fare.

By train

Eurail Romania Pass Any five days of travel in two months US$199 (first class only) and US$159 (youth, first class only). Any ten days in two months US$345 (first class) and US$279 (youth, first class only). **Eurail Romania-Hungary Pass** Any five days in two months US$269 (first class) and US$189 (youth, second class); any ten days in two months US$405 (first class) and US$285 (youth, second class).

See p.243 for Balkans Flexi Pass prices.

For Europe-wide InterRail and Eurail passes, see p.50. Because of the low train fares, they aren't nearly as essential here as they are in other European countries. For tips and tricks on maximizing your rail pass, see p.75.

By bus

Busabout doesn't operate in Romania. For buses to other countries, see Ⓦwww.eurolines.ro.

Events

● **Whit Sunday Szekely Pilgrimage** A Franciscan monastery 2km northeast of Miercurea Ciuc, in the eastern Szekely Land, hosts the year's biggest traditional folk and religious festival, which dates back to the fifteenth century and is held in thanks for the Szekely victory at Marasszentimre. Black-clad pilgrims still assemble in the yard and church interior of the city to sing hymns and touch the wooden Madonna in the sanctuary.

● **Medieval Days** The last three days of July, Sighişoara hosts this festival of arts, crafts and music. People dress in traditional costume and stage music and theatrical performances.

● **Halloween in Transylvania** What better place to be for Halloween? Celebrations, shows and tours follow in the footsteps of Bram Stoker's infamous character. Oct 31.

● **Pageant of the Juni, Braşov** To commemorate the only day of the year when Romanians could freely enter this Saxon city, the town's youth dress up in costumes – some over 150 years old – and ride through the old quarter on horseback. First Sunday in May.

● **Sambra Oilor** This festival in Bran celebrates the sheep herds' annual return from the high mountains (hurray!). Sept.

Romania online

Country info Ⓦwww.romaniatourism .com
Rail Ⓦwww.cfr.ro
Bucharest info Ⓦwww.romaniatourism .com/bucharest.html

Russia

Capital Moscow
Population 142,893,540
Language Russian
Currency Ruble (RUR)
When to go May–June and September–October, when you'll avoid the rain and summer tourist crowds

When not to go April is slushy, July and August wet (yet popular with tourists), and November–February bitterly cold
Minimum daily budget €32

Perhaps one of the strangest things about Russia is its very presence in a European guidebook. How can a land that stretches all the way from the northern Chinese border up to the Bering Strait be part of Europe? Look closer at a map and you'll see Europe's eastern borders are shaped, in part, by the Ural Mountains. Both St Petersburg and Moscow lie on the European side.

It's hard to keep up with Russia. Twenty or so years ago, the Soviets were pointing fingers, missiles and world-class shot-putters at America. Now the nation has splintered into a batch of republics with more syllables than a championship Scrabble game;

there's a new market economy, largely employing the bodyguard and bullet-proof car industry (plus the Chelsea football team); and the protesters that make the news are the ones who want communism back. Despite that, it's not as dangerous as it sounds on TV and, if you take basic precautions (see p.178), you'll almost certainly be fine.

Churchill's famous 1939 description of the Soviet Union still applies to Russia. It is "a riddle wrapped in a mystery inside an enigma". Few on the outside can begin to understand or decipher its cultural complexities. As a traveller, though, you'll get a chance to chip away at Russia's mystifying facade, even if

Average daily temperatures (°C) and monthly rainfall (mm) in Russia

	Jan	Feb	Mar	Apr	May	June	July	Aug	Sept	Oct	Nov	Dec
Moscow												
max °C	-6	-1	1	9	17	21	22	20	14	7	0	-4
min °C	-12	-11	-6	1	7	11	13	11	6	1	-4	-9
rainfall mm	36	28	33	38	51	66	81	71	58	51	43	43
St Petersburg												
max °C	-4	-4	1	8	16	19	21	19	13	7	2	-2
min °C	-9	-9	-4	1	7	11	13	12	7	3	-2	-7
rainfall mm	28	25	25	30	43	56	66	76	61	51	41	36

www.roughguides.com

RUSSIA

Metres
200
100
0

FINLAND

Murmansk

White Sea

Arkhangel'sk

HELSINKI

GULF OF FINLAND

Lake
Ladoga

St Petersburg

TALLINN

ESTONIA

Novogrod

RĪGA   LATVIA

Yaroslavl'   River Volga

Tver'

LITHUANIA

VILNIUS

BELARUS

MINSK

Smolensk

MOSCOW

Note: This map shows only the western
parts of Russia, corresponding to the
area covered by this country profile.

0   200 km

Brest   Kiev & Kharkov   Rostov &   the Caucasus Mountains   Samara

Yekaterinburg, Omsk & Vladivostok

you're just obtaining a visa, hitting the
sights, getting lost in the subway system
or trying to buy some chocolate biscuits
from a street vendor. The national
character reveals itself with enough time
and interaction.

Main attractions

● **The Kremlin, Moscow** Still the seat
of power for Russia, much of this walled-
in triangular city of churches, armouries
and palaces on Borovitsky Hill is open
to the public. You can pace the grounds
where Khrushchev engaged in the Cold
War, Stalin unleashed his raids of terror,
and Lenin orchestrated his radical vision

of government. See box on p.26 for
more details.

● **Hermitage Museum,
St Petersburg** The only museum in
the world that you might put in the
ring against the Louvre, this colossal
structure houses particularly impressive
collections of Italian Renaissance and
French Impressionist paintings, as well
as works by Rembrandt, Picasso and
Matisse. What started as the private
art collection of Peter the Great (and
expanded by Catherine the Great) finally
opened its doors to the public in 1917.
It would take years to see it all, even
if you wanted to. See box on p.26 for
more details.

- **Red Square, Moscow** Perhaps the world's most spectacular city centre, this enormous cobbled square is big enough to land a Cessna in (which 19-year-old German-born Mathias Rust did in 1987, just before taxiing to a Soviet labour camp for 432 days while his plane doubled in value and got sold to a Japanese collector). It housed enormous military parades in the Soviet era and is framed by the GUM department store (which sold consumer goods at a time when they weren't easily found), St Basil's Cathedral (the one with the multicoloured turnip spires that adorn almost every postcard) and the Kremlin. You'll also find the entrance to Lenin's Mausoleum, where the waxy, embalmed body of the former leader rests Snow White-style under a glass box.

- **Moscow and St Petersburg subways** Head underground for a real architectural and engineering wonder. After a long ride down the escalator, it's hard to tell if you've entered a museum or a five-star hotel lobby. The last thing it feels like is a subway station. The marble, sculptures and exquisite lighting make it hard to believe – in the case of Moscow, anyway – that it's the busiest system in the world, carrying eight million passengers a day.

- **The Peter and Paul Fortress, St Petersburg** Or, if you care to try your hand at Russian, Petropavlovskaya Krepost. This military fortress is as strategic as it is stunning. It was built under Peter the Great in the first half of the eighteenth century and subsequently turned into a bestselling postcard for the Russian tourist bureau. The traditional burial place for Romanov tsars, practically all of them (including Peter the Great and the last one – Nicholas II) and their families are buried here. Outside, the main spire sticks up like a lance ready to do battle with the clouds and

the "irregular hexagon" shape of the fort looks more like a symmetrical snowflake when viewed from above.

The Church of Our Saviour on Spilled Blood, St Petersburg
Emperor Alexander II was assassinated in 1881 in St Petersburg. Without conspiracy theorists or Oliver Stone around, the only thing left to do was build a church to honour his memory. This dazzling onion-domed edifice, completed in 1907, now sits on the very spot and contains – hold on to your paintbrush – 7000 square metres of mosaics.

Also recommended

- **Skate a Russian river** To make the most of Russia's arctic winter, buy a cheap pair of skates and join the locals for some free frozen fun on the lakes and rivers.

- **Ski the Caucasus** Done the Alps and want something new? Limited skiing can be found in Dombay, in the western Caucasus mountains, and Tcheget, close to Mount Elbrus. Heli-skiing is possible, but make sure you don't pay up until the helicopter comes – they're notorious for skipping out with your advance payment.

- **Experience space** If you arrive in Russia loaded with cash and don't mind spending it in a hurry, swing by the Yuri Gagarin Cosmonaut Training Centre at Star City, northeast of Moscow, and take a low-orbit flight in a MIG-29 aircraft at twice the speed of sound or go weightless on a space-training flight.

- **Take an icy dip** Join the St Petersburg Walrus Club for a plunge in the Neva River. Of course, you'll have to cut a hole in the ice first. This extraordinary winter custom occurs by

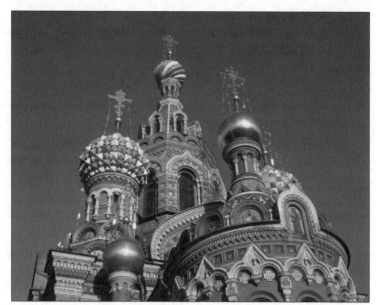

▲ Church of Our Saviour of the Blood, St Petersburg

the Peter and Paul Fortress, near the Lenin Stadium and at several other locations.

Costs

Outside of Moscow and St Petersburg, and not including any pre-booked fancy hotels, Western restaurants or luxury shopping, Russia is quite affordable and a clever budget traveller can stretch out their finances like an old T-shirt. The biggest single expense outside your €32 daily budget is probably going to be the tourist visa that got you into the country in the first place (see p.112).

Accommodation

Technically, if you're travelling on a tourist visa (see p.112), you've pre-booked all your accommodation. There is a way around this, however – the hotel/hostel you're spending the

first night with can offer invitations for any length of time, provided you spend one night with them. Hotels in Moscow and St Petersburg are expensive. St Petersburg has a campground, but that's about it. Hostels are the way to go, but you should make reservations as far in advance as you can. Private accommodation is catching on, and some offers are even affordable.

Eating and drinking

The good news is that you don't have to tip. The bad news is that a tip has already been added, and the bill isn't as cheap as you might hope. For most people, traditional fare is too bland or palate-challenging to make eating particularly enjoyable. And if you look in the places that have familiar food, you won't find the sort of prices you're hoping for. Fortunately, the vodka is cheap. And it almost counts as a meal.

Transport

Neither Eurail or InterRail passes cover Russia. Otherwise, the slow trains are cheap and there are plenty of travel agencies around to help you avoid waiting in queues at the station. Train prices seem to vary like the weather. Don't be surprised if two ticket agents at the same train station quote different prices for the same train. Local buses are also cheap and can be an excellent option. The catch is you need to figure them out; there are long, confusing queues and few English-speakers.

If you're heading there from Eastern Europe, you can get some great deals. Tallinn to Moscow, for example, costs about €50 for a one-way ticket.

In both Moscow and St Petersburg, you'll find a range of metros (over 150 stations in Moscow alone), buses, trams and trolleybuses. Tickets are subsidized and cheap. Roughly €0.50 will get you where you want to go around the city.

By train

When Eurodomino merged with InterRail in 2007, the only existing rail pass for Russia went the way of the woolly mammoth.

By bus

Busabout doesn't operate in Russia, but you can take the Beetroot Bus (Ⓦwww .beetroot.org) around the country; seven days of touring costs €530, including room and board. For buses in and out of Russia, see Ⓦwww.berlinlinienbus.de and Ⓦwww.eurolines.ru.

Events

● **Stars of the White Nights Festival**
St Petersburg's renowned Mariinsky Theatre (aka The Kirov) jump-starts summer with this taxing schedule of performances, launched by Valery Gergiev, the indefatigable conductor of the Mariinsky Opera's orchestra. May–June; Ⓦwww.mariinsky.ru.

● **Easter in Moscow** The holy day of the Russian Orthodox Church is most notably observed in Moscow's spectacular Kolomenskoe Church, with its flower-like domes soaring 70m into the air.

● **Russian Winter Festival** This twelve-days-of-Christmas-timed festival is celebrated in cities across Russia. Singers and musicians from around the world perform in the largest cities, including in Moscow's Izmailovo Park. If you get the chance, try some Russian pancakes (blini) with caviar.

Russia online

Country info Ⓦwww.russiatourism.ru
Rail Ⓦwww.poezda.net
Moscow info Ⓦwww.moscow-guide.ru
St Petersburg info Ⓦwww .petersburgcity.com

Slovenia

Capital Ljubljana
Population 2,010,347
Languages Slovenian, Serbo-Croatian
Currency Euro (€)
When to go September, when the weather's ideal for outdoor pursuits, or December–March for skiing
When not to go July–August, when the coast gets crowded, and November–February, when it's too chilly for sightseeing
Minimum daily budget €33

Sandwiched between Italy, Croatia, Austria and Hungary, Slovenia will likely be on the route of many travellers. The ones that stop for a look around will find an uncrowded gem with Habsburg and Venetian architecture and a ubiquitous assortment of impressive European churches, castles, monasteries, medieval cities and mansions from the Renaissance. Located on the southwestern side (the tourist bureau prefers "the sunny side") of the Alps, Slovenia offers incredible mountain vistas and perhaps the most affordable (and undiscovered) skiing in Europe. Think Switzerland at seventy percent off.

After the breakup of the former Yugoslavia, while Bosnia-Herzegovina, Croatia and Kosovo were enmeshed in fighting, Slovenia mostly waited on the sidelines. That is, holding free elections and voting for independence (in 1991), then fending off Milosevic and his Yugoslav army during a ten-day war before a truce was called and Milosevic backed down. The Slovenians were relatively quick to cotton on to capitalism and have already proven themselves an economic power of Eastern Europe.

Main attractions

● **Ljubljana** Narrow streets snake through the Old Town while cafés buzz with 35,000 university students. This charming, once-Roman town may not have the architectural magnificence of Prague, but it doesn't have the gaggles of tourists either.

● **The Adriatic Coast** Every country cherishes its coastline, and Slovenia is no exception. The small stretch along the Adriatic (just 100km across the water

Average daily temperatures (°C) and monthly rainfall (mm) in Slovenia

Ljubljana	Jan	Feb	Mar	Apr	May	June	July	Aug	Sept	Oct	Nov	Dec
max °C	2	4	9	14	19	23	26	26	22	16	8	3
min °C	-4	-3	1	5	9	12	14	14	11	6	1	-2
rainfall mm	33	36	38	53	69	79	56	43	41	36	51	43

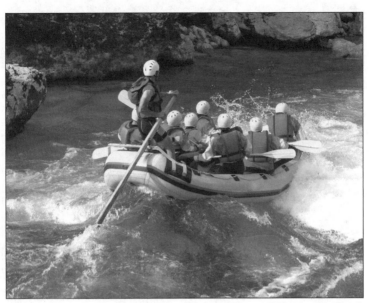

▲ Whitewater rafting, Slovenia

from Venice) is the home to Piran, with its with Venetian Gothic architecture and narrow streets, and Fiesa, edged by a clean sandy beach and tranquil boat-restricted waters.

● **Bled** This town has three draws: a medieval castle that served as a summer residence to the Yugoslav royal family and South Tyrolian bishops; a fifteenth-century belfry with a "bell of wishes" (anyone who rings it will get what they wish for); and the Alps hanging like curtains in the background, which any Slovenian will gladly sell you if you believe the thing about the bell.

Also recommended

● **Climb Mount Triglav** Action junkies and outdoor enthusiasts in Slovenia head for the triple-crested Mount Triglav (2864m), the country's highest peak. Slavs once believed the mountain to be

the lair of a three-headed deity who ruled the sky, the earth and the underworld. Today, the pilgrimage up Triglav has become a confirmation of Slovenian identity. The best routes start near Bled, at Savica waterfall and Stara Fužina.

● **Visit the Škocjan Caves** When the area was covered by the sea millions of years ago, limestone deposits were left on the bottom. A tunnel now passes through them and into an underground canyon that stretches 500m, a jungle of stalactites and stalagmites that's home to 250 types of plant and five types of bat.

● **Go wine tasting** Slovenia has supposedly been making wine since the time of the Romans, so it's not surprising that they figured out how to do it well over the years. There are fourteen distinct wine-growing regions to explore, but if you want to concentrate your palate on a specific area that doesn't require driving, make base camp in Ptuj

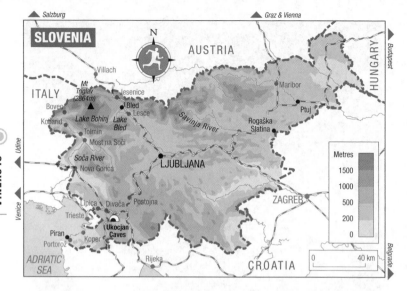

and sample the Haloze Hills and the Jeruzalem-Ljutomer districts. A bike will get you from one tasting to the next if you can't find someone willing to drive.

● **Soak in a spa** Rogaška Slatina is not just an objectionable Scrabble word, it's also Slovenia's oldest and largest spa town, with a mind-boggling assortment of cures. Everything from the rather uncomfortable-sounding "lymph drainage pressotherapy" to the scary "elecktro-acupuncture" and the mysterious "surprise bath". (Surprise! Here's your bath!) See ⓦwww .terme-rogaska.si for more treatment information.

● **Ride the rapids** Take your pick of kayaks, canoes, rafts or hydrospeed boards for the white water of the Soča and Savinja rivers.

Costs

Slovenia's still much cheaper than neighbouring Italy or Austria, though prices are increasing. To travel in comfort and style, expect to spend around €85 a day; those happy to stay at guesthouses and eat at medium-priced restaurants should get by on €55 a day. Staying in hostels and eating at self-serve restaurants can cut costs to around €33.

Accommodation

Hostels aren't plentiful, but there are some. Figure on €15–22 for bare-bones accommodation and €40 for a decent double. For €26 each, you and a travel partner can find a comfortable three-star hotel double room.

Eating and drinking

Fresh fruit and vegetables at outdoor markets are a bargain, as are breakfast pastries and street snacks. Liver and brains (fried or grilled to your disliking) are common dishes, but the strudel desserts with apple and rhubarb or home-made cheesecake are delicious, and the Italian influence means plenty of inexpensive pasta as well. A full meal, even without brains, can be found for under €7.

Transport

Eurail Austria-Slovenia-Croatia Pass Four days of travel in two months US$275 (first class) and US$199 (youth, second class). Additional days (maximum of six days) are US$40 (first class) and US$24–30 (youth, second class).

Eurail Hungary-Slovenia-Croatia Pass Five days in two months US$249 (first class) and US$175 (youth, second class). Six days US$275 (first) and US$195 (youth, second). Eight days US$325 (first) and US$229 (youth, second). Ten days US$375 (first) and US$259 (youth, second).

Busabout doesn't operate in Slovenia and nor is there a Slovenian Eurolines website, but you can find the transport info you need (if you speak Slovenian or want to make a stab at using the simple departure format) for the bus at Ⓦwww .ap-ljubljana.si, or train at Ⓦwww .slo-zeleznice.si. The trains are smooth and efficient, and local bus companies fill up on popular routes in the summer, so book ahead if you're heading to the coast.

Ljubljana is easily explored on foot, or by bike, but public transport is afford-able. A single ticket on the city's bus system costs €1 (cash) or €0.80 (token), while passes are available for one day (€4) and one week (€15). There's a 72-hour "Ljubljana Card" for €12.50 that allows unlimited bus travel and free museums. See Ljubljana website below for more details.

Events

● **Festival Ljubljana** The premier cultural event in Ljubljana sees dance, theatre and international music performances in the capital for six weeks of the summer. Past performers include José Carreras, Wynton Marsalis and Slide Hampton, and attendance for the combined events reaches 50,000. Second week of July; Ⓦwww .ljubljanafestiva.si.

● **The Cows' Ball** It's not a bovine dance ritual; just an excuse for drinking and merrymaking when the cows return to the valleys around Lake Bohinj from their high-altitude pastures. Mid-Sept.

● **Kurentovanje, Ptuj** The biggest Mardi Gras celebration in Slovenia; for ten days leading up to Shrove Tuesday there are masked balls, oodles of free-flowing wine and street performances. Mid-Feb; Ⓦwww.kurentovanje.net.

Slovenia online

Country info Ⓦwww.slovenia-tourism.si
Rail info Ⓦwww.slo-zeleznice.si
Bus info Ⓦwww.ap-ljubljana.si
Ljubljana info Ⓦwww.ljubljana -tourism.si
Bled info Ⓦwww.bled.si

Spain

Capital Madrid
Population 40,397,842
Languages Castilian (also Catalan, Basque and Gallegan)
Currency Euro (€)
When to go One of the reasons Spain is so popular is that it's good for travel all year round. The south is ideal April–June and September–October, and quite mild November–February. The north is best May–June and September
When not to go July and August can mean tortilla-frying heat and a crush of tourists. In the north, November–February can be chilly
Minimum daily budget €25

Someplace between the bullfights, crowded beaches and pitchers of sangria, you'll find the swirl of propaganda surrounding post-Franco Spain. To move beyond that, you need simply set foot in the country. There's more to Spain than most ever anticipate, and every little town seems to maintain its own architectural treasures, from the mind-blowing works of Gaudí in Barcelona to the ornate Hostal Dos Reis Catolicos, the world's oldest hotel, in Santiago de Compostela. The wealth of variety alone is perplexing. The far south still has Moroccan remnants of Moorish invaders, while the rolling green hills and

Celtic music in the north (regional instrument: the bagpipe) seem to have more in common with Ireland and Scotland. Roman aqueducts and Gothic cathedrals come together, with a few medieval castles thrown in to boot.

You can retrace the painting grounds of the famous artists (the museums are stuffed with Picasso, Velázquez, Dalí and El Greco) or watch flamenco dancers clatter the cobblestones with the hope of collecting your loose change. And if an icy gazpacho fails to cool you on a hot Andalucian day, your only choice is to make for the ocean, which is rarely far off.

Average daily temperatures (°C) and monthly rainfall (mm) in Spain

	Jan	Feb	Mar	Apr	May	June	July	Aug	Sept	Oct	Nov	Dec
Madrid												
max °C	11	12	16	17	22	28	32	32	28	20	14	11
min °C	0	2	3	6	9	13	16	16	13	8	4	2
rainfall mm	46	43	38	46	41	25	10	10	30	64	64	48
Seville												
max °C	16	17	21	22	26	31	35	35	32	26	21	17
min °C	6	7	8	10	13	17	19	19	18	13	9	7
rainfall mm	84	72	55	60	30	20	2	7	21	62	102	92

Paris & Geneva

With all this, plus a kind sky that rarely rains for more than a day or two at a time, it's not surprising that Spain is the world's second most popular destination (after France). With comparatively cheaper prices, it's an even bigger draw for the budget-minded crowd, many of whom make the short hop over the Strait of Gibraltar from Algeciras to Tangier in Morocco – a taste of Africa within a ferry ride of Europe. For this reason, we've included a mini-profile of Morocco in this chapter (see p.292).

Main attractions

● **Temple Expiatori de La Sagrada Familia, Barcelona** This Gaudí masterpiece has been under construction since 1882. You read right. And it's not expected to be completed until roughly 2080. So, even if you're with someone who has seen it before, remind them that things will have changed. You can bring your camera, but picking your favourite angle might take a few hours and nearly all two million of last year's visitors will tell you that pictures just don't do this towering structure justice.

● **Plaza Mayor, Madrid** This old-town-enclosed square in Madrid is the perfect place to buy (and pay too much for) a good coffee while you soak up the ambience. Kings have been crowned here; trials of the Inquisition held; bulls fought. Not only is it the most important historical landmark in the city, it has been beautifully preserved.

● **Beaches** The Canary Islands (a few chunks of Spain located off the coast of Morocco), Balearic Islands (southeast of Barcelona, in the Med) and the entire Costa del Sol pull in the majority of Spain's tourists who aren't looking for much more culture than a beach towel and some sun block. The sun gods willingly oblige with a blanket of warm, clear weather.

- **Prado Museum, Madrid** Even at the time it opened in 1819, the Prado was one of the most important art collections in Europe. There's far too much to see without a few weeks of museum-dedicated time, so most confine their browsing to the famous Spaniards – and even then it's a daunting pursuit.

- **Alhambra, Granada** Resting majestically atop an enormous citadel in the centre of Granada, the Alhambra is a visual overload. The Alcazaba, Generalife gardens and Palacios Nazaries take nearly a day to explore. Started by Ibn al-Ahmar, the structure's Moorish columns and domes and light-reflecting water basins inspire even the weariest traveller.

Also recommended

- **Walk the Camino de Santiago** Completing the entire journey to the city of Santiago de Compostela on foot takes most people 35–45 days, though no one says you have to do the entire thing. Some attempt this northern route across Spain on bike. See Ⓦwww .caminosantiago.com for details.

- **Watch Real Madrid or Barcelona** Perhaps never before have so many football stars been collected on two teams. Or so much money spent on them. Henri, Messi, Kaká, Ronaldo, van Nistelrooy, Ibrahimovic – see them on their home turf at the Santiago Bernabéu Stadium or Camp Nou, and there's a good chance you'll be watching them stroll to victory. See Ⓦwww.realmadrid .com or Ⓦwww.fcbarcelona.com for ticket information.

- **Go canyoning in the Pyrenees** Slip into a wetsuit, strap on a helmet and drop into the Barranco de Lapazosa. Near the Ordesa y Monte Perdido National Park, this is one of the world's most spectacular spots to splash, jump and rappel downstream in a ravine.

- **See the Guggenheim, Bilbao** Frank Gehry's gleaming metallic creation isn't on the main tourist route; if you want to catch a glimpse of this modern architectural treat, it'll take a good eight hours on a bus to get there from Madrid (six hours with the Talgo train). See Ⓦwww.guggenheim-bilbao.es for info on current exhibitions.

- **Visit Dalí's House** Salvador Dalí's surreal melting clocks and bent views can be found in many places, but if you want to step into his universe, try the Dalí House museum in Portlligat, just outside Barcelona. Ⓦwww.salvador-dali.org.

- **Ski the Sierra Nevada mountains** In late spring, you can ski all morning on 1300 vertical metres of slopes, then hop in a car or bus and head to the beach for a lazy afternoon of sunbathing: it's just 150km from Europe's southernmost ski resort to the Costa del Sol.

Costs

Away from the touristy areas, Spain can be downright affordable. If you avoid museums, bars and restaurants, you can scrape by on €25 a day with dorm living, but who wants to do that all the time? On €38–46 a day, you can live pretty well.

Accommodation
Spain has some of the cheapest accommodation, with dorm rooms ranging between €17 and €23. Pensions are particularly common, and often involve speaking into an intercom

outside the front door of an unmarked building and waiting for an elderly Spanish-speaking lady to buzz you in so you can hike up five flights and find out she doesn't have any room left. But often her neighbour or a friend down the street will, so don't despair. Out of season, you can (and should) try to bargain a bit for room rates.

Eating and drinking

Tapas in hip bars (€1.20–3.50) may be tasty, but they're far from the best way to fill up. A tortilla española (potato and onion omelette) will get you much further for your money. Don't miss out on the local wines (ask for the regional speciality), and buy them in a shop, not a restaurant, when you do your taste-testing. Also, be wary of low-priced seafood anywhere where you can't actually see the open ocean from the place you're ordering.

Transport

Spain is fairly well covered by a simple network of rail lines, with a complicated pricing system. The luxury high-speed (and expensive) AVE trains work well, with an increasing number of them departing from Madrid; budget travellers may need to hop between regional trains to get around cheaply. All this switching can be tricky and may involve an alternative route. If the local ticket sellers are reluctant to work this out (and if you speak Spanish), ring RENFE (℡902 240 202), or try playing around with the schedules on their website (Ⓦwww.renfe.com).

Bus services are comfortable and dependable and often faster than the slower trains. In Madrid, you can pick up a Madrid Card (one day €45; two days €58; three days €72), which is good for getting around on public transport and gets you admission to more than forty museums. Discounts available if you buy them online at Ⓦwww.madridcard.com.

By train

Eurail Spain Pass Any three days in two months US$275 (first class), US$219 (second class). Additional days are US$40 (first class) and US$30–36 (second class).
Eurail Spain-Portugal Pass Any three days of travel in two months US$315 (first class). Additional travel days are US$34–46 per day.
Eurail France-Spain Pass Any four days of travel in two months US$375 (first class), US$325 (second class) and US$245 (youth, second class).

For Europe-wide Eurail and InterRail passes, see p.50. For tips and tricks on maximizing your rail pass, see p.75.

By bus

A Busabout pass (see p.52) allows you to travel throughout Spain. For internal bus prices, see Ⓦwww.secorbus .es (Spanish only). For buses to other countries, see Ⓦwww.eurolines.es (Spanish only).

Events

- **The Running of the Bulls, Pamplona** The town may look like it's been invaded by pizza delivery men, but the the white outfits with red scarves are the traditional dress for running alongside a stampeding herd of bulls through a series of narrow passageways. The one-kilometre-long, early-morning *encierro* (bull run) has almost become secondary to the night-long fiesta preceding each day's run and bullfight. See p.31 for more details.

- **La Tomatina, Buñol** If you've never been trapped inside a pasta sauce factory during an explosion, here's your chance to get the next best thing: a free-for-all tomato fight in the square of this tiny Spanish town. Participants travel from around the globe to freely fling ripe tomatoes at strangers. See p.31 for more details.

● **Las Fallas, Valencia** Spectacular floats (*ninots*) of wood, wax and papier mâché are marched through the town during this six-day fiesta. Only one *ninot*, by popular vote, is saved, while the others are burned in the final night of celebrations. See p.30 for more details.

● **Carnaval, Sitges** For a wild dose of Carnaval (which can be celebrated virtually anywhere in Spain), try Sitges, near Barcelona. Expect little sleep, ample beer, and a pulsing mass of vibrant costumes. Mid-Feb; Ⓦwww.sitges.com /carnaval.

● **Feria de Abril, Seville** This end-of-April festival in Seville is a week-long party, with flamenco dancing, a horse fair and (you'll never guess) bullfights, which has become the place for Spain's socialites to mingle. Mid-April; Ⓦwww.spain.info.

Spain online

Country info Ⓦwww.spain.info
Rail Ⓦwww.renfe.es
Bus Ⓦwww.secorbus.es or Ⓦwww .alsa.es
Madrid info Ⓦwww.descubremadrid .com
Barcelona info Ⓦwww.bcn.es
Seville info Ⓦwww.turismo.sevilla.org

Sweden

Capital Stockholm
Population 9,016,596
Language Swedish
Currency Swedish kronor (SEK)
When to go June–August, when days are generally mild, lovely and long. May and September require a bit more luck for good weather

When not to go November and December. There are nice Christmas markets in December, but it's hard to count on a white Christmas. You may just get the dark, freezing, rainy part. January and February aren't much better, but at least winter activities are under way
Minimum daily budget €41

If this Nordic land conjures up images of Abba's disco outfits, Ikea's stylish discount furniture, boxy Volvos or Björn Borg's tennis headband, there's little of Sweden that will disappoint. Robyn and The Hives may grab more headlines, but Abba's music is still more popular than the national anthem; the Swedish countryside produces more giant blue Ikea boxes than berries; Volvo is softening the corners on their boxes, but still subscribes to a basic design the shape of a sauna; and Björn Borg, in addition to the headband, now has a popular underwear line.

For those slightly more tuned in to Swedish culture, there's idyllic archipelago living, the trendy glass-blowers of the Småland region, herring in the summer, and glögg (a spicy warm wine) around Christmas.

There are also 96,000 lakes, some of the best beaches in Europe and, up north, an inexhaustible supply of pristine hiking trails where there's a good chance you won't encounter another soul. Stockholm is the big urban attraction, and deservedly so, but the bicycle-inundated university towns of Lund and Uppsala clamour for a visit. And don't forget to try the meatballs.

Main attractions

● **Vasa Museum, Stockholm**
Sweden's most popular museum has just one exhibit, a mighty wooden warship that was launched from that very spot in 1628. Moments after it touched the water on its inaugural

	Jan	Feb	Mar	Apr	May	June	July	Aug	Sept	Oct	Nov	Dec
Average daily temperatures (°C) and monthly rainfall (mm) in Sweden												
Stockholm												
max °C	-1	-2	3	8	16	19	21	20	14	9	4	0
min °C	-6	-7	-3	-1	5	9	12	12	7	3	-1	-5
rainfall mm	39	27	26	30	30	45	72	66	55	50	53	46

journey, the flawed, top-heavy ship tipped over and sank, where it was preserved in the mud of Stockholm's harbour. In an ironic twist, this failure has earned more money for Sweden than if the ship had been built correctly in the first place.

● **Glass Kingdom** Hidden within the thickly forested region of Småland, several boutique glass factories can be found churning out trendy transparent glasses, bowls and sculptures. You can see the glass-blowers in action, pulling glowing orbs out of the white-hot furnaces, before buying some of their creations in the attached shop. Orrefors and Kosta Boda are the most popular,

and many of the glass artists are as well known as pop stars around Sweden.

● **Gamla Stan, Stockholm** Stockholm's Old Town rests on just one of the capital's fourteen islands. From above, it looks like a maze of tiny streets surrounding the Royal Palace (which resembles Buckingham Palace, yet, in a feat of architectural one-upmanship, was built with one more room). The Old Town is packed with tourists, but there are narrow enough side streets – several not much wider than your shoulders – to allow for some exploration.

● **Visby** This medieval port on the island of Gotland (accessible by plane

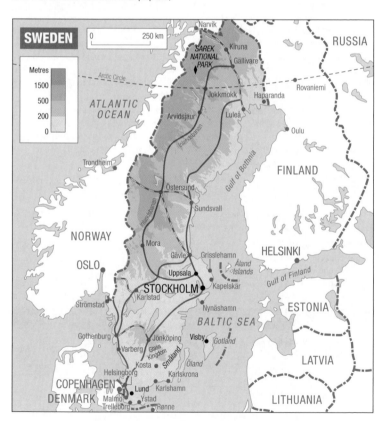

FIRST-TIME EUROPE

and just a few hours by ferry from east-coast cities) is perched on a hill, lined with cobblestones and ringed by a high stone wall. It's probably the most picturesque and charming town in Sweden, with more than forty towers and scores of church ruins remaining from the Hanseatic period.

● **Skansen, Stockholm** A vast open-air museum packed with recreated farms, windmills and 150 buildings from Sweden's past. There's a zoo with monkeys, snakes, moose and bears, plus a petting area where kids can get a little closer to goats and kittens; the kitten enclosure has become the traditional place for Stockholm's children to throw away their pacifiers (aka dummies) when they give them up for good.

Also recommended

● **Hike Sarek National Park** The glaciers, peaks, valleys and lakes of this remote northern park cover 2000 square kilometres. The trails are demanding and best suited for advanced hikers who can pack and carry what they need (there are few huts or bridges), so those who make the effort will have a vast wilderness all to themselves.

● **Kayak the archipelago** Stockholm's archipelago has 24,000 islands, and if you don't have access to a sailboat – or the ability to sail one – a kayak is the next best way to get around. Bring a tent, a good map and even a mobile phone (there's coverage over most of the islands) and book inexpensive cabins along the way.

● **Skate on thin ice** One of the most popular recreational sports in Sweden is long-distance ice-skating. You do need some special equipment, including 55-centimetre-long blades, but this

can be easily purchased or rented for a tour. More important is that you know where you're going and take safety precautions, just as the locals do. Ⓦwww.sssk.se/english/index.htm.

● **Run the Stockholm Marathon** Held on the first Saturday of June, this 42.2-kilometre race through Stockholm is one of the world's most beautiful marathons. There are other ways to get the same vistas, but few that will earn the equivalent respect from the locals. See Ⓦwww.stockholmmarathon.se for entry details.

Costs

Sweden is hardly a cheap destination, especially for the mid-range traveller who may like to dine out. If you're camping (often for free) and cooking your own food, you might get by on €18–24 a day. Figure on €41 a day at a minimum with hostel dorms, and €55–70 with cheap rooms and inexpensive restaurants.

Accommodation
Legally, you can camp in the woods for free, and even on private property (as long as it's unfenced land and more than 100m from the nearest dwelling, and even then, etiquette stipulates that you ask permission from the landowner). Getting around this way will save you a fortune and turn Sweden into one of the cheapest destinations. Otherwise, expect to pay around €21–30 for a cheap dorm bed and €52–85 for more private budget accommodation.

Eating and drinking
Falafels and pizza are the cheapest easily found fillers, but if you plan to eat out do so during lunch. Most restaurants offer lunch specials for €6–10 that include a salad bar, warm meal, cold drink and coffee. Order the same

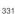

food in the restaurant at dinner time and you'll pay about €26–40 for it. Alcohol is particularly expensive, but picking up your beer or wine from one of the government-run Systembolagets will make a significant saving.

Transport

Getting around Sweden is comfortable and often quick, but never cheap. Rail and bus passes are an especially good way to move about in these parts. And that goes for inner-city transport as well (it's possible to pay €6.50 for a fifteen-minute subway ride in Stockholm if you buy a single ticket). The capital's transit authority offers clipcards for €16, which should give you about seven to ten rides, depending on distance. There's also a Stockholm Card (24hr card €34.50, 48hr card €45.50, 72hr card €54.65) that allows unlimited public transport, museum admission and boat sightseeing. For more details, visit Ⓦwww.stockholmtown.com.

By train

Eurail Sweden Pass Any three days in one month US$359 (first class), US$275 (second class), US$209 (youth, second class). Any eight days in one month US$539 (first class), US$415 (second class) and US$315 (youth, second class).

For Eurail Scandinavia Pass prices, see p.257.

For Europe-wide Eurail and InterRail passes, see p.50. For tips and tricks on maximizing your rail pass, see p.75.

By bus

Busabout doesn't operate in Sweden. For internal bus prices, see Ⓦwww.swebusexpress.se. For buses to other countries, see Ⓦwww.eurolines.se.

Events

● **Crayfish party** It's a national event without a national party or fixed date. The idea is to make friends with a local and get invited to a private bash. Swedes don silly hats as they sing drinking songs and wash down minuscule amounts of crayfish meat with schnapps (spiced vodka) and beer. Late July or Aug.

● **Midsummer's Day** The longest day of the year (at least, the closest Friday and Saturday to the longest day) is celebrated with the pagan rite of maypole dancing and schnapps drinking. There are decorations around towns, but it's essentially a family holiday. Mid-June.

● **Sankta Lucia Day** If you're in Sweden in early December, don't forget to head to church and witness a parade of white-gowned young women with candle crowns. The singing is excellent, and the traditional saffron buns and ginger snaps aren't too bad either. Dec 13.

Sweden online

Country info Ⓦwww.visitsweden.com
Rail Ⓦwww.sj.se, Ⓦwww.scanrail.com
Bus Ⓦwww.swebusexpress.se
Stockholm info Ⓦwww.stockholmtown.com

Switzerland

Capital Bern
Population 7,523,934
Languages German, French, Italian and Romansch
Currency Swiss franc (CHF)
When to go Any time. June–August is excellent for exploring nature, November–March sees the country turn into a mountain playground and April–May and late September–October bring comfortable weather, without the crowds. Skiing in the Alps lasts from the end of November until April
When not to go November–February in the cities and around the lakes is icy-cold and not an ideal time for wandering
Minimum daily budget €43

The best-known art in Switzerland may very well be the panoramic postcards for sale on racks throughout the country. When you look around, it seems the only thing missing is frames around the mountains. The best way to see the peaks, of course, is to put down your camera and strap on a pair of skis or hiking boots. Switzerland is also famous for its political neutrality, milk chocolate, yodellers, timepieces that cost more than small aeroplanes and an army equipped with tiny folding knives. What many don't know is that this teeny, wealthy, mountainous country is a potpourri of cultures speaking four languages: French, German (Switzerdeutsch is the dialect), Italian and the little-known and little-used Romansch. Together, this motley confederacy of cantons has picked up more Nobel prizes (per capita) than any other country. And you can bet your last cowbell that the sombre gaggle of bankers is going to keep the country's finances secure.

Main attractions

● **Zermatt** A glam skiing and mountaineering resort tied to the fame of perhaps the most visually stunning Alp: the Matterhorn (4478m). The car-free town is best explored on foot, and there's a cog railway that will lift you up

Average daily temperatures (°C) and monthly rainfall (mm) in Switzerland

	Jan	Feb	Mar	Apr	May	June	July	Aug	Sept	Oct	Nov	Dec
Zürich												
max °C	2	3	8	12	17	19	23	22	18	13	6	3
min °C	-2	-2	2	4	9	12	14	14	11	7	2	0
rainfall mm	61	61	69	84	102	127	127	124	99	84	71	71

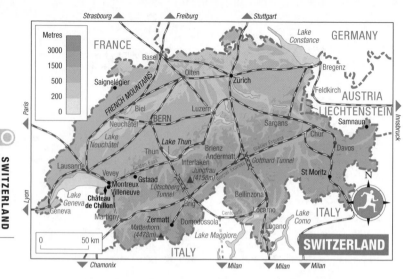

to Gornergrat for even more impressive vistas.

● **Château de Chillon** Perched on the shore of Lake Geneva, the most visited historical building in Switzerland was started in the eleventh century and has been modified ever since. Dungeons, courtyards and towers make it a fairy-tale castle and 360-degree photo op. Not surprisingly, the dreamy home found its way into the writings of Lord Byron.

● **Zürich** Geneva may have the Red Cross, but Zürich has had an explosion of trendy cafés, bars and shops. The Old Town offers a cultural afternoon of wandering – you don't need to open a numbered bank account to visit, but it certainly helps.

● **Lake Thun** Welcome to schloss (castle) country. There's Schloss Thun, Schloss Oberhofen, and Schloss Hunegg (which mixes in Art Nouveau renovations). You can visit all three on a one-day boat trip on Lake Thun and still have time to try the nearby 100-metre bungy jump.

Also recommended

● **Explore the Franches Montagnes** If you're going to head up into the mountains, you may as well avoid a superhighway of tourists gasping for oxygen. This range offers fewer visitors, cross-country skiing and gentle horses. Saignelégier is a good place to start your exploring.

● **Munch on fine chocolate** The world-famous Lindt chocolate factory is located just outside Zürich and offers an all-you-can-eat tasting treat at the end of their tour. The factory is a mesh of metal pipes labelled "cocoa butter" and "chocolate", but you'll have to sit through a rather long infomercial about the company before you're allowed access to the choco-binge room. See Ⓦwww .lindt.com for tour times.

● **Fly a glider in the Alps** Take advantage of the updraughts with a ride (or lesson) in a glider. Soar over cliffs and ride thermals as high as they'll take you (and your pilot). Switzerland is one country that deserves a bird's-eye view.

To find a local listing of flight centres, try ⓦwww.landings.com.

• **Go luging** The most famous luge course in the world is the Cresta Run, built in St Moritz for the 1884–85 season. It's now a private club, but you can try your head at it (you go head first, skeleton-style) on the ice track. Travelling 1200m at 90kmph isn't impressive for a bullet, but it's not bad for a sledge. For five runs with some instruction, you pay a small fortune (€400). Book ahead for a spot at ⓦwww.cresta-run.com/html/booking_view.cfm.

• **Cycle around Switzerland** Nine national cycle routes (3300km in total) crisscross the country, most of them well away from traffic; route maps and information in English are available from tourist offices. Eurotrek can rent you a bike, book hotels along your route and transport your gear from hotel to hotel. See ⓦwww.eurotrek.ch for tour information.

Costs

The Swiss franc may be stable and more visually compelling than the euro, but when you look at the prices, you'll wonder if you've been cheated into a bad exchange rate. Squeaking by for under €43 will be a challenge. For nightlife, restaurants and foamy lattes, you'll have to pay nearly triple that.

Accommodation

There's enough accommodation to find a room almost anywhere on the same day, but to get your choice of the cheapest digs in town in summer, try to book a few days or weeks in advance. Geneva hostels, for example, charge about €24 for a dorm room and €65 for a double. Wherever you check in, always ask for a free guest card (gästekarte, carte des visiteurs, tessera di soggiorno). This

bonus for overnight visitors gives reasonable discounts for local attractions and transport. At higher altitudes, the season is shorter and more popular (snow may not melt on those high passes until mid-June), so huts and mountain refuges should be booked well in advance.

Eating and drinking

In the south, there's an Italian influence; in the west, French cuisine; while it's German dishes everywhere else. The food is excellent – fondues, polenta, chocolates and a collection of famous cheeses await visitors – but the question is whether you can afford it. The country with the world's most expensive *McDonald's* prices doesn't welcome budget diners with open arms. Kebabs and falafels are among the most popular survival meals for the tourist. Younger travellers can also head for a nearby university cafeteria and find something filling for under €8.

Transport

Switzerland offers some of the most scenic routes in the world on funiculars, cable cars, cog railways, trains, buses and boats. All are clean, expensive and arrive and depart with the accuracy of a Swiss watch. There are several unique rail passes. For more information, see ⓦwww.rail.ch.

In Zürich, a 24-hour pass (from €3.30) is good for travel on all public transport, but a better deal might be the Zürich Card (€12.60 for a 24hr pass, €25.20 for a 72hr pass), which also allows free admission to 37 museums and a complimentary drink at 18 restaurants.

By train

Swiss Pass Ranges from any four consecutive days of travel US$276 (first class) and US$184 (second class) to one

335

month of travel US$614 (first class) and US$409 (second class).

See p.265 for France-Switzerland Pass. For prices of Switzerland-Austria Pass see p.223.

InterRail Switzerland Pass Ranges from any three days in one month €157 (first class), €117 (second class) and €75.50 (youth, second class). Eight days in one month €329 (first class), €244 (second class) and €159 (youth, second class).

Swiss Half-fare Card Fifty percent off all trains, buses, boats and most city trams for a month for US$222, US$159 (second class).

For Europe-wide Eurail and InterRail passes, see p.50. For tips and tricks on maximizing your rail pass, see p.75.

By bus

A Busabout pass (see p.52) allows some travel within Switzerland. PTT Post Buses (ⓦwww.post.ch) permit some travel with a non-Eurail Swiss pass. For buses to other countries, see ⓦwww.eurolines.ch.

Events

- **Yehudi Menuhin Festival, Gstaad** Yehudi Menuhin founded this festival in 1956 to bring chamber music to the swanky Swiss Alps resort of Gstaad. Well, it seemed like reason enough at the time. The event has grown and the concerts are held in the churches and surrounding villages. World-renowned soloists also perform. July–Sept; ⓦwww.menuhinfestivalgstaad.com.

- **Santa Claus World Championship, Samnaun** St Nick gets to show his competitive edge in this odd but colourful contest in Samnaun. There's no milk and cookie eating, but previous years have seen reindeer rodeo, sledging and skiing on primitive skis. Nov 27; ⓦwww .clauwau.com.

- **Red Bull Vertigo, Villeneuve** Watch for falling psychopaths! The world's best hang-gliders and paragliders descend on Villeneuve for a few days as part of the Acrobatics World Cup. The pros land on a tiny floating platform in the middle of a lake, where over 20,000 spectators wait for an embarrassing face plant. Late Aug; ⓦwww.redbull.com.

- **St Moritz Christmas Market** If you haven't finished your Christmas shopping come the beginning of December, this is the place to go. Tree decorations, woodcraft, dolls and snacks – nothing you actually need – are hyperinflated and put on display for purchase. Dec 3; ⓦwww.stmoritz.ch.

- **Montreux Jazz Festival** Europe's most famous jazzfest is like a tractor beam for the world's top musicians. Performers from B.B. King to Bobby McFerrin to the Black Eyed Peas – and nearly anyone you can think of in between – have played this event in Montreux, a town delightfully sandwiched between the edge of Lake Geneva and the Alps.

Switzerland online

Country info ⓦwww.myswitzerland.com
Rail ⓦwww.rail.ch
Bus ⓦwww.post.ch
Bern info ⓦwww.berne.ch
Zürich info ⓦwww.zuerich.com
Geneva info ⓦwww.geneve -tourisme.ch

Turkey

Capital Ankara
Population 70,413,958
Language Turkish
Currency Turkish lira (TL)
When to go May and October are
ideal – great weather, few tourists.
June and September have the best
weather, but they also have the crowds

When not to go December–March
is rainy and cold (though February–
March are fine on the southeast
coast). July and August are hot
and crowded, the southeast
especially so
Minimum daily budget €22

No other country provides as spectac-ular a bridge between East and West as Turkey, and nowhere more tangible as in the cultural epicentre, İstanbul. On one side of İstanbul is Europe: on the other, Asia. This quickly modernizing city (still hoping to lead the country into the EU) has retained its magical frenetic energy, mixing luxury hotels and clubs with minarets, churches and smooth-talking carpet salesmen who speak eight languages and can guess which town you're from by your dialect. With the range of poverty and wealth, European and Asian influences, Ottoman and Byzantine styles, religious and secular peoples, it seems like the country has an identity crisis. And it just may. But this fusion, combined with an outpouring of hospitality and food to die for, makes it an enormously rewarding place for the traveller.

Outside of İstanbul, there are spectac-ular ruins, several of the finest beaches on the Aegean Sea (with cheaper food and accommodation than Greece's) and some of the wildest geological forma-tions on the planet, from Pamukkale to Cappadocia.

Main attractions

- **Kapalī Çarşī (Covered Bazaar)**
İstanbul is worth visiting for the shopping alone. And the old city's Kapalī Çarşī, or "Covered Bazaar", is the logical place to start. This labyrinth of streets and passages houses more than 4000 shops, with names that recall the days when each trade had its own quarter: "Goldsmiths' Street", "Carpet Sellers' Street", "Skullcap Makers' Street". Sit down for tea with some

	Jan	Feb	Mar	Apr	May	June	July	Aug	Sept	Oct	Nov	Dec
Average daily temperatures (°C) and monthly rainfall (mm) in Turkey												
İstanbul												
max °C	6	7	11	14	18	21	24	24	21	15	9	7
min °C	1	1	3	6	9	12	14	14	11	8	4	2
rainfall mm	54	46	54	46	63	58	54	52	54	56	56	56

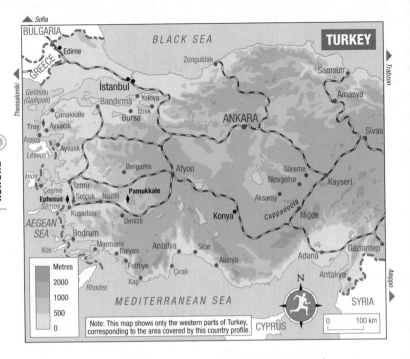

of the sellers and let them charm you into buying a few souvenirs you never realized you wanted.

● **Pamukkale** Chances are you'll catch your first glimpse of Pamukkale (translated as "Cotton Castle") on a postcard. Calcium-oxide-rich waters paint the Caldag hillside white, creating a series of Gaudí-like dripping terraces. Try to view this stunning geological formation early without thousands of people crawling all over it and turning the white surface dark with foot scum.

● **Topkapī Palace, İstanbul** One of İstanbul's big draws, this expansive fifteenth-century estate served as the centre for the Ottoman empire for four centuries and is difficult for most travellers to miss. Among the maze of rooms, you'll find inner courtyards, a throne room, a circumcision room and a harem.

● **Dolmabahçe Palace, İstanbul** When the Ottomans moved on from Topkapī Palace in 1853, they decided to build on the Asian side of the Bosphorus. It doesn't look as magnificent from the outside, but the opulence within will put even the most overdecorated Las Vegas lobby to shame. It's also where Kemal Atatürk (Turkey's first president) died on November 10, 1938 – if you want to know when, just look at the clocks, which have been set to his exact time of death (9.05am).

● **Blue Mosque, İstanbul** If you're looking for a Smurf-coloured mosque, forget it – it's the blue tilework on the insides that gives this mosque its name. If you want to walk barefoot across countless handwoven rugs while marvelling at the serenity and architecture, you won't be disappointed by this seventeenth-century Mehmet

Aga creation, known locally as the "Sultanahmet Camii".

● **Ephesus** Walking around the dry stacks of cut stone of Ephesus, it's hard to imagine that it once sat on the Aegean coast, now 8km away. And even harder to imagine the Temple of Artemis in full glory, when it was once a Wonder of the World. The site as a whole, however, has been impressively preserved.

Also recommended

● **Take a Turkish bath** Nothing scrapes off the travel grime quite like a trip to a hammam. These enormous marble steam rooms, often fitted with hot baths, showers and cooling-down chambers, can be found all over Turkey. Let a masseur scrub you with an abrasive mitt and you'll see chewing-gum-sized wads of dead skin tumbling off your body. Then he'll pound your muscles to a pulp, crack your joints, and you'll emerge feeling like a boneless chicken. In a good way, of course.

● **Explore İstanbul's sewer** Literally translated, Yerebatan Saray is the "Sunken Palace". It's İstanbul's largest underground cistern, naturally air-conditioned and renovated for public access. This one-time plumber's nightmare has been atmospherically spruced up – the water dripping from the ceiling is now accompanied by pulsing lights and creepy music.

● **Sleep in a cave** Head into the Swiss-cheese-like region of Cappadocia and you'll find a mind-boggling assortment of caves. Some of these Hittite dwellings (often called "Fairy Chimneys") have been converted into damp youth hostels that offer a nice respite from the heat. You'll also find underground cities and rock churches.

● **Pick out an "Evil Eye"** Nazar Boncuk, or "Evil Eye" charms as they're commonly known, are cheap and come in many shapes and sizes: earrings, necklaces, hatpins and so on. The little blue eye is an old superstition to ward off misfortune. Wear one and you'll likely get a smile from the locals. It's a nice way to let them know you're interested in more than snapping pictures of old ladies making carpets. Something they'll enjoy pointing out while they sell you a tea set, anyway.

Costs

You can go a long way on a minimal budget in Turkey. In the more popular spots on the traveller's trail, you can squeak by for under €22 a day; in less-visited spots, under €18. If you want to stay in slightly nicer hotels and eat some decent restaurant meals, €46 a day should do the trick. Remember to bargain for all souvenirs (see p.84) – it's part of the shopping experience and the only way to make sure you get a decent price.

Accommodation
Rooms are cheap (figure on €8–14 for a hostel), and campgrounds, when available, are even cheaper. Outside of summer, try bargaining for your accom-modation. Start by asking for a twenty percent off-season discount and see what they say.

Eating and drinking
In no other country listed in this book can you eat so well for so little. The street snacks and "fast food" around Turkey are to die for: Turkish pizzas, baklava, salted cucumber on a stick, Turkish delight, pistachio nuts, yoghurt – you won't go hungry or break your budget. Leave a bit of pocket change for a tip (five percent) and that will be fine. Offer it again if they decline the first time.

TURKEY

www.roughguides.com

Transport

Most people travel by bus in Turkey. How much you spend depends in part on your haggling and in part on what type of bus you take, from the slightly run-down to the incredibly modern. There are some express train services, but these are mostly between İstanbul and Ankara (and most are still slower than the bus). The exception is the spanking-new high-speed train that jets from Ankara to Eskisehir in under 1.5 hours. When the line is complete, Ankara-İstanbul will take three hours. Until then, you may save some time by taking a ferry, say, from İstanbul to the south, but the buses are hard to beat.

By train

See p.243 for **Balkans Flexi Pass**.
InterRail Turkey Pass Any three days in one month €70.75 (first class), €53 (second class) and €34.20 (youth, second class). Eight days in one month €171 (first class), €127 (second class) and €82.50 (youth, second class).

For Europe-wide InterRail passes (Eurail doesn't cover Turkey), see p.50. For tips and tricks on maximizing your rail pass, see p.75.

By bus

Busabout doesn't operate in Turkey. For internal bus prices, see ⓦwww .varan.com.tr. For buses to other countries, see ⓦwww.eurolines.com.

Events

● **Oiled-wrestling Festival, Edirne** Every summer, the large stadium near Edirne on the Greek-Turkish border erupts into wrestlemania. The week-long "sudden-death" format narrows the 1000-plus field of olive-oil-covered competitors down to a few slick champions. ⓦwww.kirkpinar.com.

● **Mevlana Whirling Dervishes Festival, Konya** Spin your way over to Konya (with over a million others) for this religious spectacle in the ancient Seljuk capital. The Dervishes (Sufi members of the Mevlevi Order) whirl to achieve mystical union with God. Dec; ⓦwww .mevlana.net.

● **İstanbul Music Festival** In early summer, İstanbul's Hagia Eirene Museum and Ataturk Cultural Centre welcome an international cast of performers playing traditional Turkish music, classical numbers and everything in between, from *West Side Story* to Venetian masters of Baroque. June; ⓦwww .istfest.org.

Turkey online

Country info ⓦwww.tourismturkey.org
Rail ⓦwww.tcdd.gov.tr (see ⓦwww .turkeytravelplanner.com to make sense of the timetable)
Bus ⓦwww.varan.com.tr
İstanbul info ⓦwww.istanbul.com

First-Time Europe

Directory

1 Transport   343
2 Accommodation   346
3 Red tape   346
4 Money   347
5 Travel tools   348
6 Health and safety   348
7 Working abroad   349
8 Reading resources   350

Transport

Flight booking engines

Ⓦ www.expedia.com Microsoft's online travel agency

Ⓦ www.kayak.com Searches for the best prices then links you directly to the airline or website offering the deal

Ⓦ www.opodo.com A major European flight-booking engine

Ⓦ www.orbitz.com The airlines' own group booking engine, with fares from 450 airlines

Ⓦ www.travelocity.com A leading Sabre-powered booking site

Budget travel agents

Ⓦ www.adventureworld.com.au Based in Australia with an office in New Zealand

Ⓦ www.airbrokers.com International consolidator

Ⓦ www.airtreks.com Multi-stop international specialist based in the US

Ⓦ www.flightcentre.com Offices in Australia, Britain, Canada, New Zealand, South Africa and the US

Ⓦ www.moments-notice.com Discount travel club based in the US

Ⓦ www.sta.com Britain-based agent with hundreds of offices in the US, plus branches in Australia, Canada and New Zealand

Ⓦ www.studentuniverse.com US-based student site

Ⓦ www.trailfinders.com Britain-based with offices in Australia and Ireland

Ⓦ www.travelcuts.com Canada-based, with offices in the US

Ⓦ www.yha.com.au Offices around Australia

Cheap flights within Europe

Ⓦ www.skyscanner.net Best all-round site for checking which budget carrier flies where and when it's cheapest to fly. Doesn't include charter flights, though

Ⓦ www.aerarann.com Ireland-based, with flights around the UK and connections with Aer Lingus and Etihad

Ⓦ www.airberlin.com German no-frills airline, now with international connections

Ⓦ www.bmibaby.com British Midland's budget start-up, flying from Manchester, East Midlands and Cardiff

Ⓦ www.cheapflights.co.uk Scours for the best deals offered by other discount brokers and consolidators and points you there

Ⓦ www.easyjet.co.uk One of the most popular budget carriers in Europe, with main airports at Luton, Bristol, Gatwick and Stansted, in the UK

Ⓦ www.europebyair.com Provides prices for many of the small domestic airlines like Aegean and Croatia Airlines

Ⓦ fr.xl.com French carrier with charter flights to southern Europe

Ⓦ www2.flybe.com Short for "Fly British European", it has bargain flights to 55 destinations around the continent

Ⓦ www.flyglobespan.com A Scottish carrier operating out of Edinburgh, Glasgow and Aberdeen, and heading to warm spots in southern Europe as well as Egypt, Canada and Florida

Ⓦ www.flythomascook.com Cheap flights from eighteen UK airports to the Med and beyond

Ⓦ www.germanwings.com The website has a clever click-on-map function to choose your destination. Airports are in Cologne/Bonn and Stuttgart

Ⓦ www.icelandexpress.com If you want to fly to Keflavik, this is your airline. It gets you close to Reykjavik for a shamefully good deal, and almost makes the country seem affordable

Ⓦ www.jet2.com Budget airline based in the northern UK (Leeds, Manchester, Belfast, Edinburgh, Newcastle and Blackpool) that flies to major hubs in mostly sunny spots

Ⓦ www.norwegian.no It's not easy to get around Norway on the cheap, but this site will help ease the travel expenses

www.roughguides.com

Ⓦ www.openjet.com This site queries budget and regular airlines to find the lowest fares

Ⓦ www.ryanair.com Ryanair is the Irish company that came up with the whole low-fare, anti-perk concept, and offers flights between 26 European countries

Ⓦ www.skyeurope.com The low-cost carrier of central Europe. Services Budapest, Vienna and Bratislava

Ⓦ www.thomsonflights.com Operating from airports around the UK, and offering some of the best rates to European hot spots going – especially with last-minute deals. You can even purchase extra legroom

Ⓦ www.tuifly.com Cheap flights within Europe and to North Africa, with main hubs in Cologne and Hanover

Ⓦ www.transavia.com This service runs out of the Netherlands; its main hubs are Amsterdam, Paris and Copenhagen

Ⓦ www.wizzair.com This eastern European carrier brings budget flights on 120 routes from Hungary, Poland, Bulgaria, Romania and Ukraine

Airlines and airports

Ⓦ www.airlineandairportlinks.com Links to all airports

Ⓦ flightview.com/traveltools Allows you to check the status of any flight with a real-time display of the plane in the air

Ⓦ www.sleepinginairports.net A guide to sleeping in airports

Ⓦ www.travel-watch.com/airlink.htm Links to every airline worldwide

Trains

Ⓦ www.raileurope.co.uk Europe rail passes for Europeans; see also Ⓦ www.interrail.com

Ⓦ www.raileurope.com Europe rail passes for North Americans

Ⓦ www.railplus.co.nz Europe rail passes for Kiwis

Ⓦ www.railplus.com.au Europe rail passes for Australians

Ⓦ www.railserve.com Links to rail services across Europe

Buses

Ⓦ www.eurolines.com Europe's major inter-city bus network. Tickets are typically bought per journey, but has several passes, which makes it the cheapest way to see Europe on public transportation

Ⓦ www.busabout.com Takes travellers around Europe at their own pace. It's not quite a tour bus, but not independent travel either. Offers a range of passes that allow extended travel on the network

Ⓦ www.megabus.co.uk Low-cost bus service between cities available only in the UK. Tickets are bought point-to-point, typically on their website or by phone

Cars and motorcycles

Ⓦ www.aaa.com America's Automobile Association

Ⓦ www.caa.ca Canadian Automobile Association – offers carnet info for Americans as well

Ⓦ www.horizonsunlimited.com Tips and tales on motorcycling around Europe

Ⓦ www.rac.co.uk Royal Automobile Club; offers similar services to the AA

Ⓦ www.theaa.com The UK's Automobile Association for all things automotive

Ⓦ www.viamichelin.com Driving directions throughout Europe

Ⓦ www.nationalautoclub.com America's long-established automobile association

Ⓦ www.nzaa.co.nz New Zealand's Automobile Association

Ⓦ www.rac.com.au Australia's Royal Automobile Club

Ⓦ www.europebycar.com Buys in bulk and offers discount deals with European rental companies on short-term (17 days or less) rentals and tax-free leases for longer rentals

Ⓦ www.kemwel.com Another rental consolidator. Also offers motor homes

Ⓦ www.renaultusa.com Offers brand-new cars with unlimited mileage and comprehensive insurance with no deductibles

Meet Bob...
Bob is from Bulgaria, one of the many gems you'll discover on our Mega European trip. And don't worry, he's just chopping wood for us to prepare dinner tonight.
On a Topdeck trip, we'll make sure you get to see Europe's famous sights such as the Eiffel Tower. But we'll also get you off the beaten track to see the real Europe and meet some local characters.
With over 100 trips and festivals available to you, we'll help you see the real Europe. If Europe isn't your thing, then how about seeing the pyramids in Egypt? We're all about great value trips for 18 to 30 somethings.
www.topdeck.travel
Topdeck.
share the experience

Ferries and freighters

Ⓦ www.brittanyferries.com UK carrier plying waters to France and Spain

Ⓦ www.dfdsseaways.se Services run between the Netherlands, Denmark, England and Norway

Ⓦ www.fjordline.no Norwegian carrier, servicing Norway and Denmark

Ⓦ www.freighterworld.com Will help book passage on freighters worldwide

Ⓦ www.hellasferries.gr Ferry carrier with routes between Italy, Greece and Albania

Ⓦ www.hhferries.se Sails between Helsingborg and Helsingør

Ⓦ www.minoan.gr Greek ferry operator offering routes to Italy, including Venice, Greece and Corfu

Ⓦ www.polferries.se Polish ferry operator with routes between Poland and Scandinavia

Ⓦ routesinternational.com/ships.htm Links to ferry services across Europe

Ⓦ www.vikingline.se Operates between Sweden, Finland and Latvia

Ⓦ www.silja.com Baltic operator with routes between Scandinavia and Estonia

Ⓦ www.tcpltd.com/tcpltd1.htm Canada-based freighter bookers

Accommodation

Ⓦ www.laterooms.com If you're looking for a hotel room at the last minute (or even well in advance), this service will help you find one for a decent price

Ⓦ www.tripadvisor.com Allows travellers to rate hotel rooms and other attractions. A good place to look for an unbiased review (though it is now owned by expedia.com)

Ⓦ www.hostelz.com A hostel guide with more thorough reviews than you'll find in a guidebook. And if you like what you see, you can book the room via the web

Ⓦ www.organicplacestostay.co.uk If you prefer to stay at guesthouses and small hotels that serve organic food, visit this site to find them

Ⓦ www.couchsurfing.com Register (for free) and you get tens of thousands of free sofas and guest rooms to choose from, provided you also agree to let travellers stay on your sofa when you're home

Red tape

Travel insurance

Ⓦ www.eglobalhealth.com eGlobalHealth Insurers

Ⓦ www.roughguides.com/shop Rough Guides has teamed up with WorldNomads .com to offer great travel insurance packages which should cover most needs

Ⓦ www.sosinternational.com SOS International

Ⓦ www.sevencorners.com Travel insurance provider, based in US

Ⓦ www.travelinsure.com Travel insurance services

Ⓦ www.worldtravelcenter.com An excellent starting place for finding a policy

Embassies

Ⓦ www.escapeartist.com/embassy1 /embassy1.htm Find an embassy anywhere in the world

Money

ATM locators

ⓦ www.mastercard.com /cardholderservices/atm For MasterCard users

ⓦ www.visaeurope.com/personal /findacashmachine/main.jsp For Visa cardholders

American Express travel offices

ⓦ www.amextravelresources.com Access to a list of their European offices

Currency exchange rates

ⓦ www.oanda.com Quick conversions with 164 currencies

Discount cards

ⓦ www.hiayh.org Hostelling International cards

ⓦ www.isecard.com International Exchange Student Cards

ⓦ www.isiccard.com International Student Identity Cards, Teacher Cards, Youth Cards

ⓦ www.vipbackpackers.com Discounts for select private hostels

Money transfer

ⓦ www.moneygram.com Affiliated with Thomas Cook, American Express and various banks and post offices – for sending money and paying bills urgently

ⓦ www.westernunion.com Western Union – for sending money to an overseas Western Union office

Travel tools

@ www.climatecare.org Mother Earth shouldn't pay the price just because you want to travel; yet every time we fly, we're releasing CO_2. Thisß organization provides an easy way to calculate and offset your damage (and clear your conscience) by funding sustainable energy projects

Conversions

@ www.digitaldutch.com/unitconverter Converts weights, measurements, distances, etc as quick as you can type in the numbers

Events

@ www.whatsonwhen.com Find out when and where the party is on, no matter where you go

@ www.visiteurope.com A calendar of European holidays and events with links to the National Tourist Offices of 34 European countries

Global adaptors

@ www.kropla.com/electric.htm The lowdown on what adaptors you'll need if you're bringing electrical appliances with you, and where to buy them

@ www.kropla.com/phones.htm Like above, but for phone adaptors and line checkers; all the tools you'll need, and some you won't

Language

@ www.travlang.com Downloadable online phrasebooks and dictionaries from Czech to Turkish

Online maps

@ earth.google.com Well worth the free download. Puts the spinning planet at your fingertips. You can get so hooked on it you may forget to travel

@ www.map24.com Clever map-viewing site with good zooming technology

@ www.mapblast.com Good graphics, and shows things such as hotels and petrol stations on the map as well

@ www.maporama.com Another solid online map site that allows you to zoom into nearly any spot in Europe

Times and dates

@ www.timeanddate.com

@ www.worldtimeserver.com

Weather

@ www.cnn.com/weather Global five-day forecasts

@ www.weather.com Click past the American bit and you'll find international weather listings

@ www.worldclimate.com Lists average temperature and rainfall everywhere

Health and safety

Health

@ www.cdc.gov The US Centers for Disease Control has the latest updated information on vaccinations and outbreaks

@ ecdc.europa.eu The European Centre for Disease Prevention and Control

@ www.who.org The World Health Organization site has a country-by-country health profile

Travel warnings

@ www.fco.gov.uk The UK's Foreign Office (click on "travel") is a good starting point

@ www.smartraveller.gov.au

@ travel.state.gov/travel/warnings.html The US State Department's warnings can be vague – if one spot is potentially dangerous, they put the whole country on the list

@ www.voyage.gc.ca/countries_pays /menu-eng.asp Canada's warning page

Working abroad

English teaching certificates

Ⓦ www.cambridge-efl.org Home of Cambridge TESOL programmes; allows you to find nearest location

Ⓦ www.eslcafe.com Dave's ESL Café is a TEFL forum with general job searching and classroom teaching tips and lessons

Ⓦ www.teflinternational.com Info on getting cheaper TEFL degrees in Thailand or Egypt

Ⓦ www.windsorschools.co.uk For the CELTA programme certificates

Internships and programs

Ⓦ www.amscan.org Run by the American-Scandinavian Foundation. Two- to three-month summer placements for Americans aged 21 and over; particularly for those studying engineering, chemistry, business and computer science

Ⓦ www.bunac.org Worldwide working holidays, volunteering and teaching placements; European programs are only offered in Britain, Ireland and France

Ⓦ www.cdsintl.org Programs in Germany and Switzerland aimed at young professionals seeking international experience

Ⓦ www.interexchange.org Programs in several European countries for Americans and Canadians aged 18 and older

Job searches

Ⓦ www.anyworkanywhere.com Find work, and get help with visa information

Ⓦ www.escapeartist.com/jobs /overseas1.htm Overseas jobs by region and profession

Ⓦ www.iagora.com Online community featuring entry-level jobs and internships around Europe

Ⓦ www.jobsabroad.com Allows searching by country or job type; also links to study and volunteer programs

Ⓦ www.jobs-in-europe.com A solid starting point for a job search

Ⓦ www.jobmonkey.com Search by job type, from skiing to teaching

Ⓦ www.liveworkplay.com.au A Down Under guide with useful "Working Holiday" information, complete with visa permits

Ⓦ www.michaelpage.com Professional work placement agency

Ⓦ www.monster.com Helps with available positions for skilled workers

Ⓦ www.overseasjobcentre.co.uk A resource for jobs abroad with advice and listings

Ⓦ www.pickingjobs.com Advice on finding seasonal work abroad

Ⓦ www.transitionsabroad.com A good resource, with specific tips and leads for working abroad

Ⓦ www.work4travel.co.uk Lists short-term work opportunities, such as fruit harvest, carpentry and bartending

Volunteering

Ⓦ www.earthwatch.org/europe Arranges conservation research projects around the planet

Ⓦ www.gapguru.com Focuses on volunteer projects from four to 48 weeks

Ⓦ www.gapyearforgrownups.co.uk Specializes in travel for the over-30 set

Ⓦ www.idealist.org Action Without Borders works to connect people, organizations and resources with the aim of free and dignified lives for all

Ⓦ www.i-to-i.com Hundreds of individual projects in 24 countries, for people aged 17 and over

Ⓦ www.tigweb.org Online community with information on issues and opportunities to take action

Ⓦ www.vfp.org Volunteers for Peace is a US-based organization with inexpensive international programs

Ⓦ www.volunteerabroad.com Huge directory of international volunteer programs, so you can search by location

www.roughguides.com

349

Ⓦ www.volunteerinternational.org An updated list of volunteer opportunities

Ⓦ www.wwoof.org WWOOF (World-Wide Opportunities on Organic Farms) will help connect you with farms in the region you want to be; room and food exchange for work

Ⓦ www.wwv.org.uk WorldWide Volunteering is UK-based with volunteer projects in the UK and abroad

Ⓦ www.yearoutgroup.org UK-based not-for-profit association of 35 providers of gap-year programs offering courses, cultural exchanges, expeditions, work placements or voluntary work in 92 countries

Reading resources

Online travel publications and blogs

Ⓦ www.bootsnall.com A great travel resource with many "how to do it" and "what it was like" pieces

Ⓦ www.concierge.com Inspirational ideas for themed trips (for example, top spa listings, top beaches, etc)

Ⓦ www.connectedtraveler.com Offers a refreshing perspective on cultural travel

Ⓦ www.igougo.com Swap photos and travel writing, with mileage-type points accrued for your contributions

Ⓦ www.guideforeurope.com Tips on planning, what to take, links and message boards for those heading to Europe

Ⓦ www.journeywoman.com Highlights the female perspective and offers tips and tales

Ⓦ www.literarytraveler.com Tracing steps of famous authors and learning about their inspirations are just part of the literary journey

Ⓦ www.responsible-travel.org Points out the impact of tourism and how to minimize yours while you're on the road

Ⓦ www.travelerstales.com Pushing the experiential side of guiding, Travelers Tales offers books full of true stories from people just like you

Ⓦ www.worldhum.com A travel version of *Arts and Letters Daily,* with interesting links plus original articles, interviews and reviews

Small print and

Index

A Rough Guide to Rough Guides

Published in 1982, the first Rough Guide – to Greece – was a student scheme that became a publishing phenomenon. Mark Ellingham, a recent graduate in English from Bristol University, had been travelling in Greece the previous summer and couldn't find the right guidebook. With a small group of friends he wrote his own guide, combining a highly contemporary, journalistic style with a thoroughly practical approach to travellers' needs.

The immediate success of the book spawned a series that rapidly covered dozens of destinations. And, in addition to impecunious backpackers, Rough Guides soon acquired a much broader and older readership that relished the guides' wit and inquisitiveness as much as their enthusiastic, critical approach and value-for-money ethos.

These days, Rough Guides include recommendations from shoestring to luxury and cover more than 200 destinations around the globe, including almost every country in the Americas and Europe, more than half of Africa and most of Asia and Australasia. Our ever-growing team of authors and photographers is spread all over the world, particularly in Europe, the US and Australia.

In the early 1990s, Rough Guides branched out of travel, with the publication of Rough Guides to World Music, Classical Music and the Internet. All three have become benchmark titles in their fields, spearheading the publication of a wide range of books under the Rough Guide name.

Including the travel series, Rough Guides now number more than 350 titles, covering: phrasebooks, waterproof maps, music guides from Opera to Heavy Metal, reference works as diverse as Conspiracy Theories and Shakespeare, and popular culture books from iPods to Poker. Rough Guides also produce a series of more than 120 World Music CDs in partnership with World Music Network.

Visit www.roughguides.com to see our latest publications.

Rough Guide travel images are available for commercial licensing at www.roughguidespictures.com

SMALL PRINT

www.roughguides.com

Rough Guide credits

Text editor: Polly Thomas
Layout: Pradeep Thapliyal
Cartography: Katie Lloyd-Jones
Picture editor: Mark Thomas
Production: Rebecca Short
Proofreader: Jan McCann
Editorial: Ruth Blackmore, Andy Turner, Keith Drew, Edward Aves, Alice Park, Lucy White, Jo Kirby, James Smart, Natasha Foges, Róisín Cameron, Emma Traynor, Emma Gibbs, Kathryn Lane, Mani Ramaswamy, Harry Wilson, Lucy Cowie, Amanda Howard, Lara Kavanagh, Alison Roberts, Joe Staines, Peter Buckley, Matthew Milton, Tracy Hopkins, Ruth Tidball; **Delhi** Madhavi Singh, Karen D'Souza, Lubna Shaheen
Design & Pictures: **London** Scott Stickland, Dan May, Diana Jarvis, Nicole Newman, Sarah Cummins, Emily Taylor; **Delhi** Umesh Aggarwal, Ajay Verma, Jessica Subramanian, Ankur Guha, Sachin Tanwar, Anita Singh, Nikhil Agarwal, Sachin Gupta
Production: Vicky Baldwin

Cartography: **London** Maxine Repath, Ed Wright; **Delhi** Rajesh Chhibber, Ashutosh Bharti, Rajesh Mishra, Animesh Pathak, Jasbir Sandhu, Karobi Gogoi, Alakananda Roy, Swati Handoo, Deshpal Dabas
Online: **London** George Atwell, Faye Hellon, Jeanette Angell, Fergus Day, Justine Bright, Clare Bryson, Aine Fearon, Adrian Low, Ezgi Celebi, Amber Bloomfield; **Delhi** Amit Verma, Rahul Kumar, Narender Kumar, Ravi Yadav, Debojit Borah, Rakesh Kumar, Ganesh Sharma, Shisir Basumatari
Marketing & Publicity: **London** Liz Statham, Niki Hanmer, Louise Maher, Jess Carter, Vanessa Godden, Vivienne Watton, Anna Paynton, Rachel Sprackett, Laura Vipond, Vanessa McDonald; **New York** Katy Ball, Judi Powers, Nancy Lambert; **Delhi** Ragini Govind
Manager India: Punita Singh
Reference Director: Andrew Lockett
Operations Manager: Helen Atkinson
PA to Publishing Director: Nicola Henderson
Publishing Director: Martin Dunford
Commercial Manager: Gino Magnotta
Managing Director: John Duhigg

Publishing information

This eighth edition published February 2010 by **Rough Guides Ltd**,
80 Strand, London WC2R 0RL
14 Local Shopping Centre, Panchsheel Park, New Delhi 110017, India
Distributed by the Penguin Group
Penguin Books Ltd,
80 Strand, London WC2R 0RL
Penguin Group (USA)
375 Hudson Street, NY 10014, USA
Penguin Group (Australia)
250 Camberwell Road, Camberwell, Victoria 3124, Australia
Penguin Group (Canada)
195 Harry Walker Parkway N, Newmarket, ON, L3Y 7B3 Canada
Penguin Group (NZ)
67 Apollo Drive, Mairangi Bay, Auckland 1310, New Zealand
Cover concept by Peter Dyer.

Typeset in Bembo and Helvetica to an original design by Henry Iles.
Printed in Singapore
© Doug Lansky, 2010
Maps © Rough Guides
No part of this book may be reproduced in any form without permission from the publisher except for the quotation of brief passages in reviews.
360pp includes index
A catalogue record for this book is available from the British Library
ISBN: 978-1-84836-511-7

The publishers and authors have done their best to ensure the accuracy and currency of all the information in **The Rough Guide to First-Time Europe**, however, they can accept no responsibility for any loss, injury, or inconvenience sustained by any traveller as a result of information or advice contained in the guide.

1   3   5   7   9   8   6   4   2

Help us update

We've gone to a lot of effort to ensure that the eighth edition of the **Rough Guide to First-Time Europe** is accurate and up-to-date. However, things change – places get "discovered", websites go under, and prices for meals, flights or rooms fluctuate. If you feel we've got it wrong or left something out, we'd like to know, and if you can send in the address, the price or the website, so much the better.

Please send your comments with the subject line "**Rough Guide First-Time Europe Update**" to ©mail@roughguides.com. We'll credit all contributions and send a copy of the next edition (or any other Rough Guide if you prefer) for the very best emails.

Have your questions answered and tell others about your trip at ®www.roughguides.com

www.roughguides.com

Acknowledgements

Thanks to my family; to Henrik for all his hard work on this book; to my editor Polly; to RG legend and publisher Martin Dunford; to the dozens of travel editors who gave me a break when I was getting started; and to all the travellers I've had the pleasure of crossing paths with.

Readers' letters

Thanks to all the readers who have taken the time to write in with comments and suggestions (and apologies if we've inadvertently omitted or misspelt anyone's name):

Taffeta Bourke; Arne Deubelius; Stephanie Frans; Alessandro Lorusso; Martijn Munneke; Louise Ogden.

Photo credits

All photos © Rough Guides except the following:

Title page
Couple and mountain view, Santorini © Sylvain Grandadam/Getty Images

Full page
Biker on the Zermatt, Switzerland © Rapsodia/Getty Images

Introduction
Millennium Bridge and St Paul's, London © Mark Thomas

Reasons to go
02 Leaving Korcula, Croatia © Sarah Cummins
04 Wimbledon Tennis Championships, London © Bob Martin/Getty Images
05 Students learning languages © Picture contact/Alamy
06 St Mark's Square, Venice © Mark Thomas
10 Painting in Matisse's garden © La Reeve art tours
11 Couple on scooter, Sicily © Photomax/Alamy
13 Wine-tasting, Alsace, France © E.J. Baumeister/Alamy
14 Family stay © Nick Hannah/Alamy
15 Val Veny, Italy © Roberto Caucino/istock
17 Archeological dig © Nilgun Bostanci/istock

The big adventure
p.29 Acqua alta, St Mark's Square, Venice © Claudio Bertoloni/istock
p.89 Grape-picking, France © Stockfolio/Alamy
p.115 Couple waiting in airport © Timothy Allen
p.125 Backpackers in station © Andrew Butterton/Alamy
p.143 Counting euros © Hanne Melbye-Hansen/istock
p.156 Camping in the Alps © Moritz von Hacht/Alamy
p.164 Tapas menu, Spain © Kevin George/Alamy
p.170 Internet café, Paris © David R. Frazier/Alamy
p.180 Backpacker sleeping © Westland 61/Alamy
p.188 Engaged sign © Marc Evans/istock
p.209 Traveller writing a journal © Radu Razvan/istock

Where to go
p.224 Skiing in Austria © Hermann Danzmayr/istock
p.300 Lofoten Islands © istock
p.321 Rafting in Slovenia © Simon Krzi/istock

Index

Map entries are in colour.

A

accommodation.....78, 79, 155–159, 181, 346
activity booking 35
adventure travel..............22
AIDS 193
air travel within Europe
..............................45–49
airline ticket terms 41
airlines 344
airports 344
allergies 193
altitude sickness...........194
ancestry clause, Britain
......................................92
ATMs..............................347
au pair work...................98
Austria 221–224
Austria..........................222
  accommodation 223
  attractions 221, 222
  costs 223
  eating and drinking 223
  events.............................224
  temperature and rainfall....221
  transport..........................223
  weather 221
  websites..........................224

B

B&Bs..............................157
backpacks..........123–127
The BalticStates
..........................225–229
The Baltic States 226
  accommodation 228
  attractions 225, 227
  costs 227
  eating and drinking 228
  events.............................228
  temperature and rainfall....227
  transport..........................228
  weather 227
  websites..........................229
bank cards.....................141
bargaining 84–87
bathroom fees 82
bathrooms 162
bed bugs 194
Belgium and Luxembourg
.........................230–234

Belgium and Luxembourg
....................................231
  accommodation 232
  attractions 231, 232
  costs 232
  eating and drinking 232
  events.............................233
  temperature and rainfall...230
  transport..........................233
  weather 230
  websites..........................234
bicycle rickshaws 152
bicycle tours 63
bicycles............60, 62, 152
blisters 197
blogs...................213, 350
books.............................148
border crossings 52
Britain 235–240
Britain...........................236
  accommodation 238
  attractions 237
  costs 238
  eating and drinking 238
  events.............................240
  temperature and rainfall...235
  transport..........................239
  weather 235
  websites..........................240
British Museum, London
......................................26
budget travel agents 343
budgeting 20, 71–87
Bulgaria 241–244
Bulgaria.........................242
  accommodation 243
  attractions 241, 242
  costs 243
  eating and drinking 243
  events.............................243
  temperature and rainfall...241
  transport..........................243
  weather 241
  websites..........................244
bus journey times.... 46–47
bus passes 51
buses 52, 78, 152, 344

C

calling codes 173
cameras.........................209
camping...............134, 155
canoes 153
car purchase..................56

car rental 54–56, 62–64, 182
Carnevale, Venice...........30
cars 52–56, 62–64, 182, 344
cash..............................143
cell phones 171
changing money......83, 85
cholera..........................190
climate 27
clothes 127, 128
cold sores.....................194
collect calls...................173
constipation..................195
consulates 186
cooking schools 104
Cooper's Hill Cheese Roll, Brockworth 30
costs 71–87
couchsurfing...........79, 157
country calling codes
....................................173
country cost chart 74
courier flights.................44
credit cards 140, 185
Croatia 245–248
Croatia..........................246
  accommodation 247
  attractions 245, 246
  costs 247
  eating and drinking 247
  events.............................248
  temperature and rainfall....245
  transport..........................247
  weather 245
  websites..........................248
cruise ships 153
culture shock 164–168
currency conversions, online...........................348
currency exchange........83, 85, 347, 348
cycling tours 63
Czech and Slovak republics 249–253
Czech and Slovak republics 250
  accommodation 252
  attractions 251
  costs 252
  eating and drinking 252
  events.............................253
  temperature and rainfall...251
  transport..........................252
  weather 251
  websites..........................253

INDEX

www.roughguides.com

355

D

daily costs 72, 76
daypacks 133
debit cards 141
dehydration 195
Denmark..............254–257
Denmark......................255
  accommodation 257
  attractions 254, 256
  costs 256
  eating and drinking 257
  events...............................257
  temperature and rainfall... 254
  transport...........................257
  weather 254
  websites............................257
departure list 120
Deutsches Museum,
  Munich..........................26
dialling codes 173
diaries..........................208
diarrhoea 196
diphtheria 189
disabilities, travellers with
 202–205
discount cards........72, 347
diving instruction 96
drawing........................213
drivers' licence 144
driving..............52–56, 344
dual passports..............109

E

eating.....................80, 159
Edinburgh Fringe Festival
 31
email............................169
embassies 186, 346
employers......................32
encephalitis 193
Estonia................225–229
European Union...............9
events....................29, 348

F

fact file............................7
family, travelling with 206
FAQ.................................9
farmstays.....................156
fast food 159
ferries.............60, 153, 346
festivals 30

finding work.................100
Finland 258–261
Finland 259
  accommodation 260
  attractions 258, 259
  costs 260
  eating and drinking 260
  events...............................261
  temperature and rainfall... 258
  transport...........................260
  weather 258
  websites............................261
first aid.........................132
flight booking websites
 343
flight passes 48
flights 38–49, 343
flying times 42–43
food 80, 159
food poisoning 196
food, budgeting.............80
France 262–266
France 263
  accommodation 265
  attractions 263, 264
  costs 265
  eating and drinking 265
  events...............................266
  temperature and rainfall... 262
  transport...........................265
  weather 262
  websites............................266
freighters 346

G

gay travellers 205
gear 131–136, 137
Germany 267–271
Germany 268
  accommodation 269
  attractions 267, 269
  costs 269
  eating and drinking 269
  events...............................271
  temperature and rainfall... 267
  transport...........................270
  weather 267
  websites............................271
getting to Europe............38
government jobs 98
Greece 272–275
Greece...........................273
  accommodation 274
  attractions 272, 273
  costs 274
  eating and drinking 274
  events...............................275
  temperature and rainfall... 272
  transport...........................274
  weather 272

websites...........................275
guesthouses 157
guidebooks 146–149
guided tours 62–64, 70

H

hammams.............161, 162
harvesting work..............94
health 187–199, 348
hepatitis A 190
hepatitis B 191
hepatitis C 196
Hermitage Museum,
  St Petersburg 26
hitchhiking...............57–60
HIV.......................191, 193
homestays 157
horses...........................153
Hostelling International
  Card....................73, 157
hostels 157, 159
hotels 158
Hungary 276–279
Hungary........................277
  accommodation 278
  attractions 277
  costs 278
  eating and drinking 278
  events...............................279
  temperature and rainfall... 276
  transport...........................278
  weather 276
  websites............................279
hygiene 160

I

Il Palio, Siena.................31
illegal work 93
independent hostels.....157
infections 197
insurance.....114–118, 346
International Student
  Identity Card................72
internet security...........176
Ireland.................280–284
Ireland 281
  accommodation 283
  attractions 281, 282
  costs 283
  eating and drinking 283
  events...............................284
  temperature and rainfall... 280
  transport...........................283
  weather 280
  websites............................284

itinerary.................. 19–37
IT jobs............................98
Italy 285–289
Italy 286
  accommodation 288
  attractions 285, 287
  costs 288
  eating and drinking 288
  events............................. 289
  temperature and rainfall... 285
  transport........................... 288
  weather 285
  websites........................... 289

J

jet lag............................197
job search, online...........92
journalism work 97
journals.........................208
journey times by plane
  42–43

K

kids, travelling with.......206
Kremlin and Armoury
  Museum, Moscow.......26
Kunsthistorisches Museum,
  Vienna...........................26

L

La Tomatina, Buñol 31
language study 105, 106
languages...............22, 348
Las Fallas, Valencia.......30
Latvia 225–229
letters............................175
Lithuania.............. 225–229
Louvre, Paris 27
Love Parade 31
Luxembourg........ 230–234
Lyme disease 198

M

mail................................175
manual work...................94
maps.....................149, 348
medical kit 133
meditation courses.......108

mobile phones..............171
money...........................347
money belts ...139, 144, 180
Montenegro................290
Montreux Jazz Festival,
  Geneva 31
Morocco 292
motion sickness 198
motorcycles..........153, 344
museums..................26, 80

N

The Netherlands
  293–297
The Netherlands 294
  accommodation 296
  attractions 294, 295
  costs 296
  eating and drinking 296
  events............................. 297
  temperature and rainfall... 293
  transport........................... 296
  weather 293
  websites........................... 297
news 177
NGO work.......................98
Norway 298–302
Norway...........................299
  accommodation 301
  attractions 299, 300
  costs 301
  eating and drinking 301
  events............................. 302
  temperature and rainfall... 298
  transport........................... 301
  weather 298
  websites........................... 302
Notting Hill Carnival,
  London 30

O

off-season travel.............28
Oktoberfest, Munich.......31
online travel publications
 50

P

packages, sending 175
packing........ 137–153, 180
packing lists 142,
  145, 148
painting........................213

Palio, Siena....................31
Pamplona 31
parents 32
passports 109, 110
pensions 157
personal hygiene 160
pets...............................122
phone cards 174
phones..........................170
photography........97, 106,
  209–212
place names..................151
planes...........................152
planning a trip 19
plants............................122
Poland.................. 303–306
Poland...........................304
  accommodation 305
  attractions 303, 304
  costs 305
  eating and drinking 305
  events............................. 306
  temperature and rainfall... 303
  transport........................... 305
  weather 303
  websites........................... 306
political stability..............35
Portugal 307–310
Portugal 308
  accommodation 309
  attractions 307, 308
  costs 309
  eating and drinking 309
  events............................. 310
  temperature and rainfall... 307
  transport........................... 309
  weather 307
  websites........................... 310
post 175
Prado Museum, Madrid
 27
preparation checklist....120
printing photos 210

R

rabies............................193
rail passes 50, 75
rashes...........................198
renting your property....119
restaurants...................160
restrooms 162
returning home 215–218
reverse-charge (collect)
  calls 173
river kayaks 153
robbery 179, 182
Romania 311–314
Romania........................312

accommodation 313
attractions 311, 312
costs 313
eating and drinking 313
events 314
temperature and rainfall... 311
transport 313
weather 311
websites 314
Roskilde Festival, Denmark
....30
RTW tickets 38–41
Running of the Bulls,
Pamplona 31
Russia 315–319
Russia 316
accommodation 318
attractions 316, 317
costs 318
eating and drinking 318
events 319
temperature and rainfall... 315
transport 319
weather 315
websites 319
Russian tourist visas 112

S

safety 35, 178–186, 348
salmonella 198
satellite phones 172
scams 83, 184
scuba-diving instruction
....96
sea kayaks 154
seasonal work 93
seasons 27
senior travellers 200–202
sexual harassment 183
ski jobs 93
Skype 171
sleeping bags 129
sleeping rough 158
Slovak Republic
.... 249–253
Slovenia 320–323
Slovenia 322
accommodation 322
attractions 320, 321
costs 322
eating and drinking 322
events 323
temperature and rainfall... 320
transport 323
weather 320
websites 323
solo travel 65–67
sound recording 212
souvenirs 137, 138, 214

Spain 324–328
Spain 325
accommodation 326
attractions 325, 326
costs 326
eating and drinking 327
events 327
temperature and rainfall... 324
transport 327
weather 324
websites 328
St Patrick's Day, Dublin
....30
standby flights 44
STDs 198
street vendors 160
student work 90
study abroad visas 114
studying 104–108
subways 154
summer work 94
sunburn 199
Sweden 329–332
Sweden 330
accommodation 331
attractions 329, 331
costs 331
eating and drinking 331
events 332
temperature and rainfall... 329
transport 332
weather 329
websites 332
Switzerland 333–336
Switzerland 334
accommodation 335
attractions 333, 334
costs 335
eating and drinking 335
events 336
temperature and rainfall... 333
transport 335
weather 333
websites 336

T

Tate Modern, London 27
tax 102
taxis 154
teaching English 95
tetanus 190
theft 179, 182
thrush 199
time zones 174
times and dates 348
tipping 83
toiletries 130
toilets 82, 162

tours 62–64, 70
train journey times... 46–47
trains 49–52, 154, 344
transport 151–155, 343
travel agents 40, 343
travel partners 69
travel sickness 198
traveller's cheques 142
travelling alone 65–67
travelling with others
.... 68–70
Turkey 337–340
Turkey 338
accommodation 339
attractions 337, 339
costs 339
eating and drinking 339
events 340
temperature and rainfall... 337
transport 340
weather 337
websites 340
Turkish baths 161, 162

U

Uffizi Gallery, Florence.... 27
UNESCO World Heritage
Sites 24

V

vaccinations 188–193
Vatican Museums, Rome
.... 27
vegetarians 205
video 212
visas 110–114
visa, working holiday 91
VoIP phone 171
volunteering 102, 349

W

water buses 155
water taxis 155
weather 27, 348
web surfing 176
websites 343–350
wine jobs 97
women, solo travel 67
working 88–102, 349

Visit us online

www.roughguides.com

Information on over 25,000 destinations around the world

BROADEN YOUR HORIZONS

So now we've told you about the things not to miss, the best places to stay, the top restaurants, the liveliest bars and the most spectacular sights, it only seems fair to tell you about the best travel insurance around